The Beginning of the Journey

Diana Trilling

The Beginning of the Journey

❧

THE MARRIAGE OF DIANA AND LIONEL TRILLING

A HARVEST BOOK

HARCOURT BRACE & COMPANY

SAN DIEGO   NEW YORK   LONDON

Requests for permission to make copies of any
part of the work should be mailed to:
Permissions Department, Harcourt Brace & Company,
6277 Sea Harbor Drive, Orlando, Florida 32887-6777.

Library of Congress Cataloging-in-Publication Data

Trilling, Diana.
The beginning of the journey: the marriage of Diana and Lionel
Trilling/Diana Trilling.—1st ed.
p.   cm.
ISBN 0-15-111685-7
ISBN 0-15-600135-7 (pbk.)
1. Trilling, Lionel, 1905–1975—Marriage. 2. Authors,
American—20th century—Biography. 3. Trilling,
Diana—Marriage.
I. Title.
PS3539.R56Z95   1993
818'.5209—dc20   93-18766

Designed by Lydia D'Moch

Printed in the United States of America

First Harvest edition 1994
A B C D E

This book is dedicated
to my granddaughters,
who have known me only a little
and who knew Lionel not at all.

Preface

This book is in part an autobiography, in part a biography of my husband, Lionel Trilling, and in largest part a memoir of our marriage. It is not a literary study but a personal story, an account of our family backgrounds, our childhoods and educations, our lives before we met and our life together, and a recollection of the world we lived in. When I deal with our work as writers, it is chiefly for its bearing on our personal lives: writers are what they write, also what they fail to write. Although I often cast forward in time, I end the story in 1950. Lionel and I were both born in 1905; in 1950 we were forty-five years old and there were now no significant changes in the basic pattern of our lives. This is not to suggest that after 1950 nothing of personal or professional importance happened to either of us. But with the information which I supply here, the events of succeeding years can, I believe, be sufficiently reconstructed.

In addition to the pleasure of reviewing one's own life and that of someone with whom one's life has been intimately associated, I have had two main reasons for writing this book. At the time of Lionel's death in 1975, much was written about him by friends and colleagues. In everything said, there was a curious emphasis on his grace and moderation, even upon his good manners, and since that time these are the qualities of his personality and even of his work which have been especially noted by the people who have written about him. Hostile critics have even found in the grace of his personality an evasion of the harsher realities of our social experience. There was indeed grace in Lionel's conduct of his life. His was a moderate temperament. But these are not the qualities for which he would have most wished to be remembered. They have little bearing on the nature of his thought and speak not at all to his essentially tragic view of life. There were many contradictions in Lionel's personality which were perhaps not readily visible in the classroom or in casual social encounter. But they have their place in our understanding of why he wrote as he did. It would not have pleased Lionel—I can say this with conviction— to be robbed by his critics or biographers of these various aspects of his character. It is my hope that with the publication of this book he will no longer be seen so narrowly.

My second reason for writing this book is my wish to attach autobiography to the biography of my husband. Not long after Lionel's death, as I pondered the disposition of his papers, it occurred to me that in our current spate of biographical writing I, too, might be discovered as a subject; someone going through the documents of our marriage might even perceive that the two of us together made a more interesting subject than either of us alone. If this should happen, I wanted the undertaking to be more solidly rooted in truth than was likely were the biographer dependent on existing sources. There are now few people alive with even a partially reliable knowledge of our lives as they really were. We did not have eventful lives, as this would perhaps now be understood, but our private drama had its intensity. In the early eighties, in an initial move to record our personal story, I put on tape some thirty or more interviews in which I answered questions about Lionel's and my upbringings and educations, our literary and political preferences, the good and bad turns in our personal fortunes. I at first thought that these in themselves might make a publishable volume. When this proved not to be so, I accepted the need—my need— to start again from the beginning and write this memoir.

Soon after I embarked upon *The Beginning of the Journey*—I take my title from Lionel's novel, *The Middle of the Journey*—my vision became badly impaired and I have had to write this book by dictation. It is a slow and costly method of composition and I could not have managed it on my financial own. I deeply appreciate the generous help given me by my friend and publisher, William Jovanovich. He has been unfailingly confident that though I could no longer write with my eyes, I would get the book done. It could not have been done without his patient support. I am also grateful to the John Simon Guggenheim Memorial Foundation for an award to assist me in its completion.

The Beginning of the Journey

Chapter
ONE

It was a paradox of my meeting with Lionel that although we were purposely brought together, we were not meant even to like each other, let alone marry. We were introduced by the Fadimans—that was Clifton Fadiman ("Kip" to everyone who knew him) who had been at Columbia with Lionel, and his wife, Polly, with whom I had gone to high school in Brooklyn. But the Fadimans were not matchmaking; they brought us together, or so they said, because of the euphoniousness of our names: How could they know a man named Lionel and a girl named Diana and not want them to meet? In fact, I have always suspected that they regarded us as an unlikely pair and were made uneasy by the thought of our sharing our lives: I was not sufficiently literary for Lionel and Lionel was not solidly enough fixed in the world for me. With this opinion of Lionel my father would of course have agreed. My father was a self-made businessman and would have preferred that I marry someone like Kip who, although only a year or two older than Lionel, was already an editor at the young publishing house of Simon & Schuster. When my father was first acquainted with Lionel, Lionel had neither a job nor prospects. He was studying for his Ph.D. and spoke vaguely of being a novelist. "Two damn fools can't get married," was my father's memorable blessing on us when I told him that Lionel and I had decided to marry. We were married in 1929 and my father died in 1932; the Depression had broken his health. It is one of the lasting regrets of my life that he did not live long enough to see me married to the person Lionel became. It might in some small measure have compensated him for his own financial downfall and restored the hope he had brought with him to this country as a young immigrant from Russian Poland: America had perhaps dealt unkindly with him but it had its balances and corrections.

Lionel's and mine was not a case of love at first sight, only of attraction. We were never in love in the way that people are in love in popular songs—for that kind of love I should have had to look outside reality and, like someone who is muscle-bound, I am reality-bound. Over a long lifetime, we loved each other very much, increasingly with the years, although in middle life we quarreled a great deal and often threatened each other with divorce. But even at our angriest, we were never estranged. We never stopped talking with entire intimacy and there was never a time or situation in which we could not trust and count on each other. I have never met any man to whom I would rather have been married. We probably quarreled because we held too much life in common and were battling to be disencumbered of our shared past. In our too-close union we recognized in each other our own shortcomings and blamed each other for our disappointments.

Today, there are only a handful of people who still call me Di and refer to Lionel as Li; it seems to me that, in general, nicknames are less in use than they once were. When I hear myself called Di, especially if it is linked, as it was for so many years, with the abbreviation of Lionel's name—"Di" and "Li," "Li" and "Di"—I feel as if life were being stopped for me; the train is being held at the train station. In childhood and even in my young womanhood, my name had great importance for me. I was born in 1905, when girls were not often called Diana. While for educated people the name was familiar as the name of the goddess of the hunt, I had not been named for a goddess but for my grandmother. It excited me to learn of my connection with the huntress Diana and it no doubt accounts for the fact that at girls' camp where I spent the summers of my adolescence I made archery my sport. I was an excessively fearful child; fear is the emotion I remember best from childhood. My second most important emotion was longing: I would always long for someone or something which could not be named, a transcendence, I suppose, of my capacity and experience. The extent of my fear was due to personal disposition but in some part it must also have been a reflection of the culture of my home and time. Fear is at present out of fashion; it has been largely replaced by anxiety. I am constantly surprised by the fearlessness of people today, especially young women; they move about as if the world held no terrors for them. I think of fear as something specific which proposes, if not always reliably, the existence of a cure. If I am afraid of deep water, I can stay on shore; if I am afraid of snakes, I can avoid the places where they are known to congregate. Anxiety is more diffuse and seldom offers a cure or escape. Increasingly, it has to do with how we feel as members of our nation and world. Fear may announce itself as anxiety and anxiety may be experienced as fear but we assume of anxiety that it is to be managed, lived with. Of fear, we assume that it leads to action.

I regard the whole of my adult life as having been lived in an anxious world. This began with the economic breakdown of the thirties and has been steadily reinforced with the creation of the nuclear bomb and its threat to the survival of the planet. In my childhood it was the opposite. Anthropologists speak of shame cultures and guilt cultures. Our culture today is a blame culture; it is where we have been led by our belief in every kind of determinism, economic, social, ethnic, behavioral. I grew up in a fear culture. Here are some of the things of which I and the grown-ups around me were afraid: lightning, thunder, wind, heavy snow, driving cars, driving in cars, horses, snakes, worms, germs, poisonous plants and berries, electrical appliances, gas and gas fixtures, fire, cows, bulls, all boats including rowboats, swamps, quicksand, flies, mosquitos, bees, Greek ice-cream parlors, bats, mold, rust, gangrene, spiders, caterpillars, strange cats and dogs, mice, rats of course, canned goods, bad fish, damp, drafts, whooping cough, blood poisoning, influenza, infantile paralysis, ruptured appendices, syphilis, other people's towels or tubs or toilet seats (much the same as syphilis), subways, bananas, tomatoes, oranges, oysters, fruit pits, any medicine taken even once in excess of a prescription, any two medicines taken in conjunction, foods in unusual combination with other foods, deep water, undertow, waves, leeches, toads, eels, dyes, hospitals, insanity, imbecility, brain fever, pinkeye, ghosts and ghost stories, cemeteries, Saint Vitus' dance, the poorhouse, lockjaw, rabies, heredity, sunstroke, trains, gypsies, beggars, intermarriage, leprosy, lice, nits, pimples (related to syphilis), anything swallowed without sufficient chewing, ice water, the dark, burglars.

I put last what was the most embracing of my fears: burglars. Burglars were anything that menaced me in the dark or when I was alone. Until I was nine, we lived in Westchester, first in Larchmont, then in New Rochelle. As I lay in bed alone before my sister had come to bed or if I was still awake but she was asleep, the creak of a floor or of our wicker chairs meant that burglars were about to attack me. Jack the Ripper had made his way to Westchester and was about to strangle little girls like me in our beds. Lionel told me that the greatest fear of his childhood was a piece of peeling wallpaper in his bedroom. To me that sounded like burglars, too. My parents seldom went out in the evening but on those rare occasions when they were away from home, they left us in the care of Mary, our Polish maid. Mary would put me to bed and tell me *bajki;* these were the stories she had brought with her from Poland and she told them to me in Polish. At that time I spoke Polish interchangeably with English but I have now forgotten it wholly; it was my language of terror. As I lay alone in my bed, Mary's stories would return to me; they were stories of children deserted by their parents in some faraway land and of burglars who suddenly emerged from the shadows and chopped them into pieces which they tossed into pickle or sauerkraut barrels, just like the pickle or sauerkraut barrels in our own cellar. As in surreal art, it was the commonplaceness of the detail in Mary's *bajki* which, at the same time that it gave them their actuality, added to their ability to carry me away from my actual world.

Larchmont was considerably more rural in my childhood than it is now; we grew our own fruits and vegetables and raised chickens in our backyard. Yet the neighborhood was suburban: the houses were set close to each other on paved streets and the gas street lamps were lit at night by lamplighters. I was the youngest of three children and was sent upstairs to bed a half hour earlier than my brother, who was three years my senior, and an hour before my sister, the oldest of us, with whom I shared a room. A crazy woman whom my mother, with her talent for inventive language, had named Bobolinka lived in the house next to ours. She was a Portuguese lady, Mrs. Raffaele, skinny and hook-nosed, with scraggly gray hair that hung to her shoulders in mockery of her long-ago girlhood. She was like a crazy woman in a cartoon. No one ever came to see her. Like me in my bed, she was alone, most terribly alone. Bobolinka's bedroom window was only a few yards from my bedroom window; she was closer to me than my family downstairs. It was Bobolinka's unhappy conviction that she had bugs in her hair, microbes. At night she sat at her window across from mine, a solitary prey to her delusion. Endlessly, the poor lone creature combed her lank hair, trying to rid herself of her affliction. She combed and combed and then cleared the comb by knocking it sharply against the windowsill: rap, rap, rap. It was like a communication among spirits. Bobolinka cast her shadow far into my future: I think that I still fear that I will live her frightening life and die her frightening death. My first summer at camp, when I was twelve, we had a plague of hair bugs among the campers. The camp matron in charge of cleanliness found bugs in my hair and rubbed a tarlike substance into my scalp. Even after she assured me that the bugs were gone I felt guilty and was desperately afraid that my mother would discover my secret. In high school one day I saw bugs crawling in the hair of the girl seated in front of me. This was during the First World War when we wore our hair in tangled buns on either side of our heads, called cootie traps in reminder of our soldiers tormented by lice in the trenches. I rushed home from school to the bathroom, where I raked my scalp with a fine-tooth comb. Sure enough, bug after bug appeared on the comb; I stabbed them with my thumbnail and wiped the comb clean with toilet paper. A half hour later, the bugs gone, I fell into a fevered sleep on the porch hammock. When I awoke I returned to the fine-tooth comb, but there were no longer any bugs. I never again saw bugs in my own hair or scurrying between the cootie traps of the girl who sat in front of me.

Bobolinka's death was worse for me than her life; it stays more hauntingly in my memory. She died when I was five. To me, everything important in my childhood happened when I was five—I suppose that this was when I emerged into consciousness from the spurious innocence of infancy. Not long before her death, my brother and I briefly crossed the strict boundary which separated her home and ours. None of us had ever been in her house, nor had she ever spoken to us outdoors. Then one afternoon when my brother and I were playing in the backyard, Bobolinka crossed from her yard to ours and asked us whether we knew what a microbe was. My eight-year-old brother replied that he knew the microbe in its every dimension. He fetched from our house a large sheet of paper on which he drew what in a later period would have been at once recognized as a giant zeppelin. This so much pleased Bobolinka that she asked us to her house for ice cream. Our mother had many times cautioned us that it was precisely with such seductions that children were kidnapped and lured to their deaths. Afraid either to refuse or to accept the invitation, I followed my brother's lead. I recall nothing of the inside of Bobolinka's house except darkness. She gave the two of us big slabs of soft white ice cream heaped on bananas—rotten bananas, my mother unequivocally pronounced them, shaking her head reprovingly when we reported our adventure. Putting us on notice that we were never again to repeat such an exploit, my mother spoke disquietingly of unwashed dishes and of our having eaten from God knows what kind of spoons. But in its contribution to my lasting fund of terror, even my mother's portent of the disastrous consequences of eating Bobolinka's ice cream with Bobolinka's spoons was weightless on the scale with her death. She died in a struggle, my father said; she was naked and the furniture was upside down. For several days, no one had seen or heard our neighbor and, together with the Bulldog—this was my mother's name for the local policeman— my father broke into her house. They found Bobolinka's body. It was evening and my father must just have come home from work. No, it happened on a Saturday; my mother was bathing me and had just stood me on the toilet seat to be dried. Bathroom doors were not locked in our house. While my mother was drying me, my father came in and said, "She's dead. She was naked and all the furniture was upside down. There must have been a struggle." I, too, was naked and I began to shiver uncontrollably. Alarmed, my father tried to calm me by offering me a thick roll of money and saying that I could have my pick: I could take as many of the bills as I wanted. I was already on an allowance, ten cents a week, which I was expected to save for birthday presents for my parents and sister and brother. I craved candy and spent long hours pondering the combinations which might be bought if ever I had a whole dollar to spend. Now I carefully took two single dollar bills from my father's offering. I left my father the rest. Obsessively, I returned to his statement that Bobolinka had died in a struggle, naked, and that the furniture was overturned. Which furniture was overturned, I asked myself: was it the furniture downstairs or upstairs, all of it or only some of it, and where had she been found

7

naked, upstairs or downstairs, on the bed or on the floor? Had the furniture been overturned by an attacker or only by Bobolinka herself, running away? But from what was she running? From another person, a burglar, or from herself? Perhaps from her microbes? On emotional tiptoe, daring as I could, dodging as I had to, I approached a first vagrant notion of rape; also, more soundly, an intuition of the fiercer manifestations of insanity. For all of my life, the fear of insanity has blocked the free play of my imagination and made me too intent upon reasonableness.

And yet despite my early fearfulness I entered adolescence unscarred by these terrors of my childhood, or so it must have looked. I do not mean that I had undergone a drastic emotional surgery. Perhaps even when my early life was most pervaded by fear, fear was not the dominant feature of my personality. At any rate, in adolescence I entered a kind of fear latency. In photographs of those years I stare out at the world in a way which might have led a perceptive observer, had there been one, to wonder what it was that I appealed for with such staring eyes, what comfort or assurance or forgiveness I sought, but there was now, for the unprobing viewer, a convincing overlay of composure. I had restored the daring dreams that went with my name: a Diana did not forever quake in the dark. Once more I foresaw for myself a future of boldness and romance not possible for a sister named Cecilia or for luckless female cousins with the names Mary and Sadie, Pearl, Rose, and Frieda. I am still of the opinion that had I been one of these, or even a Gladys or a Bertha, a Sylvia or a Shirley, I could not have had the life I have had. Even in bad times, my name has sheltered me and helped me to bolster my expectations. More, the knowledge that the initial *D* of my name, unlike the *C* of Cecilia or the *S* of Samuel, my brother, came from my father's side of the family rather than my mother's, memorializing *his* mother, permanently contributed to my small store of confidence, confirming me as it did in the belief—that most fortifying of beliefs, before which all that was precarious or fragile in my nature had finally to yield—that from birth I was my father's favorite.

Unfortunately, Lionel could draw no such sustenance from his name: boy and man, he longed to be a Jack or a John, a Mike or a Bill, anything except a Lionel. He bitterly envied the friends of his youth who went forward to meet their destinies armed with names so much sturdier than his. It was probably because his mother had been born in England and had spent her early life there that she hit upon this Anglicized form of his Hebrew patronymic, Lev. Of the conditions of Lionel's childhood which inevitably distanced him from other boys his age—and they were many, ranging from his dress to the fact that he was denied the usual physical activities of boyhood—not the least cruel was his name. Even in the early years of this century, when the life of the street was not yet as hazardous for a child as it is today, to announce that one's name was Lionel Trilling was a provocation. His name brought Lionel unwelcome attention even after we were married: the mother of his college friend Jim Grossman referred to him as Lionlet Trifling and, in rejoinder to an English rhyme about a writer with the improbable name of Basil Bunting, an American newspaper columnist published a couplet: "To admit defeat we are not willing / We have one named Lionel Trilling." Briefly in my childhood I felt the need of a middle name and, two Dianas being demonstrably twice as good as one, I put it about that my full name was Diana Deeana Rubin. At least in this regard, Lionel was better provided for than I: he had a middle name, Mordecai. He included Mordecai in his signature on his first published writing. But he soon came to feel that even this stern interposition between Lionel and Trilling failed to rid his name of its unmanly mellifluousness and he discarded all but the letter *M*. In the end he dropped even the *M*.

I am sure that Lionel's name has much to do with the accusation which has been brought against him that he denied his religion. With a cruder, more recognizably Jewish name, he would no doubt have been more readily forgiven his good looks and good manners. He has been charged with fabricating the name in order to disguise his Jewish origins. The Columbia uprisings of 1968 were not the first, only the most ostentatious, occasion for the accusation: as a footnote to the disorders at the University, an overaged campus radical circulated the story that Lionel's real name was Cohen and that he had changed it to Trilling to pass himself off as an English gentleman, presumably Gentile. The author of this invention was the same zealot who distributed on the Columbia campus a poster of the kind which is displayed in post offices with the pictures of dangerous criminals: below a photograph of Lionel was the legend, WANTED, DEAD OR ALIVE. FOR CRIMES AGAINST HUMANITY. Lionel never changed his name. Neither did his father. As far back as anyone knew, the family name had always been Trilling. His mother's maiden name was Cohen and this appears in any biographical dictionary in which Lionel is included. For many years, the charge that Lionel was trying to disguise his religion had currency around Columbia, perhaps elsewhere as well. Even in the late seventies, several years after his death, a Barnard student whom I employed as a part-time secretary uneasily confessed to me that her friends at school wondered about her working for the widow of someone who had refused to acknowledge that he was a Jew. Since that time there has of course been a change in the way in which the intellectual community approaches the religious issue. Increasingly, one's religious choice has become the equivalent of a political statement. On the left, to advertise oneself as a Jew is to claim honorific status as a member of a minority; minorities are presumed to be genetically virtuous. On the right, it implies that one's religious commitment falls into line with other well-tested moral and social attitudes. The charge more recently brought against Lionel is not that he denied being a Jew but that he was not the right kind of Jew: he failed to make proper public attestation of his faith. The nature of Lionel's religious upbringing is quickly summarized. He was reared in a moderately observant home. His mother, whose parents had migrated from Russian Poland to London, kept a kosher kitchen and lit candles on Friday nights, but beyond the ceremony of Friday-night prayers she took little notice of the Sabbath. Lionel's father, David Trilling, was also Russian Polish. He was born in Bialystok and came to America at the age of thirteen. Lionel's father was more given to pieties than Lionel's mother, but although he made more show than she of being an observant Jew, he was even less strictly obedient to Jewish law: outside the home he ate shellfish and other forbidden foods without apology. Lionel was bar mitzvahed but his parents belonged to no synagogue. It troubled neither his mother nor his father that their children failed to keep kosher homes when they married. It was Lionel's belief that anyone named Trilling whose forebears came from Bialystok, especially if he claimed descent from a rabbi named Trilling, was a blood relation. He was much interested in the origin of the name but was never able to determine its source with certainty. It was perhaps the name of a town in the Polish Corridor or associated with the resort town of Wassertrilling in Austria.

We met at a speakeasy; it was 1927 and Prohibition was at its height. The speakeasy was called Mario's; later, it was where Lionel and I had much of our courtship. There were more elegant speakeasies in New York than Mario's, converted East Side mansions with handsome iron gates and the imposing air of art galleries which deal only in Old Masters, but they were expensive and intimidating. We were all of us, both the Fadimans and ourselves, still in our early twenties and young for the world of illegal drinking—Lionel was a graduate student teaching part-time at Hunter College, and even Kip, already married and launched in publishing, preferred a more modest place in which to break the law. Mario's occupied the two lower floors of a run-down brownstone in the West 40's; it could once have been a theatrical boardinghouse and was now a speakeasy only in the sense that it sold illegal liquor and that its owner went through the required ritual of inspecting his customers through a peephole in the locked front door. In all other respects it was a family-style trattoria, serving excellent home-cooked food at low prices. Most important, it was safe to drink its liquor. Every day during the Prohibition years the newspapers published their grim toll of people blinded or killed by wood alcohol. We were no more deterred by their warning than a later generation would be deterred from the use of drugs by warnings in the press. There was no problem in gaining access to a speakeasy in Prohibition; anyone could turn up a "friend" whose name would open some thickly bolted door. The innocent, as opposed to the sinister, speakeasy scene is wonderfully portrayed in that rarest of American literary achievements, a good comic novel: Elmer Davis's *Friends of Mr. Sweeney.* Not the police but death or blindness was what people like ourselves had to fear from Prohibition.

My mother had died a year before I met Lionel, and I lived with my father and unmarried sister—unless a young woman was without family, it was unheard of for her to have her own apartment. As I recall the strictness of my upbringing and its deference to the proprieties which were in the service of morality, I am at a loss to explain my father's tolerance of my going to speakeasies; in fact, the attitude of both my parents toward their children and drinking. It was not consistent with their usual rules for us. Both my parents came from Poland but they came from very different backgrounds. My father had been raised in a Yiddish-speaking home in the Warsaw ghetto. My mother grew up in the native Polish countryside, close to the land and its old habits of thinking and feeling. They were also of widely different temperaments and might have been expected to bring conflicting views to the rearing of their children. But, as parents, they were indissolubly one. While they lived for our well-being—this is indisputable—they belonged to a generation of East European Jews (or at least my father did and my mother unquestioningly took his moral and intellectual guidance) for whom there was an intimate relation between happiness in the young and wrongdoing or, at any rate, between happiness and injudiciousness of a kind which leads to harm. Pleasure was not the principle of our home. We were abstemious with laughter; I learned early in life that to laugh before breakfast was to cry before dinner. Yet so far as drinking was concerned, my parents were incongruously, even irresponsibly, relaxed. Even when I was a very small child, if beer or whiskey was being served to a guest, I was given my token drink, and as a young woman when I traveled with my father I always had cocktails before dinner. Perhaps my parents had heard that the best way to curb a taste for alcohol was through early and long familiarity with it. I remember getting a food parcel from my mother at college in which, along with a roast chicken, she had included a flask of whiskey. I was carelessly unwrapping the package in front of several dormitory neighbors when it suddenly came to me that drinking was punishable by expulsion. "Oh! Gravy," I exclaimed and threw the bottle into my underwear drawer. My mother died in 1926, a year after I graduated. Living with my father in New York, I often came home drunk from speakeasies or parties where we had been drinking bootleg liquor. My father would come to my room the next morning to wake me. On the floor lay the clothes which I had unsteadily stepped out of the night before. He would shake his head and say quietly, "Drunk again, young lady?" When my father addressed me as "young lady," it usually meant that he was displeased. But he said no more than this. He went to the bathroom and drew a tub for me. Until Lionel and I decided to marry, we were never wholly sober in each other's company and until I became gravely ill a year after our marriage, I doubt that I left any social gathering without being more than a little drunk. Even after the repeal of Prohibition—in fact, until we were well into middle age—the people Lionel and I knew continued to drink too much; unrecognized alcoholism is the ruling pathology among writers and intellectuals. I have the impression that the way in which people behave under the influence of liquor has considerably changed over the years. In our younger life, people got drunk faster and tended to become either belligerent or giggly when they had been drinking. Drunkenness had its touch of theater. It was not unusual to become sick to one's stomach. We had a friend who was so squeamish that he would refuse a sandwich which had been garnished with a pickle or olive yet he made it his unofficial duty to hold the heads of sick young women at parties; he found it a useful strategy for initiating a seduction. No doubt much of our youthful drunkenness, especially our sick stomachs, was due to the poor quality of Prohibition liquor and to the strange combinations in which we drank it. At Mario's, Lionel's and my favorite drink was something called a Bullfrog, made of gin, apricot brandy, and grenadine. We alternated our Bullfrogs with Alexanders; these were made, I think, of brandy, crème de cacao, and heavy cream. Alexanders were liquid desserts but we drank them not only before dinner but through long evenings of conversation.

On Bullfrogs and Alexanders, Lionel and I got to know each other well enough to decide to marry. We did not become lovers until six months before we married. It was of the utmost urgency that this violation of the conventions not be known to our families. Even four or five years later, in the mid-thirties, when Lionel's mother discovered that a college friend of Lionel's sister, Harriet, had asked Harriet to go to bed with him, she expected Lionel (in her quaint phrase) to horsewhip him. Of our friends at the time of our marriage, we knew only one other couple that engaged in so irregular a form of courtship, and I am still convinced that if my father had found us out, he would have—he would have what? There was no talk of sin in my family or, for that matter, of virtue, whether maintained or sacrificed. I was never taught that I would burn in hell for my misdeeds. But I had my own scorching hell of the imagination, a terrible unmapped place to which I would be remanded in punishment for any major infringement of family law, and as I thought of my father's discovering that Lionel and I had gone to bed together, I could hear the creaking of its gates. Surely, going to bed with a man before marriage was the most courageous act of my life. No light penetrated the darkness of my sexual upbringing. The only teaching about sex which I received from my parents, if anything this retrograde and ugly can be called teaching, came from a sexology by one of the Kellogg brothers of cold-cereal fame—in my early childhood my father spent a brief holiday at their diet-and-exercise retreat in Battle Creek, Michigan. The volume he brought home to us from this Eden of wholesomeness opened up for at least one of his children an unrelieved vista of doom and degradation as a consequence of virtually any sexual activity—when in adult life I showed the book to a psychiatrist friend, he pleaded with me to burn it lest it fall into the hands of yet another young reader. In my high school, the girls were during one term temporarily separated from the boys and given a home-nursing course. With no apparent logic, it included a lecture on what was called sex hygiene. We were told about menstruation and that we must not allow boys to touch us lest it excite them dangerously in ways which girls did not know about—the responsibility was then ours if they went to prostitutes and contracted a venereal disease. At seventeen, I overheard my mother talking to a woman of a younger and more progressive generation than her own; she was explaining that the sexual ignorance—"innocence" was the word she used—in which she and her contemporaries reared their daughters was designed to preserve their illusions. Was she, I wonder, being honest? And if so, how extreme must have been her own disillusionment from which she hoped to shield my sister and me. At parties which I went to with Lionel when we were not yet married, we often played a game called Truth. It had the unadmitted purpose of allowing *the* question to be asked of a girl: Was she or was she not a virgin? Virgins we all were supposed to be while we waited for marriage to rescue us and, with few exceptions, virgins we all were. This was the world as I knew it, my world and Lionel's world, the world into which we and our friends had graduated from college. It was not everyone's world.

It was obviously not the world of Mary McCarthy, who was only seven years younger than I. The memoir of Mary McCarthy's young womanhood is a heavy calendar of sexual adventure: she reports of herself that she went to bed with a different man virtually every day during her early years in New York, soon after she graduated from Vassar. There is of course no such thing as a single unchallenged tendency of culture, no one response to the laws which may at any moment seem to govern our society. Mine was the corner of the world and of my generation for which necking was the chief premarital sexual activity. Neither Lionel nor I knew how to drive a car. If we wished to go to a country restaurant—and there were then many charming restaurants on the outskirts of New York— we went in my father's car, driven by his chauffeur. I am still embarrassed to remember that stolid young Dutchman; he had much to be grateful for in his phlegmatic nature. One night in the summer of 1928, the summer after Lionel and I met, as we drove home from dinner at a restaurant on the Hudson near Croton, Lionel complained of a sore throat. He had contracted scarlet fever and was critically ill for many weeks. The illness is re-created in his novel, *The Middle of the Journey,* and includes his love affair with a rose. He was not permitted visitors and I sent him a gift of Talisman roses. They were then newly bred and very beautiful; their basic color was a gentle shade of peach but they could veer to a sudden fierce bronze.

We drank too much but we and our friends, especially those of us who were Jewish—and that was most of us—are not to be confused with characters in a Hemingway novel. No Jew I knew drank with the abandon and virtuosity of the people in Hemingway. Indeed, Jewish men were at that time said to be free not only of alcoholism but also of schizophrenia; Jewish women were thought to be immune to cancer of the cervix. The author of *The Sun Also Rises,* though only a decade older than we, was of a different moral generation than ours: he was separated from us by the First World War. We were old enough to go to speakeasies and even to marry but there was an important sense in which we were still children, good Jewish children within quick and decisive call of our parents. At whatever geographic remove from our homes, we carried our mothers and fathers with us. Other than in the early Nick Adams stories, no Hemingway character has a mother or father. The lack of family and social roots in the people of whom Hemingway writes is perhaps not unconnected with whatever it is that robs him of the literary stature of Proust or Joyce or Thomas Mann or D. H. Lawrence. We and our friends were passionately in search of lives unlike those of our parents. Our parents were nonetheless always with us as we made our journeys of self-creation.

Lionel's parents did not feel the way my parents did about drinking. Except for the sweet red wine which they used for the Friday-night blessing and again at the Passover, there was no liquor in the Trilling home. In her late years, after Lionel's father died, Lionel's mother might be seen among the white-haired ladies at Schrafft's or the Tip Toe Inn on New York's West Side, bravely prefacing her dinner with an old-fashioned for her health's sake, but to the end of his life Lionel's father would have wished to restrain his children from associating with anyone whose lips had touched hard drink. A year after our marriage, I became ill with a severe hyperthyroidism and was forbidden alcohol. By the time I was allowed to drink again, I had largely lost my taste for it. With approaching middle age, Lionel's capacity for drink perceptibly diminished. Although his personality was disagreeably altered by even a single cocktail, he was unable to give up alcohol.

In the weeks after we met, Lionel and I saw each other several times. Then I went to South America with my father and was gone for close to three months. In the twenties travel was not a casual affair. Ocean voyagers were cheered on their way with shipboard parties; friends and relatives saw them off and brought presents of flowers and fruit, books, candy, toilet articles—as in an Egyptian burial, one was supplied with everything one might need for the perilous journey. Lionel and I had not yet reached the stage of official intimacy in which it was suitable for him to come to the boat where I would be surrounded by relatives, but I expected him to send me a going-away gift and when there was none I became worried: Could our friendship be this soon at an end? But he had sent a present, too late to reach me before sailing. It was Stendhal's *The Charterhouse of Parma* and it was waiting for me when I got home. I had not yet heard even of Stendhal's *The Red and the Black;* that was not the kind of thing we talked about at Radcliffe. Lionel had begun my literary education.

From earliest boyhood Lionel's life had been directed to an intellectual and literary career. He was only six when his mother told him that he would go to Oxford for a Ph.D. No one had ever supposed that he might become a doctor or a lawyer, an engineer or a physicist, an explorer, anything but what he did become, a teacher of English literature and a writer. There was no accident in his choice of profession, as there was in mine. His parents were book-reading people and his early reading was guided by them and by his young aunts, his mother's sisters. Early and late, his schooling was an extension of the clearly defined professional expectations of his home. I was not guided to books, I fell among them on my own. Reading eagerly but aimlessly in the local library, I tended to choose my books by the amount of dialogue they contained: a densely packed page daunted me. Popular authors understand the charm of telling as much as possible of a story in conversation, and it was popular novels, books of romance, which I brought home from the library by the armful. They were not "good" books; they were silly and sentimental. But I am deeply grateful for this "escape literature" which I read in my early life. It nourished my dreams and gave me an escape into possibility. My brother and sister, who were not book readers, accepted their lives as given; they never discovered my avenues of flight. I had little education in literature at college. I came out of Radcliffe badly underread. There are classical works which, if not read when one is a student, are never read, and I have many such gaps in my education. Before I met Lionel, I never thought of myself as a putative intellectual. I was not even acquainted with the word in this honorific use. Himself an intellectual, Lionel shared the attitudes and tools of the intellectual trade with me. Without him, I would no doubt have remained just another half-educated product of an expensive schooling. From Lionel, I learned not only what to read but also how to think about what I read. He gave me a literary and critical vocabulary and prepared the path to what eventually became my career. This is not to say that he made our marriage into a schoolroom or that, like the women in F. Scott Fitzgerald's later life, I was an object of his conscious pedagogy. Lionel did not undertake to teach me; I learned from him casually, unconsciously, by association. We talked a great deal, about the immediate conditions of our life together but also about books and ideas.

I, too, helped Lionel in his work but the help which I gave him, unlike his instruction of me, was not a by-product of our association; it was a wholly conscious enterprise on my side and on Lionel's as well. He was aware of it and for a long time depended upon it. Whether he was grateful for it is another matter; I think he was understandably ambiguous in his appreciation of it. Lionel taught me to think; I taught him to write. He had been writing and publishing for some years before we met but I helped him to write more attractively, with more clarity and rigor both of thought and of expression. His prose had hitherto tended to laxness. Itself not disciplined, it could allow for undisciplined thinking. Especially in the period in which he was working on his doctoral dissertation, I was relentless in my editorial address to every word he wrote—at one point, he justly accused me of rewriting a quotation from Matthew Arnold, the subject of his doctoral thesis. In a society such as ours, where despite the efforts of feminism, women continue to be treated with less generosity than men, I realize of course that whereas my statement that Lionel taught me to think will be received without murmur, I put myself at risk by saying that I played a role in his literary accomplishment. In fact, I recently tested the response which I might expect to this bald assertion: I tried it on an old friend, the editor of a magazine to which Lionel and I both contributed. He made no attempt to conceal his displeasure. "How could you teach Lionel to write?" he asked irritably. "He was a better writer than you are." Yes, he was indeed a better writer than I. But so are our famous musical artists better performers than their teachers. Lionel was a writer of broader vision than mine and of more complex purpose and in the course of time he developed a prose which I could only envy. It was the perfect instrument of his ideas, cadenced yet forceful, precisely elegant, with a curious ability to suggest that space was being saved for what the author had left unsaid. I have no sure explanation of how with my deficient literary education I discriminated as confidently as I did between good and less good writing. At college I majored in Fine Arts and learned to discriminate between good and less good painting, and until illness put an end to my ambition to be a professional singer, I studied singing and learned to distinguish between good and bad vocal performance. It may be that the same criteria apply in all the arts. But I suspect there was another, earlier element in my faith in the soundness of my judgment. Mine was not an upbringing which inspired self-confidence but I grew up with at least one unshakable assurance: my father regarded me as the brightest of his children. My sister was "good" and my brother was unmistakably a boy, but I had the best intelligence. This unspoken message of my childhood bred in me an intellectual confidence—an arrogance, if you will—which I have never lost.

I have known few men who would have tolerated as Lionel did the intrusion, however useful, of their wives into their work or who would have welcomed them into their own professions as Lionel later welcomed me into criticism. We were married twelve years before I launched my writing career. Lionel took the greatest pleasure in it; it obviously posed no threat to him. He said that he had always wanted to belong to a literary "line"; now people could think that Diana Trilling was his mother. He never condescended to me or derided me. Had he been less generous, it would have taken more than the magic of my father's communication to me as a child to fortify me against self-doubt. He was not being magnanimous on principle; he had no ideological commitment to the equality of the sexes—the issue of women's rights did not especially interest him. In the actual conduct of our lives, the two of us, in fact, silently accepted the premise that my first responsibility was to my home and family. Had this been put in words, I daresay that even as far back as the thirties and forties I would have protested it. But so long as it was not formulated, I was able to deceive myself that it was as a matter of free will and competence that I took on the tasks of the home—they were easier for me to do than they would have been for Lionel and I was better at them. We were married for forty-six years when Lionel died and for all of those years, whether or not I had work to do, I looked upon the discharge of my household obligations as my first duty. But although Lionel took my domestic role for granted, he had no wish to limit me to it; he was happy for me to branch out in any direction which appealed to me. That the addition of a professional job to a woman's homemaking occupations demands the expenditure of double energies was not a subject which was much discussed in my generation. Lionel wanted as much for me in self-realization—but how he would have hated that word!—as he wanted for himself. I wanted as much for him as he wanted for himself and more than I wanted for myself. There was nothing special about this. It was the way that nice girls were raised.

Chapter
TWO

At his death in 1975 Lionel was about to begin an autobiographical memoir. It was in these terms, as an autobiographical memoir, that he always referred to it, never as an autobiography, and I took this to mean that, walking in the broad footpath of Henry Adams, he intended to bypass his private life, or at least not dwell upon it, and concentrate upon the way in which his experience reflected, or was otherwise connected with, the social and intellectual developments of his time. The desire to do his "education" had been with him, I think, for some while, even before he drafted the notes for a talk he gave at Purdue University in 1971: I would reprint the notes in a volume of his hitherto-uncollected writings, *The Last Decade,* published after his death. It was not customary for him to speak from jottings as spare as the ones he used at the Purdue seminar and it may be that he was trying not to talk away material which he wanted for a book. Then in 1973–74 he made his first concrete move to get the volume started: he asked his research assistant at Columbia to investigate the building, ownership, and berth of a sailing ship called the *Zinita* around the year 1910. The *Zinita,* it turned out, was listed in

Lloyd's *Registry of Shipping* for 1908. It was a sloop, sixty-six feet long, cutter-rigged, designed and built by William Fife of Fife & Son; it raced to Bermuda and apparently had been moored at the Brooklyn Yacht Club. Its owner was Hyman Cohen. Hyman Cohen was Lionel's Uncle Hymie, the oldest of his mother's several brothers and, by process of natural—or unnatural—selection, the head of the Cohen family. He had been a looming figure in Lionel's childhood and, in the months preceding our marriage, his word and influence, conveyed to Lionel's mother by her sisters, Lionel's "aunties," accounted if only indirectly for much of the disapproval which met Lionel's and my decision to marry.

"Had he been born in Jerusalem," Adams wrote of himself in the famous opening pages of *The Education of Henry Adams,* reporting on the burden of his heritage as the grandson and great-grandson of presidents of the United States, "under the shadow of the Temple and circumcised in the Synagogue by his uncle the high priest, under the name of Israel Cohen he would scarcely have been more distinctly branded and not much more heavily handicapped." Lionel looked forward to opening his own "education" with the statement that born though he had been in New York, not Jerusalem, and circumcised by whoever it was in his community who performed this high office, and branded though he had been with the name Lionel Trilling, his grandfather had indeed been Israel Cohen. Israel Cohen was Lionel's maternal grandfather; he died shortly before Lionel and I met. He and his wife had emigrated to England from Russian Poland; all of their children—Lionel's mother, Fannie, was the eldest of them—had been born in London. He was an only moderately successful real-estate dealer. His wife was still a young woman when she died, leaving nine children: Fannie was then sixteen. With his wife's death, Israel Cohen moved to America with his many offspring. In America he remarried and started a second family, of four daughters. Meanwhile, Lionel's mother was surrogate mother to her eight younger siblings, the youngest still babies. In New York in 1899, at the age of twenty-four, she married David Trilling. He was older than she, though by how much we were never able to determine; it may have been as much as ten years. The Trilling home became the refuge of at least the female members of Fannie's family—Lionel's young life was overrun with women. Though I came into the family too late to know the progenitor of this numerous clan, I was made particularly conscious of Israel Cohen by his photograph on the dresser in Lionel's mother's bedroom. With his neat head and trim little beard, his slightly sunken cheeks, his delicately cut nose and sensitive arrogant mouth, Lionel's maternal grandfather bore an unsettling resemblance to Sigmund Freud. I also often heard of him as the religious arbiter of the Trilling household. Although Lionel's mother kept a kosher home, both she and Lionel's father were casual in their observance of the Jewish dietary laws—outside the home, they ate as they pleased. Israel Cohen might not wholly approve of this departure from orthodoxy but, according to Lionel's mother, he was notably flexible in his religious judgments. With grave respect, she told us of her father that he believed it to be more important to be thoughtful of other people than to be strictly adherent to law; it was, so to speak, in his name that when in the early years of my marriage I was ill and badly underweight, she slipped me a buttered roll to eat with my Friday-night chicken at her supposedly kosher table. Lionel was of course bar mitzvahed. He had his instruction in Hebrew from a newly ordained rabbi, Max Kadushin, and retained a tender memory of his young teacher. When his father died in 1943, he reached out over the years to ask Rabbi Kadushin, now returned to New York after a long period as head of the Hillel Foundation at the University of Wisconsin, to conduct the funeral service. Kadushin did not find it possible. A long time later, Rabbi Kadushin would invite Lionel and me for an evening at his apartment in New York. After a brief interval he sat down next to me and began to speak of Lionel. "He would be a good person," Kadushin said, "if he had remained a Jew." It was early in the sixties and I was not yet accustomed to these attacks on Lionel's conduct of himself as a Jew. Much taken aback, I replied: "He *is* a good person and he *is* a Jew." We soon left the house. Lionel never saw Rabbi Kadushin again.

Three of Fannie's brothers—Hymie, Izzy, and Larry Cohen—attended City College and became successful lawyers. They shared a practice in New York. Izzy married and became the father of a daughter and of the noted Harvard historian of science I. Bernard Cohen; a younger brother, Teddy, a shirt salesman, married and had a lawyer son; and a brother, Louis, who was a professor of chemistry at City College, married and fathered a son, except that Louis married a Gentile and changed his name from Cohen to Kirkman, thus substantially exiling himself from the family. Even one of the "girls," as Fannie's sisters were called, married, to everyone's dissatisfaction. But the authority of the family—moral, economic, social, cultural, aesthetic, and intellectual, but especially moral—was forever vested in, or preempted by, its unmarried members. At the pinnacle of monastic power stood Hymie Cohen, flanked by his brother Larry and the two spinster sisters, Deborah and Della. When I met them, these four unmarried Cohens were living together on Riverside Drive, surrounded by Hymie's already-extensive art collection. Soon they moved to Park Avenue, where they lived out their long lives. Marriage was more than abhorrent to the bachelor Cohens; it was intolerable. They not only held the partners of their married brothers and sisters in low esteem, but as each of the nephews and nieces came to maturity and married, he or she was effectually ostracized, until finally there was but a single representative of the children's generation with whom Hymie's household was on terms of friendship. This was the unfortunate son of the married sister, Maude; he was emotionally unwell and isolated from the world. Larry alone of the bachelor household broke the rule of celibacy. Larry had a mistress with whom he spent Wednesday nights. His absence from home on this one night of each week was borne in grim silence by Hymie and the girls. Lionel's mother said that she was sure that the lawyer brothers had protected Larry's property against any claim which his mistress might make upon it as his common-law wife.

As a boy, Lionel was thought to be Hymie's favorite—he was the oldest nephew and had the privilege of walking Hymie's dog, Roughie. Certainly it was his mother's firm belief that Lionel would inherit Hymie's estate or, at any rate, the art collection, which even at that date, when pictures did not yet have their present inflated value, was its central feature. For several summers when Lionel was in college, he went on vacation with his uncle; they camped on an island in Saranac Lake in the Adirondacks. Lionel enjoyed the fishing and the canoe trips with his uncle, but Hymie was a fussy and censorious companion and this camping experience was not always pleasurable. From his uncle's activities as a collector, Lionel got his first instruction in art, chiefly contemporary art. Hymie bought cheaply and cleverly at auctions and, in addition, bartered his legal services for paintings and sculpture. I am not sure how good his eye was; I saw the collection only once, in unfavorable circumstances—I was being stiffly entertained at lunch by Lionel's aunts shortly before Lionel and I were married. Once we married, we were not again asked to visit. The most private of private owners, Hymie never showed his pictures; I doubt that the collection ever became known. For someone as withdrawn as Lionel's uncle from dealers and other collectors, it must have been gratifying to have a nephew with whom he could talk about his acquisitions, but Hymie was able to forgo this enjoyment rather than condone Lionel's marriage. He made Lionel few gifts even while they were friendly: a Pascin lithograph and a Utrillo lithograph from an album he bought for a few dollars at the John Quinn auction, and an ink drawing by Wyndham Lewis which he also picked up at that unfortunate sale.

Lionel's interest in the *Zinita,* so strong that it persisted throughout his life and offered, if perhaps only in anticipation, the point of departure for his projected memoir, tells us something important about the nature of his thought. Occupied as he might be with literature, his mind, unlike that of so many of his intellectual contemporaries, was not bounded by books. He was never on his uncles' sailboat but it was much a subject of talk for his mother and it loomed large in Lionel's boyhood memories. He liked to speculate on how his uncle Hymie, or the three uncles acting in unison, had come to own a racing vessel. On its face, the situation was an improbable one. When they bought the *Zinita,* the uncles were still in their twenties or early thirties. They had been reared in an orthodox Jewish home in the East End of London and even now in New York lived almost entirely apart from other people. What could have inspired them to become sailors? When they raced to Bermuda, they no doubt hired a skipper, but where had they learned to navigate even in local waters and—of particular interest to Lionel—what yacht club in the first years of this century would have a member named Hyman Cohen? These were speculations which had once been understood to excite the imagination of the writer of fiction, but it was not as a writer of fiction, it was as a critic, that in 1971, at the age of sixty-six, Lionel was invited to speak of himself at Purdue. Indeed, the mild academic occasion takes significance from his statement there that even this late in his life it struck him as odd to hear himself referred to as a critic rather than as the novelist he had hoped to be. A swift overview of the family circumstances which perhaps helped shape a writer's career is permitted in even the most formal of "educations" but, more than the usual intellectual memoirist, Lionel was lured by his family past. What novelist worthy of the vocation could resist Uncle Hymie, the man, let alone Uncle Hymie, the mariner?

But Lionel was perhaps drawn to the subject of the *Zinita* for other reasons, too. Implicit throughout his work is his opposition to the disunion in our intellectual culture between person and writer, writer and person, a division which since his death has achieved a certain triumph in the literary theories of structuralism and deconstruction. He is specific—or confessional, really—about this at least once, in a letter he wrote in the fall of 1948 to John Crowe Ransom, editor of the *Kenyon Review* and founder of the Kenyon School of Letters; with Ransom and Harvard's F. O. Matthiessen, Lionel had become a Senior Fellow of the Kenyon School in the year of its founding. While the letter, addressed to someone at so marked a remove from himself in both age and social location, is predictably reticent, its tone is unpredictably that of a plaint. "It isn't that I don't like literature," Lionel writes, "it's that I don't like my relationship to literature. . . . I seem to be alienated from so many of the fine & complex figures of recent art and thought and alienated from their partisans. I find too that I'm impatient with the canonization of art that has been made by the people who have most to do with literature these days; I have considerable respect for these people yet I feel some huge discrepancy between their personal being and their evaluations of art." And he continues with this embarrassed parenthesis: "(If you will forgive the personality of my bringing you into this personal record, it is my sense of a strong intimacy between your person and your life in art and thought that accounts in great part for the admiration and affection I have for you; these have grown as in the last years I have a better chance to be aware of the intimacy between your person and your life on paper.)" Time and again, dealing with the politics of the ritualistic left, Lionel would take issue with its wish for an unconditioned universe, its vision not merely of social perfectibility but of an achieved social perfection. In his view, life itself in all its danger and folly and deceptiveness was denied in this impossible ideal. Actuality was denied. Complexity and variousness—they were his tests of reality—were denied. But nowhere as in this letter to Ransom does he ask the question so bluntly: Where do our writers live? The letter was written two months after the birth of our son and its mood was undoubtedly influenced by Lionel's new experience of fatherhood, with its immersion in the hourly practicalities of caring for an infant and with its inevitable thought of the conditioned world. But at all times not only the critic in Lionel but also the fiction writer recoiled from the gulf which for so many of our best minds separates the life of thought and the life of life. Personally and professionally he inhabited the universe of actuality. Perhaps this was what made him the person at Columbia to whom students and colleagues so frequently turned for information about doctors, psychiatrists, family problems, jobs. His one novel, *The Middle of the Journey,* is a political novel, a novel of ideas, yet even into a novel of political ideas his perception of the personal and actual intrudes in the form of charming descriptions of babies and dogs, country houses, rural rivalries. Just so, in the shape of uncles and aunts, of sailing boats and long-ago family dissension over the duty of brothers to find husbands for their unmarried sisters, his appreciation of the living texture of society would have been certain to enter his intellectual memoir. In 1953 Delmore Schwartz would publish in *Partisan Review* an essay called "The Duchess' Red Shoes," in reply to Lionel's essay "Manners, Morals, and the Novel," which had appeared in the *Kenyon Review* in 1948 and which Lionel had reprinted in his collection of essays *The Liberal Imagination* in 1950. I have recently learned that "The Duchess' Red Shoes" was in effect written to order: *Partisan Review,* or perhaps only one of its editors, Philip Rahv, felt that the moment had come for Lionel to be attacked—he was being too much praised. Seeking among his contributors for someone to take on the assignment, Rahv readily found Schwartz. While Schwartz's essay is not without cogency in its comment upon the inevitable limitations in Lionel's definition of the function of the novel, the distasteful quality of the personal sentiment which generated the piece becomes increasingly disturbing as the essay proceeds, and it reaches a climax in the ludicrous identification which Schwartz makes between Lionel's word "manners" and the "good manners" prescribed by Amy Vanderbilt in her book of etiquette. Lionel had plainly defined manners, in his use of the word, as "a culture's hum and buzz of implication." Laying out what he takes to be the indicated sphere of the novel, he rules as between the abstract and the "real": of classic American fiction he remarks that it was predominantly in the service of abstraction, whereas the nineteenth-century English novel was in the service of social and personal actuality and this was what constituted its vital achievement. The special virtue of the novel, as Lionel sees it, is its concern with the living texture of society. By its nature, the novel demands that we close the gap between the person and the life on paper.

In vain Lionel's mother had appealed to her brothers, the "boys," to invite their unmarried sisters, the "girls," on the *Zinita* to meet their friends, presumably eligible young men just waiting for this marital opportunity. It is unlikely that her brothers had friends to introduce to their sisters, even if they had wanted to undertake this unpleasing task. Their social environment was grievously limited. Fannie Trilling was far better balanced than the bachelor members of her family. But it was not easy for her to acknowledge their aberrancy; she was long habituated to their assumption of superiority. Eventually, in the last years of her life, she took permission from Lionel and me to see Hymie and the Park Avenue sisters as they truly were: small-minded, mean-spirited, overbearing in their need to dominate anyone who was not of their own household. She had from the start lacked the courage to resist their slight of her husband. Photographs show Dave Trilling to have been a rather dashing young man at the time of his marriage; at least, the flamboyance is what one sees first, before one looks behind the surface. Lionel's mother described him as having been a splendid dancer, a "spieler." Lionel remembered him as an excellent swimmer. By the time I met Lionel's father, his hypochondria was so extreme that he would not have gone within splashing distance of cold water. He had five, or was it six, weights of underwear with which to move from season to season without "shock to the system." By present-day standards, his worry about what he ate may not have been remarkable, but for someone of my generation, brought up as I had been to eat whatever was put before me and to finish everything on my plate, the fuss he made about food made him a nuisance and a bore. He was a Mr. Woodhouse without an Emma; no one was concerned to indulge him. As a boy in Bialystok, he had been slated for the rabbinate. We never learned the details of the shame which he had presumably brought upon his family. It happened at his bar mitzvah; apparently he forgot his speech. His parents shipped him off to America in disgrace. This trauma of his boyhood remained with Lionel's father for the rest of his life—as how should it not? It was never far from the mind of Lionel's mother. Lionel said that if he had a part to memorize for a school play or even a lesson to recite to his mother, his mother made sure that his father was out of their hearing lest Lionel be infected with his father's boyhood failure. How, alone in a foreign country at so young an age, with no knowledge of the language, Dave Trilling managed to maintain himself, I do not know. By the time he married he was a successful men's custom tailor, a skilled workman with an artist's conception of his craft; he told us that he often lay awake at night, pondering a better way to cut the collar of a jacket. It was as a direct consequence of Lionel's birth that Dave Trilling relinquished his tailoring to become a manufacturer of men's fur-lined coats: he did not wish his son to have to say that his father was a tailor. He had been a good tailor but he was a bad businessman and never again made a reliable living. In the Depression, when Lionel had to support his parents' household in addition to his own, he would recall with irony this decision his father had taken, presumably on his behalf. To his new business career Lionel's father brought both his insufficient practicality and his dedication to quality. Open cars were about to become obsolete but he was steadfast in the belief that the closed car was only a fad; the chauffeurs of open cars must have fur-lined coats and he put himself to their manufacture. Working with only the finest raccoon skins, he soon priced himself out of even this dwindling market. Lionel was maddened by his father's unreality. During the Depression, Lionel bought himself a much-needed new suit. It came from Macy's and cost $29.99. At his parents' house the next Friday night, he stood tensely while his father examined the strange garment, patting the shoulders and yanking at the skirt. "Son," he said at last in a tone of suffering patience, "don't you think that a man in your position owes it to himself to have a tailor-made suit?" *What* position, Lionel wanted to shout at his father. He was a lowly college instructor dependent on the yearly renewal of his appointment; he had a sick wife to take care of and parents and a sister to support. Was his a position which demanded a tailor-made suit? His father disposed of reality as met his purpose. Lionel told me of his coming home from college one evening to find his father going through the mail on his desk. To Lionel's protest, his father had replied blandly: "I'm not reading your mail, son. I'm just interested in your life." His father could not have manipulated a penny into a vending machine but if Lionel spoke disparagingly of an acquaintance, his father would urge him: "Use him as a pawn, son. Use him as a pawn." To the people with whom Dave Trilling associated in business, he was what was then known as a "perfect gentleman": clean, honest, civil, always decent in his speech. But at home his temper could be violent. It was usually directed at Lionel's mother rather than at the children, but Lionel grew up in its savage orbit. It had worsened, Lionel said, with the birth of his sister, Harriet, seven years after his own. He recalled a particularly chilling episode in which his mother was dressing for an evening engagement and asked his father to button the back of her high-necked lace blouse. Dave took the lace in his strong hands and deliberately tore it. Lionel's mother began to cry, and his father approached her a second time, as if to comfort her. Instead, he tore the blouse still further. It had been a love match, Lionel's mother told me. They had once enjoyed each other and expected to be happy together. Now it was unceasing war between them, with no possibility of victory or surrender on either side. At table, they communicated through the children. "Harriet, ask your father if he wants another potato."

"Lionel, ask your father if he wants another piece of chicken." The one sphere in which these hated wives seemed never to falter was in the duty to feed their hated husbands. When I first came into the Trilling family, I blamed Lionel's mother for the divided household. Who but women were to blame for marital conflict? I soon learned how mistaken I was. With the years, Lionel's father grew repellent to me. I disliked almost everything about him: his pieties, his hypochondria, his self-absorption, his trivial conceits. Most of all, I disliked his self-pity and the way in which he tried to ingratiate himself with me. If I remarked that it had stopped raining, he would exclaim fervently: "She's right, it's stopped raining. Leave it to Di!" If I reported that the light had gone out and a bulb needed replacement, he would nod in confirmation: "She's right. Leave it to Di!" He died in 1943; it is likely that he was in his late seventies but we were unsure of his age. At the end, he was almost wholly given over to paranoia: he thought himself surrounded by murderous enemies and he would take his medicines only from me. I did what was asked of me, but with little grace. Finally, he was confined to a nursing home on Long Island. Lionel accompanied him in the ambulance and told me that his father wept and screamed all the way. Lionel's life was dangerously dedicated to being as unlike his father as possible.

Lionel's mother was a person of far more forceful personality than her husband. She had a better intelligence and her feet were more firmly planted in a recognizable universe. I felt of her, as I felt of many women of her class and generation, that if she had been the head of the household and its wage earner, everyone would have been better off. There was nothing about her to invite competition or envy. She was of medium height, slightly pouter-pigeonish, quiet and pleasant-looking; her most arresting feature was her smooth, very white hair, which she combed back from her face and gathered in a simple knot. She liked people and listened attentively when they spoke, and when she was not being superintended by the Park Avenue brothers and sisters, she accepted people generously, on their own terms. All but two of her brothers and sisters had gone to college but, although she was undoubtedly the member of the family who would most have profited from a college education, she had not been given this opportunity. In 1986 Mark Krupnick published a book which he had been working on for several years, *Lionel Trilling and the Fate of Cultural Criticism.* By the time it was completed, he must have come to the realization that much of the biographical material which had been given him by Lionel's sister, bits of which he had included in an excerpt published in the *Denver Quarterly* some years earlier, was unreliable. He deleted these portions from his final manuscript. According to Krupnick's information from Harriet, Lionel's father was a man of learning, a student of Greek and Hebrew, and his mother was potentially a professional pianist. These were fabrications. While Lionel's father occasionally read good books, he was wholly self-taught. He had no scholarly pretensions and knew only such Hebrew as remained to him from his boyhood instruction. He knew nothing of Greek. As to Fannie's accomplishment at the piano, it was limited to an unintentionally comic rendition of "A Maiden's Prayer." Harriet had also represented her father as a furrier to celebrities and named the great Italian tenor Enrico Caruso as one of his customers. There was an obvious source for this improvisation. Lionel once saw Caruso at his father's dentist's; the singer was nervously pacing the waiting room—he wore a fur-lined coat. I remonstrated with Harriet for these statements. Why, I asked, had she lied to Krupnick? She answered that she had been trying to help Lionel. The critics were referring to his membership in the middle class, were they not? She did not understand that this was an attack; she took it to mean that they questioned his class situation. To confirm his middle-class status, she had improved upon it. There were truthful things which Harriet could have told Krupnick about their parents which directly bore on Lionel's career. Although their mother had neither training nor professional ambitions in literature, she read omnivorously: Jane Austen, the Brontës,

Thackeray, Hardy, Dickens, George Eliot, Balzac, Tolstoy, Dostoevsky, Henry James—and not only novels but also biographies and occasionally even criticism. With my Radcliffe education, I never caught up with her. She had an enviable literary memory: from the mention of a single character or scene in a novel, she could reconstruct the whole of a book which she had read perhaps twenty or thirty years earlier. Particularly striking was the soundness of her literary judgment. She offered her opinions diffidently but we never failed to be amazed by her unerring taste even in current books. Adequately schooled, she would surely have made an excellent literary scholar. If I am unable to think of her as a critic, it is because she wrote less giftedly than she read—her letters were commonplace. For a long time, Lionel assumed, not unnaturally, that it was from the Cohen side of his family that he had got his intellectual interests and aptitude. In fact, the genetic stream was richer than this. Later in life, he learned that scattered in various parts of the world were relatives of his father who had achieved considerable note in the intellectual professions, especially in science.

No child was ever more cherished than Lionel but he was not spoiled. His parents indulged themselves, not him, by the way they brought him up. They had waited six years for his birth and for the next seven years, until Harriet was born, he was an only child. It is not possible to parcel out responsibility between his mother and father for his upbringing; they had to have concurred in its more bizarre aspects. As an infant, he was grossly overfed and overclothed; in his baby photographs, his cheeks billow out over suffocating sweater collars. He was so beautiful, his mother said, that everyone wanted to kiss him and a sign had to be posted on his baby carriage: PLEASE DON'T KISS THE BABY. All through his childhood he was given his milk in beakers twice the size of normal water tumblers; and lest his stomach be chilled, it was given to him heated; it nauseated him. He had a fur blanket for his carriage and, a bit later, a squirrel coat. For a time in his boyhood, the family lived in Far Rockaway. On Saturdays and school holidays the boys of the neighborhood picnicked in little play-huts they had contrived in their backyards of old crates and cardboard. While the other boys brought sandwiches for their lunch, Lionel would be trailed by a maid carrying a silver salver with his mandatory lamb chop and baked potato: his everlasting dream of manly relaxation was to eat his lunch from a lunch pail. He never had a bicycle and I doubt that he had roller skates. When the other boys wore black stockings with their knickers, Lionel was made to wear white stockings. His father feared that he might cut his foot and, wearing black stockings, develop blood poisoning from the black dye. But perhaps the most trying of the ordeals of his youth was having to accompany his mother and aunts on their shopping expeditions; these included visits to the corsetière. At thirteen or fourteen, he was sent to camp for the summer. On the eve of his departure, his father carefully instructed him to turn his back on his bunkmates when he dressed and undressed. His mother and the aunties followed him to camp. They took up residence in a nearby boardinghouse from which they could oversee the camp activities. When they discovered that some of the older boys were stealing out of camp at night to meet the girls of the town, they reported it to the camp director; for the rest of the summer Lionel had to live with the consequences of their tale-bearing. He was not again sent to camp, nor was he permitted to go out of town to college. Other than to accompany his uncle Hymie to the Adirondacks, he was not again away from home until 1926 when, at the age of twenty-one, he spent a graduate year at the University of Wisconsin. Even this was a grudging concession on the part of his parents, and on his return to New York it was taken for granted that he would continue to live with his family. At that time the Trillings lived on Central Park West at 108th Street. The neighborhood is now badly run down and even in the twenties it was only on the border of respectability. But their own building was decently kept and their apartment was large and airy. It was convenient for Lionel to be this close to Columbia.

There were many compensations for the grave defects in Lionel's rearing—except that, unfortunately, the mistakes in our upbringings are never really compensated for. His parents did everything they knew how to do to ensure his happiness. Long before he was able to read, he was read to by them and by his young aunts. They were lavish with presents. As if to multiply the opportunities for gift-giving, they celebrated both Hanukkah and Christmas. Lionel's mother told me that always at the last moment on Christmas Eve his father would run out to buy yet another present to add to the pile which awaited Lionel on Christmas morning. This was in startling contrast to my nonreligious home, which celebrated neither Christmas nor Hanukkah. If anything, his parents were too hospitable and too interested in his friends: he was always free to bring his friends home for meals. But the generosities and kindnesses did not cancel out the humiliations of his early life. Lionel made little of them but he of course never forgot them. As I now think back upon the conditions of his rearing and the constant fuss and nervous attention directed to him, I marvel that he became the person he was. His essential character was undamaged by the extravagances of his upbringing. He was apparently able to take from his family the best of its intention for him and to discard the absurdities. Raised like a princeling, he was the least royal of people, the least self-imposing. Among the literary people I have known, he was surely the least self-indulgent and willful, the least concerned with what the world owed him. He was very good-looking, far better-looking than he appears in photographs—he was shy of the camera and some of the most celebrated photographers of his time, Cecil Beaton, Mili, Walker Evans, did their worst work on him—and very appealing to women, but this beautiful baby, whose parents felt that they had to protect him against everyone's wish to kiss him, not only disliked his looks but also sincerely envied the looks of other men with but a fraction of his attractiveness. He was similarly modest on the score of his intellectual and literary abilities. He felt of colleagues whom he plainly outdistanced that all of them knew more than he knew, reasoned better, wrote more boldly and cogently. Yet behind this inaccurate self-estimate lay a secure sense of his own worth—he was a good custodian of his strengths. He liked to quote the admonition of Joyce's Stephen Daedalus: "Silence, exile and cunning." He was not at all a calculating person but there was a considerable natural cunning in his subversion of his upbringing and in his quiet handling of his professional career.

Although Lionel frequently spoke to me about the way in which he was brought up, I know very little of his school history before college or of his early writing in grade school or high school. Neither his parents nor mine knew of private schools. He went to grade school in Far Rockaway and also on Manhattan's upper West Side and to DeWitt Clinton High School in New York. He spoke warmly of the part played in his education by his high-school teachers, especially one of his English teachers. Laughingly he recalled a favorite teacher who was drafted in the First World War: he and his classmates gave him a spyglass as a going-away present. I still have some of Lionel's boyhood books: his volumes of Kipling, his *Child's Garden of Verses,* and his worn *Treasure Island.* If any writing of his own remained from his childhood, it would have been among the papers in his mother's keeping at her death and now lost. I take it for granted that he wrote for his school publications; recently I was told that in his summer at camp he edited the camp magazine. By Lionel's own report, there was nothing noteworthy in his performance as a high-school student: he did well in English and history, poorly in mathematics and science. When he applied for admission to Columbia, he was at first refused because of his low grades in these subjects. Courageously and successfully, his mother intervened at the Columbia admissions office. His closest high-school friends went to Yale, and Lionel, too, wanted to go to Yale, but his parents would not permit him to leave home. It was in a spirit of heroic self-sacrifice that his parents consented to his year as a teaching assistant at Alexander Meiklejohn's Experimental College at the University of Wisconsin. The fact that he had the whole of his education at Columbia was, I think, definitive in his career and his life.

Chapter
THREE

At dinner at Radcliffe in the long-ago days when we sat eight to a table in the dining hall and were served by fresh-faced Irish maids in black uniforms with crisp white aprons and caps, a not infrequent topic of undergraduate conversation was ancestry. I was often tempted to interpose my own rude boast: No, my ancestors had not sailed on the *Mayflower;* they had come to America, to Ellis Island, in steerage; as a young man, my father peddled macaroons on the Staten Island ferry. What consternation I would have caused! I am afraid the statement would have been a bit exaggerated. My father sold macaroons for only a few months while he was learning English. Then he became a braid salesman—this was in the last decade of the nineteenth century, when both men and women wore straw hats in the summer. My father sold straw braid to the manufacturers of women's millinery. Born in Russian Poland, he had grown up in the Warsaw ghetto. At the age of eighteen, like so many other Russian or Polish Jews, he came to America to escape military service in the armies of the Czar. When he arrived here, he knew no language except Yiddish: he had had the whole of his education at Hebrew school, the *heder*—I doubt that my father had ever heard Polish spoken until he met my mother in America. My mother's place of birth was the Polish countryside, some fifty miles from Warsaw; she had probably never heard Yiddish until she met my father and learned to speak it in order to speak with his father. My paternal grandfather was the only grandparent I knew. He was an awesome figure to me. I never had a loving and indulgent grandparent. Broad-shouldered, full-bearded, unsmiling, he reminded me of Moses in the stained-glass window of the Temple to which we children were taken on the High Holidays. My grandfather was not interested in children; I recall but a single remark he ever addressed to any of us. My parents were celebrating their fifteenth wedding anniversary with a large family dinner at which we three children—I, the youngest, was eight—entertained with music. My sister was at the piano, my brother was first violin, and I, as befitted my age, played second fiddle to him. Our repertory consisted of trio "arrangements" by our music teacher; I remember that they included a variation on "A Hot Time in the Old Town Tonight." We were supposed to play throughout the meal, but halfway through the dinner my grandfather told us that we had done our duty and could now sit down. Although he spoke in Yiddish, we had no difficulty in knowing what he meant. Children understand approval or reprimand in any language.

There was little religious observance in my childhood home. Apparently my mother had had no religious upbringing; she had scarcely known that she was Jewish. On coming to America, my father discarded his religious rearing. The fact that we were Jewish was not established by any routine or ritual of our home. We lit no Friday-night candles and we said no prayers; Saturday was like any other day of the week. We were not kosher: we casually mixed meat and milk dishes at our table and even ate pork spare-ribs with my mother's homemade sauerkraut. But we did observe, or partially observe, the important Jewish holidays: we went to Temple—it was reformed and was never called a synagogue—for Rosh Hashanah and Yom Kippur and we fasted on Yom Kippur and ate no bread during Passover. For Seder, my father took us to the home of his older sister; I have no recollection of my parents joining us there. When I was old enough to discuss religion with my father, he explained to me that as a young man in this country he had become an agnostic. It was stupid, he said, to call oneself an atheist, since the nonexistence of God could not be proved. My grandfather gave no sign of being troubled by the unorthodoxy in which his son lived and in which his grandchildren were being reared. But he would not eat at our table. If he was with us at the dinner hour, a place was set for him apart from us, and all he ate was sardines, a tomato, and a thick chunk of rye bread. His food was served to him on a cut-glass plate and he lifted the sardines from their tin and cut the tomato with his own pocket knife. To me, the combination of sardines and tomato, eaten in this rugged fashion, was the most appealing of meals; it was my equivalent of Lionel's lunch from a lunch pail. The argument could be made, if it were called for, that Lionel's and my conduct of ourselves as Jews, though not actually determined for us by our two grandfathers, was approved by them or certainly not countermanded. While they were themselves faithful to their orthodoxy, neither of them required that his children or grandchildren substantiate their Jewish heritage with Jewish observance. Like Lionel but unlike most of the Jewish intellectuals of our generation, I had the childhood of an American who happened to be a Jew, not that of a Jew who happened to be an American.

Yet removed as he was from his own early life as a Jew, my father was intent upon his children being aware of their Jewish *being* and at least in my instance he realized this wish, though by means other than those he consciously employed. The distinguished Jewish historian Josef Yerushalmi speaks of the part played by Jewish memory in connecting Jews with one another and in preserving their sense of themselves as a people. On the surface, there may appear to have been little in my childhood to create Jewish memories but apparently there was enough to be crucial. I think that it chiefly derived from my love of my father and from his memory of himself as a child in the Polish ghetto. My father's early life is almost more vivid to me than my own; I add his past to mine, build my life upon his. At will, I conjure up the little boy he was then: I see him rising at dawn and treading the worn earth behind his tenement as he goes about the preparation for his long dark day. I see him at *heder,* bright-eyed, timid, shrewd, studying his Talmud, rocking and chanting in unison with the other little scholars, all of them hungry and sleepy and scared, all of them at the mercy of the Reb, that seedy and greedy tyrant over the young. I see him as a child of nine or ten being stealthily let out of his home to search for bread after a pogrom—he is small for his age and quick and clever, and if Cossacks are still about he will go unnoticed by them. There is no Chagall in my father's Jewish boyhood: nothing floats, there is no scent of flowers in the air. For this Jewish child there is only harshness and privation and seriousness learned too early, and somewhere the promise of enlargement, of space and light. In my childhood I had always to sleep with the windows wide open, even on the coldest winter nights, and to spend as much time as possible out of doors; my father spoke soberly of these benefits to health which had been denied him in his own young life. There was no significant difference between how Lionel and I felt about ourselves as Jews. I do not know what the memories were which connected him to his Jewish past. "I felt of him," said our son recently, "that being a Jew was for him not a matter of Jewish teaching or law but a certain unquietness, as if the world were full of ghosts which would not let him rest in a conclusion." In his more active intellectual life, religion engaged Lionel more than it did me, but except in the first year or two of our marriage, when he wrote for the *Menorah Journal* and was drawn into the quest for a Jewish identity, a search in which I refused to share and to which, in fact, I was openly opposed, we were united in being what we had essentially been raised to be: Jews without religion but Jews nonetheless.

Being Jewish was different for my brother than for me; I never experienced anti-Semitism in my early years, but he did, and the experience perhaps affects a boy differently, more personally and lastingly, than it does a girl—Paul Goodman, in an early story, "Facts of Life," writes charmingly of a little Jewish boy's creative confusion between his religion and sex. This was perhaps my brother's confusion. I had been born in the Bronx but my family had moved to Westchester when I was two years old, first to Larchmont, then to New Rochelle. In the Larchmont of those years, we were one of only two Jewish families. My sister and I played with the Lee girls on our block; their widowed mother boarded the school principal. We were welcomed by the Lees; being Jewish made no problem for us. My brother was three years, three months, and three days older than I—how he loved to spell out this magical degree of his seniority! The Gentile community of Westchester did not receive him as it received my sister and me. He often came home from school crying because he had been called a kike or a sheeny by the other boys and accused of having killed Christ. "Tell them that Christ was a Jew," my mother would instruct him in a voice of imperturbable good sense, and if this seemed not to settle the matter for her troubled son, she would add: "There's nothing I can do about it. Go beat them up!" The advice was no doubt meant to make a man of her little boy of eight or nine, but it was woeful in its ultimate influence. My brother grew up hating to be a Jew and he was something of a bully. Late in life, in a second marriage, now to a non-Jewish woman, he converted to Presbyterianism and was more content than I had ever known him to be. He was active in the church and became an elder. He was embarrassed about this before my sister and me, but there was no reason for him to be. We were glad that he was happier.

From his first employment as a braid salesman, my father progressed rapidly to become a braid manufacturer and he continued to prosper. In 1914 he took the family to Europe for a summer holiday; we crossed in elaborate fashion on the *France*. While we were in Berlin, the First World War began and for many days it looked as if we might be stranded abroad. We were booked to return on the *France* as well, but with the start of war the French Line at once closed down. Tirelessly, as if forecasting the plight of the refugees from Hitler in a later decade, my father canvassed the shipping offices until at last he found a single cabin for the five of us. It was on a British ship called, I think, the *Olympic.* The return journey was a difficult one. Threatened by submarines, we ran without lights. Our single cabin was close to the waterline, and my brother and I were flamboyantly seasick. Back in America, we soon moved from Westchester to Brooklyn, to the Midwood section of Flatbush; my father had set up his braid factory in Brooklyn's Bush Terminal. With the war, however, elaborate hats for women went out of fashion and he switched from the manufacture of braid to the manufacture of women's silk stockings and built a plant on Long Island. His new factory, I would later discover, was a pioneering venture in American commercial architecture; Nathalie Rahv, the architect wife of Philip Rahv, would tell me that she had visited it when she was a student. That, amid the poor little wooden houses in its vicinity, my father should have built this bold bare structure of concrete and glass, all functionalism and efficiency, poses the same question which is raised in many other areas of his conduct: How did he know about modern architectural design and, knowing it, come to accept it? Growing up, I was fascinated by my father as an employer and by his factory. The factory had an infirmary with an attendant nurse, and a restaurant in which one could get a hot midday meal at cost. The responsible head of his working family just as he was the responsible head of his biological family, he knew all his employees by name; if one of them was ill, he intervened in any way which he thought was helpful. The conditions which my father provided in his factory could not have been improved upon. He told me that as a young man he had been a Socialist; I always knew him as a Republican. At high-school age I sometimes accompanied the family chauffeur to pick up my father at work. I remember standing with him one afternoon at his office window, looking down at the little parking lot of his factory. There were perhaps a dozen cars in it. It was a time when cars were not yet relied upon to transport people to work, and my father contemplated this abundance with grave pride. They were the cars of his employees, he explained to me, and it was only because the people who worked for him prospered and were able to afford cars that he prospered. The successful launching of my father's hosiery business was a direct result of his trade-union sympathies. Soon after he began the manufacture of women's silk stockings, the industry was unionized. The other manufacturers set out to break the union, but my father recognized it. Alone of the owners, he was not struck. We were never wealthy; we were what is called "comfortable." My father had no imagination of wealth and he was not interested in power. Most of the intellectuals I have known made their way from what was then accepted as the lower or working class into the middle class by their own efforts. Lionel and I had our membership in the middle class secured for us by our parents.

For most of my father's relatives—my mother's, too—the prospect of earning an adequate living lay somewhere between the improbable and the inconceivable. My father helped as he could; he even created jobs for my mother's brother, my uncle Charlie, and his wayward handsome son. Uncle Charlie became the purchasing agent for my father's factory, which meant that he bought the stamps and paper clips. Regularly my father set up another brother-in-law in his own business, though just as regularly that business failed—my father said that protection of our uncle's self-respect was more important than his own loss of money. Our relatives seemed never to be resentful of my parents, despite my parents' better fortune and the help they took from them. This may have been because my mother and father had an innate innocence about money which communicated itself to the people they helped. They did not measure people by money and they largely attributed their own comfortable circumstances to luck, augmented by honesty and hard work. They had started their life together with no money at all. In the first years of their marriage they lived in San Francisco, in the Asian section of the city, and divided their two-room apartment between their living quarters and a shop in which my mother sold hats, which she made from my father's unsold braid. My sister was born in San Francisco. After my parents returned to New York, their lives became easier. With the improvement in their fortunes, they felt responsibility for their poorer relatives, but no guilt.

My parents were not book readers, like Lionel's parents. I cannot remember my mother reading even a newspaper and my father read little else. Yet from his scant reading, my father squeezed a serviceable education. At some point he had read *Les Misérables* and it had become his secular Talmud; throughout my childhood, Jean Valjean was in frequent attendance at our family table. From the injustices which had been visited upon that poor suffering creature my father spun parable upon improving parable. He had also read Upton Sinclair's *The Jungle* and Sinclair was an object of his lasting admiration: when my college friend Bettina Mikol married Sinclair's son David my father was unabashedly disappointed at not being able to find the great man in the son. The years of my girlhood and young womanhood were a period of great flowering in the American theater. After my parents moved to Brooklyn, they went to the theater every Saturday afternoon, but not for entertainment. "What do you take home with you?" my father would say, passing dismissive judgment on any play from which he failed to derive guidance or enlightenment. He was strangely in possession of information to which he had no visible access. He could assure me, for example, that the French Revolution was a middle-class revolution—but how had he come to this knowledge? While I was in college, he suggested that I take a course in logic—but how did he know that there was such a course? Yet for all his energy of mind, my father never attempted to advance his formal schooling. He never took advantage of the offerings of the settlement houses of the lower East Side, where he lived as a young immigrant. I think this was due to arrogance, and understandable. Conscious of his own quick intelligence, he was unwilling to have it look as if he were at the same intellectual level with people taking these first small steps in their education.

I would come to my interest in psychology through need: I turned to psychoanalysis because I was in emotional trouble. But my father had no doubt prepared the way for me. Intuitively he was convinced of the power of mind over body. In Larchmont he briefly made a Christian Scientist of my mother, or tried to. He dismissed his unnamed critics: "They can call it Jewish Science, if that makes them feel any better." The conversion lasted only a short time but long enough for my brother to recall tedious after-school sessions with a Christian Science reader; in the end, his enlarged tonsils and adenoids were removed surgically. When my father's best friend developed an ulcer, my father recommended a holiday from the strains of his usual life and took him on a camping trip to the Adirondacks. Neither of the men had experience of the outdoors; they must have looked a strange pair of Jewish Pickwickians. In believing when he did that ulcers were the product of stress, my father was well in advance of the medical profession. Shortly before his death, he learned of Freud and psychoanalysis: he had picked up a book by Dr. Helene Deutsch, which I had left behind me at his apartment. He tried to make an appointment to see Dr. Deutsch, but any form of psychological therapy was now out of the question for him; he was already fatally ill with heart disease. He was precociously persuaded of the importance of exercise and diet in the prolongation of life and in the countering of disease: he did elementary setting-up exercises every morning and, trailed by his car, walked a mile on his way to work. Cholesterol had not yet been heard of: for many years, with heroic consistency, he ate two poached eggs, a baked apple with cream, and a large glass of milk for his lunch each day. For some weeks after his visit to the Kellogg sanitarium, our house overran with cold cereals and ripe olives—it was a vain attempt to make vegetarians of us. Tolerant though my father was of alcohol, he was deeply opposed to cigarette smoking. When I was twenty, he offered me a roadster if I would never again smoke a cigarette. Today, gasping with emphysema, I remember my flippant refusal of his bribe.

The lust for honesty in my family was ravaging and incurable: I am its product. Honesty was interchangeable with sincerity and especially in supply where a touch of untruth would have been considerably more agreeable. If, say, my father was asked whether he liked the cake being served to him by some family member, he had no hesitation in responding with a sincere "No." My mother was the sole exception to his distaste for compliments; in general he saw no difference between praise and basest flattery. My mother was not beyond an occasional small lie. She lacked my father's taste for the literal. But she steered us children in my father's honest path. When she caught me one day with a cherry pit in my mouth and learned that I had taken the cherry from the grocer's bin, she made me repay the grocer the penny I owed him. I liked to play store and I would fill little dishes with tea, cocoa, raisins, bits of crackers, which I sold to imaginary customers. At the dinner table one evening, my mother asked me whether I had used sugar in the tea in my store that afternoon. It was wartime and there was a sugar shortage. I lied: "No." Mary was just then clearing the table; my mother turned to her and questioned her in Polish: "Did *panenka* use sugar when she was playing this afternoon?" I loved to be called *panenka*. It means "little miss," and I felt that it gave me status, but at this moment I was in irremediable despair. Even Mary could not lie—she answered that I had indeed used sugar. The room was thunderously quiet as my mother and father exchanged glances. Their silence was as severe a punishment as I ever had. I still find it difficult to tell the most trifling social lie. The need not to deviate from truth drags like an anchor on this book; it would have been impossible for me to be a writer of fiction and invent my own versions of truth. There was great emphasis on good manners in my upbringing: I was not to speak unless I was spoken to, I was not to eat until everyone had been served or to put my elbows on the table, I was not to contradict my elders, I was not to cross my legs except at the ankle. Yet there was an important sense in which I was never socialized: I was never taught to please. I was in middle age before it broke upon me that people made life more pleasant and profitable for themselves by undertaking to please others, often at some cost in honesty.

Unfortunately, my father was interested in psychology only as an aspect of physical health; he was not concerned with mind as a permanent repository of experience. While he could be highly sensitive to the needs of his adult relatives or his employees, he was more than careless of the feelings of his or anyone's children. He was of course the product of his East European upbringing; almost as a matter of principle, the culture in which he was reared inflicted gratuitous cruelty upon the young. One Christmas Eve the young son of my father's sister hung up his stocking in the inappropriate hope that Santa Claus would fill it in the night. My aunt, his mother, filled it with onions and garlic. My father thought this a splendid joke. There was no physical punishment in my upbringing; I was sometimes slapped but I was never beaten or even spanked. But I was insulted and humiliated, more by my father than by my mother. He took coarse pleasure in telling my sister or me that we were unattractive: "You'll never catch yourself a man to hang onto" was the ugly language in which, in our adolescence, he foretold our grim futures. My mother never spoke coarsely but she had her own means of keeping her small child within what she considered the proper bounds of reality. To playact in front of my gathered family when I was a little girl was to ask for ridicule. "The child is dreaming, the child is dreaming," I sang in a languishing voice and waved my arms around my head to rid the Larchmont air of its unwanted actualities. "The child is dreaming, the child is dreaming," my mother mockingly sang after me, to the delight of my brother and sister, and she waved her arms in derisive imitation of me. My father said that he would build me a stage in the toilet—the remark was critical in my life. In consigning me to the place of excrement he could not more vividly have put his ban on self-display. I permanently incorporated the prohibition into the system of law by which my life is governed. Without psychoanalysis, I would not have been enough free of it even to make a start as a published writer. My mother's mockery was diluted by her liking for fun but she, too, was sternly on guard lest I yield to the seductions of public exhibition. On my fifth birthday I was given a half-size violin and began music lessons with Professor Steinmetz, who was already teaching my brother the violin and my sister the piano—he was our local one-man conservatory and taught all instruments equally badly. Every year the students of Professor Steinmetz gave a concert in our school auditorium. I had been studying for six months when I made my first concert appearance; I was his youngest performer and my picture was printed in the local newspaper. For my solo I played an absurd composition called "The Boy Paganini"—I remember nothing about it except its inflated title. Halfway into my performance, my E string broke; the snap could be heard everywhere in the hall. Without stopping I transposed the remainder of my piece to the other three strings and went on to the end. When the concert was over I was surrounded by the admiring mothers of the other little musicians, congratulating me and exclaiming over me. My mother moved quickly among them, quieting them: "Shhh, shhh!" They must restrain their compliments lest my head be turned. To this day I expect that any success or praise will bring its swift retribution. My head need not actually be turned by a compliment for me to act out its physical consequence. All my adult life I have been prone to dizziness.

Several times while I was growing up, my mother warned me never to marry a man who did not dance. Although she spoke in jest, I could hear the regret in her voice for something she missed in her own marriage, some lightness or frivolity which would have alleviated its prevailing seriousness. Yet it was the gravity of my father's temperament which had drawn her to him in the first place. Like my father, my mother had left Poland at eighteen but she left an old rural Poland of which my father knew nothing. Her maiden name was Forbert, neither a Polish nor a Jewish name—perhaps a soldier in Napoleon's army had lingered on after the Russian campaign. The youngest of a large family, she had been orphaned while still an infant and brought up by an older brother and his wife. My mother had more formal schooling than my father: she attended gymnasium and in addition to her native Polish spoke fluent German and even a bit of Russian. For me, the fact that she rode to school on horseback cloaked the whole of her early life in a romantic glow. She left Poland because of the sister-in-law with whom she lived: her brother's wife was so stingy, my mother said, that she bought teacups with bumps in the bottom so people would think that they were stirring sugar in their tea. Such extravagance of speech was typical of my mother. She made up wonderful on-omatopoeic words which still are part of my unspoken vocabulary and she gave drama and color to even the most commonplace communication. My uncle Charlie had preceded her to America, and when she got here my mother lived with him and his wife. While she learned English, she worked as a model in the garment district. Her employment as a model soon turned out to be too morally hazardous for her and she apprenticed herself to a milli-ner. She never spoke of this as a sexual harassment, only as a nuisance. She never ceased to be vain of her figure.

My parents often told us children how they had become ac-quainted: my uncle Charlie had met my father and invited him to visit so that he would meet my mother. My mother, indignant at being matchmade, at first refused to come out of her bedroom. But curiosity then got the better of her and she peered in at the parlor door. My father was seated in a rocker and he was so short, my mother said, that his feet barely reached the floor. She was about to flee, but she heard him talk and was captured by his intelligence. My mother's careless exaggeration of my father's lack of height would always embarrass me—she was a few inches taller than he. It seemed not to bother my father. There was another story, in which the two of them were caught in a blizzard and my mother had to clear a path for my father so that he would not be lost in the snowdrifts. On his side, my father said that he married my mother so that his children would have a chance to be taller than he—and see how successful he had been! More momentously, he said that he fell in love with her when he heard her sing. At this, my heart stood still: after all, it was I who had inherited my mother's voice. I doubt that my mother had any awareness of the loveliness of her voice. Naturally, effortlessly, she sang at her housework; no one ever thought that she might study singing. She never sang for company; it was I who was asked to sing for guests.

My mother was not a beautiful woman but people treated her as if she were. Everyone, my father's friends, my brother's friends, the neighborhood storekeepers, the family chauffeur, was a little in love with her. I was confused and disturbed by the behavior to her of my father's old camping companion. In the summer of my sixteenth birthday, my mother and father went to Poland to visit their relatives. On their return, we children met them at the pier; my father's friend was there as well. No sooner was the gangplank lowered than he rushed up to the deck and lifted my mother in his arms to carry her down to us. His display of intimacy seemed not to trouble my father but it troubled me: it gave me an unformulable but disquieting perception of the tangled emotions which lay behind this seemingly simple friendship. Five or six years later the wives of the two men died within a few months of each other; both men then courted the same woman. She married my father's friend, but he did not live happily with her or long. He took his own life shortly after my father died.

I grew up with the belief that my mother was greatly dependent upon my father. This was both true and untrue. Her relation to my father was much like my relation to Lionel: she was dependent upon him but also entirely competent on her own. From Westchester my father commuted by train to work in New York. In winter there were often heavy snowfalls which delayed his return home. When this happened, my mother would stand at the window, silently staring out into the darkness; she was the very image of operatic despair, Madame Butterfly piteously watching for her Pinkerton. If my father took even the briefest business trip, the whole family flocked to Grand Central Station to see him off; my mother had only to enter that august structure to begin to cry. Yet in my father's absence she was her same busy competent self— or so it appeared to me. She died of pernicious anemia in her early fifties, after seven years of steadily deteriorating health, but until she became ill, which means until I, the youngest of her children, was thirteen or fourteen, her domestic energies were formidable. In my early childhood, in addition to her other duties of marketing and cooking and seeing to her children, she made most of my clothes, including my coats and of course my hats. She took care of a sizable kitchen garden with the help of a professional gardener only one half-day each week. She fed the chickens and gathered their eggs; she even cleaned the coops. In Larchmont we had a cold pantry next to the kitchen and a storage pantry in the cellar. On their shelves stood row upon row of fruits and vegetables which my mother had put up for the winter: carrots and beets and beans, peaches and plums, rhubarb, strawberries, raspberries, huckleberries. She dilled her own pickles and, on a weird contraption which stood in the cellar, a kind of domestic guillotine, she chopped cabbage for sauerkraut. In the backyard she plucked the feathers of ducks and geese, washed them and set them in the sun to bleach; she made them into pillows and billowing comforters for our beds. Spring and autumn housecleanings were giant campaigns against despoiling time: every closet in the house had to be turned out, everything aired and scrubbed. With Mary, my mother lifted the rugs and hung them on clotheslines in the yard. The two of them beat them with sticks. Both our Larchmont house and the house to which we moved in New Rochelle were heated by coal furnace, and my mother cooked on a coal stove. A furnaceman came mornings and evenings, but between his visits either my mother or Mary stoked the furnace and hauled the coal scuttles from the cellar to the kitchen. My father had no part in these burdensome routines. I never saw him do anything around the house more strenuous than hosing down our dog, Toodles, on a hot summer evening; this was in itself an unlikely enough activity for someone bred in the ghetto, where pets were unknown. On snowy winter mornings, when the milk and bread were delivered by sleigh and the bell tolled at the firehouse so we would know that there was no school, my mother rose even earlier than usual to clear the porch steps and front sidewalk for my father. It took a long time for me to learn that in our society it was the men who were expected to do the heavy work. When Lionel and I were first married, it frightened me to see him lift heavy luggage or furniture. I took this to be the work of women.

Our return trip to America in 1914 after the outbreak of war in Europe had to have been a difficult one for my parents, but neither my mother nor my father betrayed undue anxiety. Our port of departure was Liverpool; we had to get to England from Berlin. Although the fighting had only just begun, the Berlin train station was already jammed with carloads of wounded German soldiers; there were heads wrapped in bloody bandages at every window. We children had little American flags pinned to our clothes to indicate that we were neutrals. On the train we shared a compartment with a demonic British nun, who displayed to us her collection of bullets: the merciful ones, she said, were those of the British—they did their work swiftly and cleanly; those of the "enemy" tore agonizingly through the heart. For many hours we were without food, until at last we stopped at a station in Holland where my father got off to buy sandwiches, *schinkenbröts,* at the station restaurant. A whistle blew and the train took off without him; we had lost not only our father but also our money and passports. My mother remained wholly in command of herself. In her excellent German she arranged with the conductor that we would get off at the next station. Meanwhile, the conductor would wire back to tell my father where to meet us. It turned out that my father had not, in fact, been left behind. He had been unable to reach us until we got to a station. Our return voyage across the submarine-infested Atlantic could not have been more hazardous. In mid-ocean there was a fire on board, and it was rumored that as we neared New York we rammed and sank a fishing vessel. Until we sighted the Statue of Liberty my mother gave no sign of her strain. Only when she saw that at last we were home did she allow herself to cry.

Dr. Marianne Kris, the last of my psychoanalysts, suggested that my mother had perhaps suffered a nervous breakdown after my birth. She was speaking conjecturally but her speculation was confirmed by my sister's response when I showed her a picture of me at the age of ten or eleven months. Although it was a posed studio photograph, I was accompanied not, as one would expect, by my mother or some other family member but by a strange young woman, Slavic in appearance yet distinctly not one of our Polish maids. I appealed to my sister as to someone who had been six and a half years old when the picture was taken and would presumably be better able than I to identify my companion. My sister pushed the picture from her. I was never again to question her about our childhood, she said fiercely. "I remember nothing!" I now recalled that my mother herself often casually spoke of a nervous breakdown. I had never thought to inquire about its circumstances. It was the assumption of our home that mother was "nervous." I took this to mean that she worried unnecessarily, especially if we children were not home when we were supposed to be. If it was true that she was away for a year or more after my birth or even that she was home but unable to be in charge of the house or of her children, this together with Bobolinka's close presence would be enough to account for much of my early fear-fulness and for the insecurity which, in one manifestation or an-other, all three of us children shared. There were also aberrancies in my mother's conduct which support the belief that she suffered a breakdown after my birth. When our cat had kittens, my mother drowned the unwanted litters in a kitchen pail. This could have been done in the yard or in the cellar, out of my sight, but it was always done, as if by unrecognized purpose, in my full view—I still see their bloated little bodies rising to the surface of the water, their tails limp at their sides like bits of wet string. Could this happen to an unwanted little girl? One awful day the cat chose to give birth to her kittens under the dining-room table. While I stood by, screaming, my mother had Mary prod the laboring creature with a broom: a baby kitten which was in the process of being born was squashed and the bloodied rug had to be taken outdoors and scrubbed. With her well-cared-for hands, my mother twisted the necks of chickens or, alternatively, chopped off their heads. Yet if a baby chick was ill, she bedded it down in soft cotton batting in an old sewing basket which she set at the back of the coal stove for warmth. Delicately, she would pry open its little mouth and feed it pepper-water with an eyedropper. I remind my-self that my mother was country-born and that what I saw as bru-tality was perhaps the habit of her country upbringing: chickens are food, cats are expendable. But it was not as a country wife or a country mother that my mother presented herself to the world or raised her children. She did hard physical work but she was never disheveled. She was never crude in her speech or tolerant of crudeness in our speech or behavior. Yet when my brother wet his bed—or was it I? He and I once talked about this and he insisted that it was I and not he who had misbehaved and been pun-ished—she spread the discolored sheet on the hedge in front of our house for all the neighborhood to see. More and more, I come to think that insofar as my parents are to be blamed for the emo-tional difficulties of my later life, it is largely due to their inconsistency of behavior. The father who told me that he would build me a stage in the toilet was—I keep it in mind—the same father who was unsparing in his concern for his employees. The same mother who allowed a cat to be beaten while it was in labor could not have been more tender of an ill baby chicken. A child has to know the nature of her emotional universe; she has to know where she stands. I never had firm emotional ground under my feet. One day in kindergarten our teacher talked to us about being kind to animals. I listened intently as she told us that there was a Society for the Prevention of Cruelty to Animals to which we could report any abuse of our animal friends. She gave us SPCA buttons and, wearing my button, I rushed home from school, exulting in my new power. My mother and sister and brother were in the kitchen; the ubiquitous Mary was with them. Ringingly I cautioned my mother that kittens were never again to be drowned in our house. I snapped my fingers and announced grandly: "I can have you arrested as easy as that!" Shouts of laughter greeted my threat and for the rest of my life, long after my parents were dead, until my brother and sister also died, I had only to venture a claim to power for one or the other of them to respond with a snap of the fingers: "I can have you arrested as easy as that!"

Lionel and I had been married for several years when one day he chanced on a book by an American journalist, Virgilia Peterson, a memoir of her marriage to a member of the Polish nobility, Prince Sapieha, and of a visit she made with him to his family in rural Poland. Delighted, Lionel declared that he now had the key to my upbringing: I had been raised in sixteenth-century Poland, a child of the landed aristocracy. The Polish town which my mother came from, Plozk, did indeed have a twelfth-century cathedral with the tombs of Polish kings; but the distance between her family and royalty, or even between her family and the Sapiehas, was wide and unbridgeable. The old ways of the landed aristocracy and in particular its superstitions could nevertheless have readily filtered down to her class. My mother's medical practices had to have come from a culture steeped in folk magic. If, as a child, I caught cold, she rubbed the soles of my feet with garlic; if I got a foreign object in my eye, she licked it out with her tongue, or tried to. If she had to catch up a hem or otherwise sew something I was wearing, she gave me a piece of thread to chew so that my insides—or was it my brains?—would not be sewn together. I recall a day when we had tuna fish for lunch and my mother was suddenly seized with the idea that the fish was tainted; she rushed us children to the kitchen and rubbed our tongues with lettuce leaves. The Sapiehas and their class were elegant worldly people but the culture around them was cruel and primitive.

Apart from whatever in the tension between us might be traced to a breakdown after my birth, my mother and I were perhaps also too much alike in temperament to live together without friction. There were moments of tenderness in my early childhood, when I lay with my head in her lap or nuzzled my nose in her neck, but by the time of my adolescence I felt as if there were nothing I could do that did not displease or anger her. Yet hurtful as this was, the strain in our relationship was finally, I think, less damaging to me than was the permission she gave my brother and sister to act upon their envy of me, the last-born of the family. Their teasing and torment of me was permitted by my father as well. I had few playthings as a child—this was an aspect of the puritanism of our home. Especially precious to me was my set of dolls' dishes, which hung on a bracket in the pantry. My brother one day tossed a tennis ball at the little cups and saucers until every piece was smashed; although my mother was close by in the kitchen, he was not stopped or reprimanded. I loved the paraphernalia of business offices and I had hoarded a collection of bills of lading and ledgers. My sister threw them into the furnace. Unheeded by my parents, my brother would press his mouth to my hand or arm and kiss it until I was in a frenzy of rage. My sister tickled me mercilessly. I tried to fight them off but they were bigger and stronger than I. Even after college, I was still punching and scratching my sister. Throughout my childhood, whenever I told my family something which my brother could suppose gave me an advantage over him, he accused me of having made it up. For instance, on my return from camp one summer, I reported a visit we had had at camp from the famous Rose Pastor Stokes; she was an immigrant garment worker who had married a wealthy society man and become a figure in the news. As my parents sat by without comment, my brother declared categorically—in the face of my protest that Rose Pastor Stokes had even borrowed my riding pants—that the visit had never taken place. It was never openly said by my parents that I was not to outdistance my brother or sister; I knew, however, that they must not in any way be threatened by me or surpassed by me. I was not to surpass my brother because he was a boy and I was not to surpass my sister because she was handicapped—she had a slight curvature of the spine and was slower to learn than I. I was not consciously aware of it until middle age, but this requirement put upon me by my parents was of central importance in my life. I internalized it as firmly as I internalized my parents' ban on self-display. It has outlived my brother and sister and still disarms me for normal competitiveness. I populate the world with sibling surrogates: brothers to whom I must allow ascendancy over me for no other reason than that of gender, sisters to whom I must atone for having been born with a quick mind and a straight spine. My son was an only child: I often assured him that this was a happy fate. When I encounter someone with loving, proud, encouraging, protective brothers and sisters, I am filled with envy.

Chapter
FOUR

I had followed my brother to Erasmus Hall High School in Brooklyn. He was a senior when I was a freshman; if we passed each other in the school corridors, he pretended not to know me. It was understandable. In 1917 when the glamourous Irene Castle cut her hair, she set a fashion for women. My parents opposed it. They also believed that schoolgirls should not pin up their hair. My hair hung down my back; it was no longer in curls but it was dismally childlike. The girls with whom my brother associated were precocious worldlings; they not only wore their hair up but also wore high heels and silk dresses to school. I wore blue serge middies with matching pleated skirt. My brother moved in what was reputed to be the school's "fast" set. While I could not have said what was the speed at which he and his companions traveled or to what destination, I, like everyone else in the school, had heard colorful stories of parties in the art teacher's studio and of study hours diverted to a nearby pool parlor. My high-school friends were girls. We were not budding intellectuals; we were yearners, hankering after the mysteries of art and love. We formed a club which met at one or another of our homes to read poetry and listen to Victrola records of Paderewski and Kubelik. With the lights dimmed, cautious lest a mother suddenly come in upon us, we drank ginger ale laced with grape juice—we had been promised that in proper proportions it was an intoxicant. Our eyes grew heavy. In these early years of the century, political protest had not yet reached the campuses of the universities, let alone the high schools. Nevertheless, fired by idealism, I helped organize a third political party at Erasmus to combat our corrupt old two-party government. Unsuccessfully, we ran a colored boy for student president—it would then have been insulting to refer to him as a "black"; at that time the use of the word "colored" rather than "Negro" indicated a decent relaxation in matters of race. But my friends and I were not always and only high-minded. There were spring afternoons when I twisted my hair into spit curls at either side of my face, pasted a bit of black paper at the corner of my eye for a beauty spot and, in the company of one or more of my girlfriends, went to Brooklyn's Prospect Park to pick up boys. At the park lake, we rented a flat-bottomed boat and rowed out until we were close to a boat with boys in it, so close that our oars grazed and there was the danger that they might interlock and that we would all of us go overboard together.

Although I was not the first member of my family to go to college, I was the first on either side to graduate from college; my brother briefly went to Cornell but flunked out at the end of his freshman year. He made no further attempt to advance his education; he entered my father's business. My father is the only person I have ever known who did not want his son to follow him in his business or profession. My mother prevailed upon him to yield to my brother's wish. It turned out to be a costly mistake. At the start, my brother was gifted in business. But this was in the early twenties; in 1929, when he was twenty-seven, the stock market crashed and his life was drastically altered. In the flourishing economy of the late twenties, my father had decided to add a new wing to his factory. He took a substantial bank loan, using not only his business but also his personal assets as collateral. The market collapsed and the bank took over his business and threw him out. My brother was made head of the company: changes of this kind, however ill-advised, seem always to be demanded in proof that a business is making progress. It was a catastrophic development for both of them. My father lost everything he had ever worked for, and although my brother had no part in my father's downfall, the fact that he had replaced his father tortured him with guilt for years to come. The bank insisted that he run an open shop, and as he entered and left the factory he was booed by my father's old union employees. For years he struggled to keep the company afloat, until at last he admitted defeat; he was never again able to find employment for his talents, and indeed the talents themselves disappeared. Soon after the loss of his business, my father became ill and in 1932 he died. My mother had not lived to see the change in his and my brother's fortunes: she had died in 1926, well before the Depression.

My mother opposed my going to Radcliffe: she wanted me to go to college in Brooklyn or New York but she was overruled by my father. My father had not had a sudden access of parental permissiveness; he did his best to circumscribe my new freedom. I had to be accompanied by my sister on my train journey to Boston—my long-dreamed-of arrival in college was ruined. The night before I left for college he made a last effort to control the company I would keep while I was away from home. I had been corresponding with a student at the Massachusetts Institute of Technology, the friend of a friend of mine; my father had confiscated a letter from my unknown correspondent and confronted me with it:

Dear Diana [it began]
belongs over here but I am putting it over there.

"Who is this man you're writing to?" my father demanded in a voice which plainly conveyed his opinion that anyone who violated the conventions of letter writing was bound to be a villainous seducer. "You are never again to have anything to do with him!" I felt that I had even to conceal from my parents the fact that our dormitory rules permitted us to stay at a Harvard dance until it ended—after a Yale-Harvard game this could be 5:00 A.M. Actually, my parents had little to fear in my life at Radcliffe, certainly not in the sexual sphere, which was of course what concerned them. My closest college friend, Bettina Mikol, was only an extreme instance of the sexual inexperience and ignorance which characterized most of my college contemporaries. We were allowed to entertain our professors at dinner in the dormitory, and Bettina and I were invited to one of these polite ceremonies. The dinner-table conversation turned to the news of the day: a Siamese twin had married. "Imagine!" Bettina declared, bright-eyed. "Imagine having to propose in front of another person!" She was not being playful; at the age of eighteen, this was the extent of her knowledge. A girl I knew in our hall married at the end of her junior year. She came back to finish college but she was not again allowed to live in the dormitories. The Dean warned her that she was not to answer any questions about the marital mysteries put to her by the other students. Another of my dormitory acquaintances broke her engagement when she discovered that after a Harvard hygiene lecture her fiancé had specifically asked questions about sexual hygiene. We were largely self-governed in the residence halls but each of the dormitories was presided over by a house mistress, a middle-aged woman who was either a widow or a spinster. The house mistress was not a role model. No one spoke of role models; we were expected to make our futures without the aid of precedent. Her job was to keep us in charge and see that we behaved like ladies. Miss Whitney was the house mistress of Barnard Hall, the dormitory in which I lived during my first three years of college. She was by far the most appealing of the house mistresses. I liked to visit her in her sitting room with its New England clutter: its old family books and photographs, the travel scenes and writing cases and book stands, its plethora of clocks and vases and bric-a-brac. Miss Whitney had her own store of prejudices: she refused me permission to double-date with a Chinese girl in the dormitory because she considered it improper for me to be seen in the company of Chinese men. Unlike the other house mistresses, all of whom seemed stifled by respectability, she leavened her exercise of propriety with humor; it was fun to have a house mistress who posted a notice on the door of the dormitory: "If you have to salute your escort, please don't do it under my window." The love of Miss Whitney's life was her cat, James Barnard. She would invite anyone of whom she was especially fond to plant a kiss on James's wet little nose. One night James Barnard gave birth to a litter of kittens; with perverse instinct, he chose as the place for the accouchement the bed of the most maidenly resident of the hall. The occupant of the bed awoke to see the strange event which was transpiring on her bed and became hysterical. The hysteria continued for several days while she tried to persuade the college authorities, if not to dismiss Miss Whitney, at least to make her give up her pet. Again and again, she assured us that if her mother had wanted her to know such things, she would have told her about them. Obviously, there were "things" about which none of our mothers had told us. No one in the dormitory—not Miss Whitney, not any of us who had been privileged to salute her cat—had recognized that James Barnard was not a male.

Like my brother, I, too, did badly in my freshman year at college. I was luckier than he; I was able to rescue myself. I had similarly never had to study in high school; now I insolently cut classes and disregarded the assigned reading. At midyear I flunked all my courses, including a course in European history taught by the eminent Harvard historian Charles H. Haskins. Professor Haskins took the trouble to consult my high-school records and immediately identified the nature of my problem: I was not studying. He warned me that unless I got to work, I could not stay in college. The idea of repeating my brother's failure filled me with fear:

by the end of the term, I had raised my grades to passing or better. I had only a smattering of a literary education at Radcliffe: one course in Romantic and Victorian poetry taught by the celebrated John Livingston Lowes and a half-course in Tolstoy—I have no way to account for the course in Tolstoy. In 1969–70 Lionel would be the Norton Visiting Professor of Poetry at Harvard and we would live in Cambridge for the year. We were invited one evening to speak to a group of Harvard and Radcliffe undergraduates at a dormitory gathering. The first question was courteously asked of me: What courses had I taken at college to prepare me for the profession of critic? "None," I had to reply. This seemed to surprise my listeners, but in the Radcliffe and Harvard of my day criticism had no independent standing in the study of literature and even had it been taught, it is not likely that I would have enrolled for it. I was not an English major; I majored in Fine Arts, then a relatively new subject in the curriculum. What drew me to art history was a first survey course which I took in my freshman year—in my time, and perhaps still, Radcliffe and Harvard freshmen were let sink or swim with no guidance in the selection of their courses. Fine Arts 1c and 1d, as the survey course in art history was then called, was the most beguiling of the five demanding subjects I selected as a freshman. The most diligent and disciplined student might have sunk under the load.

Although Lionel and I entered college in the same year, 1921, and at the same age, just after our sixteenth birthdays, to compare our college experiences, mine at Radcliffe and his at Columbia, is to conclude that the concept of cultural contemporaneity has no meaning. To be sure, we were differently prepared for college. Lionel had read, or had had read to him, many good books and reading had been an approved activity of his home. He had uncles and aunts who were college graduates, and it had always been taken for granted that he would go to college and even to graduate school. My family was ambivalent about books. On the one hand, my parents recognized the essential part they played in education and thus in the Americanization of their children, a process to which they were wholeheartedly dedicated. But on the other hand, they looked upon books as an enemy: books drove a wedge between parents and their children. Their ambition for me when I grew up was that I would marry—or fail to marry. Neither eventuality required that I go beyond high school; too much education might even lessen the possibility of my marrying. More important, however, than any difference in our family cultures was the difference between the colleges we chose. Lionel's intellectual and professional life was directly shaped by Columbia. My intellectual life was shaped by Lionel. If Lionel had not shared the benefits of his Columbia education with me and I had been left with only the arid discipline of my Radcliffe schooling, I very much doubt that I could have become a critic. The Radcliffe-Harvard education of my day was a training in scholarship. It did not encourage the exercise of the critical intelligence.

For many years, even before it became a part of Harvard, to be accepted by Radcliffe was a badge of uncommon academic distinction. This was not how it was when I went there. I chose Radcliffe, Radcliffe did not choose me. I picked it as one might pick a name from the telephone book. I was not interviewed or in any way personally evaluated; I had only to pass the four standard college admissions examinations. I had heard of Vassar and Smith while I was in high school, and Mount Holyoke and Bryn Mawr, and even of Goucher, but I discovered Radcliffe in a library catalog. There were no college counselors in my high school or anyone to assist us in making our application; there were not enough of us interested in college to make this necessary. What attracted me to Radcliffe was the fact that it was an all-women's college and yet not isolated in the country. I wanted to avoid what I supposed would be the sexual competitiveness of a coeducational college but I also wanted to be near a men's school and near a big city. That Radcliffe shared the faculty of Harvard did not, I fear, significantly influence my choice. Fifty years later, in 1971, I would return to

Cambridge and for several weeks live in my old Radcliffe dormitory. I was doing an extended series of interviews with Radcliffe and Harvard undergraduates. As Lionel once had occasion to point out to our son's nursery school, all educational institutions live by self-congratulation. Although in 1971 Radcliffe was already giving up its independent status and merging into the dominant male university, it was still possessed of an unbecoming immodesty: to have been admitted to Radcliffe was to have been touched by the hand of God. Yet the pleasure which the students had in having scaled this Everest of educational institutions was far from absolute. Their achievement was blighted by their loneliness. Loneliness was the complaint not only of the Radcliffe students whom I interviewed but also of the Harvard men who were now moving into the Radcliffe dormitories—the reason, indeed, that most of the men gave for making the move was their hope that it would be easier for them to make friends with women than it was with men. But apparently the expectation was not being realized; they continued to be lonely alongside equally lonely young women. Sometimes the men and women went to bed together: this was not from the desire for a sexual encounter; it was an effort of intimacy. The close proximity of a body of the opposite sex seemed not to produce any sexual excitement. It never occurred to any of these young people that they might themselves be responsible for their loneliness. They regarded it as a given of life, wholly external to themselves, and spoke of it as one might speak of an unpleasant phenomenon in nature, a hailstorm, say, or poison ivy. One evening a group of students took me to dinner at a dormitory cafeteria. We walked there in a straggly line. As I entered the door, it was all but slammed in my face by the student who had preceded me. No one guided me through the unfamiliar routine of the eating hall; no one thought to fetch me a tray or a glass of water. In the course of the meal, we inevitably returned to the subject of how hard it was to break through the barriers separating them from one another. I listened for several minutes and then said bravely: "Wouldn't it perhaps help if you did simple polite things for one another, like holding the door or offering each other a glass of water?" They stared at me in wonder: What did offering someone a glass of water have to do with the conquest of loneliness? These were pleasant young people, generous and kind. They and the other students whom I was meeting were much nicer to me than the students of my generation had been to people older than themselves: if the students in the hall in which I was staying saw me leave for the evening, they went out of their way to wish me a good time; if there was a dormitory dance, they knocked on my door and insisted that I come out and join them. Yet they had the manners—in particular, the table manners—of people trained only in the pursuit of their own interest. It was at table that their separation from each other was most plainly visible. They addressed their food with a strange intensity, as if they were absorbing power with every mouthful. As the food bowls moved around the table, although everyone was careful not to take more than his or her fair portion, it never occurred to them to help another person, even an older guest, before serving themselves. For all their affability, they inhabited the world alone.

I knew no one in the Radcliffe of my day who was lonely, not after the first weeks of school, and no one who believed that loneliness was the human fate. We had far less public conscience than students of a more recent generation. We were less alert to the world's burden of injustice and conflict and far less conscious of our obligation as citizens. But within the social group we were connected with one another. We might not delight in the company of this or that resident of the hall but sociability was the premise of our daily experience. There is no question but that the friendliness with which we lived together was fostered by a certain formality in our dormitory arrangements. Breakfast and lunch were hurried affairs but our evening meal was ceremonious. For dinner we changed our clothes, if only to put on a fresh blouse, and gathered promptly and quietly outside the dining-hall doors. No one sat down until the house mistress had said grace and taken her place at the head table. The tables seated eight and were set with spotless white linen; we were waited upon by maids in uniform. Whoever happened to sit at the head of a student table was pro tem its hostess and took on a hostess's duty to see that her guests were properly cared for. Everyone was unostentatiously attentive to the needs of everyone else; no one would have thought to use the salt or pepper without first offering it to her neighbors, and everyone helped sustain the conversation and was involved in it— even the dreariest table companion was not knowingly excluded. The way in which we comported ourselves might not always be the practice of our homes—it was far from the practice of my home—but all of us accepted the established rules of propriety. Soon we were ourselves the bearers of tradition. From this steady exercise of courtesy, with its concomitant recognition of the existence of others besides ourselves, we developed our personal friendships and through our civility we confirmed and even helped create a society which could embrace all of us as individuals. We never doubted the good purpose of all society, particularly that of our own country, and we never questioned the idea of progress. We were taking our own small step in what would always be the brilliant forward march of history. It would have been inconceivable to us that only four short decades later, when I used the word "society" in just the sense in which I use it here, to denote the social entity within which we make our lives as individuals, the young New York literary critic to whom I was speaking would interrupt with the caustic comment: "Society? What's that? There's no such thing as society." His comment was not idiosyncratic. Even in the early sixties this sentiment was widespread among intellectuals and in the years since then it has of course been variously adumbrated in our intellectual culture. It was on this response and what it implied of rootlessness and fragmentation, both of them, as I saw it, the product of a culture in bondage to defeat, unwilling or unable to empower its continuing existence, that in 1964 I based the Foreword to my volume *Claremont Essays.*

I suppose that it was an important factor in my choice of my two closest friends at Radcliffe that although our families were differently located on the economic spectrum, we had basically the same origins: we were all three of us the daughters of immigrant Jews who had not allowed either their foreign birth or their religion to determine the kind of lives they led as Americans. That is to say, we were assimilated Jews—the designation was not yet thought to be pejorative. But even in the twenties our impulse to join in the full life of the college set us apart from the majority of the Jewish students. These were chiefly day students, girls who commuted to Cambridge from Boston and its environs; there were few Jewish girls in the dormitories. The Jewish day students huddled together in self-imposed segregation; it was a precursor of the black separatism of a later period. As residents of a dormitory, my close friends and I were suspect; the commuters rejected us along with the resident Gentile population. I cannot recall ever having had a conversation with a Jewish day student at Radcliffe, whether in a classroom or at the library or at a college assembly. The day students ate together in the Agassiz lunchroom, studied together, talked only with one another. But my close friends and I were also drawn together by something else: our shared attitude toward the prevailing social habits of Cambridge. In the strict social atmosphere which surrounded us, we thought of ourselves as rebels. This was not because we refused the prevailing conventions but because we reserved the right to choose which of them we would accept and which reject as an infringement upon our freedom. We were in fact little rebellious. Often we came close to outconforming the conformers: one of my friends had calling cards engraved so that she could follow a dinner at a professor's home with a properly documented dinner call. But prepared as we were to accept the customs of this strange country, there were proprieties which were binding upon our schoolmates which we disdained. The majority of the students at Radcliffe in my day were New Englanders, the daughters of small-town teachers and ministers. My friends and I felt of them that their imagination of life was sadly limited by their ready compliance with social dictate. The battle over hats was typical of the issues on which the three of us took our unpopular stand. In my junior year Radcliffe acquired a new dean, Bernice Brown. She was unusually young for the position, not yet thirty and, perhaps because of her youth, overly concerned with decorum. One day Dean Brown announced that she would not greet any Radcliffe student whom she met in Harvard Square not wearing a hat. Bettina and Dorothy and I risked this harsh punishment: we continued in our undecorous dress and I debated the issue of hats versus no hats in our Radcliffe newspaper with the president of student government, Vera Micheles, later Vera Micheles Dean of the Foreign Policy Association. Shortly before he died Dwight Macdonald would tell me that as a college student he had been similarly engaged in a protest of hats—Yale underclassmen had had to wear hats when they went outdoors.

But controversy even as moderate as this was infrequent at Radcliffe; the ruling Radcliffe style of my day—it was of course the style of Harvard as well—was one of complacency and polite accommodation. We were old for our age but also childlike; most Radcliffe girls seemed to have skipped the turmoil of adolescence. In high school I had counted the days and hours until I would go to college and be liberated from the oppression of my home, both actual and fancied. I ached to escape my parents and my brother and sister. I ached to escape my own skin. The independent life I envisioned for myself as a college student was largely inspired by the boarding-school stories I had read at the age of nine or ten. It had little to do with the widening of my perception of the world and much to do with fudge-and-pajama parties. If Radcliffe was not a place for fudge-and-pajama parties, neither was it a place where there were sown the seeds of a free life of the mind. Wherever we gathered, we chatted amiably but we never exchanged ideas or offered one another any intellectual challenge. Argument, however impersonal, was frowned upon as bad manners. We avoided even the mildest disagreement lest it give offense; there were no hills and dales in our intercourse, only the smooth plains of the acceptable and ordinary. The one passion we permitted ourselves was eating. Our interest in food was considerably more compelling than our commitment to thought. The pathologies of anorexia and bulimia were not yet known; there was no one of us but was healthily overweight. On each floor of the residence halls there were kitchenettes in which we could prepare between-meal snacks. When we were not eating in our rooms, we were eating in the ice-cream parlors or cafeterias of Harvard Square. The teaching fellow at MIT who later married my friend Dorothy never forgot the night that he took the two of us to a concert and then to the Harvard Cafeteria for a late-evening refreshment. Both Dorothy and I had dinner-size bowls of lamb stew.

All college education was then more rigorous than it is today, and Harvard was more demanding than most; our courses required long hours of study. We had strict afternoon and evening quiet periods in the dormitories; at examination time we were at our desks far into the night. What we were learning were facts, more facts, and yet more facts, how to gather them, how to memorize them and how to put them together in orderly fashion. The discipline was character-building but it was not conducive to thought. Since any intensity of idea bordered on the ill-bred, no one carried back to the dormitory any topic for discussion which had arisen in a classroom. I once tried to involve the girls at my dinner table in the metaphysical problem of appearance and reality—I was taking an elementary course in philosophy. My overture was received much as a discussion of business would be received in a club designed for escape from the sordid affairs of commerce. Few of us read any books which had not been assigned in our courses. The dormitory subscribed to several current magazines but I cannot remember reading them. An English course was required for graduation. With Professor Lowes, who must then have been working on his celebrated study *The Road to Xanadu,* I probed Coleridge's unconscious for the source of his literary allusions but I graduated from Radcliffe without having read a line of Homer or Dante or Chaucer, without knowing anything of Shakespeare beyond the one or two plays we had read in high school, scarcely knowing so much as the names of Montaigne and Tocqueville, Austen, Trollope, Flaubert, Dostoevsky, Emerson, Thoreau, Hawthorne, all of them writers with whom any educated person, even one who majors in art history, might be presumed to have an at least superficial acquaintance. And of present-day authors—also present-day artists—I knew even less than I knew of the past. In 1927, two years out of college, I had not yet heard of Proust or Yeats or T. S. Eliot. Lionel told me about them. In my senior year a young man named Alfred Barr, a newcomer to Harvard, one day to become the celebrated head of the Museum of Modern Art in New York, lectured to the art-history students on the modern masters of painting. The lecture was wordless, which was its own form of drama. Without comment other than to name the author of each picture, he flashed slides on the screen while the audience sat silent and staring. This was how I first learned of Matisse and Picasso, Cézanne, Derain, Duchamp, Léger, Braque.

With the approach of graduation, I was offered two positions by Professor Paul Sachs. He was one of my teachers and a powerful member of the Harvard Fine Arts Department and of the international art community. Among the several courses I had taken with him was his new, soon-to-be-famous museum course. One of the positions he now offered me was to assist him as director of Harvard's Fogg Museum. The other was to start a Fine Arts Department at Mount Holyoke. They were striking opportunities for a nineteen-year-old, yet for all the consideration I gave them, he might have been proposing that I do missionary work in China. In common with so many college women even today, I graduated from college wholly lacking in the professional definition which one finds in virtually any man of similar ability and training. I was as competent, I think, as the Harvard men alongside of whom I studied at the Fogg. But I could not imagine myself in the important positions which they naturally looked to and eventually held. I was without the fundamental prerequisite for a successful professional career: a firm sense of goal. The fact that I had become a serious student did not mean that I had become a serious candidate for professional employment. Perhaps none of the clever, hardworking women students in the department were. It was our male contemporaries who went on to become the leading museum directors and curators of the country. So far as I know, none of the gifted Radcliffe art historians of my time made a notable career in the field. In the wake of the First World War and woman suffrage, even young women who were securely fixed in the middle class were coming under pressure to "do something"; that is, to engage in a paid activity outside the home. The new demand had nothing to do with professional commitment or professional ambition. It represented only the wish to be free of the confines of domesticity. This is not enough on which to build a career. But my lack of professional seriousness was only one factor, and not the most important, in my rejection of Professor Sachs's offers. There was no point in my weighing the proposals he made to me because I knew that my family would not allow me to accept a position away from New York. The unspoken but unnegotiable agreement by which I had been permitted to go away to college was that as soon as I graduated I would return home where I belonged. My mother was now very ill with pernicious anemia. A dying mother might want to have her daughter at her side and a daughter might want to be with her dying mother: I wish I could say that this explains my response to Professor Sachs, but the truth of the matter is that even had my mother been entirely well, I would have made the same answer to him. My four-year leave of absence from home had run out. I had not been sent to college to prepare for an independent life, either emotional or financial. There was no need for me to be financially independent, because my father was there to take care of me. From time to time, he would say that I must know how to support myself in the event that this was required. He meant, of course, in the bleak event that I was without a man to take care of me. He never pressed the point. To have been emotionally independent of my family would have run counter to its interests. It surprised me to meet girls at Radcliffe who spoke unabashedly of their love for their mothers and fathers—I had never before met anyone who would admit that she loved her parents. In the world as I knew it, you honored and obeyed your parents, and if obedience and respect developed into affection, it was by unexamined accident and it was never spoken of. Now I also discovered that these loving daughters lived anywhere they chose when they finished college. I attributed this to the fact that as Gentiles they were free of the close ties of Jewish family life.

In the same years that I was at Radcliffe, Lionel was at Columbia. We both graduated from college in 1925, just before our twentieth birthdays—it was the habit of public schools, when we were young, to have their bright students skip grades, so that it was not unusual to enter college at sixteen. Our college experiences could not have been more unlike. If I now speak critically of my Radcliffe education, this must not be taken to suggest that I was disappointed or discontented at the time. My Radcliffe years were thoroughly enjoyable; as graduation approached, I felt that I would never again live so agreeably, in circumstances so suited to my taste, among people whose civility announced itself not only in their choice of language but in the very intonations of their speech. Cambridge, with its uncared-for winter streets, its ugly sprawling book-filled houses, their curtains never drawn so that in the dark and cold of a late winter afternoon the passerby could peer in at the windows and see the family gathered before a blazing fire, perhaps at tea, perhaps reading, was all I wanted of peace and charm. Severe as I may now be in judging my college education, I have never ceased to appreciate the setting in which I received it and the high gravity of its purpose. In particular, I appreciate the grounding it gave me in history, that most useful of teachings. My sense of the past remains skeletal but it has at least been of enough substance to make a major contribution to the enjoyment I have had in art, in travel, in politics, in all the occupations of my life. On one of our stays in England, my sister came to visit Lionel and me and I took her around London and on a sightseeing trip to Windsor and Oxford. She failed to respond as I hoped she would, and suddenly it came to me that nothing I was showing her—not Westminster Abbey or Trafalgar Square or the Tower of London or even Windsor Castle—had meaning for her. This was, for her, a world naked of association, naked of history. My knowledge of history, scant as it is, comes from my training in the history of art. To know anything of the history of art is to know something of the history of civilization. Yet if I compare my education with Lionel's, the conclusion is forced upon me that I spent my college years, if surely not in a cultural vacuum, in a cultural parish. This is not to be accounted for by any disparity in the education of men and women. Radcliffe was a separate institution from Harvard but it had the same faculty, the same mandatory courses, and the same range of electives. Our professors crossed Cambridge Common from Harvard to repeat to their female students the same lectures they had just delivered to their male students—how vividly I remember George Lyman Kittredge, the flamboyantly bearded Shakespeare scholar, clutching his green bookbag against the savage Cambridge winds which propelled him in our direction! What made for the difference between Lionel's experience and mine was not any difference between Radcliffe and Harvard, but the difference between Columbia and Harvard and between the intellectual climates of New York and Boston. I had no intimate men friends at Harvard but I had close working associates at the Fogg. We studied next to each other in the museum library and even joined forces in such advanced courses as Professor Sachs's museum course. These male contemporaries who went on to fill leading posts in the colleges and museums of the country were undoubtedly well-schooled connoisseurs, jam-packed with the necessary learning of their trade. I never knew them as inquiring minds or eager minds. Even today the academic study of art history, altered as it is since my day, still discourages speculation as if it were a subversion of reliable scholarship. The art historians are perhaps still atoning for the improvisations of a Berenson. But at Harvard it was not only in art history but in all the disciplines that the amassing of information was the primary aim. When Professor Sachs suggested that I work with him at the Fogg or start a department of art history at Mount Holyoke, he was not recognizing some special gift of critical intelligence in me—I had none, and had I had, it would have been a handicap. I was quick, diligent, and retentive. I reasoned well. But I was intellectually passive, and it was the combination of these qualities, both positive and negative, which won his approval. There was an occasion when I did undertake to do my own thinking at Radcliffe instead of relying on the lectures and secondary sources. The consequence was of a sort which could not inspire me to repeat the experiment. For my term paper for Professor Lowes, I had decided to compare Swinburne's treatment of the Tristan legend with Matthew Arnold's. I did almost no secondary reading for the paper; I applied myself to the poems. The class was a large one, and our papers were graded by a course assistant. He gave me a C minus. When my paper was returned to me, it resembled an illuminated manuscript, its margins were so richly decorated with the instructor's queries: "Source?" "Source?" "Source?" I was not being charged with plagiarism. He was accusing me of using other people's ideas without acknowledgment—students did not have ideas of their own.

Literary criticism, as we now define it when we distinguish it from book reviewing, on the one hand, and literary exposition or literary scholarship, on the other, was obviously not born at Columbia. But it was born in New York City and it had its fine early flowering at Columbia in the years in which Lionel was an undergraduate. There is a certain defiance of history in fixing the place and date as I do, in New York in the twenties: Was Coleridge, then, not a critic? Or Hazlitt, Carlyle, Ruskin, Tocqueville, Sainte-Beuve? Were the Transcendentalists of our own country not critics in at least an important part of their intention—if not literary critics, then literary-intellectual critics at a time when we had not yet become familiar with that ubiquitous hyphen? And what about Henry Adams, blood father of mid-twentieth-century criticism at its most alienated, which is to say, at its most exigent? Yet the fact remains, quite in the face of so daunting an array of figures from the past, that in the twenties there developed in this country, New York its birthplace, a new kind of critical attention to the arts and society which appeared to be indigenous, without nameable antecedent. The First World War had newly brought America into the community of nations and it had been followed by the Russian revolution, which newly demonstrated the role of mind in politics. There now emerged in this country a new life of idea. With varying degrees of urgency, mind—conscious mind—had tried throughout history to influence the way in which public, no less than private, responsibility was exercised. There must be many explanations of why a new and strenuous effort along this line now announced itself in America. That it appeared in New York is easier to account for. We casually speak of the intellectual life of New York City in the mid-twentieth century as New York Jewish intellectual life. This is not because it lacked its distinguished practitioners who were not Jews but because so many of its influential figures *were* Jews, not only self-conscious but self-advertised Jews whose parents had come to this country from East Europe to escape religious and political oppression. These first-generation Americans were importantly concentrated in New York City and they gave its tone of significant contention to the intellectual life of America for several decades. One might conjecture, indeed, that one of the reasons why criticism as we knew it in earlier decades of this century has now disappeared, or has certainly shown a marked decrease in vitality, is that it is practiced by people reared at a generational remove from the contentious tradition of their European-bred forebears. At Columbia or New York University or the City College of New York, New York produced young intellectuals the character of whose thought, whatever the politics to which it might attach itself, had its roots in the Jewish European rather than the American past. The Jewish intellectual tradition was a sternly questioning one. The study of the Talmud is the disputation of law; there is nothing accepting about it, or genteel, or accommodating. Somewhere in every Jewish intellectual, even the mildest-seeming of them, there is—or was, in this period in which criticism was our most notable contribution to literature— the disputatious child-scholar of the ghetto.

In the twenties, Columbia took only a small quota of Jewish students and those it took were not untypical of America's first generation of Jewish intellectuals and critics. The vitality of thought at Columbia in these years in which Lionel was an undergraduate also happened to coincide with, and be nourished by, an uncommon outburst of literary energy throughout the world. Wryly, I note that, like Lionel, I, too, was in college when Yeats, Thomas Mann, Joyce, Proust, Kafka, Rilke, D. H. Lawrence, Bernard Shaw, T. S. Eliot, all these literary masters of our century, were alive and writing—Proust lived until 1922, the year in which Lionel and I were college freshmen. America did not produce figures as imposing as these but it made its contribution: Sherwood Anderson, Dreiser, Faulkner, Willa Cather, John Dos Passos, F. Scott Fitzgerald, Hemingway were all of them writing during Lionel's and my time in college. At Radcliffe I knew nothing of any of them except Sherwood Anderson. I read Anderson's *Winesburg, Ohio* when I was only recently out of adolescence and it spoke to me as personally as Salinger's *Catcher in the Rye* would speak to a later generation of young readers. But I read it in intellectual isolation.

There was no one I knew at Radcliffe with whom to share a literary adventure or test its value.

At Columbia—or at least in Lionel's corner of Columbia—the flow of ideas, literary or nonliterary, was inexhaustible. Lionel was in the class of 1925: with the classes which immediately preceded and followed it, it is still remembered for its intellectual distinction. Recalling his college years, Lionel often spoke of the Hartley Hall group—not all the members of this gifted enclave lived in that Columbia residence hall but it was where they tended to congregate. Many of Lionel's Columbia generation and many of the Hartley Hall group—Meyer Schapiro, Jacques Barzun, Clifton Fadiman, Francis Steegmuller, Edgar Johnson—would become known in one or another sphere of the intellectual activity of the country. All the literature students, Lionel among them, wrote as undergraduates for *Morningside,* the campus literary magazine. Jacques Barzun, who majored in history, also wrote for the *Spectator* and the *Jester.* The latter was a lively but less exalted campus publication—Barzun recalls that although he was part of the Hartley Hall group, the other members of that austere company thought him vulgar or commonplace (the language is his) because he lent himself to so unworthy an enterprise. Jacques and Lionel were acquainted as undergraduates but it was only when they began to teach together in 1934 that they became close friends. There were no courses in criticism at Columbia, any more than there were at Harvard. Criticism was not an approved activity in the academy; when the young Mark Van Doren came up for promotion at Columbia, he had to be forgiven the fact that he published book reviews. Lionel and his college friends were their own teachers of the critical craft and teachers to each other. They were not all of them destined to be critics, and it was not even literary ambition which brought the Hartley Hall people together. Their careers were widely varied. Henry Rosenthal became a rabbi; Meyer Schapiro was soon one of the outstanding art historians of the country; Herbert Solow became a political journalist; James Grossman became a lawyer; Victor Lemaitre joined the FBI. Their common bond was books: books and the ideas generated by books. This was what bridged their professional divergence. Their intellectual curiosity led them everywhere, back to the classics of drama, philosophy, and history, and head on into confrontation with the most innovative thinkers of their own day. In striking contrast to my Radcliffe and Harvard contemporaries, Lionel's Columbia contemporaries were well acquainted with the masterworks of modern writing and art and wholly at ease with the idea of modernism itself. Schooled though they were in tradition, they were calmly knowing in their approach to what has come to be viewed as the revolutionary cultural change which took place in the early years of this century. While the alteration in style and taste which occurred in art at the beginning of this century bore witness to a radical alteration in culture, for Lionel and his college friends it did not constitute the absolute rupture between past and present which the polemic of modernism has made it out to do and still would make it out to do. Shortly after the campus uprisings of 1968 a young instructor of English at Columbia told me that his students no longer consented to read anything written before 1900. They made only a single exception, he said: for Blake. The reporter was a self-conscious left-winger and he was obviously pleased with his news. It confirmed his presence at the death of stale old history and at the birth of a new world unencumbered by the past. On behalf of cultural pluralism, the present-day college curriculum would also thin out the traditional culture of the West to make place, whether deserving or not, for the work of minorities; and in the name of gender equality the women's movement makes a similar sweep of history—whatever in the literature of the past fails to serve its polemical end it would discard as the legacy of dead white males. It would have been unthinkable for Lionel and his Columbia friends to be moved by ideology in their judgment of literature. They fully recognized the challenge to tradition in the new art of the century but they felt no call to position themselves on a cultural barricade. There were technical difficulties to be mastered in T. S. Eliot or Joyce but they read these and the other writers of their time as they had read Hardy or Conrad before them and Dickens or Stendhal before *them*. Nobody said: "This is modernism. Let fly your flags of youth and rebellion!" The modernist writers were not yet being taught at Columbia; the English survey course, not unlike my art-history courses at Harvard, stopped well short of the contemporary. But one could pursue an interest in contemporary writing at its most radical without having to renounce the traditional literature being taught in the classroom and without having to commit oneself to the overthrow of anything except ignorance.

The cultural excitement of a period can pass a young student by unless it appears to him in the shape of an individual person, someone with a name and face and voice. Mark Van Doren, beguilingly elfin and yet a rugged representative of what an American, a "pure" American, might ideally look like, was this agent of their cultural times for Lionel and most of his college friends. John Erskine also taught at Columbia in these years and he, too, brought the outer world of the arts to the campus; he was not only a professor of English but a gifted pianist and the author of a bestselling novel, *The Private Life of Helen of Troy*. It is my impression that Lionel was only moderately responsive to Erskine as a literary figure. What he appreciated in Erskine was the fact that he had created the famous Columbia honors course. It was the course which came to be called the Colloquium. Lionel, Kip Fadiman, and Meyer Schapiro took the course in its first year, 1924. The Colloquium met once a week in the evening in small groups for the discussion of the great works of literature and philosophy and history. Each section was taught by two teachers, and only juniors and seniors were eligible for it. The standard of admission was high. For many years Lionel and Jacques Barzun would teach the Colloquium together. A list of their students is a Who's Who of the gifted undergraduates of the thirties, forties, and early fifties;

it includes Fritz Stern, John Hollander, Louis Simpson, Quentin Anderson, John Berryman, Theodore deBary, Jeffrey Hart, Donald Keene, Charles Frankel; also Michael Sovern, who later became president of Columbia. In the years in which Lionel taught the Colloquium, the last book in the sequence of the great classics of Western thought was Freud's *Civilization and Its Discontents.* In 1924, when he was himself a student in the course, the last book in the sequence had been William James's *Principles of Psychology. Civilization and Its Discontents* was not published until 1930, when Lionel had been out of college for five years.

Only ten years older than the youngest of his first ravening students, Mark Van Doren was already, in the early twenties, a practicing member of the writing community, a published poet and critic, married to a writer, Dorothy, brother of a writer, Carl— both Mark and Dorothy were editors of the *Nation* in the period before I began my writing career at that magazine. Even Mark's sister-in-law, Irita, was a writer and editor. In the Van Dorens the literary dream of a young college student was given human, almost familial, lineaments. The Van Doren image would alter as time went on and writing for publication came to be thought of as a work like any other. But for years any Columbia undergraduate with literary ambitions took his poems and stories to Mark for approval; Lionel did and all his hungry friends did. He represented the possibility of being a teacher, yet also a writer: you could earn your living as a teacher without sacrifice of the "creative impulse," as it would then have been honorifically described. This was no doubt important for Lionel. Today we take it for granted that writers, even poets and novelists, teach. In the early twenties teaching was thought to be fraught with peril for a writer. It was regarded as a bondage to respectability and thus inimical to the free play of the creative powers.

Lionel was apparently not easy to know as a young man. Jacques Barzun remembers that as an undergraduate he had a sort of "standoffish" quality. "He affected," said Jacques, "a sort of superior bohemianism—very gentle, not at all aggressive, but it indicated that the Hartley Hall people were made of finer stuff than the rest of mankind." Another Columbia contemporary and friend, Jim Grossman, recalls Lionel's "Proustianism," his air of elegance and his pretension to a worldliness which he could not actually claim but which he considered appropriate to a rising young literary fellow. Poor Lionel! As man-about-town he had a long way to go and would never really make the course. Several times during our courtship, he took me to restaurants which he could not afford and in which he was plainly not at ease. He was drawn to them by literary curiosity; he wanted to know how things arranged themselves in the big world. To a degree the standoffishness stayed with him throughout his life. It was a shield against timidity and self-doubt, a continuation of the protection he had contrived for himself in an upbringing which grievously ignored the prides of developing young manhood. Even as a boy, he had looked to literature for his strategies of defense. Going to school one day—this was on Manhattan's upper West Side—he was besieged by a group of street boys and pelted with snowballs. Some of them had rocks in them. He had been reading the Norse myths and told himself that he was Balder, favorite of the gods, and could not be hurt. He was not hit. Fortunately, he was not tempted to this kind of self-fictionalization as an adult. Yet he always retained a certain air of unassailability. There were people whom this seemed to disturb. In middle life, he lectured at the University of Chicago, and Saul Bellow, who taught there and with whom he had become pleasantly acquainted in the early fifties when Bellow was writing *The Adventures of Augie March,* invited him to have a drink after his talk. For their drinking place Bellow chose a bar in a desperate quarter of the city; it was the gathering place of drunks and deadbeats, a refuge of people who had been irreparably damaged by life. What other explanation of Bellow's choice could there be than the wish to test Lionel's ability to handle himself in such surroundings? With our marriage, Lionel's youthful literary affectations quickly disappeared. If there are those who would have welcomed this as evidence of his advancing maturity, I am not among them, or at least not in hindsight. In his book on Matthew Arnold, Lionel tells us that when the young Matthew Arnold was rid of his earlier dandyism, he stopped being a poet and spoke of himself as being "two parts iced over." Behind Lionel's Proustianism lay his hope of being a novelist.

Lionel was still an undergraduate when he met Elliot Cohen, the editor of the *Menorah Journal.* With this meeting there began one of the lasting friendships of his life and surely its most difficult. Although Elliot was only seven or eight years older than Lionel, he always presented himself as someone of a distant generation. He had been born in Mobile, Alabama, the son of a small-store keeper, and went to Yale. He had even briefly stayed on at Yale as a graduate student in English. But at that time there were obviously no prospects for a Jew at Yale and he soon came to New York, to the *Menorah Journal.* The *Menorah Journal* had been started as an organ of the Menorah Society, a series of clubs for Jewish college students. Elliot quickly rescued it from the parochialism into which it had settled under its previous editor, Henry Hurwitz. The magazine remained a Jewish magazine but he rid it of its insistent sectarianism and made it into a widely read journal of intellectual opinion. He had a great interest not only in sports, especially baseball, but also in the movies; he was particularly fond of American comedy and comedians, not the pseudointellectual stand-up comics of a more recent day but the old-time vaudevillians and the crazy men they spawned: Lou Holtz, Ed Wynn, W. C. Fields, Jimmy Durante. Without instituting regular sports reporting or film reviewing in his magazine, he opened its pages to the popular culture of the time, especially Jewish popular culture, in a way which was new and provocative.

One of Elliot's first clever moves was to solicit contributions to his magazine from Columbia's gifted undergraduates, Lionel among them. Lionel was still in college when he wrote his first story for the *Menorah Journal;* it was called "Impediments" and appeared in the issue of June 1925, shortly before his twentieth birthday. It is unlikely that he would have published at so early an age if Elliot had not sought him out, and there is no reason to suppose that he would have concentrated as he did in his early fiction on his experience as a Jew if Elliot had not been editing a magazine specifically directed to Jewish affairs. Elliot employed his belief in the diversity of the intellectual undertaking as a lure with which to bring new young writers, people like Lionel and his Columbia friends, for whom the fact that they were Jews had hitherto had little authority in their intellectual lives, into an investigation of their Jewish identity. At twenty, twenty-one, twenty-two, what a young writer wants above all else is to see himself in print. He is not inclined to worry about where he may be led, into what intellectual or political or cultural commitment, by contributing to this or that periodical. Is it a Jewish magazine which solicits his work? Very well, he will write as a Jew. Especially in youth, the literary personality is protean; the self is multitudinous. A young writer can in all honesty bear witness to beliefs whose implications and ramifications he does not fully appreciate—and this can be entrapping.

Eventually Lionel did a good deal of reviewing for the *Menorah Journal,* but in the four years between his college graduation and the time we married his chief contributions to Elliot's magazine were stories. After the first of them, the grimly brilliant "Impediments," his next story was a venture in social reporting, "Chapter for a Fashionable Jewish Novel." The story was almost as swaggering as its title. Among his high-school friends Lionel had numbered several wealthy German-Jewish boys who went to Yale— Lionel had hoped to go with them. "Chapter for a Fashionable Jewish Novel" is about the world of these well-fixed young people: German Jews had to suffice as Lionel's Guermantes. Written in a more confident political climate than ours today, one in which the democratic preference could still be taken for granted and did not have to be certified at every step, this youthful story dares to see society as class-defined. Indeed, it relishes its observation of class assumptions and manners. Lionel would be forty-two when he published his only novel, *The Middle of the Journey*. *The Middle of the Journey* is a novel of ideas; its subject is the politics of the intellectual left. The novelist of ideas was perhaps already visible in the author of "Impediments," but the sharp-eyed young man who wrote "Chapter for a Fashionable Jewish Novel" had, one must think, a different future in mind for himself than as a writer of political fiction. Surely he would have preferred that his social and political ideas unfold from the abundance and accuracy of his social perceptions rather than depend upon expository statement. Early in our acquaintance, I asked Lionel why he was taking a Ph.D. if he intended to be a novelist. He replied that fiction had altered in our century and that the novelist had now to be a man of learning—he was foreseeing the work of Sartre and Camus, of the later Thomas Mann, of Nabokov and Bellow. His seemingly neutral response had for me a tone of personal problem. I felt that he was revealing an uncertainty about himself as a novelist, recognizing the greater pull which criticism had for him. Had he been born a quarter of a century later, so that he would have begun his career in the fifties instead of the twenties, he might better have been able to reconcile the two impulses and not given up fiction for criticism. He might, like Bellow, have made criticism a natural element in his fiction. In the fifties, in a world perhaps too complex for our imaginative grasp, the social novel as Lionel and I knew it when we were young, as a net in which to gather as much as possible of the significant variety of life, was ceasing to be an option. Where there is no society, how can there be a novel of social observation? On Lionel's twenty-fourth birthday, my brother gave him a present of a gold-headed black evening stick. Although Lionel never subscribed to the soggy warning repeated by E. M. Forster in one of his novels, to distrust every enterprise which requires new clothes, it was already plain to him that in the life which lay ahead of him a gold-headed evening stick was not his most necessary article of apparel. He carried the stick only once, to a white-tie dinner at the home of Columbia's President Nicholas Murray Butler on the evening that Butler undertook to ensure Lionel's promotion to a Columbia professorship. I still have the stick though it had no place in our "real" life, as we like to call it. It symbolizes for me the research to which Lionel would first, last, and always be dedicated: his inquiry into the nature of society as this may be dealt with not only in fiction but in criticism.

Elliot Cohen's influence on the intellectual history of his time has yet to be assessed. The writers he gathered around him at the *Menorah Journal* are now referred to by the historians of our intellectual culture as "the *Menorah Journal* group", and in their time they did indeed represent a small but important intellectual constituency. The *Menorah Journal* stopped publication in the early thirties for lack of funds, and for a short time Elliot worked in the Communist movement; he was a fellow traveler, not a Party member, and headed the National Committee for the Defense of Political Prisoners, a Communist-front organization. But he soon broke with Communism and became a passionate anti-Communist. He was the founding editor of *Commentary,* a new Jewish magazine which came to be boldly stamped with this view. At Elliot's death in 1959 Norman Podhoretz, who had been a student of Lionel's and been recommended by Lionel for a position at the magazine, became the editor. Podhoretz was a left-wing liberal when he began at the magazine; he initiated his incumbency as editor with an extended campaign in which he announced the birth of a "new, *new" Commentary* which would not be in thrall to Elliot's anti-Communism. Podhoretz's liberalism was not proof, however, against the unprecedented assault of his liberal friends upon his autobiographical volume *Making It.* It was a crudely boastful book and recorded a life in which the desire for popular success as this might be defined in Hollywood had manifestly superseded the values of a well-trained and highly endowed intellectual. But from the reviews one might have supposed that he had written *Mein Kampf*. By the end of the sixties Podhoretz had moved far to the right, and since then he has made the magazine into a commanding voice of neoconservatism. It is perhaps a question how much the influence which Elliot exercised throughout his functioning life is to be attributed to the power of his ideas and how much to the force of his personality. Few people take up as much space as Elliot Cohen occupied in the lives of his friends and surely few are as fear-inspiring. Everyone was intimidated by Elliot: when Marjorie Nicolson, the acclaimed scholar of seventeenth-century literature who had known Elliot at Yale's Graduate School and was now a formidable member of the Columbia English Department, heard that he was planning to attend a lecture she was scheduled to give at Columbia's English Graduate Union, she wanted to run away. He was unusually fertile with ideas but badly blocked as a writer and looked to other writers to act as his literary surrogates. In fact, he so thoroughly intruded himself into the articles he commissioned that he might often be regarded as virtually their coauthor—I remember that after leaving a discussion I once had with him of a piece he wanted from me, I felt that the piece was already written, or spoken, and that there was nothing left for me to write. To be associated with Elliot and yet maintain one's intellectual independence, one had constantly to battle the imposition of his mind and will: it was like extricating oneself from under a suffocating encumbrance. The need to assert his remarkable self was undoubtedly a primary motive in Elliot's character. There was no situation, however trivial, which he did not have to dominate. He was unable to acknowledge an introduction lest it be taken as evidence of his submission to the person being introduced. When we once spent a summer as neighbors on Long Island and played tennis with him, he unfailingly made us wait while he fetched his racquet and changed his clothes. Even to read a book was too great a capitulation to its author. He was one of those Jewish intellectuals of the thirties and forties for whom the *New York Times* was the Talmud and all its commentaries but he never read books, not really; he circled them in some private rite which drew out their indispensable content and lodged it in his capacious head. It was the head of an Assyrian king, aquiline, massive, high-domed. For some years he wore a heavy black beard and it has occurred to me that perhaps he was the physical prototype of Rouault's bearded king, that figure of cruel power who so portentously invades the first pages of Lionel's story "The Other Margaret." If so, he would not have got there through Lionel's conscious intention, only by the avenue of dream. He suffered chronically from congested sinuses; one heard him breathe heavily through his nose. His teeth were abnormally white. While his customary expression was one of sullen withdrawal, when he loosed the smile which was usually held in hostile reserve, it was mesmerizing; it was a smile of unalloyed love. It was disconcerting to contemplate Elliot's hands and feet; they were much too small for his body. In 1959, after an extended hospitalization for depression, he committed suicide by smothering himself. The hands with which he pulled the plastic clothes bag over his head were helpless hands, the hands of an inept child.

By the time of Elliot's death, Lionel was no longer a young man; he was in his mid-fifties and all too sadly accustomed to speaking at the funerals of friends. He spoke at the service for Elliot Cohen, but until the last minute, as I sat next to him and waited for him to be called upon, I was not sure that he would be able to stand, he shook so violently; and when he spoke, though it was in his usual quiet tone, I could see the whitening of his knuckles as he clung to the lectern. This was no ordinary friend who had died and certainly no ordinary editor, nor was he a literary mentor such as male writers often seek in their teachers. Lionel never had such a figure in his writing career, not in Elliot, not in Mark Van Doren. For Lionel, Elliot was a figure in some primal line of influence, someone in a writer's mysterious and terror-ridden universe of father-gods.

While I was at college my parents moved from Brooklyn to an apartment in New York. We no longer had a house with a yard and trees and garden; this had been left behind in Westchester and Brooklyn. We now lived on Manhattan's West Side, on West End Avenue at 84th Street. The new location considerably added to my unhappiness at having to leave Cambridge. In the twenties, the very words "West End Avenue" were, for some ears, synonymous with vulgarity; to live in this section of the city was to live with the crudest ostentations of new wealth. Only a few years earlier, most of its residents had been impoverished immigrants, living on the lower East Side and struggling for a foothold in their new country. They had first made their way to Washington Heights and the Bronx; West End Avenue was their next step on the journey to Central Park West and, eventually, the upper East Side. Their financial climb was not accomplished in silence; they noisily advertised their rise in the world. The men were flashy and brash, their wives were loud and demanding. In their showy clothes, laden down with diamonds, the women overran the local shops; at lunchtime, their rude voices filled the Schrafft's restaurant on Broadway at

83rd Street. On Sunday mornings the husbands strolled boastfully back and forth on Broadway between 79th and 86th Streets; on these Sunday parades the wives brought up the rear, diminished by their menfolk. My mother and father were untroubled by their new surroundings; although they themselves had no taste for show, they were apparently able to tolerate it in others. Too, my mother was now very ill and seldom left the house. But I felt implicated in the coarseness, degraded by being in such close proximity to it; I was ashamed to give people my address. In Cambridge, the only permissible ostentation had been that of modesty. One recognized a Boston millionaire by the seedy dress of his wife and daughters.

My first year back in New York stays with me as a bleak and lonely time. Most of my high-school friends had disappeared and my Radcliffe friends had either scattered or were still in school. Halfheartedly, I looked for work. I am among the fortunate of this century in having had little direct experience of anti-Semitism; the little I have experienced was largely concentrated into my first year back in New York after I graduated from college. American anti-Semitism in the twenties was neither virulent nor organized but it was widespread. To be a Jew in the professions, especially those associated with high culture, was a sizable handicap. University teaching was in most instances closed to Jews; there were student quotas in the private colleges and even stricter quotas in the med-ical and law schools. The condition was not protested; both Jews and non-Jews seemed to take it for granted, as if it were a natural manifestation of life in society. Hitler had not yet alerted us to the danger in even the mildest racial prejudice. To improve their chance of success in the professions, many Jews Anglicized their names if this had not already been done for them by their fathers. Lionel was rare among Jewish intellectuals in having a name which had never been changed; such names as Hook, Howe, Phillips, Bell, Kazin, now proudly enshrined in the literary-intellectual history of our century, were probably not the names borne by the fathers of these distinguished figures when they left Europe. There was even some degree of "passing" by people who argued that since they observed no religion, there was no reason for them to bear the opprobrium of being Jews. Passing was considerably more prevalent and urgent at Harvard where the social establishment was more tightly knit and powerful than at Columbia. The matter of one's social origins seemed to be of particular importance in the Fine Arts Department: several of the art-history students of my Harvard and Radcliffe generation were Jews but they kept it secret; I was the only person in the department to acknowledge my religion. Professor Sachs had a curious place in the social hierarchy of Harvard and Cambridge. It was generally known that he was a Jew by birth but it was never spoken of; it was as if his independent wealth as a member of the Goldman Sachs banking family had given him an invincible weapon against social exclusion. He lived at Shady Hill, which had once been the home of Charles Eliot Norton; his museum course met at his home and he generously allowed his students to use his library and to have access to his fine collection of drawings. He frequently entertained students at evening gatherings. But despite his interest in my professional future, he never invited me to an evening party at his home: I apparently failed to qualify for this more familial association. With disarming naïveté, as if he were reporting a scene at which he had been an innocent bystander, he one day told us in class of a gathering in his home at which, as so often happened in the Cambridge of that time, the conversation had turned to ancestry. Noticing that one of the guests, a Chinese student, was not taking part in this improving exchange, Professor Sachs had courteously asked him how far back he could trace his forebears. Only three thousand years, the Chinese student answered sadly. Professor Sachs failed to tell us what lesson he had drawn from this reply. A long time after I graduated from college, I heard that one of Professor Sachs's daughters had married a Jewish doctor, a man much esteemed in the Harvard community. The report dramatized for me the change which had taken place in the American response to religious discrimination in the wake of the Holocaust. But in 1925 Nazism was still in the future: my Jewish name stopped me at the door of both the Metropolitan Museum and the new Frick Art Reference Library. I came with high recommendation from the Harvard Art Department but neither place granted me an interview. Yet to conclude that because I met religious prejudice in trying to find a job it was only or even chiefly anti-Semitism which put an end to my career in art history is to overlook my personal contribution to my defeat. I was as little serious in looking for work in New York as I had been in weighing the offers made to me by Professor Sachs. My job-hunting efforts were desultory and undirected, the fumblings of someone who had but little notion of where she wanted to go and who was therefore destined to go nowhere. All the Radcliffe art-history students of my year graduated with honors, perhaps not the high honors we hoped for when we studied as hard as we did for our final examinations but with enough distinction to promise that we would have little difficulty in finding employment. So far as I know, none of us did much better than I did. Somewhere between college and the professional world for which we had presumably been trained, we women lost our way. We were professionally schooled but not emotionally schooled or properly directed for professional achievement. Before the year was out, I gave up all thought of becoming an art historian, all thought, indeed, of a professional career.

With no job, no classes to attend or papers to write or examinations for which to prepare, the days of my first year back in New York stretched out endless and empty. I was often still in my bathrobe at four or five in the afternoon, the same old red corduroy bathrobe which I had worn as the fire captain of my Radcliffe dormitory. I was living in some shadowy world between the normal lassitude of adolescence and depression. In the next room, my mother lay dying. By now she was almost wholly bedridden, yet each evening as the hour approached when my father would be coming home from work, she rose and, sitting precariously on the edge of the bed, combed her hair and managed to pull on a dress.

We had a maid to do the cooking but on faltering legs my mother went to the kitchen to apply the finishing touches to our evening meal. My mother left me a substantial legacy of determination. To the end, we were untrusting of each other; there lay between us a lifetime of failed communication. All parents are mysteries to their children. As we grow older, we try to re-create and comprehend these people who produced us. I now often ask myself: What were my parents really like? When I remember my mother as I do, do I remember her as she actually was or do I once more conjure up my old substitution for reality, my old collection of impressions, many of them perhaps false, which I randomly put together over the years and which I call my mother? Do I remember my father as he really was or only as I have come to think he was? I am on firmer ground, I think, when I speak of my father than when I speak of my mother. My mother was more volatile and elusive than my father and I was jealous of her and angry at her and had, in her instance, more reason for distortion. I was twenty-one when she died, yet in many ways I was still a child, insufficiently grown to take her into my imaginative universe. She died in the fall of 1926, at the age of fifty-three, in the hospital to which she had been moved for a blood transfusion. The transfusion was a counsel of desperation; there was no hope that her life could be saved. I was in the room with her while it was performed. Blood banks did not yet exist and to receive someone else's blood was a momentous undertaking. The patient received the blood directly from its donor: it was a transaction between two persons visible to each other, physically connected by their arms. Beyond cure, my mother should have been spared this last ordeal. She turned her head away from the young man who sat at her bedside and closed her eyes as his arm was tied to hers. It was only when the transfusion was over that she permitted herself to look at the stranger whose blood was now in her veins. He was young and clean, probably a student, and she smiled at him tenderly and thanked him. The day before she died, she asked me to sing to her in her hospital room. There was no one else in the room, but I was frightened by the thought of singing to my dying mother. Scarcely above a whisper, I sang a Russian lullaby. Several months had to pass before I let myself realize that my mother was dead. On a winter day, I stood at the window of my father's apartment and looked out at the season's first snowfall. I thought of my mother's body freezing in the cold ground and my heart ached. I sometimes think that my heart has never stopped aching, whether with my masked and injured love for my father or my injured and buried love for my mother. In asking me to sing for her, was she thinking, I wonder, of mortality and of her life continuing in mine. My voice was hers—but so was a great deal else of me: her love of fun, which she tried to repress, whether through distrust of herself or in deference to my more serious-minded father; her love of drama and exaggeration, which was so much in defiance of our family's commitment to unembellished truth; her domesticity; her practical good sense. Lionel was unalterably formed by his parents' intellectual aspirations for him; it was by their earliest design that he chose his profession. Late in life, as his unreasonable irritability with his mother subsided, he readily acknowledged the part played in his career by her intention for him. Like Freud, who attributed his success to his mother's confident expectations for her "goldener Siggy," Lionel attributed whatever he had achieved in his career to his mother's expectations for him. But one saw little of either of his parents in Lionel's adult personality. His mother had excellent literary judgment and also her own strengths of character, but it was not from her that Lionel derived the complexity of his intelligence or his stubborn resistance in adversity. There would seem, however, to be no aspect of my mind and no activity of my mature life whose source cannot be traced to one or the other of my parents. Only the mix is mine. If from my mother comes that part of me which wanted to sing, from my father comes the larger and sterner part of me which has kept me at my desk, writing as I have written. Despite the restrictions put upon me in my upbringing, I was permitted some degree of success in whatever I ventured; I have taken care not to exceed the limits which my parents set for me. My political idealism is my father's and so is my political realism. When I was small, my mother used to say, not without exasperation, that when I grew up I would be a lawyer; perhaps influenced by my father's evocations of Jean Valjean, she would say that she could see me standing at the bar of justice, pleading for some poor father who had stolen a loaf of bread to feed his starving children. When I graduated from college, my father spoke of my becoming a political journalist—he admired Walter Lippmann. I have not been strictly obedient to these prophecies: I am neither a lawyer nor a political journalist, not literally, but as a critic and a member of political defense committees I have frequently been involved in issues of law and much of my political writing can be described as political journalism. I had just begun to write a column for the editorial page of the *Herald Tribune* when that paper ceased publication.

I started to study singing soon after my mother died. When I began, I had no idea of a professional career in music; my teacher was responsible for turning me in that direction. It was not wise of her; she should have recognized that I lacked the emotional stamina and firmness of purpose for a musical career. At no point would my study of singing be the ruling discipline of my life; my technique was disciplined but I was not, not enough for professional success. Even for my time, the vocal technique in which I was being trained was old-fashioned; it harked back to the turn of the century and the era of Melba and Patti and Tetrazzini, when what made for the art of vocal performance was not musical showmanship or skill as a singing actress but one thing only: confident and beautiful sound. A good voice is of course in the first instance a gift of nature. But the ability to put it to reliable use depends upon its production. A properly produced voice is steady over the whole of its range; each note is linked to every other in an unbroken chain. It never wavers in pitch and it lasts through a singer's lifetime. This, at any rate, was how it once was. Listening today to

101

the great singers of the past on even the thinnest of old recordings, one hears with awe this assured and uninterrupted flow of sound. But the old technique seems now to be forgotten. The present-day vocal ideal is as remote from the ideal of an earlier era as the novel of Pynchon or Vonnegut is from that of Dickens, or the poetry of Wallace Stevens from that of Keats or Shelley. Today's celebrated opera stars, in particular the women, brutalize their magnificent native endowments. They achieve "effects" which are perhaps pleasing to listeners reared on the tonal extravagances of pop singers but which in actual fact are a cover for their uncertain breathing and pitch. Their elaborate vocal devices, their darkenings and brightenings of tone and their dramatic shadowings and intensities, are borrowed from the popular theater. The technique in which I was trained did not invite such deceptions. Once one's method of production was established—but this was no easy matter; it was the most strenuous work I have ever done—one was freed for the speaking of one's musical mind. Yet of course the musical mind and heart are inseparable: singing is nothing if not the public exhibition of private feeling and thus it was not readily allowed the child whose father had declared that she might most fittingly enact her dreams in the toilet. I was not kept from being a singer by lack of talent, only by my deeply ingrained fear of self-exposure plus, hardly a minor consideration, the same deficiency of intention which characterized whatever I did at this period of my life. My teacher was a dignified old lady who did her best to counteract my upbringing. "Wear a red dress! Step through windows!" she would say to this student of hers for whom the purchase of a red dress would one day initiate a three-month period of agonizing dizziness and who would soon develop a lasting fear of height. There came a moment when she even urged me to leave home and live with her. She was not the only teacher who wanted to detach me from my family. A retired Shakespearean actress who visited at my summer camp saw me as a potential dramatic actress and suggested that I live with her to prepare for the stage.

With my mother's death, my sister and I shared the running of my father's home; a maid did the cooking and cleaning, my sister and I alternated in planning the meals and doing the marketing. This was not a new occupation for me: I had been only nine when my mother, accompanied by my sister, had gone to the Mayo Clinic in Minnesota for an operation and I had been left to supervise the home—our Polish maid spoke no English. With my mother dead, my father indulged his liking for travel. He took it for granted that my sister and I would travel with him; grudgingly I accompanied him to Canada and the Midwest, to Florida and Cuba and South America. On ships or in hotels, wherever he could suppose that a potential seducer lay in wait for me, my father was the most indefatigable of chaperons. One late evening on our boat to South America he came on deck in search of me wearing his dinner jacket over his pajamas; he had neglected to replace his false teeth and Milk of Magnesia dribbled down his chin. Yet he gave me some of my most treasured travel memories. As a child and again as a young woman, I saw Europe when it had not yet been trampled upon by this hard century of ours. When I first saw Switzerland, women in native costume sat at their embroidery or lace-making in front of the shops of Zurich or Interlaken and bands played in the crowded beer gardens; awestruck, I stared up at Trimelbach Falls from my seat in a horse-drawn carriage. The serenity of northern Italy had not yet been violated by the roar of motors: sailboats were placidly in command of Lake Lugano, and on Lake Como the occasional appearance of a motorboat was a surprise and amusement. Everywhere on the dusty roads of the Italian countryside there were roadside shrines at which the faithful left their offerings, a rose or a tiny spray of field flowers. One afternoon in Italy our carriage had to stop for a funeral procession: the mourners were on foot and one of them, bent and weary, carried a full-scale picture of the local saint. The Paris I first saw with my father was still the Paris of Proust: it was the Paris of the Place Vendôme and the Rue de Rivoli, of the Hotel Continental and of the Château de Madrid and the Pavillon d'Armenonville in the Bois de Boulogne. The Germany of my childhood was a land of toy church towers and magical castles to which, again, I traveled by carriage. When I returned in 1967, the Rhine would be a river of blood. I felt badly used in having to accompany my father to South America after my mother's death, yet that journey, too, could never be duplicated for me. We moved slowly down the west coast of South America on a Grace liner. For a reason which was never explained to me, my father was treated like a guest of the line: at the desolate ports of Talara and Salaverry, wherever the ship called in Ecuador or Peru or Chile, we were taken ashore in a Grace Line launch and received along with the dignitaries by the local consul. Usually he was British but serving our country as well. Without much understanding of what I saw, I watched the meetings between the representatives of the copper companies who were traveling on the boat with us and the strange lonely people in these forsaken towns, but I somehow understood that I was being given an outsider's first veiled glimpse of the workings of dollar diplomacy.

My father's best friend was also recently widowed; he had a daughter a bit older than I. With the loss of their wives, the two men may have conferred on their new parental responsibilities. Fairly or not, I blame my father's friend for the fact that my father now began to talk about the need to find a husband for me. Actually he did nothing about it; it was only talk. But it was dispiriting and humiliating talk and brought me into threatening reach of a culture which I despised. Matchmaking was an unconcealed activity on West End Avenue. In the hunt for eligible young men, parents took their daughters to Lakewood or Atlantic City or to the big hotels of the Catskills. These resorts were serviced by semiprofessional marriage brokers: $30,000 or $40,000 bought a young lawyer or doctor. The possibility of parental interference in my marriage had been made real for me by what had happened at college to a slightly older friend of mine, Theresa Goell. Theresa was the daughter of a wealthy Brooklyn real-estate dealer; at the end of her junior year her father snatched her from school to marry a man he had chosen for her. She was soon divorced and her new status enabled her to make a splendid life for herself: she became a world-renowned archaeologist of Turkey. I attended Theresa's wedding; at the dinner her father asked me what my father was doing about finding a husband for me—I was not yet seventeen. Fortunately for me, my father was more ambivalent than Theresa's father about ruling a daughter's life: he did not force a husband on me or even seek one for me but settled for pressing me—without success— to attend the parties and dances at his golf club on Long Island in the hope that I would meet a proper husband there. I had never had the normal social life of a young girl of my class and genera-tion. Although my parents had friends, they were as socially iso-lated as themselves; they did not constitute a society where I could meet other young people. On my own, I was too sexually timid to have boyfriends. In high school I never went to parties and by and large even my social life at college was limited to female friends. That my father's golf club was scarcely the place to remedy my impoverished condition is attested to by the strange occurrence at one of its Fourth of July celebrations. In consequence of this re-port, my father stopped trying to entice me to join the festivities at his club. As we heard the story, it was a warm and clear evening and the buffet tables for the Fourth of July supper had been set up outdoors on the clubhouse terrace. They were laden with tempting foods: whole turkeys and hams, roasts of beef, seafood platters and salads. The guests had gathered and the meal was about to begin when the company was seized by a kind of hysteria. It was as if word had arrived of the approach of famine. The guests rushed for the tables and without even taking plates grabbed what-ever they could reach, whole hams and turkeys, fistfuls of seafood or salad. With the food dripping on their summer finery, they spread over the golf course and the clubhouse lawns. The next morning, the club attendants found half-eaten turkey carcasses and remnants of seafood and salad on the club greens.

On my return from South America, I took a position at the National Broadcasting Company as an assistant to the writer and producer of a children's radio serial called "The Gold Spot Pals." Other than to subvert the possibility of a singing career, I can think of no reason for my taking the position: my father housed and fed me and gave me a generous allowance; I had no need for my salary. In fact, while I worked at the broadcasting company I had more money to spend on myself than Lionel and I would have to live on for many years to come. "The Gold Spot Pals" was a weekly program which advertised Gold Spot shoe leather. A group of youngsters, together with an Irish singing policeman and an Italian organ-grinder with monkey, wandered the streets of New York having adventures. The cop sang, the organ-grinder ground, the children performed like the robust little professionals they were: singing, playing their musical instruments, providing the occasion for the older members of the cast to display their skills as well. The children never wearied because they wore Gold Spot leather shoes. A large part of my job was to shepherd these stage youngsters, usually trailed by their mothers, on publicity tours. With writers and photographers, we went to Coney Island, to the city parks and zoos, to the Palisades across the Hudson, wherever there was the setting for a fabricated adventure. In the evenings I helped my boss, Raymond Knight, entertain the people with whom he wished to ingratiate himself; this required me to drink rather more than I should have. In the history of radio, Raymond Knight probably has his small niche: he was, I think, the first radio producer to incorporate a studio audience in his programs and the first to broadcast such unaccustomed sounds as the tap of dancing feet. I was still taking my singing lessons and I never canceled a lesson because of my job. I even managed to salvage an hour each day for practice. But my teacher often commented on how tired I looked.

Tiredness was not my problem; tiredness yields to a good night's sleep. I was off course and it would take a multitude of changes in my life—marriage; ill-health so severe that I was near death; long years of psychoanalysis, some of it useless or worse, some of it lifesaving—before I would find my way. When I met Lionel, I had not yet gone to South America or begun to work at the National Broadcasting Company. But I was already hoping to be a singer. When I spoke of this to him, he was understandably cautious in his response. Every family has its daughter or cousin or aunt who sings; Lionel's sister, Harriet, had a charming voice. I invited him to one of my lessons; he would not be able to be with me in the studio but he could listen from an adjacent room. The day after his visit, I delightedly burst in on my teacher: Lionel had liked my voice! She failed to share my excitement. "Why do you have to have his approval?" she asked coldly. "It's your voice, isn't it?" If this statement were made to me in our present period, I would of course immediately recognize that I was being spoken to in the language of women's liberation. In 1928 there was no such cultural context for my teacher's terse remark. I was being confronted with the naked question: Was I able to function on my own or did I mean to be dependent on the approval and wishes of my husband, do only what he thought I should do? My reply was an avalanche of tears. Now I look back upon this scene and realize that it was not I who was out of step with my times in being concerned for Lionel's opinion of my voice and relieved because he thought it was of professional caliber. It was my teacher who was being extraordinary in proposing that I take charge of my own life. Undoubtedly there were women who, even in the twenties, believed that they were the custodians of their own fates, but I did not know them. I knew no woman in my generation who would have continued in a career which her husband did not want her to pursue. In fact, as good a way as any to describe the domestic culture in which Lionel and I began our marriage and, as time went on, made our close relationships is to note the absence among our friends of women who in any significant fashion challenged the established conventions of the relation between husbands and wives. Almost uniformly the women who were our close friends deferred to their husbands in the arrangement of their joint lives and in their important decisions. This was so even when the women worked and their earnings were essential to the family economy and even where they might give the outward appearance of independence or even of being in command of the home. Whatever their pretense of emancipation, the women of our acquaintance exercised only such control of their lives as their husbands granted them. They were ingenious indeed in contriving new ways to indulge the men to whom they were married, accommodate their eccentricities, subordinate themselves to them. They went nowhere that their husbands did not want them to go and did nothing that their husbands did not want them to do. Had their husbands not wanted them to work, they would not have worked—this was true of me and of all my married women friends. As time demonstrated, Lionel's belief that my voice was of professional quality could not guarantee that I would have a musical career. I soon relinquished this dream. But I would not have dreamed it for as long as I did without his encouragement. It is possible that he felt worse than I did when I gave up the hope of being a singer. In our middle life, well after I was launched in my writing career, he and I often talked about singing: he wanted me to write about it, but except for a short piece which I wrote in the *Nation* about Caruso when his wife published a memoir of their marriage, and a piece about Puccini which I contributed to a volume called *Atlantic Brief Lives,* a biographical dictionary edited by Louis Kronenberger, I never found the opportunity. When Lionel and I talked about singing, it was usually to talk about vocal technique and its resemblance to sports, the similarity between a properly placed note and the "ping" of a well-struck tennis ball, or the apparently unnatural route one travels, whether in poetry or sport or music, to attain to the appearance of naturalness and ease. Good vocal production was disappearing even while Lionel was alive. I now find it painful to go to the opera. The women's voices, in particular, are spread and breathy. Scarcely anyone sings on pitch; were I now to write about singing, it would be an excursion in nostalgia. A singer used to be made fit for the communication of music as someone might once have been made fit for the performance of a high religious ceremony. But today, in this art as elsewhere, discipline bows to the impertinence of self-presentation.

For his intellectual times, Lionel was unusual in his enjoyment of singing. Few of his literary contemporaries went to the opera, though in the universities there were always a few lovers of the operas of Mozart. It was rare for intellectuals—I speak here of America; I would learn that it was different in England—even to attend symphony concerts. In the fifties the poets Robert Lowell and William Meredith were given foundation grants to attend the Metropolitan Opera; it was hoped that they would write librettos for contemporary composers, as Auden did for Stravinsky. The project seems not to have been productive. Back at Radcliffe, my close friends Bettina Mikol and Dorothy Farber and I had spent many evenings going through Italian opera scores. I sang while Dorothy, who had a piano, an old upright, in her room, accompanied me. Bettina was our audience. Often we talked about the kind of men we wanted to marry and I would say that I wanted to marry a man who was equally at home in the top balcony of Carnegie Hall or tea dancing at the Hotel Plaza. Did I suppose that this was an easy demand to fill? I now know that it was not. There were many times when Lionel sat with me on the floor of the top balcony of Carnegie Hall—it was the "seat" one purchased by slipping a dollar to the door attendant—and often he stood with me through opera performances in New York or London. He would have liked to tea dance at the Plaza but even for a literary man he danced badly; dancing made him almost as awkward as having his picture taken. But there was one magical evening when he lost his self-consciousness on the dance floor: he could have danced all night. In 1966 Truman Capote gave his famous black-and-white ball at the Hotel Plaza; it was the great social event of the year. The party, it seems, was the fulfillment of a dream he had cherished for many years. The guests were masked and no color was permitted in their dress; it was mandatory that one wear black or white. We had never known Capote well; he was not part of our literary world. We had met in 1943 or '44, not long after the publication of Lionel's book on E. M. Forster, when I was waiting for Lionel near a ticket window in Grand Central Station and Capote approached me, emerging as if from a bottle. He recognized me from a photograph he had seen at Leo Lerman's. Looking like a bright-eyed but wizened child, he spoke in a high squeaky voice which rang clearly above the noise of the crowded car in which we traveled together to Connecticut. Why, he demanded, had Lionel, in writing about Forster, not dealt with Forster's homosexuality? Lionel explained that he had not known of Forster's homosexuality when he wrote the book; the possibility had occurred to him only when he was reaching its end. It was obvious that the mere sound of Capote's voice roused the passengers in our railway car and as he went on to speak of Forster's homosexuality, one could feel the air thickening with hostility. But if Capote was aware of danger, he gave no sign of it. In the next twenty years, we encountered him only infrequently; he was becoming a professional celebrity and made his life among the people who support the life of celebrity. But we were pleased to be invited to his party. I had never been in the company of so many lovely-looking people. On the evening of Truman Capote's ball Lionel discovered that dancing to rock 'n' roll released him from the necessity of leading a partner and this enchanted him.

In the spring of 1929, we decided to marry and I gave up my job at the National Broadcasting Company. It was the moment when I should have held on to it; with marriage, I would for the first time need the money. I was not guided by practical considerations; Lionel had not criticized my job but I knew that he had no respect for it. Soon I had to stop singing: I developed a severe thyroid dysfunction and had to be operated on. I was told that the removal of my thyroid did not affect the vocal cords but the physical and emotional exertion of singing became too great for me. I have never again sung. After I stopped, it was some years before I could listen to music and even longer before I could listen to vocal music.

Lionel's mother could not have been unprepared for his announcement that we were going to marry: from his love affair with a rose when he was ill with scarlet fever, she had to have guessed that he had fallen in love with the girl who sent it. At Christmas I gave him a present of a Feron tennis racquet. This, too, had to suggest that we were growing in intimacy—it was not the gift of a casual friend. Yet when Lionel told her that we were going to marry, his mother fainted, or made to faint, and his sister, Harriet, a lively and pretty girl of sixteen, obediently fell prostrate at her side. Lionel's mother had never shared the aversion to marriage of her bachelor brothers and sisters. She assumed that Lionel would one day marry. But "one day" was out of sight and mind. The immediate reality of losing her son to another woman required an accommodation for which she was not ready. There was little which was personal to me in her protest of our marriage or even in the encouragement which her opposition to it had from her relatives. I would perhaps have been more cordially received if I had been blond and beautiful, or of German rather than East European origin, or the daughter of a certified millionaire. Yet I suspect that even these splendid attributes would not have outweighed her conviction, or that of her brothers and sisters, that it was Lionel's plain duty to stay home and provide his mother with the support, both emotional and financial, which she had need of as the wife of so inadequate a husband. The opposition to our marriage came to a climax at Passover that spring. Lionel's mother's family regularly came to the Trillings' house for Seder; it was the one time of the year when her relatives sufficiently overcame their contempt for

Lionel's father to accept his hospitality. The Seder service would always be important to Lionel. After his father's death, managing as best he could with the little Hebrew which remained to him from his instruction for his bar mitzvah, he would lead the service at his mother's table, and when his mother became too old to prepare the elaborate meal, he gladly switched the Seder to our house. We stopped having a Seder only because our brothers-in-law, my brother and Harriet's husband, persisted in clowning during the service. If we were to have a Seder, Lionel wanted it to be taken seriously. Having told his mother that we planned to marry, he asked her to include me in their family gathering and, realizing that there was nothing she could do to prevent our marriage, she consented. The uncles and aunts were already assembled when I arrived. Unsmiling, they stood in a stiff circle in the living room: Uncle Hymie and Uncle Larry, Aunt Deborah, Aunt Della, the married sister, Aunt Maude, and Maude's expendable husband, Uncle Doc, who was a physician in the Department of Health but whose professional existence was acknowledged only when a member of the family was ill. Taking me around the room to introduce me, Lionel's mother was nervous; she was trying to please Lionel but she was frightened at seeming to break ranks with her family. I put out my hand to each of the uncles and aunts as I was introduced. It was refused. One after the other, each of the relatives turned his or her back on me. It was a massive and deliberate affront, and as I recall it today, I have to ask myself why Lionel and I did not at once leave the house but remained through the long service and dinner. After all, we could not foresee that Lionel's mother would one day be free of the influence of her brothers and sisters and be my friend, not theirs. The time did indeed come when they no longer exercised power over her and she and I became close to one another. Eventually she became more of a mother to me than my own mother had been. But this took many years to happen, and at the Seder Lionel and I could have no prevision of a happier future. It was from cowardice that we remained at the party or, more precisely, from the inability to defend ourselves in an appropriately assertive way. I do not think of either Lionel or myself as lacking in courage. At some cost, we took unpopular political and cultural positions throughout our careers; they could have been avoided and our lives would have been much easier. Over the years we had severe personal problems which we met with fortitude. But we were both of us crippled by a curious diffidence in our dealings with people. Lionel would sooner have gone into battle than rebuff an offending waiter and I could more readily challenge Sidney Hook in political debate than defend my place in line at a supermarket. We once engaged the young son of friends of ours in London to drive us on a holiday in France. He turned out to be the most sullen of companions, dissatisfied with everything in our travel arrangements, but rather than tell this young man to pull up his socks and do what he was paid to do, we devoted our holiday to mollifying him. When it was apparent that he was displeased with the pension into which we were booked in Avignon, we moved to the best hotel in the vicinity and ate our dinner each night in its expensive garden restaurant, Lionel meticulously consulting our young chauffeur on his preference in wines. There was nothing that Lionel or I could ever have done to establish a peaceable relation with his uncles and aunts. Like all people who live by their angers, they were endlessly fertile in creating grievances. We wanted a quiet wedding with only our immediate families present: the uncles and aunts took this as an insult directed specifically to them. When we relented to the point of saying that Uncle Hymie could attend the wedding as their representative, the compromise was rejected. No relation of Lionel's sent us a wedding gift. When Lionel and I were settled in our first apartment, we invited Aunt Deborah and Aunt Della to tea. Lionel's mother reported that the "aunties" spent the next night weeping because, as they had come in, I asked them if they would like to take off their hats; they were reminded, they said, of *Hedda Gabler*. It was unavoidable that Lionel had soon to break with his uncle Hymie. They quarreled on the telephone a year or two later. Lionel never told me the reason for the rupture but from the next room I heard him call his uncle a bastard. Lionel was twenty-five when he stopped speaking to his uncle and lived to be seventy. The Park Avenue uncles and aunts were longer-lived than Lionel; all but Uncle Larry were still alive at Lionel's death. As I write, I am told that Aunt Della is still alive, in a nursing home, at the age of a hundred and three. I know nothing of the disposition of Hymie's art collection but if it is intact, at today's prices it must be worth a great deal of money. I never heard Lionel say a word of regret for his sacrifice of the inheritance which his mother had always thought would be his.

The day after the Trillings' Seder, Lionel and I were walking near Columbia and ran into Irwin Edman, a professor of philosophy who had been Lionel's instructor and was now a friend. Had we attended a "real Seder," he wanted to know. I answered, laughing: "A real Seder, with all the fixations." I was trying to dispel my distress of the previous evening with humor, and as the weeks went on and Lionel's mother, unable to prevent our marriage, turned her attention to how we would live after we married, both Lionel and I took what refuge we could in laughter. Harriet was her mother's ambassador, or perhaps her investigative agent. When she herself married, Lionel's sister became an unexceptionable suburban wife and mother, but at sixteen and seventeen she had much to overcome in her upbringing. "Harriet darling, fix your mouth," her mother would suddenly address her at table, by which she meant that Harriet was to purse her lips into a rosebud and thus simultaneously make herself both more ladylike and more seductive. On the theory that if a girl did not know how to cook, her husband would have to provide her with a maid, her mother kept Harriet out of the kitchen—it was not surprising that after her marriage Harriet became so zealous a cook. In these early encounters of mine with Harriet she was memorably and absurdly her mother's spokesperson, a sixteen-year-old come to question me about the home I intended to set up for her brother. What kind of sheets and pillowcases was I going to buy, she inquired, and assured me that Lionel could sleep only on pure linen. With what kind of cutlery would we eat? Lionel was accustomed to eat with sterling silver. Through her daughter Lionel's mother was of course undertaking to control our lives; but I suspect that in communicating these requirements she was also trying to impress my family and me with her social standing. Her motive was not unlike Harriet's in her interview with Mark Krupnick.

It had not occurred to either Lionel or me that my father would want Lionel to ask his permission to marry me. We broke the news of our engagement at an awkward moment, when my brother and his wife were visiting and Lionel was at the house for dinner. I was in bed with a severe sore throat. At the end of dinner everyone gathered in my bedroom. "Father," I croaked from bed, "Lionel and I are going to get married." My father's face reddened and he started from the room, but he stopped to deliver his opinion of my news. "Two damn fools can't get married," he announced harshly. He was of course not saying that he thought us stupid, only that he thought us lacking in practical good sense. Further and perhaps more important, he was saying that we were deficient in experience of life. The latter judgment he particularly applied to Lionel. He had a parable for the occasion which he soon told me. There once was a boy who had been brought up in entire isolation, never permitted to see anyone other than the rabbi who was his guardian. When the boy was grown, he one day saw a woman. "What's that?" he asked the rabbi. The rabbi replied that it was a goose. "I want a goose," said the young man. Although Lionel's means of earning a living were all but invisible, my father never questioned him on how he planned to support me. He readily accepted our wish for a small wedding and he gave me a wedding gift of $5,000 with which to buy such clothes as I might need and furnish a home. In 1929 it was a substantial sum of money but I am afraid that, as a daughter, I was deeply afflicted with ingratitude. I took his gift as my due and when my father commented on my not having an engagement ring and offered to buy one for me, I replied rudely: "I don't like diamonds. You can buy me an emerald." Like Harriet, my father did once interrogate me about our future home but with a different purpose from hers. It was sex which was on his mind, as always. We had taken a two-room apartment in Greenwich Village, and I explained to my father that each of the rooms was to have a double use. The living room would be my practice room and the bedroom would also be Lionel's study; we would sleep on a studio couch. It was my incautious mention of a studio couch which apparently inflamed him. Why, my father demanded, could we not have a normal bedroom like other married people, with twin beds. My sister was similarly preoccupied. Shortly before our marriage she took Lionel aside to inform him that I had an appendicitis scar. "If you don't already know it," she added maliciously.

We were married on June 12, 1929, in my father's apartment. Through the years we would dutifully take note of the date but we would be honoring our marriage, not our wedding. We would never look back on our wedding with pleasure. In 1929 one married in a place of worship or a public hall. More moderately, one married in the home of one's parents or in a magistrate's office—not even the most inventive young couple married on a beach or in a lifeboat or at the entrance to a mine shaft—and one adhered to the traditional marriage service. We did not suppose that we could improve on its language. I knew no one who had a big wedding. The people we knew demonstrated their enlightenment by the simplicity with which they made the transition from the single to the married state. But if we resisted Lionel's mother's wish to extend our wedding party so that it would include her brothers and sisters, it was only to capitulate to the rabbi, Henry Rosenthal, who performed our ceremony. Henry was Lionel's close college friend, the antagonist in Lionel's first *Menorah Journal* story, "Impediments." From college he had gone on to the Jewish Theological Seminary; he had just graduated. Henry was the logical person to officiate at our marriage, not because of his religious dedication but because he and Lionel were close friends. In the twenties, religion had no place, or only a negative place, in the literary-intellectual life of the country; the words "intellectual" and "religious" were indeed all but mutually exclusive. The people with whom we were acquainted would have hesitated to be married even in the auxiliary facilities of a church or synagogue lest it falsely suggest that they were believers. There were a few practicing Catholics among the literary intellectuals but among our Jewish friends Henry was virtually alone as an observant Jew. Elliot Cohen edited a Jewish magazine but it was not a magazine directly concerned with religion, only with Jewish culture. The search for their Jewish identity which he urged upon his writers was not so much a religious quest as the search for what we would now call ethnicity, a celebration of the habits of thought and conduct, even the habits of speech and the tastes in food, which distinguish a particular social group. Yet remote as we were from religion, we were tolerant of Henry's choice of the rabbinate as his profession. Being young, we were tolerant of most things. Out of respect for the cloth, as he put it, Lionel's father would refuse to turn off a preacher on the radio; in a sense this was the kind of respect we gave Henry's religious commitment. Like Lionel in "Impediments," we preferred not to see the extent to which Henry's religious protestations were the expression of his moral arrogance.

I would not have thought to describe any of Lionel's friends, in college or after college, as sunlit. But of them all, Henry Rosenthal was surely the least illuminated; the darkness of Elliot's personality or that of his friend Herbert Solow was substantially relieved by wit. Henry was the only intellectual I have known who was never funny. His most familiar mood was that of scornful superiority. Whom or what he was triumphing over was not made specific, but that he lived a life of unremitting challenge was unmistakable. Our wedding was his first official act after ordination and he brought to it all the fervor of his new authority. Today, the observances upon which he insisted—that we marry under a *hoopa,* that my face be veiled and that I not see Lionel on our wedding day until I was summoned to his side under the canopy, that the service be largely read in Hebrew and that Lionel step on a glass at its conclusion—may not seem very burdensome, but they were inconsistent with our upbringings, especially mine, and did violence to our secularism, certainly to mine. The most troublesome of his requirements was that the marriage be witnessed by two Jewish males not of blood kin. How I came to hate that phrase, "not of blood kin," which Henry intoned as if it were itself an article of faith! Lionel and I had wanted our marriage to be witnessed only by our immediate families; we found it difficult now to choose two men guests from among our friends without being invidious. For one of our unrelated witnesses we finally hit upon my father's old friend and camping companion; the choice was appropriate if only because I had known him all my life. There was nothing appropriate in our choice of our second witness, the man on whom my sister was currently pinning her hope of marriage. His presence at our wedding apparently frightened him away forever. He was a horrid person and should not have been included in our intimate gathering. The ceremony was to take place in the late afternoon and be followed by dinner. As Lionel was about to step under the *hoopa,* my father went to the bathroom and did not emerge for forty-five minutes. In the meanwhile, I waited alone in my bedroom. I had a sheaf of Talisman roses spread on my arm; the florist had neglected to clip the thorns and they bit painfully through the sleeve of my dress. At the other end of the apartment, Lionel was having his problems. He had had a suit made to order, his last tailor-made suit for many years. The sample from which we picked the fabric had apparently been cut from between the red stripes. Lionel felt that he looked like a barbershop pole.

My sister was in charge of our wedding dinner. To put my sister in charge of anything which had to do with food was to invite disaster. My mother had been an excellent cook, my father was something of a gourmet; my sister was a culinary sport in the family. She had once helped run a camp for undernourished children, and the children went on strike because they felt they were being insufficiently fed. She hired the caterer for our dinner and supervised the menu. The dinner was food as theater. There were twelve of us at table: Henry, Lionel and I, Lionel's parents and sister, my father and my sister, my brother and his wife, our two male witnesses not of blood kin. The meal began with wedges of honeydew melon: they had been made to look like battleships—down the middle of each wedge ran a row of smokestacks made of maraschino cherries; little American flags flew at their sterns. The main course was squab nested on beds of green beans. From under their warm bodies rolled small white potato balls, like freshly laid eggs. But it was the dessert, a bombe, which was the high point of the drama. From above a wide skirt of spun sugar rose the upper half of a doll bride; one dug under her skirt to reach the hidden sweet. Far in the past my father had laid down champagne for the improbable day when one of his daughters would marry. It had gone sour and his old friend had to rush home to replace it from his private store. Lionel and I had invited a few intimate friends to stop by for wedding cake: Jim Grossman and his soon-to-be-wife, Elsa, the Fadimans, Dorothy and George Calingaert, Bettina and David Sinclair. Their arrival did little to relieve the gloom. No one seemed to rejoice in our marriage.

We had rented a cabin for the summer near Westport, Connecticut, and my father lent us his car and chauffeur to drive us there the next day. As we left the Fifth Avenue Hotel, where we had spent the night, it occurred to me to stop at Lord & Taylor's to buy my sister a present in appreciation of her help with the wedding dinner. What I was doing, of course, was apologizing to her for having married while she was still single. Lionel

accompanied me into the store and decided that since I was buying a present for my sister, he would buy a present for his sister,
too. But why should he apologize to Harriet for leaving her behind? Harriet was young, pretty, manifestly marriageable. It angered me that Lionel should want to ask the sixteen-year-old
Harriet's forgiveness for claiming his own life. We had never seen
the cabin we rented for our honeymoon; the arrangements were
made by phone. I had proposed that we use some of my father's
wedding gift for a trip to Europe, but Lionel felt that he could not
afford the time for travel. He had to study for his doctoral examination: he had never read Meredith. But he had also never been
in Europe, and it would be twenty-seven years before he made his
first trip abroad: soon after our marriage, I developed a travel phobia which persisted for many years and controlled our vacation
plans; it was a long time before I was able to travel further than
Long Island or Connecticut. Lionel was not phobic about travel
but, like many people who have no idea that travel is hedged around
with restrictions for them, he was made uneasy by being out of his
familiar surroundings; it was as if he were stripped of his identity.
When he did eventually go to Europe, it was without me and he
did virtually no touring; he chiefly visited with English literary acquaintances. He was not a good traveling companion. When in
later years he and I would travel together, I would have always to
make the arrangements: choose the hotels and restaurants, plan
the sight-seeing expeditions. Once, in Venice, I rebelled at having
to make all the plans and, presenting him with a stack of guide-
books, I insisted that Lionel arrange our schedule for at least this
one day. The task defied him. At the end of a half hour, he suggested lamely that we might visit St. Mark's.

Our cabin in Connecticut was on a dirt road up a small hill
off the Black Rock Turnpike, some ten or twelve miles inland from
Westport. Two other families had homes on our road, a farmer
named Freeborn who lived a half mile below us with his wife and
young daughter and our landlords, the Rortys, who lived a quarter

of a mile beyond us, where the road ended. Jim Rorty was a poet who had for a while worked in a New York advertising agency; with the money he had saved, he moved to the country to write. Rorty was our first literary exurbanite and the first person we knew who spoke of Madison Avenue not as a street but as a condition of life. His wife was Winifred Rauschenbusch, of a well-known public-spirited Midwestern family. We had no acquaintance with either of the Rortys when we rented their cabin; I cannot remember how we came to be in touch with them. Although the cabin was not actually in a valley, it had no outlook, and as the summer went on we came to feel hemmed in and airless. Otherwise, it was entirely adequate, furnished simply but decently, lighted by kerosene lamps, heated by a good-sized fireplace in the living room. There was no bath but we had an inside toilet, and a shower had been rigged up outside the cabin door. It took courage to use this improvised facility early in the day, but after the sun had heated the pipes it was manageable. We pumped water for the kitchen sink. For cooking, there was a two-burner stove fueled by bottled gas; to bake or roast, one set a portable oven over the gas burners. At intervals, a meat truck with excellent meat drove up the hill. For the rest of the marketing, we were dependent on the Rortys' telephone. Once a week, a block of ice was deposited for us beneath a tree at the foot of the hill; Lionel would lift it into a towel and carry it up the hill to our icebox. When the ice gave out, which it inevitably did after a few days, we put our perishable foods in a bucket which we lowered into a well in the pump house across the road from the cabin. Neither of us had difficulty in adapting to the primitive conditions of the Rortys' cabin: Lionel could draw upon his experience camping out with his uncle Hymie and I had spent many summers at girls' camp. Our rent for the summer was $300.

Three months are a long time for a newly married couple to be removed from other people, with only each other for company. There were no beaches or other places of amusement within walking distance and we had no car. Apart from our casual exchanges with our landlords and an occasional neighborly word with the farmer down the hill, we were wholly dependent upon each other for conversation. The airlessness which I ascribe to the cabin may have been a reflection of the claustral nature of the human situation. Both Lionel and I were born in July; we were glad to have our families come to celebrate our birthdays with us. On my tiny stove with its portable oven, I prepared elaborate birthday dinners. Throughout the summer we had only one other visitor. One afternoon Francis Steegmuller, whom Lionel had known at college, chugged up our hill in his battered old car—many years later, in Florence, he would produce a local sensation by calling for us at our pensione in his Rolls-Royce. In August the Fadimans rented a weekend cabin in the Stonybrook section of Westport. The house was owned by Rose Pastor Stokes, the very lady who my brother had insisted had never visited my summer camp. The Fadimans, too, were without a car, but Lionel and I were so starved for company that, like characters in a D. H. Lawrence novel, we walked eight or nine miles each way to spend an evening with them. That was the house in which the Fadimans were broken in on while they were away in the city; although nothing was taken, they knew the house had been entered because a can of spaghetti in tomato sauce had been emptied into Polly Fadiman's underwear drawer.

At camp I had frequently gone on overnight hikes. Wrapped in ponchos and blankets, we had slept on the ground under the sky—there would be fifteen or twenty of us and we would sing and call out jokingly to each other in the dark until we at last submitted to sleep. In Connecticut Lionel and I were alone in the night, on an unlighted road off a deserted country highway. The night was heavy with fear for me—the Freeborns and the Rortys were too far away from us to call out to for help, should there be need. I would wake in the night and strain to distinguish among the country noises. Nature had lost its innocence and I was back in my Westchester childhood: once again the night was peopled

with "burglars," those faceless creatures who had been my noctur-
nal companions as Bobolinka's neighbor. At my side, Lionel lay
peacefully asleep; if I had tried to wake him, it would have been
useless. Years later, when we had been married a long time, I would
tell Lionel that I was one day going to write his biography in terms
of his relation to sleep. Though he had, really, no knowledge of
insomnia, if he was not asleep the moment his head touched the
pillow he was convinced that he was its victim; he would jump
from his bed and go to another room to read. But when he was
once asleep and meant not to wake until the next morning, he
could be pinched, punched, and pummeled and not stir. This, at
any rate, was his conduct as a husband; it was not at all his behavior as a father. Our small son, himself an erratic sleeper, had but
to call "Pop" for Lionel to spring from bed, sharp-eyed, eager. I
accused Lionel of sleeping *against* me: I meant by this that he was
entirely capable of waking but deliberately refused to be wakened
by me. I now realize that I was probably unfair in my judgment of
his pattern of sleep. I am told that his cousin Bernard Cohen and
even Bernard's daughter, Franny, fall asleep as promptly and thoroughly as Lionel and, like him, believe that they are insomniac if
the process is delayed by so much as a moment; like Lionel, they
are also unwakeable. In Connecticut, Lionel lay at my side, sleeping his inviolable sleep while I lay stiffly awake, readying myself
for the hostile intruders whom we would soon have to battle. Often
in the first dawn, when the sun had barely mounted the hill, I
would hear a thumping noise across the road, or perhaps it was
scraping; yet on the other side of the road there were no houses,
only our pump house in an empty field. Tense with terror, I tried
to identify the marauders: Who were these people and against whom
did they direct their murderous intentions? Shortly before we returned to New York, Mr. Freeborn explained to me that these
early-morning sounds were the sound of deer come to sharpen
their horns on our pump house.

We had been told by the Rortys that in return for weeding

their garden, we could take all the vegetables we needed for our table. When Jim Rorty saw us at work under his window, he would sometimes come out to talk to us. He was the cheeriest of Irishmen, always in a chuckle, but his jokes were apt to be lost on us. He was an ex-Communist and an anti-Communist when Lionel and I scarcely knew that there had been a Russian revolution. He liked to mock his old Party comrades and told us, for example, that he had named his cat Mike Gold because he was so lazy and stupid—Lionel and I had never heard of the Communist writer Mike Gold. Jim's wife, Winifred, was of a more somber disposition than Jim. She was a tall rawboned woman who talked very little and joked not at all, but she was efficient at flattering Lionel and snubbing me. Her and Jim's son, Richard, now a well-known philosopher, had not yet been born, and as I think back on Winifred I realize that she must have been still in her early or mid-thirties. I thought she was advanced in middle age. Certainly she commanded a moral universe beyond my reach; it was the universe of country living as this is experienced by women of sensibility who in moving to the country from the city believe that they have been cleansed of all the falsities and contaminations of modern civilization. As the summer progressed, I became increasingly embarrassed at having to do my corrupt marketing in her hearing. One evening when Jim was away from home, we invited Winifred to have dinner with us. She was disapproving of the lamb stew I served her: "You put our beautiful garden peas in a stew," she rebuked me softly. Winifred lacked the confidence to be a successful flirt but she did contrive that evening to reach the point of any story she told while I was in the kitchen. She would come back to mind a quarter of a century later when Mary McCarthy and her then-husband, Bowden Broadwater, returned to New York after having lived for a year or two in Newport and invited us to dinner. We had never before visited Mary, though we had often met at *Partisan Review* parties. Mary wanted to establish literary connections in New York. A mutual friend, the harpsichordist Sylvia Marlowe, would later tell me of the remarkable preparations which Mary made to entertain us: she not only submitted menu after possible menu for Sylvia's opinion but also borrowed several paintings from an art-dealer friend on 57th Street as decoration for her living room. There was only one other guest, the composer Virgil Thomson; it was fortunate that he and I found much to talk about, because Mary, like Winifred Rorty, concentrated the whole of her attention on Lionel and excluded me from the evening. "What makes an intelligent woman suppose that the way to attract a man is to be rude to his wife?" Lionel later pondered. Winifred was the first of a long line of women who would have me understand that in choosing me for a wife, Lionel had gravely underestimated his own worth. A quarter century after we were the Rortys' tenants, I got to know Jim at the American Committee for Cultural Freedom; the Committee occasionally engaged him for jobs of research. With the passage of time, there was no longer the old overrun of laughter in his personality and a strange vacancy seemed to have crept into his eyes. I saw Jim and Winifred together for the last time when we briefly visited them at the farm they now owned in New Jersey. As we drove up, Winifred was sitting on a bench in front of her door. She was shelling peas; they were no doubt too beautiful for a lamb stew. She looked worn and dreary, like an overworked farm wife, and as I contemplated her I was filled with wonder that this sad and vulnerable woman should once have so much intimidated me.

One of Lionel's responsibilities at our honeymoon cabin was to prime the pump in the pump house each day. Swinging his thick ash walking stick in front of him like a scythe, he crossed the field to discharge this duty. He had great affection for his ash stick and carried it with him wherever he went. On walks he swung it like a golf club, driving fallen apples down the road—I still have the stick and, more than sixty years later, it still smells of apples. We had returned to New York before Lionel told me why he never left the cabin without his stick, especially if he was going to the pump house. When we had been in Connecticut for only a few days, he had seen a snake wriggling out of sight beneath our cabin. He described it to Mr. Freeborn, who had identified it as a moccasin and poisonous. It probably lived under our cabin with its mate. I have an immoderate fear of snakes but Lionel's fear was, if possible, even greater than mine. Yet he not only stayed on at the cabin and each day walked through the thick grass to the pump house; he kept his worry to himself. Now I understood why he had not allowed me to sit on the ground outside our door and why, soon after our arrival, he had gone to New York on an undisclosed errand: he had gone to Abercrombie & Fitch to buy a snake-venom kit. That summer Lionel interrupted his reading of Meredith to write a story about a snake. It was not precisely the snake under our house but it was unmistakably his own personal and private snake, the secret sharer of his jealous fantasies about me. Lionel's snake story was never published, nor do I recall that Lionel ever attempted to publish it, and it now appears to be lost. Although the emotions of the story were excessive, it was a remarkable piece of fiction, perhaps the best Lionel wrote. I, too, wrote a story that summer, to while away the time. Although it was a first venture in story writing, it was not autobiographical; I made up a story about a young American girl in Florence. I had not yet visited Florence but I was able to supply the geography from my college courses in Italian art. On my return to New York, I boldly sent my story to Elliot Cohen at the *Menorah Journal*. Where else? It was never possible for Elliot simply to accept or reject a manuscript; he had to talk around his decisions. I went to Elliot's office for what I supposed would be an editorial conference, but my story was not mentioned, not then or ever, though Tess Slesinger later told me that Elliot spoke well of it to her. In 1929 I still hoped to be a singer; I had no thought of being a fiction writer or a writer of any kind. But how can I now say what it might have meant to me if Elliot had told me he liked my story? It may be, of course, that he thought poorly of it but spoke in praise of it to Tess out of mischievousness, in order to make us competitive with each other or simply to undermine her confidence. Shortly after my friend Elinor Rice published her first novel, she met Elliot at a party at which he greeted her: "How's the author of one novel?" Angrily, she retorted: "Better than the author of no novel!" Ours was a society in which there could be few more significant accomplishments than to write a novel. Young writers did not talk of the slow difficult process of building a literary career or producing a body of work but only of "a" novel, the single much-to-be-heralded volume which would justify a life and no doubt remake the world.

We had no piano in our cabin but I nevertheless practiced singing each day. Often I stopped in despair: my voice sounded as if it were being released from a tight coil. I had forgotten how to produce it. It was one of several early signs that I would not make a career in music. I had also lost, or begun to lose, my hold on whatever it is in the life process which keeps us at peace with ourselves and steady in the world. I was not yet phobic; I did not yet experience panic—symptoms of this dimension would not appear for close to two more years. But as the summer went on, instead of becoming more used to the country, I was becoming increasingly uncomfortable, especially when Lionel went alone for a walk or even when he left me to go to the foot of the hill for the ice. One August afternoon Jim Rorty rattled up to our door in his old Ford; a fire had broken out in the nearby woods and the men in the neighborhood were being rounded up to combat it. As Lionel drove off with Rorty, my heart began to race with fear. It was not fear of the fire or of danger to Lionel but fear without source or object, incoherent, senseless. Before Lionel left I had begun to prepare dinner. I tried to resume this quieting occupation, but I was unable to. There was an enormous rock in back of our cabin and I went out and climbed it. From its top I could scan the horizon: I had no notion of what I was looking for, whether for Lionel or the fire or only for an indication that there were other people in the world. But I saw nothing; we were in a valley from which there was never anything to see. Wagner was not in my repertory—it was much too heavy for my voice—but the "Ride of the Valkyrie" was the loudest music I knew. Standing on top of the rock, I began to sing it to the empty countryside. Perhaps I was trying to drown out my fear or perhaps, however vainly, I was using what means I had to call someone's attention to me—as a child, I had not been permitted to call my parents when I woke frightened in the night. By the time Lionel returned, I had recovered my composure and was once more preparing our dinner. I was unable to tell him what had happened in his absence, nor would I have wanted him to know. Soon after Labor Day we moved back to New York and into our first apartment. We were relieved to put the summer behind us.

Chapter
SIX

Our first apartment was at One Bank Street in Manhattan's Greenwich Village, a few blocks south of 14th Street. The building was still in process of construction when we signed up for it before leaving for Connecticut but it was ready for occupancy on our return. A structure of soft tan brick, it looked as if it would crumble at a touch but it still stands where so much around it has fallen to time; it has even begun to take on the charm of urban endurance. But it was surely one of the least attractive buildings in its neighborhood. On a street of sturdy old brownstones, it was six stories tall, with an elevator, and everything about it was typical of the commercialism of its period, including its shiny linoleum-tiled lobby and its manned switchboard. Our apartment was on the fifth floor and consisted of two rooms and a bath. The first of the rooms, the living room, had a galleylike kitchenette which was hidden from view by a heavy curtain of gray monk's cloth. The kitchenette had a stove, a sink, and a small gas refrigerator, which was the earliest form of mechanical refrigeration. Both the living room and the bedroom, which also functioned as our dining room and Lionel's study, were of decent size. But there was nothing about them or about anything in the apartment—no irregularity in the shape of the rooms, no bay window or wood-burning fireplace—to suggest that in moving to the Village we had left behind us the staid uniformity of the apartments in which we had lived with our parents. We searched very hard to find an apartment in a brownstone in the Village which we could afford. None was to be found. Our rent on Bank Street was $90 a month.

When we had settled into our apartment, Lionel began to work at the *Menorah Journal* as a part-time editor; his salary was $45 a week. This meant that we were spending almost half his monthly earning for rent. We married at a moment when prices were high and they continued to be high for some time even after the stock-market crash of October 1929, only a month after our return to New York. But it was not impossible for two people to live on $2,400 a year—it was the starting salary of a Columbia instructor. A Columbia graduate fellowship at the time was $1,800 a year. While it was not easy for married students to live on this stipend, many young couples managed it. Our friends Jim and Elsa Grossman were married a few weeks after us. Jim, who had been editor-in-chief of the *Columbia Law Review,* now had a position in a highly respected New York law firm at a salary of $25 a week. When he married, his salary was raised to $35. Elsa had a responsible position in the story department of a large motion-picture company and earned $25 a week. The Grossmans saved money on their combined earnings. While Lionel and I were not extravagant, not in the sense of being drawn to display or acquisition, our tastes were not in keeping with our income. We also seemed not to be aware that money was not self-renewing and we used it without regard to whether or not we had it. For instance, although when I married I had all the clothes I would require for the next few years, walking through Bonwit Teller's one day I saw a hat which appealed to me and I bought it. It cost $35, almost the whole of Lionel's weekly pay. Lionel was dismayed by this incautiousness, yet he regularly clipped newspaper advertisements of clothes which he wanted me to buy. They were no less out of our financial reach. I liked to cook and I quickly got used to our kitchenette. It never occurred to either of us that we must forgo foods like shrimps or roasts of beef—in 1929 these were not as expensive as they are today but they were surely too costly for us. We ate in restaurants infrequently yet when we did, instead of patronizing a modestly pleasant place like the nearby Waverly Inn—itself beyond our means—we went to the Café Lafayette on University Place, a well-known French restaurant to which my father had sometimes taken me. Both Lionel and I were for many years heavy smokers; when at last we had to give up cigarettes, one of the things which made it difficult for us was that our self-image was being violated: we preferred to look like people who smoked. Just so, we preferred to look like people who were not constrained by concerns about money—to stay within our minuscule income, we should have had to subscribe to an entirely different principle of living, one of vigilance and prudence. Actually we could not afford to go to any restaurant, however modest, and certainly not to the theater or opera, and we should have had to live in Brooklyn or Queens or in some such cheerless section of the city as Washington Heights. Our Bank Street apartment was a disappointing substitute for the atmospheric walk-up in which we had hoped to live, but in the Village we were at least among people of whom we could assume that they, too, aspired to more than mere solvency. On our own street, diagonally across from us, lived Edmund Wilson, whose literary essays, soon to be published in his volume *Axel's Castle,* were just now appearing in the *New Republic.* Walking to and from the subway, we could see him at his desk in the window of his brownstone and feel that we were of his free and enlightened kind.

When our apartment was ready for occupancy, the furniture we had ordered before we left for Westport was ready to be delivered. One of Lionel's aunts, Aunt Blanche, the wife of his uncle Izzy, was in the business of buying home furnishings from wholesalers on commission. She was not a decorator, only a commissionaire, and was not responsible for our choice of furniture. Through Aunt Blanche we bought portentous seventeenth-century pieces, which were better suited to a feudal manor than to a two-room apartment in Greenwich Village: an oak refectory table which must have been close to eight feet long, four high-backed three-legged oak chairs, a massive oak credenza. In 1967 Lionel and I would be sent by the Ford Foundation to Germany—we were a strange company, headed by Irving Kristol and including Dwight Macdonald, Stanley Kauffmann, Norman Podhoretz, Robert Manning, and our future Senator from New York, Daniel Patrick Moynihan. In Cologne our group was entertained at dinner by an industrialist in the Ruhr. Although I was a member of the group, its only female member, he would not allow me to join the discussion after dinner in his library; and in 1967 no male member of the company protested my exclusion. The antique furniture we bought on Bank Street belonged in our host's baronial mansion. In addition to these Italian or Spanish pieces we also bought a desk, which would serve as the whole of my work space until Lionel died and I moved into his study, a sofa improbably upholstered in antique velvet and a club chair covered in antique satin. I needed a piano and we bought a small Hardman & Peck. With the rest of the $5,000 which my father had given me, we bought carpets and floor-length crewel-embroidered draperies, tan Wedgwood dishes, garnet-colored Czechoslovakian glasses and dessert plates. We had silver circles fired into the Wedgwood plates. It was an odd scheme of decoration for a pair of putative bohemians and can be explained, if at all, only by our dislike of the dull minimalism of the functional furniture of the time, plus, of course, our wish to put as much distance as possible between ourselves and the taste of our families.

With our first year of marriage, we were launched on our life-long state of indebtedness. Over the years, for reasons both good and bad, we had constantly to borrow money; it would be 1970 and we would be sixty-five years old before we paid off the last of our loans. To report of someone that he lived a lifetime of debt has a splendidly romantic ring: it suggests a life of adventure and recklessness, of high spirits and the defiance of respectability. I wish I could say of Lionel and myself that we were ever adventurous or defiant of respectability other than in thought, or that we were reckless or even high-spirited. In the Depression and through all the bad years of our lives, we were stubborn and enduring, uncomplaining in adversity—we had spirit but we were not high-spirited; they are not the same thing. We never threw off the yoke of our upbringings. There was no lack of respectability, only a lack of good sense, in the way we spent money when we had none. We enjoyed having people to dinner and were especially improvident in our expenditures for food. But could anything be more respectable than a three-rib roast of beef? Fortunately it was Prohibition and our friends drank only at speakeasies or parties. We soon recognized that we were getting ourselves into serious financial trouble, and in an attempt to improve the situation we devised a budget. It consisted of a series of envelopes marked "Rent," "Food," "Laundry," "Utilities," "Newspaper," "Spending Money," and, last and most capaciously, "Miscellaneous." In the course of a week, if the contents of one envelope disappeared, we borrowed from another; by midweek all the envelopes were empty. As the winter drew to its end, we began to sell our wedding presents, first the silver flower bowl which had been given to us by one of my father's more ambitious salesmen, then a silver water pitcher and a set of silver holders for demitasse cups. In mid-spring, we sold our antique furniture at auction, everything except the desk. The Depression had begun and people were not crowding the auction rooms: we retrieved only a fraction of its cost. Sometime that winter, I briefly went into business with my brother's wife: we bought furniture on commission, like Aunt Blanche. I detest shopping, especially for the home, and could not have chosen a less congenial means of earning money. After a few months we dissolved the

133

partnership. The money I had earned disappeared as all money disappeared.

I would always be in charge of our family finances; Lionel earned the money, I paid the bills and verified our bank statements. Lionel was not to be relied on even in the use of a checkbook. Later in his career, his Columbia paycheck went directly to the bank. His salary was never physically in his hands, and this came to symbolize for me his disconnection with his financial life. Nothing in his upbringing had prepared him for the handling of money. When he went to college, his parents were in straitened circumstances, but whether from a misguided sense of pride or from generosity— probably both—they never required him to contribute in any way to the cost of his education. He had a job or two as an undergraduate but nothing of consequence: one summer he earned a bit of pocket money by washing instruments in his uncle Louis's chemistry laboratory at City College and another summer he briefly worked for a commercial genealogist. Even after he returned from his graduate year at the University of Wisconsin and began to teach, although he continued to live at home he was never allowed to feel that he was paying for his room and board. He regularly gave his mother money but she always received it as if he were making her a gift. Yet despite his lack of experience in the earning and management of money, he became, if surely not a money-maker as the world knows that species, a steadfast provider. Soon after the collapse of the stock market, when he was still a very young graduate student, earning only a part-time salary of $45 a week, with no prospects, he took over the support of his family. It was a daunting responsibility but he never shirked it or allowed it to alter the career he planned for himself or his standards as a writer. In the thirties and forties literary people often talked about "selling out." It was an accusatory term and was applied to writers who went to Hollywood or into advertising, or who in whatever fashion were felt to have cared more for money than for the preservation of their talents. Today no one keeps so sharp an eye on the moral life of writers, but I doubt that this is because we are more generous in our personal judgments than we used to be; probably it is because we no longer make the distinction we once made between serious and nonserious writing. Lionel would not have known how to sell out, but money was crucial in determining the work he did. Many of his best literary essays were written because we needed money. He wrote several introductions to books for which he was paid between $300 and $500. This was more than one was paid for a review and he could also sell the introduction as a magazine article and later reprint it in a collection of essays. As time went on and his name got to be known, he became a book-club editor and, later still, he produced or shared in the production of several textbooks. A good number of the pieces reprinted in his volume *A Gathering of Fugitives* first appeared in periodicals published by his book clubs, and *Prefaces to the Experience of Literature,* one of the volumes in the Uniform Edition of his work which I edited after his death, is entirely made up of the short introductory pieces he wrote for that textbook. He seldom in later life spoke of the heavy financial burden which had fallen upon him as a young man, but it had a lasting effect on him. We had our only child in 1948. With Jim's birth Lionel became increasingly anxious to accumulate a small capital fund against our old age. He was determined that his son should never be burdened by us as he had himself been burdened by his parents.

Even at our remove from Wall Street, we and our friends had to realize that the stock-market crash was a calamitous event, but months had to pass before we recognized the profound alteration it would make in our lives and the life of the nation. Both of our fathers were financially destroyed by the crash but it took time for us to comprehend the degree of their disaster. In the twenties writers and intellectuals deliberately distanced themselves from public affairs; their refusal to talk or think about politics was how they guaranteed their intellectual purity—I was not surprised when J. Robert Oppenheimer, testifying at his loyalty hearing before the

Atomic Energy Commission in 1954, declared that in the late twenties and early thirties he had no radio and read no newspaper. Today, as I reconstruct the first months after the collapse of the market, the period between, say, November 1929 and the summer of 1930, what I am chiefly struck by is how slowly the Depression made itself felt and how normal life appeared to be until we experienced its full impact. From the start one heard stories of personal tragedy; people lost their fortunes and jumped from windows. The newspapers reported these financial suicides as they reported the deaths and blindings due to wood alcohol. A friend of my sister became insane over the loss of his family's money; it had been entrusted to him and he accused himself of having betrayed his trust. But these were extreme responses and did not represent the look of America at the time, or at least not the look of New York. Throughout the winter of 1929 and the spring of 1930, the life of the city was much as it had always been. Restaurants continued to be patronized, theaters and concerts were as well-attended as ever. In our own circle, the collapse of the market and the possible consequences were scarcely spoken of—it was as if, in a more recent time, the Berlin Wall came down without any of us stopping to comment on it. We sold our wedding gifts to a Village jeweler, not to a pawnbroker. He correctly assumed that we were young people who had got out of our financial depth; he did not regard us as victims of a national catastrophe. Lionel and I continued to have dinner guests and to buy our shrimps and roasts of beef. Indeed, our mishandling of money, I now realize, only actually began after the Depression, or at least after the collapse of the market. On the eve of 1930, we gave a New Year's party to celebrate the arrival of the new decade; it was unclouded by any intimation of national anxiety. The widespread move to Communism among intellectuals, which would be so conspicuous a phenomenon of the thirties, did not announce itself overnight. It was a response not to the crash on Wall Street but to the economic and social consequences of the crash as these gradually revealed themselves. As the decade went on, it was of course also a response to Stalin's brilliant manipulation of liberal sentiment in the democracies.

Lionel was miserable in his part-time job at the *Menorah Journal* during this first year of our marriage. Neither then nor ever did he tell me what happened there, but as I got to know Elliot Cohen and Herbert Solow, who was Elliot's close friend and coadjutor at the magazine, I could guess how humiliating the experience must have been for him. Cohen and Solow were not the kind of people to respect Lionel's good temper. They took it to be a defect of character: a vigorous intelligence was not this courteous and peaceable. Even after Elliot came to know and like Lionel, he was confounded by Lionel's placidity. With this deficiency, how did he manage to win intellectual regard? The untiring argumentativeness of the writers around the *Menorah Journal* was of course not special to that magazine; when *Partisan Review* began to publish, the writers for that magazine would be just as challenging. But *Partisan Review* was less claustral. Although its editors were likely to find their friends among their contributors, they did not have the close and overbearing connection with their authors that Cohen had with his. Cohen's and Solow's was a genius of hostile intimacy. In 1934 Tess Slesinger published a novel, *The Unpossessed,* which has since acquired a cult reputation; it was reissued in 1966 with an Afterword by Lionel. We had first known Tess as Herbert Solow's wife; the two lived in Brooklyn Heights in the home of Margaret DeSilver. In 1930 the Solows were divorced and Tess moved to Hollywood, where she remarried. She died at an early age, having written only the one novel. The leading male characters in *The Unpossessed,* Miles Flinders and Bruno Leonard, are generally supposed to be portraits of Cohen and Solow. This is neither entirely true nor untrue. A third male character has sometimes been said to be Lionel, but this is mistaken. The third male in the book is based upon a friend of Tess, Melvin Levy. There is no question but that Cohen and Solow were the models for Flinders and Leonard but in their re-creation the originals were importantly falsified. In his Afterword, Lionel writes of Tess's book that it was "not only a literary enterprise but also a personal act. It passed judgment on certain people; in effect it announced the author's separation from them and the kind of life they made." With her divorce from Herbert, Tess did indeed separate herself from the life lived by Cohen and Solow. She freed herself from what, in her view, both men represented in denial of direct feeling and even of biology. But it is necessary to understand that by the time she wrote her novel a new factor had entered her judgment of these earlier relationships. Her assessment of her former husband and her former editor was influenced by the politics she had newly embraced in Hollywood. Briefly in the early thirties, both Herbert Solow and Elliot Cohen were Communists, not Party members but strong sympathizers. But disillusionment had quickly set in, and by the time Tess wrote *The Unpossessed* both men were passionate opponents of Communism. In the meanwhile, Tess's own life had taken an opposite turn. Married to a Hollywood writer and producer, Frank Davis, she came to profess the Communist-oriented liberalism of the movie colony and this was the political bias from which she wrote about her earlier associates. It could not but distort her perception of them. But there was also another explanation of the lack of accuracy in Tess's re-creation of Cohen and Solow. She was an intelligent woman and a talented writer but she did not have the intellectual power to reproduce the way in which they thought and talked. As a record of Cohen's and Solow's conversation, the talk of Flinders and Leonard is almost parodic. While it would have been possible for Lionel to be in the professional company of a Miles Flinders or a Bruno Leonard with little more than distaste for their aggressiveness, to work each day with the real-life Cohen and Solow was a different matter. It was to be in the company of people who deeply threatened his sense of his own intellectual capacities.

It was not the kind of furniture we had on Bank Street but the fact that we *had* furniture—a sofa, chairs, even carpets and curtains—that made us objects of suspicion to the people around the *Menorah Journal*. Our two-room abundance marked us as members of the hated middle class. As the years went by, the envy which lay behind this judgment became all too apparent to me, but in 1929 I suffered the disapproval of Lionel's *Menorah Journal* friends unaided by any insight into their own hidden ambitions. Contempt for the middle class and its ambitions is of course as old as the middle class itself. In nineteenth-century France the painter Boudin was fiercely criticized for putting people in middle-class dress on the otherwise-unpolluted beaches in his seascapes. Its mockery of the narrow-mindedness of the American small-town middle class was undoubtedly a major element in making Sinclair Lewis's *Main Street* one of the most widely read books of the early years after the First World War, and its ridicule of the middle class was probably central to the success of Mencken and Nathan's *American Mercury*. Although the *American Mercury* was an essentially conservative magazine addressed to middle-class readers, much of its claim to seriousness could be traced to its derisive view of the American bourgeoisie—the "booboisie," as Mencken called it. Mencken's magazine was surely not Cohen's model of serious journalism but the *Menorah Journal* breathed the same cultural air as the *Mercury*. The writers whom Elliot gathered around him were similarly attuned to the danger of submission to the values of the middle class. I would learn that even before we had our apartment, even before Lionel and I were married, I had come under criticism at the *Menorah Journal* for my deplorable middle-class origin because of my fur coat: it was sand-colored broadtail with a collar of sand-colored fox and I had been wearing it the day that Lionel introduced me to Elliot Cohen. The three of us had lunch at the Longchamps restaurant on lower Fifth Avenue. Although Elliot was already at the table when Lionel and I arrived, he did not, of course, rise to greet us—he acknowledged the introduction with a twitch of the nose and the little rush of sound which I would come to identify as his attempt to clear his congested nasal passages. Over the years I discovered of Elliot that he was considerably less competitive with women than with men but on our first meeting he was not disposed to be charitable to this girl whom one of his writers was planning to marry, and my fur coat had much to do with the poor opinion he formed of me, especially when, throwing it back over my chair, I exposed to view my initials embroidered on the lining in gold braid. It was plain that Lionel was not only marrying a middle-class girl; he was marrying a West End Avenue middle-class girl, than which what creature was less to be recommended! I would not have condescended to explain that the initials had been supplied by the furrier without my consent and that although I wanted the lining ripped out, I had not had the heart to ask this of him. Often in our early months on Bank Street I tried to persuade myself that I was being wholly accepted by Lionel's friends and that I was only imagining that they disapproved of me. But this was not so. Before the year was out, Eliseo Vivas, a teacher of philosophy who wrote for Elliot's magazine, told me of the unfortunate impression which my coat and the furnishing of my apartment had made on the people at the *Menorah Journal*. He was not apologizing for the harsh judgment which had been passed on me; he concurred in it. Later, his report was confirmed by Herbert Solow.

I doubt that our rabbi friend, Henry Rosenthal, took any notice of our apartment or of what I wore. He was not concerned with my class origins but with something more elusive, my ultimate fitness as a wife for Lionel. Henry was the same age as Lionel, perhaps even a bit younger, but he was already married to a woman named Rachel, the daughter of a renowned Talmudic scholar, Rabbi Tchernowitz—the name Rachel had always to be accented on the second syllable, Rachél. Rachel brought a touch of the unknown and foreign into our little parish. She was older than Henry and had had a previous marriage but a veil of silence was drawn over her earlier life: she never told us to whom she had been married or where she had been born or where she had lived or had her education. If at one moment we assumed that she came from Russia, it was only, the next moment, to have to shift the location to France or Italy. With her Europeanism and her obscure past, her redundant figure, and her strangely accented name, Rachel was irremediably unlike the other wives of our acquaintance, and indeed both she and Henry regarded the rest of us as but poor specimens of our sex: thin-bodied, thin-blooded, deficient in physical and emotional substance. When it would be discovered that the flush in her cheeks was due to tuberculosis and she was sent to Switzerland to cure, her illness seemed all too appropriate. Fevered and foreign, she had always belonged in the pages of *The Magic Mountain*. By 1929 we had all of us read at least this one novel of Thomas Mann. None of us was as yet acquainted with the work of Henry James. We were therefore unable to appreciate the wonderfully Jamesian opposition which the Rosenthals created between Rachel's densely European consciousness and the meager American consciousness of Elsa Grossman or myself. As the year progressed, Henry had much to distract him from my deficiencies as a wife: his own wife was seriously ill and many miles from home. But he remained the tireless student of my American bloodlessness. The question which seemed unceasingly to absorb him was: If I were pricked, would I bleed? Rachel left for Switzerland on a late winter evening, and Lionel and I went to the pier to see her off. We had no wish to intrude upon their leave-taking but we felt that there ought to be someone with Henry after Rachel's departure. The foghorn moaned as the ship pulled away from the dock. It was not a happy moment, not a moment of new beginnings. The world seemed hopeless and forlorn and I began to cry. I should have thought that Henry was lost to his grief, but instead he looked at me sharply: "I didn't think you would cry," he said. Rachel returned from Switzerland cured and was soon restored as a target of Elliot's and Herbert's wit. Herbert referred to her as "La Swamp" and Elliot said of her that she was the kind of woman who made her draperies out of dress material and her dresses out of drapery material. Henry and Rachel said of Elliot that he was a black soul.

In January Lionel had his oral examination for his Ph.D. It was a mild afternoon and I accompanied him uptown and waited for him on the steps of Columbia's Philosophy Hall. The examination went well enough; it made no particular impression on his examiners but Lionel passed. We had looked forward to celebrating the completion of this first stage of his doctorate with dinner at Robert's, an expensive French restaurant frequented by publishers and successful theater people. Though Lionel was still feeling the effects of a recent flu, we foolishly held to our plan. Lionel celebrated with the world's most expensive chicken hash. Even when he was well, he was never at his happiest in restaurants. He never seemed to order what he wanted. At home, he was the least finicky of eaters and enjoyed everything which was served to him, but a restaurant menu seemed to paralyze him with indecision and he would vacillate between extremes of choice, only to settle on something which disappointed him. Then he would look piteously at my plate and wonder why he had not ordered what I ordered.

Between April 1927, when he was twenty-one, and June 1929, when we married, Lionel had published some thirty reviews and stories. Considering his youth and the fact that during these same years he was a graduate student and part-time teacher, it represents, if only in point of quantity, an impressive start to his critical career. But more striking than his productivity is the range of subjects with which at this young age he felt competent to deal. For the *Menorah Journal* he chiefly wrote about Jewish fiction; he reviewed novels by Lester Cohen, Ludwig Lewisohn, Louis Untermeyer, and Paul Rosenfeld. More variously though seldom at greater length than an extended book note, he also reviewed for the now-forgotten literary section of the *New York Evening Post,* a periodical for which he had begun to write as far back as December 1927. In the *Post* he commented upon books as diverse as Glenway Wescott's short stories, Amiel's *Journal,* Julia Peterkin's *Scarlet*

Sister Mary, Joseph Auslander's *Hell in Harness,* studies of Thomas Lovell Beddoes and Swinburne, Stendhal's *Lamiel,* Henry Morton Robinson's *Buck Fever,* the stories of Saki, William Clyde De-Vane's *Browning's Parleyings,* V. Sackville-West's *Aphra Behn,* Horace Kallen's *Indecency and the Seven Arts;* also, de Gobineau's *Pleiades,* Virginia Woolf's *Orlando,* Hugh Kingsmill's *Matthew Arnold,* Richard McKeon's *The Philosophy of Spinoza,* Philip Guedalla's *Conquistador,* Wyndham Lewis's *Childermass.* That the reviews he wrote for the *Menorah Journal* focused as they did on the Jewish content of the books he was discussing could be justified, even in my unsympathetic view, by the nature of the periodical. It was, after all, a journal of Jewish affairs and it was natural that the reviews should emphasize writing by and about Jews. It was about his fiction for the *Menorah Journal* that Lionel and I came into conflict. In the August 1927 issue of the magazine, he published a story, "Funeral at the Club, with Lunch," and in the issue of May 1929 he published a story, "Notes on a Departure." Both were inspired by his year at the University of Wisconsin and dealt with the emotions he had experienced as a Jew in that alien environment. In the twenties and thirties, the word "authentic" was not much in currency. In essence, my complaint against Lionel's Wisconsin stories was that they were inauthentic. In my knowledge of Lionel, he was a Jew as I was a Jew, fully conscious of his religious heritage and of what, in difference from non-Jews, it might account for in the attitudes he brought with him into the world. But no more than mine was his day-to-day life defined by the fact that he was a Jew. Obviously there could have been moments in his year at Wisconsin when he felt removed from the people around him; his was indeed another kind of background and ethnic tradition than that of the majority of the teachers and students whom he met there. But the year had been entirely comfortable for him. It had not been a year of isolation or alienation. He had worked well and made friends. His religion had not come between him and the people among whom he lived as it did for the protagonist in his stories. I accused him, and not only him but several of his college contemporaries who were also writing for the *Menorah Journal,* of having allowed the sectarian requirements of the magazine to dictate their feelings as Jews. I charged him with seeking a "Jewish identity" because this was a passport to publication: understandably he wanted to be in print and in order to be printed in the *Menorah Journal* one had to write as a Jew. We argued the matter strenuously, sometimes angrily. I think that this was the only time in our marriage that I deliberately undertook to combat an intellectual position which Lionel had taken. In our years together, there would be many times when we disagreed, but we were never again this significantly divided. I do not know how much Lionel was shaken by my opposition. He eventually changed his view of the importance of a Jewish identity but there is no reason to think that this was because of me. Most of his friends who had come under Elliot's influence in the mid- and late twenties changed their position on the Jewish issue in the next years, as did Elliot himself. But in the meanwhile, the contest between Lionel and me was not an even one: I had formidable adversaries at the *Menorah Journal* and a highly visible opponent in Henry Rosenthal. With Rachel in Europe, he was often at our house. But Henry's situation as a Jew was not Lionel's: with his religious upbringing, it was not necessary for Henry to seek a Jewish identity—the fact that he was a Jew had always been the dominant factor in both his public and private consciousness. My argument with Lionel on the Jewish issue could not have made his job at the *Menorah Journal* any easier for him. Today I recognize what, in our protracted conflict, I failed to appreciate at the time: how free he was of the animus which we can now anticipate whenever the issue of religion is raised among intellectuals. I was harsh in my characterization of Lionel's motives and those of his friends who were similarly discovering themselves as Jews, but Lionel never retaliated by attributing personal motive to me. He never accused me of wanting to hide his or my religion. This would not have occurred to him any more than it occurred to me. In the not very long run, I was the victor in our controversy, but what won the battle for me was not any inherent rightness in my position but a development in history. With the deepening of the Depression, the writers around the *Menorah Journal* stopped thinking of themselves first as Jews and only secondarily as members of their nation. They were suddenly catapulted into citizenship; they began to ask what there was in the social, political, and economic structure of the country which had brought it to its present crisis. They turned to the study of Marx and became Communists or Communist fellow travelers.

Although Henry Rosenthal had as acute an intelligence as Cohen or Solow, he was not given to polemic as they were. He was a more inward, Dostoevskian character, tormented by ultimate questions of good and evil. For a short time in the thirties he, too, would become a Communist, but even as a fellow traveler calling for the triumph of the world proletariat he had to have been conspiring in the failure of the Communist hope—for how could virtue be known other than by its defeat? He was not a good choice of intimate for Lionel at this stage of Lionel's life, or perhaps at any stage; even after Lionel had reason for confidence in himself, he was easily discouraged. I never learned on what terms Lionel stopped working at the *Menorah Journal* and whether there was a clear moment or statement of opposition between him and Elliot Cohen. Whatever happened, he and Elliot remained friends for the rest of Elliot's life. It was not an entirely comfortable friendship; Elliot had little respect for other people's independence of mind, and bludgeoned his friends with his ideas. Himself badly blocked as a writer, he tried to turn his more productive friends into his literary spokesmen. Yet despite his attempts to commandeer Lionel's mind and typewriter, Lionel never found it necessary to terminate their relationship. With Henry Rosenthal there could be no such mediation of friendship. One could never deflect the full force of his moral urgency; he was an absolutist in friendship as in all things. Lionel and Henry never quarreled; the friendship simply ended. Henry went out of our lives and, disappearing from our lives, he seemed to disappear from life itself. He held only one position in the rabbinate, at the 92nd Street YMHA in New York. It was while he was at the "Y" in the mid-thirties that he apparently decided that the rabbinate was no longer his vocation. He left to take a degree in philosophy. Occasionally in the next years he returned to visit Mark Van Doren at Columbia: Van Doren had been his teacher and had spoken admiringly of him in an essay about his former Jewish students, which he wrote for the *Menorah Journal*. Still admiring, Van Doren repeated to Lionel one of Henry's current pronouncements: Love, Henry had told Van Doren, was quenched wrath. Lionel did not consider this a self-evident truth; he preferred to believe that love had a more independent source. I have no recollection of Lionel's seeing Henry again after they stopped being close, but not long ago I surprisingly found among Lionel's papers the reprint of an article by Henry in the *Review of Religion*, "On the Function of Religion in Culture." The reprint is inscribed to Lionel "with love" and the inscription is dated February 1941, close to a decade after they stopped seeing each other. My own last firm recollection of Henry is in the early thirties, at a small gathering of friends in our apartment on upper Claremont Avenue. Dark and saturnine, he sits apart from the other guests, sucking his inevitable pipe, his lips curled around its stem in their usual scornful smile. More than by any act of social grace, it is by holding himself this aloof from the rest of the company that he means to put his mark on it. The effort is misbegotten; no one is paying him any attention. After leaving the rabbinate, Henry became a teacher of philosophy at Hunter College; I know nothing of his career there. He should not, of course, have been either a rabbi or a college professor. He should have been a novelist: he was the most gifted of the young writers we knew, if one can call someone gifted who was this impeded in the realization of his talent. So far as I have been able to find out, he never finished the novel on which he was working at the time I knew him. He read part of it aloud to Lionel and me: it was about his boyhood in Louisville, Kentucky, and as we heard him Lionel and I felt that we were listening to our American-Jewish Joyce, not the Joyce of *Ulysses* or *Finnegans Wake* but the Joyce of *Portrait of the Artist as a Young Man*. Perhaps Henry destroyed the novel because it promised a degree of success which frightened him. Or perhaps he gravely underestimated it. As a Communist fellow traveler, he sometimes wrote for the radical press under a pseudonym. His writing as a Communist was indistinguishable from the mechanical polemics of the time. For his doctorate in philosophy, he wrote a book on Spinoza. I never heard it spoken of.

With marriage I had entered Lionel's world; it was with his friends that I now chiefly associated. My career as a critic still lay in the future but unconsciously I may have been preparing for it. They were not easy companions, these intellectuals I was now getting to know. They were overbearing and arrogant, excessively competitive; they lacked magnanimity and often they lacked common courtesy. But they were intellectually energetic to a degree which I had not previously encountered and—this particularly attracted me—they were proof against cant. A received idea was an idea to be resisted; piety in thought was the equivalent of nonthought. I did not give up my old friends for Lionel's friends but they now had a less central place in my life. The question is often asked: What do we mean by an intellectual? Is an intellectual anyone who has an advanced education and is interested in activities of the mind? Is everyone in the so-called intellectual professions an intellectual? Are our Nobel scientists intellectuals? What about John F. Kennedy? Adlai Stevenson? A distinction must be made between power of mind and intellectual power; they are not always the same thing. To be a success in business requires power of mind but not power of intellect. For an intellectual, the mind is primarily an instrument of speculation. It operates in a sphere where the consequences of thought are not necessarily put to the test of reality, as they would be, say, in a scientific laboratory or in politics. William Phillips once defined an intellectual as anyone who wrote for *Partisan Review* and his fellow travelers. He spoke laughingly but not without seriousness. My response to William was that an intellectual was anyone who called himself an intellectual. Intellectuals own the word and quickly identify their kind, or so it once was.

In the spring of our year on Bank Street, I wrote a play with my college friend Bettina Sinclair. Its title was *Snitkin,* the name of its central character. Bettina had a full-time job and could work only in the evenings and on weekends, but our play was finished in a few weeks. The character of Snitkin was Bettina's invention: Snitkin was a West End Avenue clothing manufacturer who aspired to be a detective. My part in the collaboration was to supply the West End Avenue atmosphere and dialogue. Neither Bettina nor I had any knowledge of playwriting and we never deceived ourselves that we were making a contribution to the American theater. We had no ambition beyond entertainment. When the play was finished, we made the mistake of reading it to Lionel and Henry. They were not amused; in fact, they could not have been more disapproving if we had been conspiring to poison the culture of the country for the next hundred years. After a futile half hour of trying to explain our modest intentions, Bettina sensibly went home. Alone, I held the fort against the two of them until, completely frustrated, I broke down and began to cry—Henry could once again marvel at my strange capacity for emotion. The battle went on long after Henry, too, had gone home. At two in the morning, in a climax of rage, Lionel threw his favorite pipe from our fifth-floor window and stormed from the house. I was frightened that he meant never to return and rushed to the window for one last look after him. He was standing in the gutter, motionless, bent over his shattered Dunhill: so might one bend over the body of a fallen comrade! Despite Lionel's and Henry's attack, Bettina and I put our poor *Snitkin* in the hands of a play agent, Leah Salisbury, but we no longer had pleasure in it. When I now think back on our playwriting venture, it seems to me that our play had an amusing idea and some amusing dialogue but that as professional playwriting it was a failed effort—we were not philistine, we were incompetent. In the next weeks I forgot about *Snitkin:* I was ill and ordered to bed. After a brief period of bed rest, I went to Boston to be operated on. When I returned to New York in the fall, I was told by Leah Salisbury that Morrie Ryskind, a well-known play doctor, had expressed interest in our Jewish detective and I traveled to Westchester to speak with him about it. The meeting led to nothing and I relegated *Snitkin* to the embarrassing past.

In a world in which the least pressing of exchanges could involve strenuous mental exertion, Lionel and I and our friends had at least one topic of talk which we could pursue without any great exercise of mind. We talked incessantly about sex, sex, and more sex, with particular emphasis upon adultery. Elliot Cohen was only a little older than we but he was never included in these discussions: we were as constrained with him as with a parent. For the rest of us, sex took up as much conversational space as in later years we would give to politics. What were the rights and wrongs of adultery? Could a marriage sustain the unfaithfulness of one of its partners? Here we were, barely launched in our marriages, and all we could seem to think about were new partners. The discussions almost always divided by gender, the men holding the line for monogamy while the women were strong for experience. Kip Fadiman was an exception to the usual male viewpoint. "Couples, couples, couples," he would mutter in despair as he contemplated the imprisonment of matrimony. When we speak of the nineteenth century and the "other Victorians," we assume that there existed at that time a sexual code or, at any rate, a set of accepted standards of sexual behavior, from which the "others," a small minority of the population, deviated. There are of course "others" in all societies. Who, one wonders, were the "others" in America in the twenties? Were they the Hemingways and Fitzgeralds and Millays, the writers whom we associate with the sexual rebellion of the First World War, or were they ourselves who in point of age were so close on their heels and yet so different from them in conduct? We and our friends had been schoolchildren during the First World War but for the writers who had been born only a short decade before us the war was the central experience of their lives—their imagination of life had been quickened by their knowledge of death. In 1929 Edmund Wilson, who was of the war generation, published a novel, *I Thought of Daisy,* set in Greenwich Village; its central character was said to be drawn from Edna St. Vincent Millay. The Village of *I Thought of Daisy* was not the Village in which Lionel and I had our transitory residence. Ours was the Village of Wilson's *Axel's Castle,* a different place from Daisy's place, one in which the moral and emotional upheavals of war had been brought, if only in their public aspect, under the rigorous control of mind. Even in our own generation, who were the "others," those of us who hoarded our bootleg copies of *Lady Chatterley* or *Ulysses* in token of a sexual freedom which was all too firmly anchored in caution, or those who followed in the footsteps of their daring predecessors? Mary McCarthy, recalling that, fresh out of Vassar, she went to bed with a different man each day, sometimes with more than one, tells us that she began to worry that she might be promiscuous. I felt sinful because I went to bed with Lionel without being married to him. We had no apartment of our own in which we could meet and we were afraid to go to a hotel lest we be seen; we borrowed the apartments of our married friends. Our women friends had no reluctance about lending us their beds but they worried that their husbands would disapprove of the illicit use to which their homes were being put. Was it the husbands or the wives who were the "others" of these households? Of contradictory standards of sexual behavior even within a single family, let alone within a single historical period, there is obviously no end. The author of *The Group* thought it was a joke to go to Dr.

Hannah Stone's birth-control clinic for a pessary. My first visit to Dr. Stone was not a joke. I was afraid that I might be seen going into the building or that there might be a police raid and her office records become public. I worried about a hiding place for the bulky little object with which Dr. Stone supplied me: how should I hide it from my sister? The gentle lovers of Noel Coward's *Brief Encounter,* the 1946 film which continues to make its moving impression of truthfulness, could not permit themselves the consummation of their adulterous attraction. The force of their guilt is matched only by the contempt of the friend in whose flat they had hoped to make love. During the first year of our marriage, Herbert Solow and Tess Slesinger were divorced and Herbert asked Lionel and me to be the witnesses of his trumped-up adultery—we were to surprise him at home in his flagrant act. Lionel suggested that it would perhaps be more convenient for us if we came to Brooklyn on a Saturday afternoon instead of a weekday evening. "The *afternoon?*" Herbert repeated in dismay. "Am I to be perverse as well as an adulterer?" In part he was joking, but only in part.

Largely through the *Menorah Journal* Lionel was making new friends. He frequently asked them to dinner. This was how I met Alfred Kreymborg, though I was familiar with his whimsical play *Six Who Pass While the Lentils Boil;* we had regularly performed it at my summer camp. Recently he had published a well-received autobiography, *Troubadour.* Kreymborg no doubt thought of himself as a strolling minstrel and perhaps this was how strolling minstrels actually looked, like clerks in a failing business. His wife, Dorothy, and he addressed each other as "friend." While we were at dinner, Bettina dropped by and sat chatting with us. She carelessly used the word "screw"; the Kreymborgs were at pains to dissociate themselves from such conversational license. When he was leaving later in the evening, Kreymborg asked Lionel if he could cash a five-dollar check. As he wrote the check, he suggested that we might want to keep it for the signature. Only a short year later I would see a signed copy of *Troubadour* on a sale table at the Columbia University Bookstore. The price was twenty-five cents. He was not being boastful, just unaware of his dependence, of the dependence of all writers, on the calendar of culture. It is a short day between the dawn of fame and the darkness of anonymity. Once the stock market collapsed, there was no place for minstrels.

Had there not been an economic depression, Edward Dahlberg would have invented it. On an afternoon that spring, he appeared uninvited at our door. I was home alone. He was ragged and dirty; as he crossed the living-room floor, the loose sole of his shoe flapped like a dismal metronome. I concluded that he must be destitute and starved and although it was three o'clock in the afternoon and I had long since eaten my lunch, I pretended that it was now my lunch hour and set out all the food we had in the refrigerator. Dahlberg ate ravenously; he murmured something about having just come from the Bowery. Not until he was ready to leave did he explain that his mission in going to the Bowery was to get material for a story; he had put together the appropriate clothes for the assignment. Dahlberg was surely the least appealing literary person I have ever known. His meanness of spirit was unrelieved by charm or humor or even by a lively play of mind. Without knowing what I meant, I would insist to Lionel that he must be a bigamist; he looked like a bigamist. He had come to literary attention when D. H. Lawrence wrote the introduction to his first novel, *Bottom Dogs. Bottom Dogs* was a fresh and gifted work of fiction; he never again wrote anything which was its equal. As the years went by, he fell in love with big words, dictionary words; his language became ridiculous in its inflation. We stopped seeing Dahlberg soon after we moved uptown. He insulted Fadiman in our home and we asked him to leave.

Lincoln Reis was also an unhappy, short-term acquaintance of our early marriage. Lionel and I first knew Reis when he was a graduate student in philosophy. Later, he became the model for the non-hero in Mary McCarthy's *Groves of Academe,* the trouble-making college instructor who refuses to confront the actual reason for his academic failure and blames his inability to hold a job on the machinations of his political opponents. Even as a very young man, Reis was a highly efficient plunderer of one's peace of mind. He was given to taking out of context anything he heard one say about a mutual friend, supplying it with an unfavorable emphasis, and repeating it to the person of whom it had been said. Before we realized how necessary it was to be on guard with him, he did considerable harm to Lionel's relation with Mark Van Doren and wholly destroyed Lionel's and my friendship with Philip Wheelwright, a young philosophy professor at New York University and the founder, with James Burnham, of the critical journal *Symposium*.

Throughout our year on Bank Street, Lionel's mother would visit us only by invitation. She did try to keep track of us by telephone. She worried that we might be seeing my father more often than we saw her. She also worried that I might not be giving Lionel proper food; when he accommodatingly developed a mild digestive disturbance, she said that it was because I fed him delicatessen. Presently his stomach disorder disappeared, but soon after our marriage he developed a back problem which would continue to trouble him all his life. In X-rays one saw a visible spur on the sacroiliac, yet the pain was an emotional barometer: when he was low in spirits, it was bound to be accompanied by discomfort in his back. He could do strenuous exercise but standing on his feet for any length of time or moving slowly around a room, as at an art exhibition, produced severe pain.

Apart from an appendicitis operation when I was in my sophomore year at college, I had always been in good health, but we had not been living on Bank Street very long when I began to notice that I was having difficulty climbing the subway stairs. My appetite was also diminishing rather dramatically and I was losing weight. My heart raced; my hands trembled. I consulted the doctor who had treated Lionel for his scarlet fever. In the first of a long series of medical errors which, without shortening the span of my life, have considerably reduced its quality, he pronounced me "healthy as a horse." When my condition worsened, I decided to see the doctor who had taken care of my mother in her last illness. He at once ordered a metabolism test. The diagnosis was obvious: I was suffering from a severe hyperthyroidism. A normal metabolic rate is plus or minus 10. Mine was plus 70. My pulse rate was 135. I was sent to bed and put on iodine. For some time I was not told that I would need an operation or that I was gravely ill. I had never heard of my germless disease nor, apparently, had my father. But he had his own explanation of my sudden ill health: sexual excess. He dispatched my brother to have a man-to-man talk with Lionel. No one I have ever known, not Alfred Kreymborg, not Henry Rosenthal, not Elliot Cohen, no one was less qualified to be a sex counselor than my brother. He was a walking repository of all the sexual fears and superstitions of our early century. There were just so many apples on the tree, he now warned Lionel: he spoke as if it were Lionel's tree which had been too often shaken and Lionel who had in consequence become ill. We tried to laugh off my brother's visit but we were not emotionally free to be intelligent. Lionel reported the visit to the doctor, who said tartly that instead of giving us sexual advice, my father ought to give us money. He had known my father in better times. He must in fact have telephoned my father, because the next afternoon my father appeared at my bedside carrying two large bags of groceries: he had brought me asparagus and artichokes and strawberries, all the foods he could think of which would tease a reluctant appetite. The visit was embarrassing for both of us. As my father prepared to leave, he awkwardly inquired if I needed money. I replied just as awkwardly that I could use ten dollars if he could spare it. But the memory of a father who can take care of his daughter's needs does not die easily. In Boston, with no thought of the financial realities, I arranged for a private room in the hospital and for private nursing after my operation. I suppose that I counted on my father to pay the bills but he was unable to help, and Lionel and I struggled for years to meet them, until eventually the hospital forgave the balance.

Women's liberation, that most successful revolution of our century, has cast a wide net. By now it reaches even the aging men of my generation. They are in their seventies and eighties and have never in their lives performed a domestic service. They were brought up taking it for granted that it was their natural right to be waited upon by women. Now they serve the coffee at dinner or help clear the table and with these token gestures persuade themselves that they are doing their modern bit and sharing in the labors of the household. I doubt that they have much imagination of the range of tasks involved in running a home, even a modest home without children. When I became ill as a young bride and was ordered to bed, the whole of the responsibility of our home fell upon Lionel. In terms of his preparation for the task, the situation was of a different order of magnitude than it would be today. Men had then no training or experience in fending for themselves. Unless he was professionally engaged as a chef, no man knew how to cook. No man knew how to clean a house or even to make a bed—no man I knew had ever made his own bed until he entered the army. Indeed, from earliest childhood, men had been conditioned to believe that if a man engaged in the work of the home, he was robbed of his masculinity. When I became ill, Lionel had his part-time position at the *Menorah Journal* and he was also supposed to be starting his doctoral dissertation. Now, in addition to this work, which was the kind of work which a man was presumably intended to do, he had to see to the myriad duties which were presumably mine alone: marketing, cooking, dusting, sweeping, making the beds and changing the bed linens, sorting the laundry and seeing that it was delivered and returned, serving the meals and clearing up after them. There were only the two of us to cook for and wash up after but frozen meals did not yet exist, nor dishwashing machines. More than most men of our acquaintance,

Lionel had been helpful around the house, or tried to be. When we had guests to dinner, he swept the carpets or helped set the table; he liked to polish silver and never objected to going on last-minute errands. But this help had been his gift to me. It was not his duty or my entitlement, and I was grateful for it, as one is always grateful for help which can be withdrawn at will. Now it was different: he was no longer a volunteer. To make things worse, he was not skillful in cooking and housework. I would lie in bed, torn between guilt and impatience. It was unfair for him to have to do the housekeeping, it was not what he was supposed to do, but if he *had* to sweep the carpet, could he not put both hands on the carpet sweeper instead of gliding it about this loosely and aimlessly? I corrected him; he got angry. My criticism embittered him: Was he not already doing more than anyone had a right to expect of him?

In the course of my marriage, I would have many illnesses, none as serious as the first of them but all of them burdensome to Lionel, and I would experience much remorse because I asked more help of him than other women asked of their husbands. But men get sick, too, and their wives take care of them and is there a man in the world who feels that he must apologize for putting this burden on his wife, as I felt that I must apologize for burdening Lionel? When I was ill on Bank Street, no member of either of our families and no woman friend offered us help. Surely this presents a cultural paradox. If caring for the home and the ill is women's work, how did it happen that neither my sister nor Lionel's sister nor Lionel's mother nor my brother's wife nor any woman of my acquaintance ever cooked a meal for us or in whatever way relieved Lionel of his unmanly duties? In later years, when, say, I was recuperating from an operation and my women friends or women relations came to visit me, they never offered Lionel assistance. On the contrary, they were pleased to let him bring them a cup of tea along with mine.

In the early summer, accompanied by Lionel, I went to the

Lahey Clinic in Boston. The Clinic specialized in thyroid disorders. We traveled by boat on the old Fall River Line; it was cheaper to go to Boston by night boat than by train and normally it was more fun. When we got to Boston, instead of going directly to the Clinic, we made a detour to Cambridge. I wanted Lionel to see Barnard Hall, my old Radcliffe dormitory, in which I had lived for three of my four college years, and to meet Miss Whitney, its house mistress. The hall was about to be closed for the summer. Miss Whitney was going through the ritual of counting the table linens and seeing that the furniture in the reception rooms was covered with summer sheets. The house mistress had probably been in her late forties or early fifties when I lived in Barnard Hall. In the five years which had passed, her appearance had not much altered: with her high pompadour and stiff-necked blouse, she still looked sternly patrician. But her sweet humor was missing, the curl at the edge of her mouth as she suppressed her laughter and the mischievous light in her eyes; and certainly there was no evidence of what I had used to believe was her affection for me. Her greeting was distant and formal and after an exchange of courtesies, she quietly made it plain that she had to get on with her work. It embarrassed me to have Lionel witness our meeting; it was as if I had boasted a relationship which never existed. Soon after my visit to her, Miss Whitney died. She had known that she had a fatal cancer when I saw her and that she was closing the dormitory for the last time. She inquired of me why I was in Boston and I replied as casually as possible that I had come for an operation. She had not pressed me for details. At the Lahey Clinic it was arranged that I would enter the New England Baptist Hospital and I checked in that afternoon. I had again to rest for several weeks before being operated on.

Lionel took a furnished room in Cambridge. After paying his rent, he had a dollar a day to live on. This had to suffice for food, cigarettes, newspaper, his subway fare to Boston. He lived chiefly on bananas until it occurred to us that if he visited me at my

dinner hour, he could finish the food on my tray; I had no appetite. He was acquainted with no one in Boston or Cambridge. Although he had never met Conrad Aiken, he knew that this writer
whom he admired was a Cambridge resident and he telephoned to
ask if he might see him; he had especially liked Aiken's novel *Blue
Voyage*. The visit left him lonelier than before and forever shy about
intruding upon a writer because he liked his work. Our families
could not afford to come to Boston and I have no recollection of
their writing or phoning us. There were several calls to my hospital
room from Lionel's sister, Harriet, who had taken a first job, as a
camp counselor, and wanted his permission to go home. Routinely,
the thyroid patients in the hospital were taken to the laboratory
for metabolism tests. We were a sad lot: here one of us would be
in tears while there another of us was thrashing on her cot and yet
a third beat a compulsive tattoo on the counterpane. After I had
rested for several weeks, Dr. Lahey operated on me. Midway through
the operation, it was halted. It was too dangerous to continue; the
remainder would be performed in a second stage. The hospital had
no postoperative room or intensive-care unit—no hospital did in
those days—and I was returned to my private room. It was no
doubt fortunate that I had a private room and a private nurse: in
the course of the night, half returned to consciousness, I opened
my eyes to find myself surrounded by men and women in white,
doctors and nurses laboring over me. I was lying naked, spread
eagle. Tubes were stuck everywhere possible in my body. I had
become a female Sebastian. I was being drained, they later told
me, of the toxins which were flooding me. Without explanation, I
understood that I might be dying. I absorbed the fact as I might
have absorbed the information that a bulb had dimmed in the
fixture over my head. When I woke the next morning, a large-
bosomed nurse was standing at my bedside inviting me to sit up
and eat my breakfast; I was being urged back to life with a cold
fried egg. She was a very cheerful nurse. "You almost died last
night," she told me. "But we're not finished with you yet. You'll

have to have another operation." Between the two stages of my operation, we traveled back to Westport, where Lionel and I boarded with the Freeborns, the farmers who lived below our honeymoon cabin. Mrs. Freeborn was a good farm wife and a good country cook: she became in part the model for the country wife in *The Middle of the Journey* with whom Laskell boards while he recuperates from his long illness. A specialist in white foods, she fattened me up for my second operation with creamed fresh farm chicken, mashed potatoes, huge white dumplings. The second operation was gentler than the first and in mid-September I was able to return to New York. I steadily regained my strength but I never wholly regained my health. I have, in fact, never since that summer had a day in which I have felt wholly well, although slowly and almost perversely my health seemed to improve with age. I find it comforting to be told that today hyperthyroidism no longer requires surgery; what is now prescribed for it is a dose of radioactive water.

Back in the city, our first act was to move uptown to a cheaper apartment, closer to Columbia; we took an apartment at 160 Claremont Avenue. The southern end of Claremont Avenue, between 116th Street and 120th Street, where I have now lived for many years, is largely the property of Columbia University and the neighborhood has considerable charm. But the street badly deteriorates as one goes north and the buildings no longer belong to Columbia. Our apartment at 160 Claremont Avenue was at the undesirable northern end, near 122nd Street. If for Lionel and me the building in which we had lived on Bank Street represented a concession to middle-class propriety, the building into which we now moved had no such pretense. It had long since surrendered any claim to class status. On Bank Street our rent was $90 a month. When we first moved to 160 Claremont Avenue, the rent was $70 a month. But the Depression deepened and our rent was reduced. By the time we left in 1933 we were paying $50 a month.

Chapter
SEVEN

We were in our first year on upper Claremont Avenue when Lionel began to lie to me and say that he was going to the library when, in fact, he was going to the movies. I am unsure how I found this out; perhaps he eventually confessed it to me. He had frequent recourse to this refuge: like someone unemployed and homeless, he sat through long blinding hours of double features in the moving-picture theaters of Times Square. He was not unemployed: he no longer worked at the *Menorah Journal* but he had a part-time teaching position in the evening session of Hunter College. Yet in a career which had scarcely begun, he felt defeated, robbed of expectation. His experience of working in the company of Cohen and Solow at the *Menorah Journal,* followed by my illness and operations and by his lonely weeks in Cambridge, had taken its toll in confidence. He also had before him, as did his young literary friends, the discouraging example of Kip Fadiman's quick rise to literary recognition. On the basis of but a few pieces for the *Nation,* Fadiman had become in the early thirties the most enviously noticed critic of our generation. All his life Lionel would suffer from depression. As pathologies go, his depression was mild but it was nevertheless a clinical symptom and a more troubling phenomenon than mere dejection or downheartedness. For no perceptible reason he would suddenly fall into an extreme bleakness of mood and be unable to function with appropriate spirit. At these times he regarded me as his enemy and acted toward me as if it were I who were the cause of his despondency—there was always anger at the heart of his depression. Yet no one of his acquaintance and no one with whom he worked outside the home was aware that he was subject to these alterations of mood. Except when he was alone with me, he never allowed his depression to show. But even apart from these shifts of mood, he was not to be described as a happy person. Indeed, he thought poorly of happiness and of people who claimed to be happy or desired happiness above other gratifications in life. He often repeated the question which Philip Rahv put to us with such gusto. Rahv had been born in Russia and had trouble pronouncing the letter *h*. "Oo's 'appy?" he would inquire with obvious relish. Lionel would have replied that it was not the serious people of the world. Seriousness was the desirable condition of man, especially literary man. At best, the poet might be amiable, like Keats. The standard to which Lionel held himself as a writer made it virtually inevitable that he be disappointed by his own performance. Even late in his career, in the face of incontestable achievement, he would feel that he had accomplished little of what he had intended to do and that the little which he had done was of only dubious worth. He never kept a conventional diary but at irregular intervals he recorded his personal journey in a series of untidy notebooks. In one of the notebooks for the year 1952 there is a revealing entry:

> I hear on all sides of the extent of my reputation—which
> some even call "fame." In England it seems to be very
> considerable, and even in this country it is something,
> and in France there is some small trace etc. At Cam-
> bridge someone gave 3 lectures on me. I contemplate this

with astonishment. It is the thing I have most wanted
from childhood on—although of course in much greater
degree—and now that I seem to have it I have no understanding whatever of its basis—of what it is that makes
people respond to what I say, for I think of it as of a
simplicity and of a naivete almost extreme.

The only time I knew him to receive a compliment with pleasure,
as conventionally one is expected to, was when, though he was
himself of course not a Nobel Laureate, he was among the guests
invited to President Kennedy's Nobel Prize dinner and was greeted
by the President on the receiving line: "Oh, it's you." After the
evening's entertainment we were asked to join a small party in the
President and Mrs. Kennedy's quarters. Leaving the White House
that night, Lionel was unreservedly happy and for once allowed
his assessment of his personal situation to include the right to pleasure.

In the fall of 1930, after a year which would have threatened
the firmest self-confidence, there was no doubt but that Lionel's
circumstances were problematic. He had settled on the topic for
his dissertation but he had scarcely begun the reading he would
have to do for it and he knew that many years of hard work lay
ahead of him before he would receive his degree—just how many
years even he at his most disheartened would not have predicted.
His job in the evening session of Hunter was dull and humiliating
and it offered no prospect of permanence. Even the neighborhood
in which we now lived contributed to his discouragement. Upper
Claremont Avenue was not then a dangerous neighborhood; as in
most residential areas of the city, one could walk about even at
night without fear of attack. It was not noisy and crowded as it is
now. But it was a neighborhood without hope; it promised no
future. Our apartment house was more solidly constructed than
the building in which we had lived on Bank Street—it was built
in a more substantial era—but its blank façade was latticed with

water stains and rusting fire escapes which were an invitation to burglars. A few months after we moved into our fifth-floor apartment, we were robbed of all the mementos of my younger life which I had brought with me into marriage: my infant ring with its ruby birthstone, my infant locket and chain, the green enamel lapel watch which my father had bought for me at the Paris Exposition of 1925, the old Russian earrings which had once belonged to Lionel's father's grandmother, which he had given me as an engagement present.

Hunter was not new to Lionel; he had been teaching there when we met. At this period of the century it had a questionable reputation: appointments in the college were said to be in the gift of Tammany Hall. The night session in which Lionel was now teaching was even less self-respecting than the day session. Most of the evening students had full-time jobs and came to class weary and unprepared; they were in college not to learn but in the vain hope that merely having a college degree would give them the possibilities denied them in the life into which they had been born. The college faculty was cynical and bored; working in an atmosphere of political patronage, it had lost whatever intellectual energy it might once have brought to the profession of teaching. Teaching in the evening session, one was paid by the hour and not paid if one failed to meet a class. If I remember correctly, Lionel's pay was $3.65 an hour for his undergraduate class and a bit over $5 an hour for his graduate course—graduate classes ran for an hour and a half. Should an insufficient number of students register for a course, the course was dropped. When it looked as if Lionel's graduate course would be undersubscribed, I and two of our friends registered for it; it was worth our investment of $45 to ensure that the course was given. I have often been asked why I never taught. I did teach, for one evening at Hunter when Lionel was taken ill; we could not afford to lose his evening's pay and I taught in his stead. I had no problem with his undergraduate course. It was a course in composition and I read aloud a story by Katherine Mansfield; then we briefly discussed it. His graduate class was what ended my teaching career. The subject that evening was Ruskin. As a student of art history, I had read one or two of Ruskin's essays, but this had provided me with far from a sufficient knowledge to teach him. I planned to read at least one other essay on my ride downtown but unfortunately I met an old friend on the bus and was prevented from doing this preparation. There were only three students in the class. Two were as ill-informed as I, but the third was not only intelligent but probably the best student in the college. Lionel had spoken of her at home. She was also beautiful and, as I had gathered, more than a little attracted to her instructor. She quickly guessed that I was Lionel's wife and that I was ignorant of my subject and set about torturing me. By the end of the evening I had vowed never again to teach.

The economic breakdown in the country was at last becoming real to us. In the Village we had lived at the classless edge of bohemia, nibbling at its seductions. We foolishly supposed that if we rejected the economic authority of the society, we were immune to its dangers. Now it was being borne in upon us that with or without our assent, we were part of the economic and social organization and were to be spared none of its actuality. Lionel's father's fur business had always been precarious but at its worst he had been able to maintain some kind of footing, however slippery. Now, with the crash of the market, he was unable to meet his rent and modest payroll; the business soon ground to a halt. My father's fate was less predictable but no less extreme. In an expanding economy he had taken a large bank loan to build a new wing to his factory. The market collapsed and his collateral became worthless. The bank took over his business: my father was removed and my brother was installed in his place as head of the company. My father's dignity as he confronted the loss of everything he had worked for gave his ruin an added dimension of pathos. For the time which remained to him, he and my sister lived on his paid-up life insurance. The insurance had been meant for his children and it was painful for him to use it. He felt that the money was not rightfully his. Soon he developed heart disease and for the next three years he quietly waited for death.

Lionel's family had no paid-up life insurance to live on; his father had taken out his insurance at an unusually late age and it had not accumulated any cash value. When I first knew Lionel's parents, before the collapse of his father's business, I thought of Lionel's mother and father as essentially timid people, eager to please. Now, in adversity, they seemed to become inordinately self-willed. All our first winter on upper Claremont Avenue, Lionel's father battled with us over his insurance. Neither he nor we had the money with which to meet the premiums but he was determined to hold on to his policies. We spent similarly futile hours of argument about the disposition of his precious shells, the outer garments of his fur-lined coats. Several dozen of them remained in his inventory. The policies and the shells, the shells and the policies: Lionel's father's celebration of his two assets, as he called them, became the litany of our first year uptown. When he at last yielded to our urging and consented to their sale, it was as if he yielded on life itself. He began to drift into a universe of fantasy which had probably been beckoning him for some time. A first manifestation of the paranoia which would persist and increase throughout the twelve years of life which remained to him was his belief that he was in debt to a porter who had once worked for him in his fur business. Furtively he appealed to Lionel for money with which to placate this unseen adversary. In the spring of 1931 Lionel took on the support of his family; it was an inevitable next step in his life, like the succession to the throne of a crown prince on the death of his father, the king. Lionel's mother had always looked to a future in which Lionel would replace his father as head of the household; that future had now arrived. Actually, there was no practical alternative to Lionel's assumption of the support of his parents and sister. There were no jobs to be had and even had there been, his father was not employable. Though his mother was only fifty-five, fifty-five was then thought to be a great age, virtually terminal. Too, she had never worked for a living and with her upbringing could not have imagined herself in even the most genteel employment. Lionel undertook to give his family $100 a month. In his hourly teaching at Hunter this must have been close to the whole of his earnings. In the next academic year, 1931–32, he had a fellowship at Columbia with a stipend of $1,800. Although usually one was not permitted to work while holding a fellowship, he was allowed to continue his evening teaching at Hunter because of his family responsibilities. In the fall of 1932 he was made an instructor in the Columbia English Department, with a salary of $2,400. His monthly contribution to his family was now half his salary. It was not enough for his family to live on and it left us without enough to live on. There was a short period when my sister squeezed $85 a month out of her household money to help us. Without collateral or cosigners, we were unable to borrow at a bank but we borrowed from everyone we knew, small frequent sums, usually not more than $50; occasionally it might be as much as $100. It was a great deal for our friends to lend us. No one charged us interest; our friends had not yet come to think of money as something with which to make more money. Of the people we asked for loans, only Herbert Solow refused us; sounding very grand, he said that he would not cooperate in Lionel's self-destruction. What he meant, of course, was Lionel's sacrifice for his parents. Though Solow was alone in refusing us money, he was not alone in thinking that Lionel conspired in creating his financial difficulties. Even our more generous friends felt, and made Lionel feel, that in supporting his parents he was masochistically contriving his own ruin. It seems always to have been Lionel's fate to have his virtues regarded as shortcomings. At the *Menorah Journal* Cohen and Solow thought his peaceableness a weakness of character, and when I became phobic and abnormally dependent upon Lionel's being with me, our close friends thought it neurotic of him to sacrifice his freedom as he did in order to stay with me—with the exaggeration which was usual in his pronouncements on marriage, Kip Fadiman assured Lionel that there was only one test of a good marriage, the distance a man could put between himself and his wife.

While the loss of his money and business was bound to alter my father's sense of himself, it never altered his behavior to his children or ours to him. Whatever his private emotions of diminished pride, there was no diminution in the authority he had for us or in the respect we accorded him. But with the loss of their financial independence, the relation of Lionel's mother and father to Lionel and me was forever reversed: we became the parents, they the children. Lionel's father steadily receded into his darkening world. He took no account of how his household was being managed; from time to time he would emerge to ask Lionel for money with which to meet some personal obligation such as a bill for his medications—he lived at the border of addiction, always frightened that his drugs would give out. Lionel's mother made no outright demand for more money than Lionel gave her but her relation to us was charged with dissatisfaction: the money we gave her was insufficient; she felt that she was not getting her due. The best of Lionel's mother's strength of will in those years was directed to avoiding a change in her standard of living. Lionel had been sent to Columbia rather than City College, where the tuition would have been free; Harriet, now in college, was similarly sent to New York University instead of Hunter. She was not made to work on Saturdays or during vacations. We were never told where the money came from for Harriet's tuition but her mother's long-cherished diamond rings and diamond brooch, once the property of *her* mother, disappeared and we surmised that they were sold for this purpose. What was perhaps most extraordinary was that the Trilling household continued to employ a daily maid. To be sure, the pay for a maid in the Depression was only $1 a day. But one could also feed a family of four on $1 a day. The fact that it was our money that Lionel's mother was spending made it impossible for us to tell her how she should spend it. Had she been asked to justify the way she handled her domestic affairs, she would almost certainly have said that she had to keep up appearances for Harriet's sake: if Harriet was to make a proper marriage, she must come from a proper middle-class home. And, in fact, once Harriet married, her mother dropped all pretense to a station beyond her means: she happily did her own housework and after her husband died rented out their bedroom and herself contentedly slept in the living room. As the years went by, Lionel's mother and I grew close to one another. I came to think of her as a fond and generous parent, much to be relied upon. When I was pregnant and began to miscarry, she stood by me as I cannot suppose that my own mother would have, insisting that I had not lost the baby and helping me to withstand the doctor's opinion that I should have a curettage. How reconcile the woman she became with the woman who in the early years of the Depression had so little heed of us and our needs? Throughout our first year on Claremont Avenue, Lionel's mother gobbled up Lionel's energies like an ill-conditioned child. At one point the pressure became so great that Henry Rosenthal, in his role of rabbi, intervened with her on Lionel's behalf, reminding her that Lionel was only at the start of his professional life and that she must give him the peace and freedom to find his way. I, too, pleaded with her to retract some of the greedy demand she put upon Lionel; in response she sternly cautioned me that the one thing she would never forgive me was interfering with Lionel's career. Although it had to be plain that my father no longer had money, Lionel's mother still apparently solaced herself with the idea that I was an heiress and had only to dip into my private reserves for her financial problems to evaporate. It was not uncommon in her time and class to suppose that people had secret legacies or other hidden sources of money. Lionel's mother was always enviously conjecturing of one or another of her women acquaintances that she was "climbing the marble steps." This meant that the woman was secretly squirreling away money from her housekeeping allowance. In the earlier years of this century the private universities took it for granted that their instructors were not financially dependent on their university earnings. When our friend Alan Brown was a young instructor of English at Columbia and asked for a raise because he now had two children in school, his head of department assured him that it was always legitimate to invade capital for the education of one's children, and at Yale this confidence was carried even further. At Yale it was assumed that anyone who taught there must be rich enough to own a boat: one of the senior professors in the Yale English Department, taking leave of a junior colleague at the start of the summer vacation, urged this impecunious young friend of ours to be sure to moor in his harbor should he be cruising off the coast of Maine.

Lionel's mother's Park Avenue relatives had not forgiven Lionel for marrying. Although they were themselves little hurt by the Depression, they made no move to help their sister. They were pleased that the burden of his mother's support had now fallen on Lionel and that marriage had not permitted him to escape his duty to his family. A few years later, one of the aunts, Aunt Deborah, softened and gave Lionel's mother $25 a month. She taught school and had her own income. The only other assistance Lionel's mother had from her relatives came, most strangely, from uncle Louis, the chemistry professor at City College who had been read out of the family when he married a Gentile. He, too, began to give her $25 a month—with their steady paychecks, teachers in the city school system had suddenly become people of substance. But Louis's help continued for only a short while: his wife did her own housework and when she discovered that Lionel's mother had a maid, she put a stop to Louis's contribution. The emotional pressure which his mother put upon Lionel and the constant intrusions upon his time were not the most troubling aspects of his relation with his family during these years of the Depression. Surely the worst feature of the situation was his parents' lack of appreciation of what he was trying to do for them. Lionel's father lived until 1943. For as long as he lived he never spoke a word of gratitude to Lionel. But his father was of course not the family member who mattered; it was his mother's acknowledgment that he was doing everything he could for her which Lionel wanted and needed. As the years went by, Lionel's mother often spoke in praise of me; she would say that I had been more than a daughter to her. She never said that Lionel had been more than a son, that he had been her mainstay and the mainstay of her household. To thank him would, I suppose, have been to recognize a dependence which she preferred not to admit to.

The part played by Lionel's mother's wish to maintain her place in the middle class is not to be minimized in any account of her behavior in these difficult years. Often there was reason for Lionel to feel that she cared more for the appearance of class than for his well-being. Yet paradoxical as it may seem, it was finally neither money nor social status which was most important to her, but something else, something she called "culture." The word "culture" was also often used by her Park Avenue sisters but what it meant to her sisters was going to the Boston Symphony concerts on Thursday afternoons and having the right opinion as to whether Toscanini or Koussevitsky was the better orchestral conductor. By "culture" Lionel's mother meant much the same as Matthew Arnold had meant: the sum of assumptions and ideals which, in the absence of a presiding religious faith, offers us our moral guidance. Without minimizing the tangible advantages of a well-financed membership in the middle class, she gave her ultimate regard to the intangible advantages of learning and high aspiration. In this, she was the superior of her Park Avenue relatives. Lionel was irritated by his mother's invocations of "culture." He felt that she was laying claim to territory which was not hers. But I think he was mistaken and that it was her sincere way of referring to what she most valued in life. There was always less talk of money in my family than in Lionel's—my father had more of it. But for my father, too, there was a contradiction between the importance he ascribed to money as proof of worldly success and his scorn when money was offered in evidence of a successful life. More than Lionel's mother, who would always maintain certain of the religious practices in which she had been reared, my agnostic father associated idealism with religion or, more specifically, with being Jewish. He believed that Jews were people of especially high moral purpose, and he took pride in Jewish philanthropies, as in anything which transcended economic self-interest. With this as the teaching of my childhood, it was with troubled amazement that I read an article in *Commentary* during the Reagan years celebrating self-interest as a step-in-progress in the moral and political evolution of the Jews.

In December 1932 my father died and I inherited a third of the $200,000 insurance trust which was all that remained of his estate. It was inviolable and had not been cashed in like his ordinary policies. The trust was administered by the Guaranty Trust Company; after administrative fees, my share of the principal was something over $60,000. It was a substantial sum for the time. The principal was to be distributed in four quarters at five-year intervals. In the meanwhile, I had the income. If I remember correctly, in the first quarter, while the principal was intact, the income was between $2,000 and $3,000, virtually the equivalent of Lionel's salary at Columbia. But even with this boost in our finances, we were unable to meet our expenses: in addition to our obligation to Lionel's parents, we were soon having to pay for psychoanalysis. But now at least we could borrow more widely than before—for the duration of the trust we would owe the whole of each quarterly distribution by the time I received it. My inheritance was not salvation for us but, as I think back upon the situation, it is hard for me to see how we could have managed had we not had it. Lionel did everything in his power to earn extra money but we were never able to catch up with ourselves. Without my inheritance, he would either have had to find a more lucrative way to supplement his salary as a teacher than the various jobs of writing and editing which he took on—and I cannot imagine what the way could have been—or we would have had to live a very different kind of life, a life of poverty. But a life of poverty is a life of despair. We lived moments of despair but never a life of despair. It was painful for Lionel not to have his mother's gratitude for the help he gave her, yet it would turn out that he was himself unwilling to be grateful for the help we had from my father. We were in middle age when one day we were talking with Elliot Cohen about our early experiences and I spoke of how important it had been to have my inheritance, how it had given us the financial hand we needed when we saw no other means of rescue. Lionel became bitterly angry at me, as if I were crediting my father with the support which he, Lionel—and Lionel alone—had provided. But I was not slighting him; he was slighting my father. For all Lionel's effort, we would have sunk under the weight of our indebtedness if it had not been for the money my father left me.

On my return from Boston I had resumed my singing lessons and I practiced each day, or tried to. But the machine had run down; there were days when it refused even to start. I have no recordings of my voice. Recordings could at that time be made only in a professional studio. With Lionel dead, there is now no one who heard me sing when I was singing at my best and I sometimes ask myself: Did I have enough of a voice to justify my ambition for a professional career in music or was I pursuing an idle dream? The question is pointless. A voice which cannot be put to professional use is not a professional instrument. I stopped my lessons and have never sung again. In the spring of 1933 we moved into a garden apartment in the East 70's where I saw my teacher for the last time: I had invited her and the sister with whom she lived to tea. People occasionally know more about the lives of their friends than it is useful for them to know, but perhaps more frequently they know too little. My singing teacher knew nothing of the neurotic problems which were now besetting me and which put an end to any possible career I might have had as a singer. She blinded herself even to the physical threat which had been posed by my illness and operations. Having counted on me to justify her own career as a teacher of voice, she now fitted me into what must have been a heavy history of failed promises and even of professional betrayals. To confirm her belief that when I stopped studying with her I set myself up as a teacher of singing, she asked me slyly that day whether I had many pupils. I replied that I did not teach, but I doubt that she believed me. I am never able to make myself believable where I am not already believed.

Today, I casually use the words "neurotic" and "neurosis" as if they had always had a place in my vocabulary. In 1931 when I experienced my first panic, not only was the language of psychological disorder altogether foreign to me but I had no idea of what was clinically meant by panic. I had had premonitions of emotional disturbance during the summer of my marriage when we were living in the Rortys' cabin in Westport. I had been on the verge of panic the day that Lionel went with Jim Rorty to fight the neighborhood fire, and there had been forebodings of phobia in my uneasiness when for any reason I was left alone on our Westport hill. But I had not recognized these as signals of trouble to come. It was not until two years later, in the spring of 1931, that I had my first full-blown panic. I had gone to bed one night feeling entirely well but restless. While I lay in bed, waiting for sleep, I was all at once overwhelmed with terror. This is to say that I now realize that I was in the grip of terror. At the time I would not have thought to describe what I felt as fear—until one learns that terror can take so extravagant a form, one does not readily connect an experience of panic with anything so commonplace. I was unable to speak or move, unable to tell Lionel what was happening to me. I clung to him, praying for release from whatever awful thing had attacked me. Finally, the panic subsided. In my ignorance of psychic illness, I attributed the episode to indigestion: I had perhaps eaten a tainted food whose poison penetrated to my brain. But the attack recurred several times in the next weeks and I began to be afraid to stay home alone or to go any distance from home without someone with me, preferably Lionel. I could no longer be persuaded that I was suffering from a physical disorder and I decided to consult a neurologist. Neurology was my closest approach to psychology or psychiatry. It was my bridge between body and mind. The neurologist I consulted was Dr. Israel Wechsler. I think he was recommended by some connection with the *Menorah Journal.* Dr. Wechsler was not a voluble man. He checked my blood pressure and reflexes. Then quietly, almost timorously, conscious of the treacherous waters into which he was heading, he questioned me about my sexual life. Did I have normal sexual desire, normal gratification? I thought him rather silly: even a child of my benighted generation had to wonder how a doctor defined the normal in sexual desire. Dr. Wechsler's next question to me hangs in my mind like a balloon in a comic strip. Why, he asked, did I want Lionel always to be with me? The question implied an element of choice in my symptom, as if I had been presented with a list of fear-provoking conditions from which I had chosen this as the disorder to inflict upon myself. If there was indeed purpose in a symptom, was there not also accusation in bringing the choice to my attention? Vaguely I was annoyed, yet I responded unhesitatingly: I wanted Lionel to be with me because I wanted to be more dependent upon him than he was upon me. I am reporting a conversation of many years ago and over time I have frequently pondered this reply which I made to Dr. Wechsler. Although even today I am not sure that I fully comprehend what I was saying, I think I do understand what in essence I was revealing about a hidden motive in my burgeoning neurosis. Lionel was little dependent upon me. He was considerably less dependent upon me than most men of my acquaintance are upon their wives. He sought and usually took my advice and, like any partner in a working marriage, he relied on me to be in his corner. He would come to depend upon me for help with his writing, although at the time that I saw Dr. Wechsler this had not yet begun. I was using the word "dependent" imprecisely. What I was trying to say was that I wanted Lionel to be more commanding, more in charge of me. I wanted him to be more like my father even if this would involve a curtailment of my freedom—perhaps especially if it curtailed my freedom. I wanted him to be the chaperon my father had been. The fact that he did not exercise parental authority over me exposed me to all the illicitness and temptation I had been taught to fear. If Dr. Wechsler knew what I was revealing to him, he kept it to himself. He prescribed a mild sedative, liquid Luminal.

The Luminal was in my handbag as we traveled to Yaddo several weeks later. I was uneasy about traveling but it was not yet a phobia. We had been invited to the writers' and artists' retreat in Saratoga for the summer. Officially I was invited as a singer but actually I was a marital appendage; no one that summer asked me to sing or spoke to me about singing or even heard me practice. Each of the guests had a studio and my studio was at a remove from the main house. I had no identity other than as Lionel's wife and he had little enough professional identity of his own. A place at which writers and painters and musicians pursue their creative work free of cost and free of the responsibilities and interruptions of their usual lives, Yaddo was—and remains—the best known of these colonies which sprinkle the country. The estate on which it was located had originally belonged to the Spencer Trasks—I think Mr. Trask had been a banker. It was now presided over by Mrs. Elizabeth Ames, a pretty, soft-spoken woman in her early middle age. No one who was at Yaddo the summer that Lionel and I were there spoke either of Yaddo itself or of Mrs. Ames except as mad— not only the writers but whoever could put pen to paper was determined to write a novel about it, with Mrs. Ames as the villainess. Yaddo had known tragedy; the Trask children had died there and were buried on the grounds. But this alone was not what accounted for its eeriness. The guests were housed in the mansion, as it was always spoken of. It was the main house, where the Trasks had themselves lived, and it had apparently been little changed since their occupancy—its decoration attested not only to their wealth but also to their extravagance of taste. The vast central hall was connected to the upper floors by a grand staircase at whose foot stood a huge Russian sleigh. The hall was itself covered with a rug woven to look as if the sun played upon it at all hours of the day, even in the rain. Although some of the upper rooms were still bedrooms, as they had always been, others had been made into workrooms or studios. Frequently their earlier inhabitants had etched their signatures or poetic sentiments into the windows, no doubt with diamonds. For Mrs. Trask life had apparently been a perpetual high-minded house party and this was the spirit in which Mrs. Ames undertook to run the colony. The guests who were at Yaddo when Lionel and I were there would have been model residents in my Radcliffe dormitory. Everyone was quiet-voiced and decorous, prompt to meals, conformable in dress and speech. At dinner we engaged each other in courteous conversation and, when the meal was done, we lingered politely in the central hall over our coffee. In recent decades there has been a stringent retrenchment at Yaddo: services have been drastically reduced and former guests are solicited for funds to maintain the colony. But in 1931 a stay at Yaddo was for most of us an unprecedented experience of luxury. In addition to a handsome bedroom, each of us had our workroom or studio. Both the house and the grounds were fully staffed and the food was consistently the best I have ever eaten. There was nevertheless something about the place, perhaps its wish to persuade so motley a group of hopeful writers and artists that they were the house guests of a dead millionaire, which infected even the servants. One of the elderly waitresses was said to have worked for the Vanderbilts. As she passed a platter of chicken to Lionel one evening at dinner, he lightly inquired whether the chicken was "public or private"—the vegetables which were served to us at Yaddo were grown on the estate and he was asking whether the estate also raised the chickens. "Public, like Yaddo," the waitress snapped. There was also reason to suppose that the housemaids had the auxiliary function of spying for Mrs. Ames, for how else could she have known that Lionel and I slept in only one of our twin beds or that, oblivious of the rule which forbade our visiting in each other's rooms before four in the afternoon, I had allowed one of the guests, a photographer, to take my picture by the morning light in his studio? Mrs. Ames was hard of hearing and preferred to communicate with the guests by note. A few days after our arrival, Lionel received a note asking if we intended to use our second bed; if not, the maid could be spared the necessity of making two beds. My ill-timed picture-taking brought me two notes in rapid succession. In the first, I was informed that having broken a Yaddo rule, I would have to leave the next day. The second note instructed me that I was to leave by the early-afternoon train, "without lunch." The financial appeals which are now sent to former guests of Yaddo contain many reminders of the colony's worthy yesterdays. These include fond recollections of Elizabeth Ames, who was early and long in charge of the colony. No doubt Mrs. Ames changed with the years: I indeed heard that she had a love affair with one of the guests and that she was much altered by it; she became kinder and less suspicious. When Lionel and I knew her, the best that we or any of our fellow guests would have said of her was that she must be forgiven her behavior because of her sad past. Her young husband had been killed in the First World War.

Lionel and I had our twenty-sixth birthdays at Yaddo; we were not children. But professionally we were nowhere. I had no professional commitment of any sort and although Lionel had published a great deal, more than many of his literary contemporaries, he had not made himself felt in the writing community: nothing he wrote was referred to by other writers and no one sought him out for any activity connected with the literary life. But there were few of our fifteen or sixteen fellow guests at Yaddo who had as yet advanced far in their careers. The only one who even approached fame was Evelyn Scott, a Southern novelist who had written a much-praised novel, *The Wave;* we could none of us have foreseen that in the next years she would be written out of American literary history as thoroughly as dissidents in Stalin's Russia were written out of Soviet history. Malcolm Cowley, also at Yaddo that summer, had already acquired a modest renown as a poet and critic, and Sidney Hook was beginning to be known as a teacher of philosophy at New York University. Marc Blitzstein was at the start of his career as a composer, and B. H. Haggin had not yet begun his long and distinguished career as the music critic of the *Nation.* Max Lerner had yet to win recognition as a journalist. We were a promising group, not a company of stars. Sassy and provocative, Blitzstein was the most entertaining of the guests. Hook was the most vigorous-minded. Long a student of the philosophy of John Dewey, he had recently become a Marxist. In the course of the summer he converted several of us, including Lionel and me, to Communism.

The thirties made Communists of many Americans, not so much among the working classes, in which with the breakdown of the economy one might perhaps have expected to find a desire for revolution, but among intellectuals and other members of the opinion-forming classes. In the wake of the stock-market crash many intellectuals became disaffected from capitalism and turned to Marxism as the remedy for our manifestly faulty system of social and economic organization. It was now no longer a mark of moral superiority for writers and artists to stay aloof from politics; on the contrary, it was imperative that they have political opinions and make them known. To this day we still speak blithely of "card-carrying Communists," as if in the earlier years of this century to have been a dedicated Communist meant that one had to be a member of the Communist Party. Actually, only a small minority, a handful of Communist sympathizers, were Party members. The great majority were fellow travelers, people who in one or another degree were committed to the Communist cause and who, whether

179

they were wholly conscious of it or not, took their direction from the Party but did not submit to its discipline. This was how the Soviet Union wanted it. Even early in the decade, but increasingly as time went on, Stalin was more interested in extending the political influence of the Soviet Union in the democracies, where it would add to the strength of his country in world affairs, than in enlarging the national Communist parties. But although the American radical movement of the thirties was in this sense a movement of revolutionary idea rather than a movement of revolutionary action, for intellectuals the imagination of political change was always one of violence and barricades. American intellectuals were not drawn in any number to the Socialist Party; the Socialist Party was a party of reform, not a party of violent class conflict, and it was therefore felt to be both cowardly and ineffectual. As the thirties went on and Roosevelt restored the nation to economic stability, the desire for an American revolution on the model of the Russian revolution almost entirely disappeared. The radical zeal of earlier years of the decade was now replaced in this country by a liberal zeal of self-criticism. Liberalism came to feel that while we might not be in a position to emulate the Soviet Union, neither were we in a position to feel superior to it; we had our own house to clean. This development, too, had Stalin's approval. In fact, he helped initiate the change by creating the "popular front": in 1935 he announced that the Communist movement had abandoned its old hostility to other factions of the left and would now lead a movement against fascism in which all well-meaning people must join. Stalin's presumed leadership of a world union against fascism brought into being the period of his greatest influence in the West, certainly among intellectuals. Today, with the defeat of Communism in Europe and the dissolution of the Soviet Union, it requires a considerable effort of historical memory to bring back to mind the extent to which Stalinism dominated American culture in the years before the Second World War: in art, journalism, editing and publishing, in the theater and the entertainment industries, in the legal profession, in the schools and universities, among church and civic leaders, everywhere in our cultural life the Soviet Union exercised a control which was all but absolute. The submission to Stalinism by our opinion-forming population was not always politically conscious. It represented the fashionable trend in what was presumed to be enlightened thought.

Lionel's and my intimacy with the radical movement of the early thirties would have a deep and lasting effect on our thinking about politics and society and on the kind of work we did for the rest of our lives. It made anti-Communists of us: from our first-hand knowledge of the authoritarianism and dishonesty of the Party and its cynical betrayal of its own proposed goals, we came to our early understanding of the nature of the Soviet dictatorship and of the workings of Communism throughout the world. Neither of us was ever a Party member; at our most ardent, we came far short of making this much of a commitment. But as members of the National Committee for the Defense of Political Prisoners, a Communist-front organization with which we were connected between mid-1932 and the spring of 1933, we were sufficiently close to the Party to become well acquainted with its operations. Lionel's understanding of the ways in which Stalinism worked within the culture was of course central to his novel, *The Middle of the Journey,* and made a connecting theme among the essays in the most widely read of his critical volumes, *The Liberal Imagination.* As fiction critic of the *Nation* in the forties, I would write as an avowed anti-Communist, and as a free-lance writer after I left the *Nation* I frequently dealt with issues of Communism and anti-Communism. In the mid-fifties I became a member of the Executive Board of the American Committee for Cultural Freedom, whose parent organization, the Congress for Cultural Freedom, was a long-unacknowledged child of the CIA. This was during a brief period in the history of the CIA when that organization was unaccustomedly ambivalent about its relation to Communism. Unlike the Congress for Cultural Freedom, the American Committee for Cultural Freedom was always forthrightly and unambiguously anti-Communist. It was not easy, through all these years, to be an anti-Communist in a predominantly "liberal" intellectual community. It meant that one swam against the cultural tide. To be an anti-Communist and also a liberal—that is, to be an anti-Communist without sacrifice of liberal principle—is even more difficult now that neoconservatism, often of the extreme right, claims so many anti-Communists.

Sidney Hook did not remain a Communist for long: he soon confronted the character of the Soviet regime, its absolutism and injustice and cruelty, and for the rest of his life he was a passionate opponent of Communism. But at Yaddo in the summer of 1931 he was still ignorant of the range of Stalin's power and the means by which it had been arrived at and was maintained. As he instructed us in Marxism, he could speak of the dictatorship of the proletariat as if it were merely a neutral tenet of revolutionary theory rather than the screen for a murderous tyranny. He spoke not at all of life in a society in which one could be dragged from bed in the middle of the night, never to be seen or heard of again. The Communism to which he introduced us was that of a practical utopianism: in Soviet Russia one supposedly saw the inevitable first step in the worldwide move to banish capitalist greed and inequality. We of our generation were felt to be the witnesses to a great political and social experiment. We had been given the opportunity to embark on a brave new voyage of discovery. The rhetoric was as swollen as our hopes. Hook's dialectical skills were formidable. One did not doubt his story that as a boy of ten or eleven he had converted his orthodox father to atheism; in 1948, during Henry Wallace's presidential campaign, Mark Van Doren had the temerity to engage Hook in political debate and was publicly annihilated. In his later years Hook became boastful in a fashion which I do not associate with him as a younger man and this has much obscured the admiration I once had for him. In his autobiography, published shortly before his death, he immoderately tells us that it was he who supplied *Partisan Review* with its politics. More germane to my concerns, he also reports that in 1936, when Lionel was about to be dropped from his job at Columbia, it was he, Hook, who planned the strategy which won Lionel his reinstatement. These assertions are untrue. While Hook was indeed an advisory editor of *Partisan Review* and, like everyone close to the magazine, expressed and no doubt argued his political viewpoint, a magazine edited by William Phillips and Philip Rahv and Dwight Macdonald did not depend upon him for its politics. His was only another voice. He also had no part in either the restoration of Lionel's position at Columbia or, as he would have us believe, Lionel's subsequent promotion to a professorship. After Lionel's death, I discovered and published a detailed day-by-day record which Lionel had himself made in his notebooks of the events which surrounded his projected dismissal. Yet even with this evidence, Hook refused to concede that he had not salvaged Lionel's teaching career.

Under Hook's guidance, Lionel and I bowed to historical necessity and embraced the new revolutionary faith. We were not alone among the guests at Yaddo that summer in believing that in Communism lay our best hope for the future. Malcolm Cowley lacked Hook's pedagogic energy but he was already an eager fellow traveler and would remain so for most of his long life. Max Lerner was only at the start of his professional achievement but he was already turned to the left, and Marc Blitzstein was already at work on his now-famous revolutionary opera, *The Cradle Will Rock*—in the evenings he played excerpts from it for the rest of the guests, singing all the roles in his curiously harsh, cracked voice. Another convert of Hook's that summer was a young woman named Catherine Bauer, a disciple and friend of Lewis Mumford, who had come to Yaddo to write a book on city planning. Unable to get on with her work, she blamed her lack of progress on the breakdown of capitalism: How could one write in a society unable to feed its own people? She was the first person I knew to attribute her personal problems to our weak and malign economic system. As the decade wore on and throughout the forties it would become routine for writers to blame their personal failures and shortcomings, or those of their fictional characters, on the society. In the novels which I reviewed for the *Nation* in the forties, capitalism was responsible for all the woes of mankind, from stuttering to sexual impotence.

I was singing so badly that summer that it embarrassed me to think that I might be overheard while I practiced. I had no place to spend my time except in my workroom and, to pass the hours in which I had nothing to do, I wrote another play. This time my lone venture in playwriting was called *The Young Wives' Tale*. It dealt with marital infidelity—what else? Not surprisingly, it had little action and much talk. *The Young Wives' Tale* never reached an agent; I have a copy still but cannot bring myself to read it. There was actually little reason for me to feel as lost and lonely as I felt at Yaddo. Although Mrs. Ames was not pleasant to me, all the guests were friendly. Malcolm Cowley and Marc Blitzstein and Max Lerner were so kind to me that summer that I was never afterward able to hold them wholly to account for their political transgressions. But what place could be better suited to the ripening of neurosis than an artists' colony where fifteen people have been taken out of their accustomed world, mandated to be creative, and put under the rule of a woman as seemingly sympathetic as Mrs. Ames, yet in reality so willful and manipulative? The directress of Yaddo was conspicuously cordial to Lionel: despite her impaired hearing, she heard everything he said, even when he mumbled. She heard nothing I said but she did hear that I had visited another guest at a forbidden hour and she expelled me from Yaddo like a delinquent schoolgirl. It was humiliating and frightening. We had no money; our apartment in New York was tenanted, and I had to stay with my father. Three weeks later, she relented and asked me back.

Part of the period in which I was on probation from Yaddo I

spent with Polly and Kip Fadiman in Boonton, New Jersey. Together with three other couples—Elinor and George Novack, Rose and Norman Warren, Ann and Felix Morrow—the Fadimans had rented a large house called Derrygally for the summer. In 1931 communal living had not yet become a way of life for people with little money. The four couples at Derrygally were not only ill-chosen for so intimate an arrangement, but they seemed to be peculiarly gifted in noncooperation: they were in a perpetual state of disharmony, punctuated by fugitive alliances for the purpose of aggression. The duties of the household had been sensibly parceled out among them at the start of the summer but none of the party was disposed to stay with the schedule. It was only by divine intervention that food got bought and cooked and the dishes washed. Two of the women, Rose Warren and Ann Morrow, commuted to work in New York. Ann, the mildest of creatures, was a legal secretary; at any hour of the day, even on her return from the hot city, she looked as if she had just licked herself clean, like a well-loved kitten. Rose Warren, who was making a successful career in, I think, the manufacture of expensive fabrics, was a classic beauty, smooth and elegant. There was something anomalous in the fact that the Warrens and the Morrows were longtime friends. Boisterously Jewish, Felix Morrow was famous for the response he had made to the professor of philosophy at Columbia who was interviewing him for admission to a graduate seminar and who remarked with obvious malice on the distinction of Felix's family name. "I wouldn't know about that," Felix had replied cheerfully. "I'm the first in my family to bear it." Except among their literary friends, the Warrens were at pains to conceal their religion and inauspicious family backgrounds. But in the privacy of Derrygally, Rose happily returned to her native Yiddish. As a child, I had thought of Yiddish as the language of invective but I now learned that it was also the language of poetry—on Rose Warren's tongue, it was liquid and melodious, the language of a gentle heart. Novack and Fadiman were vacationing. If I remember correctly, Norman Warren was looking for a job. Alan Wald, who has come to be considered an authority on the New York intellectuals, has written of Warren in such a manner as to suggest that he was an important figure in the New York intellectual world. No one I knew among Warren's contemporaries looked upon him other than as someone whose serious ambitions were too heavily overlain with frivolousness to promise fulfillment. In 1931 Felix Morrow was still a student; in the style of his scholarly East European forefathers he was being unabashedly supported by his wife. Polly Fadiman was pregnant and often sick to her stomach. She blamed her morning nausea on the sight of Felix at breakfast, splashing and dripping his coffee, naked beneath the dressing gown which failed to span his substantial girth.

At Derrygally as at Yaddo, much of the talk focused on the promise of revolution. On a soft summer evening, amid the sweet murmurings of the countryside, I heard Felix Morrow reassure his wife, Ann, on what would happen to them when Communism triumphed. "What will you be, Felix, after the revolution?" Ann inquired anxiously. "A commissar, of course, darling," Felix replied with humorless conviction. Only George Novack among the people at Derrygally failed to heed the call of history. George was the softest-mannered of the Derrygally husbands. In 1931 he had not taken even a first step in the general movement to the left; it would not have been possible to foresee that only a few years later he would become a professional revolutionary and for the rest of his life be a committed Trotskyist. But in 1931 one could also not have surmised that the indolent Felix Morrow would one day go to jail for his radical activity. Felix, too, became a Trotskyist and worked in a Trotskyist union in Minnesota, the only union controlled by this dissident Communist faction. He was convicted of criminal syndicalism and jailed for several years. Trotsky is today long dead and except among historians largely forgotten but until his death in 1992 George Novack was still a dedicated Trotskyist: full of years, cherished by his ever-dwindling band of comrades, he was for the Trotskyist movement "the old man" which Trotsky once was for his followers. Felix's life would take a different course from Novack's, away from the revolutionary struggle. When he became disillusioned with Communism, he turned to the occult and still later, even more remarkably, he became a psychotherapist.

By the time I was invited back to Yaddo, even the short train journey from New York to Saratoga had taken on menacing proportions. My bottle of Luminal no longer lay in my handbag during the train trip; it was clenched in the fist which I would soon raise in salute to the workers' fatherland. I reached Saratoga shaken and worn. Lionel had come to meet me at the station but, alas, this was not the Lionel I had expected to see. In my absence he had grown a mustache; it was red, scant, and unbecoming. But it was not for aesthetic reasons that I was dismayed. Emotionally I was unable to handle the change in his appearance. I trembled with anxiety before the unknown; in the next months and years any change in my familiar circumstances, even a sudden shadow across a window or an unanticipated sound, filled me with terror. I was like a child whose world must not be altered lest she be left without protection against all the unnamed dangers of a hostile universe. Lionel could shave off the offending mustache but he could not keep the world unchanged for me. We returned to New York at the end of the summer to discover a new city. Everywhere in the streets there were now beggars; soon there were apple vendors at all the street corners. Milk stations sprang up; hungry people waited in long lines for a bit of nourishment. The veterans of the First World War had been promised bonuses, which had not been given them. During the winter of 1931–32 the demand that this promise be kept became steadily more urgent and in the spring a company of hungry, ill-clad former soldiers, armed now only with their need, marched on Washington. On the order of President Hoover, General Douglas MacArthur fired upon them. Upper Riverside Drive was soon a shantyville. The unemployed and homeless constructed pitiful little huts for themselves from crates and sheet metal. They were scarcely more shelter against cold and rain than the play-huts which we children had built for ourselves in our backyards in Westchester. When they found food, they cooked it in old tin cans over fires made of paper with an occasional stick or precious piece of wood picked up in a gutter. Today, as I write, more than sixty years have passed since the Depression of the thirties and once again our poor and homeless are in the streets. But the situation is different from what it was then. Now the needy live amid relative plenty. It may not be the abundance of the eighties but compared to the thirties ours is still a land of plenty. Today our homeless live outside the structure of society. We call them an "underclass," by which we mean that they have no place in our class-defined society. They have extruded themselves and we extrude them. Many of them have been released from mental institutions and are unable to make their way in the world or care for themselves. Most of them have come to think of their own little doorway or cardboard box as home; they refuse the public shelter which is sometimes offered them; they are a derelict population. In the Depression of the thirties there was not this drastic a division between those in want and the rest of the population. The Depression of the thirties was a great leveler. While only a minority was actually pushed to the extreme of begging and homelessness, no one felt economically secure. When you gave a nickel or a dime to someone soliciting on the street, it was not an act of charity as this is commonly denominated but an act of comradeship, virtually an act of identification. Those who were able to give money instead of asking for it felt that theirs was but a temporary advantage over those whose luck had already run out. It had run out for both Lionel's father and mine.

Weisbecker's at Broadway and 110th Street was my first experience of a supermarket, a department store of food, selling meat, fish, vegetables, groceries, all under the same roof. From where we lived at 122nd Street, it was a long walk to 110th Street, especially on the return trip, when I had heavy bundles to carry. But the ten cents it would have cost for carfare bought a pound or more of fish. Fish had not yet made its commanding entrance into the American middle-class diet. In deference to the Catholic students we had had fish at college on Friday nights but it had put a strain on our religious tolerance. Its appearance on our tables during the Depression was not dictated by considerations of health: no one had yet heard of cholesterol. Fish was a cheap substitute for meat. Once the economy improved, we quickly returned to our meat-eating habits. Each day the canopy at Weisbecker's advertised a fish "special"; it usually cost as little as five or six cents a pound. Lionel's mother read fish as dependably as she read Henry James; she taught me to look the poor dead creatures in the eye to be sure they were fresh. The government provided regular advice on low-cost nutrition; the newspapers published sample menus, guides to feeding a family of four on five dollars a week. It could actually be done for less. Lionel and I no longer asked people to dinners of shrimp and roast beef but we invited our friends to what we called Sunday tea. It was really a light supper. We no longer went to restaurants or the opera but we went to the movies; one could see a double or, if one had the endurance, even a triple feature for a dime. We sternly disciplined ourselves not to think about clothes. I remember that I finally bought three dresses at Macy's for $5.99 each, but I made the mistake of lending one of them to a friend who needed it for a job interview. She must have been very nervous and perspired heavily in it; I had to throw it away. It was a financial calamity.

In editing the Uniform Edition of Lionel's work after his death, I put together a new volume, *Speaking of Literature and Society*. It allowed me to publish various short pieces which had not previously been reprinted. Among them was a sampling of the early reviews Lionel wrote not only for the *Menorah Journal* and the *New York Evening Post* but also for other periodicals to which he had begun to contribute: the *New Freeman,* the *Nation,* the *New Republic.* Everything Lionel wrote for publication in these early years, with the exception of the snake story which he wrote on our honeymoon and a long essay, "The Changing Myth of the Jew," was published. "The Changing Myth of the Jew" was discovered by Elinor Grumet in the American Jewish Archives in Cincinnati, where she was working on a history of the *Menorah Journal*. The essay was in galleys; it had been about to be printed when the magazine folded for lack of funds. Probably written in 1930, when Lionel was not yet twenty-five, it is a creditable piece of historical criticism—I published it in *Commentary* in 1978. But not all of his early writing was of this quality. In much of Lionel's early work the prose is self-conscious and slack; it lacks the sinew to carry any significant weight of idea. It was in the interminable writing and rewriting of his *Matthew Arnold* that Lionel developed the firm but flexible style which we associate with his mature years. To augment his income at the start of the thirties, he lectured as well as reviewed. It was a trying time and the shadows under his eyes had deepened. Misleadingly, they spoke of romance to a woman lecture agent; she promised him a profitable future on the women's club circuit. In later life Lionel could be an attractive public speaker but he did poorly at the start. For his first lecture he badly misconceived the nature of the assignment and composed a talk with the rousing title "Joyce, Mann, Proust, Wyndham Lewis and the Modern Temper." He was not re-engaged. In a more relaxed vein, he was successful in talks to small groups of women in the suburbs. For a fee of $10 he not only lectured for an hour to gatherings in Westchester or Connecticut but stayed on for refreshments and friendly talk with his women listeners. One of my great mistakes as his business adviser was to urge him to raise his fee for these lectures from $10 to $15. The engagements came to an abrupt end.

In pictures taken of me in this period, my face is strained and drawn, without the light of joy or curiosity in my protuberant eyes, that lasting remnant of my hyperthyroidism. My body is toneless, exhausted. My life was toneless and exhausted. I remember of myself in these years that when I woke in the morning I lay in bed for a long time, waiting for the will to start another day; I lacked the strength to do the things I wanted to do. I had been told at the Lahey Clinic that for the next year I was to avoid alcohol, cigarettes, and coffee and tea, and that I was not to become pregnant. The temporary ban on smoking was hard for me; I often smuggled cigarettes. But I scarcely noticed the prohibition against pregnancy. My college friends were starting their families but these were my friends of the past. The people with whom Lionel and I associated were almost all of them childless and intended to stay childless. I was part of a childless culture: we talked about everything in the world *except* the rearing of children. To start a family was perhaps the least pressing item on the intellectual agenda. The men were for the most part too emotionally unstable or self-absorbed to want to share their lives with offspring, and the women felt as their husbands wanted them to feel. The economic precariousness of the time reinforced our personal insufficiencies. The nation could not look to a future and neither could its thoughtful citizens.

Lionel and I were married nineteen years when we had our first and only child. While somewhere in my plan for life I had always taken it for granted that I would have a family—and I suspect that Lionel had the same expectation—the subject never came up between us. We never set ourselves a timetable for starting a family and never noticed the passage of the years. We lived our lives as if life were forever. To live one's life without a sense of time is to squander it. For more than a decade Lionel and I squandered life not in pleasure but in fearfulness. We were afraid to be fully grown up and to be in command of ourselves and others, even children. Ours was a successful marriage on the score of this shared impediment as well as on the score of more attractive features. It was one of those unconscious conspiracies between a man and a woman which make a successful marriage so remarkable an accident. It would be 1947 and I would be forty-two years old before I opened my eyes on the world one morning with the astonishing realization that if I ever meant to have a child, it had to be now. It could no longer be put off. In psychoanalysis, one of my analysts suggested that in the early years of my marriage I chose to have panics instead of babies. She even ingeniously tried to establish the proposition that various important manifestations of my neurosis appeared at nine-month intervals. It was an audacious speculation and had the appearance of an "insight," one of those triumphant invasions of the terra incognita of the unconscious which makes psychoanalysis worth paying one's money for. But in reality it had no support in anything I subsequently learned about myself or about the source and meaning of my fears. Had I had a child when I first married, it would probably have worsened rather than helped me avoid my emotional problems.

Chapter
EIGHT

The year 1932 was momentous in Lionel's life: it was the year in which he was made an instructor in the English Department at Columbia. His appointment came as a surprise to him: he had not been promised the position nor had there been anything in the behavior of his dissertation director, Emery Neff, to suggest that the post would be offered to him. Actually the appointment was as surprising to Professor Neff and the other senior members of the department as it was to Lionel. It was made unilaterally, even imperially, by Professor Ashley Thorndike, who was then head of the department. Lionel had an only limited acquaintance with Professor Thorndike. Why he had singled out Lionel for the position would always remain a mystery. Several of Lionel's college friends, Fadiman among them, would very much have wanted the appointment; the fact that it went to Lionel was always a source of bitterness to Kip. But where it failed to cause envy, it brought no response of any visible sort. His family and mine were impressed but, other than that, word that Lionel was now a Columbia instructor made no difference in his standing in the literary community. An instructor's salary was $2,400 a year, which was something of an improvement on the $1,800 which had been the stipend of his fellowship. With two households dependent upon his support, the increase did little to relieve our financial distress.

The year in which Lionel began to teach at Columbia was also the year in which I began to work in the radical movement. In the summer of 1932 I volunteered to help Elliot Cohen at the office of the National Committee for the Defense of Political Prisoners— the NCDPP, as it was always referred to. This was not entirely or even primarily a political move on my part. I was aware from the start that genuine as was my concern with the political and economic crisis of the country, my more pressing reason for becoming involved with the NCDPP was psychological: I needed something to take me out of the house and into the company of people I knew. All my irrational fears, and in particular my fear of being alone, were steadily becoming more troublesome. Although Lionel was with me as much as he could be and far more than I had any right to ask, there were hours when he of course had to be free of me. Eventually I would meet the problem by hiring a paid companion but I had not yet reached the stage where this humiliating step was feasible. I became involved with the radical movement as a substitute arrangement. In the McCarthy years, when people's political lives would be put under such severe inspection, I often wondered what an investigating committee would make of someone like me who would testify that, yes, she had worked for the Communist Party, or certainly for an affiliate organization, but that what had brought her into the radical movement was not so much a political impulse as a need to escape the fear of being alone.

Elliot Cohen was no longer engaged in Jewish affairs. The *Menorah Journal* had ceased publication for lack of funds and, together with his old *Menorah Journal* friend, Herbert Solow, he had transferred his interest to the radical cause. He, too, had come to believe that capitalism had run its course and that Communism was the only answer to the crisis confronting the country. Lionel and I had become Communists through the persuasive reasoning of Sidney Hook at Yaddo but one did not have to be indoctrinated by so gifted a dialectician to turn to Communism as the cure for our failed economy. The lure of Communism was everywhere in the air, at Yaddo, at Derrygally, everywhere in the city; one had only to be open of mind and generous of heart to accept its promise. The time had come for radical change; a Marxist-Leninist revolution along the lines of the Russian revolution was the obvious next step proposed by common sense and history. With the overthrow of the czarist regime, Russia had been released from repression and tyranny, given a new life such as we must now claim for our own country. That in actuality Russia had been released from the tyranny of the czars only to come under Stalin's murderous rule was a disillusionment which still awaited us—awaited those of us, that is, who would allow ourselves to recognize this disturbing truth. The NCDPP was an early Communist-front organization, an "innocents' club," as we would disdainfully come to call its kind. In common with all such groups—and they were numerous even this early in the thirties—it had been created to draw people of liberal good will into the Communist orbit while hiding from them the fact that they were under Communist domination. It was clever of the Party to have put Elliot Cohen in charge of the NCDPP; he was notably gifted at promotion and fund-raising. He was never a Communist Party member. His zeal was not of the sort to impel him into the faceless ranks of those who submit to organizational discipline. He nonetheless thought of himself as a Communist and would not have hesitated to admit his support of the Party. At least for the time being, he had no reluctance about working under Communist control.

When I started at the Committee Elliot and I were not yet friends but I was enough comfortable with him to feel that his office provided me with a safe haven from my phobias. He, on his side, was glad to have my assistance. Elinor Rice, George Novack's wife, with whom I had become friendly at Derrygally, was also a recent convert to Communism and similarly volunteered to work at the NCDPP. There were undoubtedly members of the Committee who were as ignorant of its connection with the Communist Party as the Party wished them to be, but this was not the case with Elinor and me. We joined the Committee because of its connection with the Communist movement. Were it to have been the liberal organization which it pretended to be, we would have shunned it. New as we were to the radical movement, we had already absorbed this first important tenet of the Communist faith: liberalism was the enemy of revolution. In the years leading up to the Second World War, it was on the radical left, not on the conservative right, that the "L" word was a word of opprobrium, seldom spoken without its attendant pejorative adjective, "mere." To think of oneself as someone on the left and yet to raise any question about the goals or practices of Communism was inevitably to earn the sad accusation that one was a "mere" liberal. And yet, in fact, the relation between Communism and liberalism was far from this simple. While on the one hand Communism scorned liberalism as a masked partner of capitalism and thus the enemy of revolution, on the other hand it looked for and found its chief support among liberals. Indeed, it was from the supposed kinship between Communism and liberalism that most intellectual sympathizers with Communism drew their sense of moral validation.

The proliferation of Communist-front organizations was a significant political and cultural phenomenon of the thirties and forties. The Friends of the Soviet Union, the League of American Writers, the League of Professional Groups, the League of Women Shoppers, the League Against Imperialism, the National Student League, the Lawyers Guild, the League Against War and Fascism: these were but a few of the many groups inspired and controlled by the Communist Party. There had only to be a cause or social group for there to be an appropriate Communist-inspired committee; the influence of the most popular of these organizations, the League Against War and Fascism, might well be envied by the best-financed Washington lobby of our present day. Each of the groups had its own ostensible purpose. What connected them with one another and made them a powerful force in the society was their shared submission to the dictate of Stalin: recent research shows that the rule of the Comintern, the international body of the former Communist organization, was even more absolute than scholars previously supposed. With their imposing lists of sponsors—writers, artists, Hollywood and Broadway celebrities, lawyers, teachers, clerics—the Communist-front organizations were for two decades a formidable instrument of Communist propaganda in the Western democracies, a major force in the creation of political opinion and in the decisions of government. Today we are still unwilling to recognize the extent to which the Communist-dominated culture of the time was reflected in Roosevelt's foreign policy, right up to his tragic concessions to Stalin at Yalta, which put another sixth of the earth's surface under the yoke of Soviet Communism. It is more comfortable for us not to be reminded that Roosevelt's closest personal adviser, Harry Hopkins, was a much-trusted friend of Stalin.

But pronounced as was the political influence of Communism in this country, even more marked and certainly more persistent was its influence on the culture. Political correctness is not an invention of recent decades; it is the natural successor to cultural Stalinism. It satisfies the same need and proceeds from the same cast of mind. In the universities and throughout the publishing and entertainment industries a chain of Communist command was in place to see that the preferences of the Soviet Union found their suitable cultural expression and that the supporters of Communism were justly rewarded. It was a bad time for a writer to become known as an anti-Communist or even as a member of a dissenting radical faction. It was hard for him to be published and his published work was attacked. The visual artist had an equally hard time. The group shows were likely to be organized by fellow-traveling artists and it was they who decided who should exhibit and how the work should be shown. If there were jobs available, it was the Party adherents who filled them. Communist sympathizers distributed assignments and opportunities. It was politics which made and broke reputations. There was no energy of opposition comparable to the energy of Communist fellow-traveling.

Until Elinor and I graduated to higher responsibilities at the National Committee, we did the women's work of revolution, stuffing and licking envelopes for Elliot's fund-raising appeals; a joke of the period was that the revolution would be won by whoever captured the mimeograph machines. Each innocents' club had its own letterhead with its own lengthy list of distinguished sponsors. To have one's name on a Communist-sponsored appeal or protest considerably enhanced one's standing in the cultural community. For a previously unknown writer to find himself in the company of John Dos Passos or Theodore Dreiser was like election to an exclusive club, and for a writer of faltering reputation it could be a quick road to re-establishment. Elliot Cohen brought great personal charm to this competition for "names" with which to ornament a committee: he captured Sherwood Anderson for the NCDPP. The interest which the author of *Winesburg, Ohio* could perhaps no longer command on literary grounds he now recovered as a radical activist. I briefly met Anderson at the office of the NCDPP and once or twice relayed messages to him. On this small acquaintance he entrusted me with the use of his name: he empowered me to dispose of his signature as I saw fit. A similar authority was given me by another member of the Committee, the president of one of our city colleges; he had never met me at all. No one foresaw the day when one's appearance on a letterhead or among the signatories of a Communist protest would constitute evidence of subversion. But for that matter, it seldom occurred to any of us that political action might have political consequence.

The office of the NCDPP was on a low floor of a shabby building on Broadway and 10th Street; the offices of the ILD, the International Labor Defense, a group which was presumed to be no more than the legal arm of the Party but which was actually a highly important agency of the international Communist movement, were on a higher floor of the same building. A few blocks away, on 13th Street, were the headquarters of the American Communist Party, the famous "Ninth Floor." In *Scoundrel Time,* a disingenuous Lillian Hellman reports, not without boastfulness, a mission which she undertook for Henry Wallace in the 1948 presidential campaign. Wallace asked her to help him be rid of the Communist Party's embarrassing endorsement. As Hellman tells the story, it is clear that she had no difficulty in penetrating Party headquarters and in talking with the top Party dignitaries. She fails to realize what this tells us about her relation to the Party. No one at the NCDPP would have thought to approach the "Ninth Floor." It was our local Kremlin. The Party used us as sympathizers but it did not trust us. It even put a monitor in the office of the NCDPP, Comrade Grace. If Comrade Grace had a last name, we never learned it. We never learned even the first name of the man she lived with; she spoke of him only as her "Comrade lover." Comrade Grace was more than a Party stalwart; she was an Ethel Rosenberg in the making. Many years later I would attend a debate in New York's Town Hall on the guilt or innocence of the Rosenbergs and, thinking of the cruel waste of Ethel Rosenberg's life, the memory of Comrade Grace would flood back over me—what had happened to her, I wondered, and to others like her. Comrade Grace would also have gone to her death unshaken in her Party loyalty. Her commitment to the revolution and to the Communist Party as the agent of our glorious future made Elinor and me feel like middle-class frivolers, but we could at least bring the benefit of our middle-class upbringings to the Committee. Before we had come to the NCDPP it kept no records, but the two of us had been reared in orderliness and at once set up a filing system to keep track of the people we solicited for funds and what contributions we received. This later turned out to be useful to me in extricating myself from a tangle of Party lies.

Early in the thirties Lionel was not enough known even for his name to be useful to the Communists. He was rarely asked to sign a petition or protest; even at election time in 1932, when it looked as if everyone was being mobilized to support Foster and Ford, the Communist Party candidates for president and vice-president, he was not included in the parade of luminaries. No doubt he felt hurt because of this neglect. I know that I felt hurt for him. My father took a different view of the situation. He was now terminally ill and housebound. It worried him that Lionel's job at Columbia might be jeopardized should it become known that he was a Communist sympathizer. I recall trying to amuse him one evening by telling him of a political debate which Lionel and I had attended at the Morningside branch of the Socialist Party, near Columbia. The subject of debate was Communism versus Socialism, and we attended it with Elinor and George Novack. Earl Browder, head of the American Communist Party, spoke for the Communists; McAlister Coleman for the Socialists. Taut of body and speech, Browder seemed to Lionel and me to be conspicuously victorious in the confrontation. In the loose and crumpled appearance of the Socialist speaker we read the weakness and inevitable defeat of the Second International. Alone of the four of us, George Novack gave the evening to Coleman: he was frightened, he said, by the intransigence of Browder's position and by his implacable manner. (It was a year later that Novack himself became an intransigent revolutionary.) My father was disturbed by my story; he felt that Lionel should not be seen at such occasions. He knew nothing about universities but, like any newspaper reader, he knew of the political conservatism of Columbia's President Nicholas Murray Butler and his ambition to be president of the United States. Assuring my father that Lionel had not put himself at risk by attending the Browder debate, I explained that several members of the Columbia teaching staff had been present. These included Corliss Lamont, a son of the Morgan partner Thomas Lamont. "A Communist like Corliss Lamont, Lionel should be," my father responded wryly.

Apart from attending the regular meetings of the NCDPP, Lionel took little part in its activities; he was too occupied with his teaching and his dissertation, not to mention the always-pressing need to make money. I kept him abreast of what was going on downtown. Occasionally we went to a Communist rally. Once or twice we went to an open meeting of the John Reed Club, the Party's intellectual front; it was the most austere of the Party's affiliates and differed from the general run of front organizations in the fact that its members were either Party people or known to be reliable fellow travelers. While nothing transpired under the supervision of the John Reed Club which had not been directed or approved by the Party, its open meetings were designed to create the illusion of Communist democracy by encouraging the discussion of doctrine between Party members and undifferentiated Party sympathizers. Big or small, all Communist gatherings concluded with an oath of allegiance to the revolution: standing erect, arm upraised and fist clenched, one sang the "Internationale." I never joined in this revolutionary ritual without guilt and embarrassment. Was I sincere in my commitment to Communism? I asked myself. Did I really desire an overthrow of the American system of government and a restructuring of our society?

> Arise, ye prisoners of starvation.
> Arise, ye wretched of the earth!
> For justice thunders condemnation.
> A new world's in birth.

The militancy of the revolutionary anthem excited me but I was unable to sing it without feeling inauthentic. I had never missed a meal in my life, let alone been a prisoner of starvation, nor was I among the wretched of the earth, or certainly not for economic reasons.

Lionel and I never brought up between us the question of whether or not we were sincere Communists: there are certain doors which must not be opened a crack, lest they reveal what is better left unseen. That fall of 1932 my friend Bettina Sinclair returned from Russia. She and her husband, David, had spent the year abroad, the last months in the Soviet Union, where David's father, the novelist Upton Sinclair, had an accumulation of uncollected royalties. In Moscow, David worked as a physicist; Bettina taught English to minor officials in the Kremlin. The Sinclairs had long been Socialists, members, in fact, of the Morningside branch of the Socialist Party. They were seasoned opponents of Communism and had no stars in their eyes as they took their first measure of life in the Soviet Union. The poet E. E. Cummings was also visiting the Soviet Union at the time and their paths crossed. His eyes were clouded by the expectations he had brought with him. In *Eimi,* the book he wrote about his stay in Soviet Russia, Cummings calls the Sinclairs "blouse" and "spouse" and savagely satirizes them for their unwillingness to be co-opted into the service of Stalin. It was from the Sinclairs that Lionel and I had our first instruction in the truth of Soviet Communism. It was from them that we first learned of the inequities and injustices of Soviet society, the swollen lives of the bureaucrats with their caviar and dachas and fine cars and the sordid poverty of the working masses. It was they who first told us of the abrogation in Soviet Russia of all the freedoms we take for granted in a democracy: the freedom to speak, to vote, to travel, to work where one chose. From them we first heard of the brutality of Stalin's regime, the fear which lay over the land and over every Soviet household. They told us of people dragged from their beds in the middle of the night and never heard from again and of children taught to spy on their parents for the secret police. They were telling us of the failed Communist utopia and we had no wish to hear them. We preferred Cummings's happy inventions. I knew Bettina too well to be able to accuse her of lying. Lionel and I dismissed her and David's report as a deficiency of imagination: the Sinclairs were Socialists and by habit "mere" reformers and temporizers, unable to understand that hardship and even a degree of inequity must necessarily attend the reconstruction of a society—it was a saying of the time that you could not make an omelet without breaking eggs. This was how we accounted for every disturbing report which came out of the Soviet Union: Russia was making omelets.

In becoming involved in the radical movement, joining a Communist-front committee and going to its meetings, sharing its internal struggles, signing protests and petitions, one became "active," what the French honorifically call "engagé." In the thirties this was of great importance to intellectuals. The cultural pendulum had made a wide swing since an earlier decade when intellectuals defined their integrity by their aloofness from public affairs and by their unabashed concern for the private life of mind. Now it was incumbent upon them to step out of the airless confines of thought in which they had taken refuge and to embrace the experience of their world and time. I am afraid that our culture is still paying a price for this sacrifice of the private life of mind to the public life of action: mind has not regained the prestige it once had in our society. The idea that action is preferable to thought or even that political activity can be usefully separated from the activity of mind was of course not something which Lionel ever accepted. The primacy of mind, independent of the coercions of social or political fashion, would always be the unannounced premise of his work. He nevertheless had an emotional problem about his inviolate commitment to thought. He had had an unusually protected childhood. He had not been allowed a boy's normal life of action and, in consequence, any kind of action had a special charm for him. War, politics, business, finance: all of these were for Lionel the "real" world, from which he had been excluded by the excessive love and protectiveness of his parents. They offered themselves to his imagination as somehow sturdier and—in a way which he did not stop to examine—even worthier pursuits than his own quiet pursuit of teaching and writing. This was no doubt the reason why, on an immediate level of experience, he so much enjoyed what, on a deeper level of both experience and principle, he did not approve, the Columbia uprisings of the sixties, especially in their first days. At the outbreak of the 1968 disturbances, he was made a member of a three-man faculty committee charged with reassessing the disciplinary arrangements of the University. For three days he was on campus around the clock; when he finally came home for an hour or two of sleep, the police insisted upon escorting him—rumor had it that Harlem was about to march upon the University. He was sixty-two years old at this time but I never saw him less tired or in better spirits, and in the next weeks, as a member of a larger faculty committee whose consultations were as unending as they were fruitless, he was full of appetite for the emergency. He was at last sampling the life of action which had always been denied him. Ruefully he told me how much he liked it. Yet whatever its gratifications, it did not enlist his best talents. He had no gift for political leadership or political maneuver; he was not among the several members of the Columbia faculty for whom the campus insurrection led to a significant advance in their University careers, nor would he really have wished it to. He had, actually, the career which was best suited to him. Unlike most people of whom we feel that in their choice of profession they employ but one of several aptitudes and perhaps not the best of them, so that of a teacher of literature we think what a splendid doctor he might have made or, of a doctor, how successfully he might have performed in law or in business, Lionel was by profession much what he was by native disposition. He was not designed for any but the work he did, least of all for the life of "doing." As the Columbia uprisings continued, he was asked to sum up for a television program what was happening at the University and what outcome could be anticipated. Because of his personal manner as well as the quality of his writing, people looked to him to be wise. He *was* wise, but not with the terse and confident wisdom of the public man. He was disappointing at such public moments. Even as a putative radical, he was always and only a private man who needed to sit at his desk and quietly wrap himself around an idea until it flowered into useful thought.

There were no major factional divisions in the NCDPP before Lionel and I and our small group of friends broke with the Committee, but sometimes there were disagreements between Elliot Cohen and Herbert Solow, those passionate contenders; they were our Bukharins and Plekhanovs, full of theory and factional vigor. One such dispute even spilled over into our apartment: I was ill with a mild case of jaundice and it was arranged that there would be a small evening meeting of our NCDPP friends at my bedside to try to iron out the difficulty which had arisen. The two battlers could bring seconds. Surprisingly Solow consented to this peacemaking operation and put in an appearance. Elliot not only failed to materialize but held his old crony Louis Berg captive in his apartment in the Village. Uptown, we were not serious for long; we were soon making fun of ourselves and our disputes. Mimicking the bombastic Communist rhetoric of the day, we dispatched a telegram to Elliot protesting Berg's imprisonment: "We demand the immediate unconditional release of Louis Berg. Hands off Communist China!" Decades later, in a piece I wrote about a poetry reading at Columbia by Allen Ginsberg and his friends Orlovsky and Corso, I commented on the difference between their radical generation and mine. The thirties had not been generous or kind. They encouraged a righteous social anger which still persisted as one of the less attractive legacies of progressivism. They also licensed unseemly personal ambitions: Felix Morrow had aspired only to be a commissar but Lionel's rabbi friend, Henry Rosenthal, had wanted to be in charge of the American Cheka, the revolutionary tribunal which would decide who was to live and who was to die in Communist America—his dread prototype in the Soviet Union had been the sainted Dzerzhinski. Yet it had been a time of much good-natured fun when even our most intense political arguments were larded with humor and self-mockery. "Intellectuals of the world, unite; you have nothing to lose but your brains," we parodied the assurance given by the *Communist Manifesto* to the working classes of the world that they had nothing to lose but their chains. There was surely a connection between our readiness to make fun of ourselves and our unreliability as revolutionaries— nothing in the letters of Bartolomeo Vanzetti or in the prison correspondence between Ethel and Julius Rosenberg suggests that they were given to humor at their own or anyone's expense, nor are there any passages of fun in those two exemplary novels of revolution, Conrad's *Under Western Eyes* and Henry James's *The Princess Casamassima.* People who mock themselves are perhaps not to be depended upon to kill their class enemies. But the fact that we laughed at ourselves does not mean that we should be laughed out of history. In the fifties a panel discussion of the radical thirties was held at Columbia. The speakers were Mary McCarthy, Arthur Schlesinger, Norman Mailer, and Norman Podhoretz, and Lionel was the chairman. The audience was large and it came to the meeting full of anticipation. It learned very little that evening about our sorry decade. Neither of the Normans had been part of the thirties, and Schlesinger's approach to the decade was that of an admiring historian of the Roosevelt administration. Lionel, as chairman, did not take things in hand as he might have. Mary McCarthy's contribution to the discussion was a light-minded romp through her fellow-traveling youth. She made the radicalism of the intellectuals the target of her sharp wit and allowed it no seriousness of purpose. Not long after that evening Dwight Macdonald published a similarly frolicsome memoir, coyly and uncharacteristically entitled "Reminiscence of Politics Past: A Backward Glance O'er Roads Once Travell'd More Than Now." Both reminiscences, both Mary McCarthy's and Dwight Macdonald's, were unworthy of their talented authors and did a disservice to history. The radicalization of the intellectuals in the thirties was serious in its intent. In consequence of the stock-market crash, America was in desperate condition. The people who turned to Communism as the way out for a country robbed of hope were taking a wrong road but they did not yet know what dictatorship meant or how total is totalitarianism. Nazism had but recently come into being, and as for the Soviet Union, willfully or not we knew little of what was actually happening under Stalin. In subscribing to Communism we supposed that we had the welfare of our nation at heart. The error we made had its source in an idealism which indeed demanded correction but of which we need not be ashamed.

In early 1933 Hitler marched on Germany. Ignorant as we were of Nazism, we recognized that this was a dangerous development for that country and a crucial event in world affairs. All of us at the NCDPP, even Comrade Grace, waited expectantly for the Communist Party and the Social Democratic Party of Germany to unite in opposition to the Nazis. The fact that this union was never permitted and that the workers of Germany, even the most politically conscious of them, the Communists, did nothing to stop Hitler significantly contributed to our suspicion of Stalin and thus to our impending break with the radical movement. The only united front between the German Communists and Socialists which Stalin was willing to countenance was a "united front from below," a manifestly impossible union of the rank and file of both parties without official leadership. Although, acting alone, neither party in Germany could have stopped Hitler, if they had acted together there was the likely chance that they could have saved their country. The Nazi-Soviet Pact was still six years in the future but apparently Stalin had already decided to ally himself with the German dictator. He feared a Soviet Germany as he feared an independent Communist country anywhere outside the Soviet Union. In addition, in playing Hitler's game he hoped to buy time to build his own military strength. Comrade Grace was able to absorb her disappointment over Hitler's unimpeded advance; to cope with disappointment was part of her habit of Party obedience. The rest of us lacked her rebounding faith. We could not understand Stalin's refusal of a united front in Germany and we interpreted it as another evidence of his accustomed attitude to Socialist parties everywhere: he preferred that Nazism triumph rather than that the Communists share power with the Socialists.

What chiefly occupied us at the NCDPP in the early months of 1933 was the Scottsboro case. A group of black youngsters had been riding a freight car in the South when they had been apprehended and charged with the rape of two white girls, young prostitutes who were also riding the cars. They were being held for trial in Scottsboro, Alabama, which was how the case had got its name. Under the law of the place and time, the Scottsboro boys were threatened with execution. The American Communist Party was in charge of the defense. All of us at the Committee believed that the Scottsboro boys were innocent; there has never been reason for me to alter this opinion. It soon became clear, however, that the Communist Party was not concerned with the justness of their cause. It had come into the case for its own political motive: the case gave the Communists exactly the opportunity they sought to dramatize the condition of blacks under capitalism and thereby strengthen their influence both in the black community and among white liberals. When it came to our break with the NCDPP, what we felt was a betrayal of the Scottsboro defendants was a central issue in our decision to leave the Committee and the Communist movement. As defense counsel, the Party had hired Samuel Liebowitz. He was a well-known criminal lawyer who had made his reputation defending gangsters, including Al Capone. Certainly Liebowitz had no record of defending civil liberties or victims of such injustice as was involved in the Scottsboro case. His choice as defense counsel dismayed us. To make matters worse, after he was signed on by the Party, he launched a bizarre public romance with Communism, traveling the country lecturing on its behalf. He was an unabashed opportunist and, as we soon came to realize, a fitting representative of the Party which hired him.

We did most of our work for the Scottsboro case in Harlem. While in the thirties New York's African-American population was more strictly segregated in that section than it is today, Harlem was not then as much cut off from white New York as it is now and there was considerably less racial hostility than at the present time. White tourists regularly patronized black nightclubs and restaurants. I had frequently had dinner with my father at Frank's, a restaurant on West 125th Street; the country was not yet committed to integration and Frank's was not publicized as an integrated eating place but its clientele was casually mixed. It was nevertheless with some trepidation that I ventured into the shabby hallways of Harlem's apartment buildings or attended evening meetings in that unfamiliar section of the city. In our circle of friends, unless a man were directly bent on sexual conquest, no relation with a woman took precedence for him over the company of other men; a woman could not count on the offer of male escort, whatever the hour or however uncomfortable the circumstances. The residents of Harlem whose support we were seeking were chiefly writers, musicians, and entertainers. In the usual Communist fashion, we were looking for "names"; names would earn us money. Providentially Elliot Cohen had attracted young John Hammond to the work of the NCDPP; Hammond helped clear the way for us. He was the son of a prominent New York family and from an early age widely known and liked by the jazz musicians of Harlem. Despite their public achievements, the residents of Harlem on whom we called for support lived in a manner which would not have been tolerated by their opposite numbers in the white community. Their buildings were ill-kept, their apartments dark and charmless. An exception was Striver's Row, a street of private houses which had been designed by Stanford White and which were now occupied by successful business people and professionals. The women of Striver's Row were very snobby: they were willing to support the fashionable Scottsboro cause but they were not easily persuaded to associate with the Comrades. For me the most memorable of the many more generous-spirited men and women we worked with in Harlem was W. C. Handy, the composer of "St. Louis Blues." Handy, too, was reluctant to leave Harlem, even for a meeting at our apartment on upper Claremont Avenue. While Lionel and I might think that we lived cheek by jowl with Harlem, for Handy ours was an all-white neighborhood and a building in which he might be refused admission or made to ride in a service elevator. With Hammond's help and Handy's, we mounted a gala benefit concert in Harlem. Handy and Cab Calloway were the featured performers and did "St. Louis Blues" together so brilliantly that the audience was lifted to its feet. Handy was among the many people of Harlem who were misused by the Communist Party. I still feel remorse for whatever part I played in his exploitation. He cared deeply about the fate of the Scottsboro boys and said that if they were executed, he would write a Scottsboro blues. He added that it would not be a blues you could dance to.

There was no limit to the Communists' entrapment of innocents: while I was working at the NCDPP we spawned a subsidiary committee, the Prisoners Relief Fund, whose ostensible purpose was to provide small comforts—cigarettes, books, newspapers—to political prisoners and financial aid to their families. In actuality, it was of course only another means of bringing new sympathizers and more money into the movement. This new shadowy enterprise was housed in the same office with the NCDPP and Elliot put me in charge of it; it was in this committee that I had my most direct experience of the Party's deceitfulness. He one day directed me to send out a letter appealing for help for the families of the Scottsboro boys. Usually Elliot himself wrote these fund-raising letters, but on this occasion the appeal appeared to have been written in the office of the ILD. Instead of having me sign it with the name of one of our celebrated supporters, Elliot instructed me to put my own signature to it. It was a moving appeal: the families of the Scottsboro boys were in great need but, because of the case, the state of Florida was denying them the public assistance to which they had a claim. The letter was generously responded to. But in addition to money it brought a letter from the Florida relief office, listing item by item, pound by pound, the food which had been distributed to the Scottsboro families. The letter went on to inform me that I would be reported to the federal authorities for using the mails to defraud. I was badly frightened but even more I was furious at having been used in this fashion to circulate the Party's lies over my name. Without stopping to consult Elliot, I stormed upstairs to the offices of the ILD. There a Party functionary listened to my complaint with galling patience. "But Comrade," he finally condescended to answer me, "what difference does it make if they got a little sugar or flour? Does this wipe out the injustices of capitalism?" I returned to my desk and to the file which Elinor and I had created as if for just this emergency. To everyone who had sent us money for the Scottsboro families, I now sent a second letter in which I confessed to the earlier mistaken statements. I assured the contributors that if they wanted their money back, they had only to ask. In the next few days, no one requested a refund and several people even sent additional donations—I seemed to have hit upon a new method of fund-raising, the appeal to honesty. Although I never heard further from the authorities, the incident was decisive in my growing alienation from the Party and the radical movement. The Party lied even where it would have been to its advantage to tell the truth. I soon learned that Elinor was also coming up against the Party's untrustworthiness; she had discovered that it diverted funds which were specifically intended for the Scottsboro defense to cover the costs of its national convention. We did not regard these misdeeds as trivial. Like the Party's engagement of Samuel Liebowitz as lawyer for the Scottsboro defense, they paralleled on the domestic scene the lack of principle in Stalin's refusal of a united front in Germany. We had begun, that is, to recognize the great deceit and betrayal of this century: the promise that in ridding us of the evils of capitalism, Communism would rid us of the baser human motives generated in an unjust social and economic system. Communism was not the fulfillment of an ideal. It was itself a movement of power, and like all movements of power it was fed by ambition and self-interest. In

April 1933, less than a year after Elinor and I had come to work at the NCDPP, we and our friends left it. Lionel of course left with us. It was not the intention of our little group to be a political faction. We were joined in disillusionment as we had once been joined in hope. But under the guidance of Cohen and Solow, we did in fact turn out to be a political faction, or certainly to look like one. With their taste for dispute and political maneuver, the two of them inevitably took us in charge. Elinor and I, believing ourselves to be partners with them in the common venture of resigning from the Committee, were for a time content to follow their lead. But they were pursuing a political end of their own: they were making the Trotskyist case against the Stalinists. They turned our resignation into a Trotskyist coup. Elliot was never in any official sense affiliated with the Trotskyists. Solow did briefly become a Trotskyist but this happened, I think, only after we had left the Committee. By the line they pursued, however, they metamorphosed all of us into Trotskyists. They used us as the Communist Party used its fellow travelers. The Communist press had a rich vocabulary of invective: it often spoke of the liberal opponents of Communism as the "running dogs of capitalism." In leaving the NCDPP under the superintendence of those two masterminds, Cohen and Solow, Elinor and I were the running dogs of Trotskyism.

Trotsky had a strange role among anti-Stalinists. In Trotsky's opposition to Stalin we found a ready platform from which to launch our criticism of the official party. The commander of the Russian civil war was the "good" revolutionary, somehow innocent of doctrinal or personal responsibility for the regime he helped bring into being, miraculously exonerated of complicity in the violence of its birth. We seem to have been persuaded that his "dictatorship of the proletariat" would have been different from that of the other revolutionary leaders. For no reason except his intellectual distinction, we endowed him with the humanity which was missing in Stalin and even in Lenin. It was as if his good prose was the guarantee of a superior morality: he wrote too well to be a tyrant. Everyone we knew owned a copy of Trotsky's history of the Russian revolution. Habitually, affectionately, our friends spoke of him as "the old man." But to the Stalinists he was of course a villain. They eventually murdered him. I once overheard Comrade Grace and a group of the female Comrades consulting on how best to tell their children what had become of the commander of the Red Army; they were like a group of progressive-school mothers taking advice of one another on how best to toilet-train their babies. In Moscow in 1937, at the trial of the old Bolsheviks, the court accused Trotsky in absentia of having plotted a fascist takeover in the Soviet Union. Although by then we and most of our friends were dedicated anti-Communists, we promptly rallied to Trotsky's defense. It apparently never occurred to us that were he in power instead of Stalin he would similarly persecute his enemies. This fantasy of Trotsky's moral distinction has had a curious persistence. As late as 1971, when I asked a class of Harvard and Radcliffe undergraduates if any of them knew who Trotsky was, one young man shot up his arm. "Wasn't he the one who was in favor of peaceful revolution?" In response to the accusations against Trotsky in Moscow, a commission of Americans was set up to investigate the charges brought against him. The commission was headed by John Dewey and held its hearings in Mexico City, where Trotsky was then living. Lionel joined the Dewey Commission but did not go to Mexico. Both of us supported the inquiry. In one of her late memoirs, Mary McCarthy refers to me as a Trotskyist but this is an error. Neither Lionel nor I was ever a Trotskyist, nor even much of a Trotskyist fellow traveler. But as between Stalin and Trotsky, we for a long time took the side of the latter.

Our group at the NCDPP made no secret of its disapproval of the Scottsboro defense and well before the meeting at which we resigned from the Committee it was known by the ILD that we were about to make this move. For the meeting itself the ILD lined up its regulars to bolster the vote for the Party and to swell the chorus of abuse with which we were met. Many of the "members" who were gathered for the occasion had never before been present at a meeting. Among these illegal voters was the beautiful Helen Schneider, wife of the poet Isidor Schneider. Over these long years, I still think of the Schneiders as pre-eminent among the forgotten dead of the hoped-for Communist revolution in this country. They have their unmarked place in history as people whose lives were destroyed in the pointless and degrading service of Stalin. Or it may be that only Isidor's life was destroyed; Helen's was perhaps fulfilled as it would not have been if she had remained the discontented housewife she was when Lionel and I knew her. Even on shortest acquaintance, one had to be aware of Helen's unsatisfactory marriage. She looked like a flower which, ready to bloom, had been denied this natural consummation. Isidor was sallow and stooped and peered out at the world from behind thick rimless glasses. He was graceless in his movements; one felt of him that his body was an encumbrance. Once in a conversation which had nothing to do with sex he suddenly perpetrated what he took to be a bold sexual joke: he defined a gentleman as a husband who put his weight on his elbows. We were embarrassed. Still young when we knew him, Isidor had already achieved something of a reputation as a poet. He had also won critical attention with a novel in the experimental mode, *Dr. Transit;* somewhere it no doubt survives as a reminder of the territory which his imagination claimed for itself before it was enslaved by the Communist orthodoxy. Lionel had met Isidor at the *Menorah Journal* and from time to time we saw him and Helen. They invited us to dinner one evening at their apartment in Sunnyside, a residential section of Queens where they lived with their infant daughter. Sunnyside had been designed by Lewis Mumford and was planned precisely for people like the Schneiders who, though they had little money, were rich in the confidence that mind could govern all the undertakings of society. Everything about the Schneiders's apartment testified to their modest and estimable ambitions. The neat living room was lined from floor to ceiling with Isidor's books, many of them about China. There was even a closet in the living room which with its door removed provided additional space for books; its walls were lacquered in red and the shelves were edged in gold. Because of the anchovy torture, I can never forget our dinner at the Schneiders'. Before we even sat down, Helen proudly told us of the treat with which the meal would begin. On each of our plates there lay three crackers and on each cracker lay a silver-skinned snake, its coiled body glittering in the candlelight. It was not conceivable for me to put these venomous creatures in my mouth and sink my teeth into their gorged bodies. And yet how, in courtesy, in minimal appreciation of what the occasion meant to Helen, could I refuse her treat? Life in its ungenerosity has never permitted me to faint. In a sweat I swallowed the anchovies whole, all three of them, very fast, one after the other. It was one of the bravest acts of my life. The Communist movement rescued Helen Schneider from the discontents of her marriage. Within the Party she perhaps found men who were better suited to her needs than Isidor; report had it that she became the lover of one of the black Communist leaders. Determined to hold on to his wife, Isidor followed Helen into the Communist movement and became a writer for the Party's literary journal, the *New Masses*. The gently myopic poet became one of the Party's most dependable hatchet men, a well-practiced and efficient literary executioner. Although over the next years Lionel and I lost track of Helen, Lionel sometimes ran into Isidor. Their relation had never been intimate and it was now known that Lionel was an anti-Communist, yet at the last of these encounters Isidor opened his heart to Lionel as if desperate for someone to whom he could pour out his story. Amid the crush and bustle of Macy's then-famous bookstore, he confessed to Lionel that he had never meant to be a Communist. He had intended only to be a poet and a private man. He had lost control of his life; it had moved in a direction he had not chosen for it. There was nothing unusual in intellectuals who were close to the Party, or even Party members, criticizing the Party to non-members: the novelist Joseph Freeman made a habit of cornering one with his complaints. But Isidor was admitting to more than dissent from this or that aspect of the official line. He was confessing to having surrendered his life for his marriage. He was still a craven servant of the Party when we last heard of him.

A few days before the meeting at which we resigned from the NCDPP, Whittaker Chambers came to see me on Claremont Avenue. He came to ask me to help him with his spying operation for the Soviet Union. Lionel had been casually acquainted with Chambers at college, but this was not a visit to Lionel; it was a visit to me. He had been watching for Lionel to leave the house. He told me that instead of taking the elevator in our building he had walked up the back stairs so as not to be seen. In one degree or another everyone who seeks personal or social salvation in Communism is pursuing an illusion, but Chambers brought an added dimension of pathology to the quest. He was a Soviet agent. Such, at any rate, was our assumption and the assumption of everyone around us. Years later, during the famous Hiss-Chambers case, in which Chambers accused the former official of the State Department of having also been a Soviet agent, one of Chambers's former colleagues at *Time* magazine would write that Chambers's involvement in Soviet espionage was the best-known secret of the decade. Chambers promptly stated the business on which he had come to see me: he wanted me to receive mail for him. In spy language, he was asking me to be his "drop." Today, as I look back on this visit from the distance of more than half a century, a passage of time in which we witnessed not only the apotheosis but also the total dissolution of Soviet power, what most impresses me about Chambers's request is the emotion with which I received his invitation to be a spy or at least an accomplice in his spying. From the start of our conversation, I knew that I was not going to do what he asked of me. Yet I was enormously flattered that he thought me capable of such an assignment and I was ashamed to refuse him.

With good reason, I regarded myself as preternaturally fearful, yet here was this man of the world, this man of two worlds, who believed me to be enough courageous to be a semi-spy. I felt greatly complimented. Obviously my pleasure had little to do with my politics: I was on the verge of resigning from the NCDPP and of giving up the radical movement; I had done with the adventure of Communism. I struggled for a way to refuse Chambers without sacrifice of his good opinion of me. To gain time, and also in the hope that I sounded clever, I asked him whether the mail which I would receive for him would be of a kind I could open. He replied quietly that he preferred that it not be opened. I said that I would have to discuss the matter with Lionel and he nodded his agreement. It was just then that the phone rang with the message that my father's best friend, my mother's friend as well, who had carried her down the gangplank on her return from Europe, had committed suicide. He had put his head in the gas oven. Badly shaken, I tried to reach Lionel at the University but he was nowhere to be found. His business finished, Chambers had been about to leave, but he saw how troubled I was and sat down again. All at once the underground man became the tenderest of companions. He spoke softly of death by one's own hand: his brother, he said, "did this for himself"—his consciously bare language stays in my memory. Today, with the recollection of this visit and of the risk to which it invited me, I recall another and perhaps even more dangerous risk I skirted in my life. It was when I was eleven or twelve years old and living with my family on Ocean Parkway in Brooklyn. On a pleasant spring evening, when my parents supposed that I was visiting with a friend in a neighboring house, she and I and another girl had gone out on the Parkway to pick up boys. It was after dark and the Parkway, never as active in those days as its imposing name would suggest, was largely deserted. The three of us took our stand on the gravel bicycle path adjacent to the main thoroughfare and waited. Several cars went by without noticing us but finally a car stopped and three men alighted and

217

approached us. They were not boys, they were grown men, and they stood for a moment studying us. Then they offered to take one of us for a ride. "Which one?" my friend asked brazenly. The speaker pointed at me: "The little one in the middle." It was a long block to my house but I was not conscious of running until, breathless and trembling, I was inside my front door. Then, too, I had been flattered that of the three of us I was the one whom the men had chosen. But the point was that even at that early age, as again now, I had not surrendered to the flattery; my rearing had triumphed over seduction. Why, then, had I for so many years needed my painful fears in order to hedge in my life and reinforce my upbringing? Was my infant education in lawfulness and caution not enough to counter the lure of the forbidden? Was impulse this raging a torrent within me? A few days after Chambers's visit, we left the NCDPP. Word of our defection spread quickly. Chambers telephoned, as he had said he would. But now his voice was cold and hard. He assured me that he knew my answer. I wanted to explain to him that it was not a political but a moral decision which I had come to, but he was not interested in an explanation. When the Hiss case broke fifteen years later, Chambers became a daily figure in the news and, to liberals, a figure of evil. They had no difficulty in believing that he had been a Soviet agent. They refused, however, to believe that Hiss had taken this same idealistic step. I did not attend the Hiss trials but wrote about the political significance of the case for *Partisan Review*. I believed then, and still believe, that Chambers was telling the truth about Hiss. Lionel wrote *The Middle of the Journey* before there was a Hiss case. In his novel, Whittaker Chambers is substantially the model for the character of Gifford Maxim. Shortly before he died, Lionel wrote a new introduction for a reissue of *The Middle of the Journey* in which, speaking of his use in the book of his old college acquaintance, he referred to Chambers as "a man of honor." It was a careless phrase: a spy is never a man of honor, not even if, like Chambers, he engages in espionage on principle and not for money.

Diana (above)
and Lionel
(right) as infants

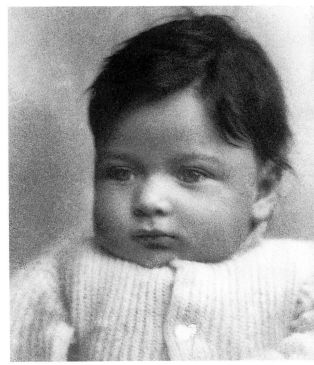

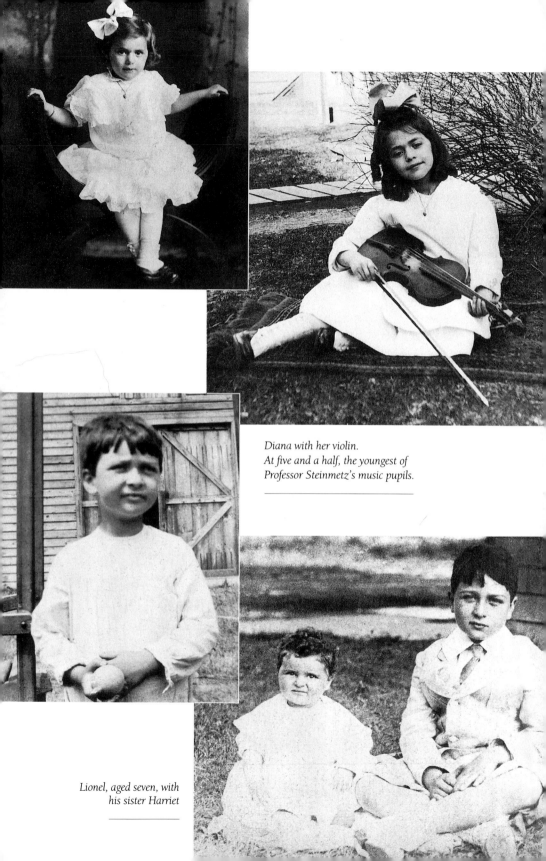

Diana with her violin.
At five and a half, the youngest of
Professor Steinmetz's music pupils.

Lionel, aged seven, with
his sister Harriet

Lionel's maternal grandfather. He bore a striking resemblance to Freud.

Diana's paternal grandfather. She confused him with Moses.

*Lionel's parents in the mid-thirties, pictured
at their usual distance from each other.
Lionel's father died in 1943; his age was
not accurately known. Lionel's mother died
in 1964 at the age of eighty-nine.*

Diana's parents in the twenties, when
her mother was already seriously ill.
She died in 1926 at the age of fifty-three.
Her father died in 1932, aged fifty-nine.

Still in high school, Lionel had reached his full growth.

Diana at seventeen in the men's Brooks Bros. coat much favored by college girls of her generation.

*Lionel and Diana at the time of
their marriage, June 1929. In July
they had their twenty-fourth birthdays.*

TOP: *Lionel and Diana in Riverside Park, near Columbia University, 1942*

MIDDLE: *Jim Trilling*

BOTTOM RIGHT: *Diana in Westport, Connecticut, 1950. Picture taken by Lionel.*

From the little which I myself knew of Chambers, I, too, felt that while he would perhaps have killed for his cause, he would not lie to destroy a friend.

In the interval between our leaving the NCDPP and the Hiss case, we saw Chambers several times. Each time had its mild drama. Again unannounced and unexpected, he had dropped by at our apartment on East 77th Street—we had moved there from upper Claremont Avenue in the late spring of 1933. Other than that he appeared to be under great emotional strain, we had no clue to the reason for this visit. Our 77th Street apartment was a garden apartment; there was no elevator to avoid, but this visit had its own air of furtiveness. When Chambers heard movement at the rear of the apartment, he looked up sharply. "Who's that?" he demanded. We explained that a maid was washing the dinner dishes in the kitchen. "Send her home," he ordered. He was like a jungle animal that evening, sniffing at hidden danger. He left without telling us why he had come. Another time we passed each other in an Alice Foote Macdougal restaurant in the West 50's. It was a tearoomy place done up like an old plantation, even to strings of bright kerchiefs hanging on clotheslines. There could not have been a less probable place in which to meet a Soviet agent—I suppose this means that it was the most probable place in which to meet a Soviet agent. When Chambers saw us, he darted out of the restaurant. After he left the Soviet underground, Chambers's life was of course in grave danger. In self-protection, he undertook to establish an identity aboveground: if people had recently seen him alive, the GPU could not so easily eliminate him. He was a gifted writer and was readily engaged for the staff of *Time*. It was later in this period that he turned to his old college acquaintance Herbert Solow for help in coming aboveground. Solow considerably shared his taste for intrigue and conspiracy and was energetic in assisting him. Among other things, he took him to a Halloween party at the Brooklyn home of Anita Brenner, an old friend of ours, and her doctor husband, David Glusker. Anita, an anthropologist, had been brought up in southern Texas on the Mexican border; she had got her Ph.D. with a much-praised study of the interpenetration in Mexico of Christianity and paganism, *Idols Behind Altars.* Her celebration of Halloween had indeed all the paraphernalia of a pagan festival: masks, pumpkins, skeletons were everywhere. When Solow shepherded Chambers around the room, it was as if he were introducing yet another apparition. More than one guest mockingly greeted him: "Whose ghost are you?" It was some years since Chambers had visited me on Claremont Avenue and I now knew rather more about the workings of the Soviet Union's secret apparatus than I had known then. I knew that it included murder when this was felt to be required. As Chambers came up to me, I put my hand behind my back. I did not feel friendly to an agent of Stalin who could have the blood of innocent people on his hands. Chambers flushed and turned away. Apparently this wound did not heal. The last time Lionel and I saw him before his great confrontation with Hiss was at a cocktail party at the apartment of Nigel Dennis, then the book editor of *Time.* As soon as Chambers caught sight of us, he fled. People have taken it to be proof of a deranged mind that Chambers hid his papers in a pumpkin. In *Scoundrel Time,* that compendium of errors, Lillian Hellman tells us how impractical a pumpkin is as a hiding place. Facts are facts, she reminds us, and she points out that, as everyone must know, pumpkins quickly rot and Chambers's papers would have been destroyed in such a hiding place. The relevant fact here, however, is that the pumpkin which was used by Chambers was never indoors. It was in his garden and the so-called "pumpkin papers" were not papers, they were microfilm. More, the film was in its hiding place for only one night. It occurred to me during the trial that there was a ready explanation for Chambers having chosen a pumpkin in which to hide his microfilm. Unconsciously this had no doubt been suggested to him by the decoration at Anita Brenner's Halloween party. After all, that had been an important evening for him. His appearance had been part of his effort to stay alive. Solow communicated my conjecture to Lloyd Stryker, the attorney prosecuting the case, but although Stryker thought it a reasonable speculation, he felt, probably correctly, that it would not be helpful to Chambers to make it public.

In leaving the NCDPP, Lionel and I made our first public move as anti-Communists or, more accurately, as anti-Stalinists— it was a while longer before we opposed Communism in all its manifestations. We never again raised our voices on behalf of the workers' homeland. But even as late as the late thirties, traces of Lionel's earlier Marxism are still to be found in his writing. In 1937 *Partisan Review* began publication as an independent journal of Marxist opinion; that is, as a revolutionary journal independent of the Communist Party. Lionel was able to live comfortably with the revolutionary program of the new periodical. He appeared in its first issue and continued to be one of its contributors throughout its years as a Marxist publication.

Chapter

NINE

In *The Truants,* a memoir of his association with *Partisan Review,* where for an extended period in the forties he was an assistant editor, William Barrett states that Lionel's interest in Freud probably had its source in his successful analysis—he puts the word "successful" in quotation marks as if to shield himself against the charge of overestimating the usefulness of any psychological therapy. This speculation is anything but correct. Lionel was indeed psychoanalyzed; he was in analysis over a long period of his adult life. But I doubt that he would have described his treatment as successful, with or without quotation marks. He frequently had difficulty in writing and he was prone to depression. Analysis did not rid him of his problems. The depression was not of a sort to be confused with ordinary low spirits or with philosophical despair. He was never what one would describe as a cheery person; no one would have thought to accuse him of taking a smiling view of life. But even when he was in the depths of a depression it did not control his view of the world or color his perception of reality. It was a specific self-limited clinical symptom, a frequent but transitory state of feeling which comported easily even with his youthful verve and certainly with the grave energy of his middle years. Few people—perhaps no one but myself—knew of this affliction. He was at pains not to disclose it even to his closest friends. While a spell of depression might last for only a few hours, it usually lasted for several weeks and when he was in its grip, although he had been afflicted in this way well before we met and indeed had put this on record in the snake story he wrote on our honeymoon, he acted as if I were its self-evident cause; he talked freely enough with other people in these periods but much of the time he kept a hostile silence with me. Mealtimes, unless we had guests, were especially unpleasant: he not only refused conversation with me but was angry at his food. He pushed a potato away from him on his plate as if it were his contemptible enemy—I had seen his father make the same gesture. But should a guest have arrived at the next moment, his appetite would have been miraculously restored. Over the years, psychoanalysis somewhat diminished the frequency and force of these attacks but he was never cured of them. His difficulty in writing also manifested itself irregularly and it, too, was largely immune to cure. There were times, usually when one least expected it, that he wrote at a secure and steady pace. Other times he was severely blocked. Throughout the early years in which he worked on his dissertation, he seemed unable to organize his ideas and put them coherently on paper, but in its last years his *Matthew Arnold* proceeded at a normal speed. He amazingly wrote his next book, his *E. M. Forster,* in six weeks. For the whole of his career Lionel's performance as a writer varied this dramatically. For instance, his essay on Keats reads as if it had poured from his pen in an easeful flow of affection and wonder, but its composition was agonizingly slow. He worked on it for the better part of a year. On the other hand, his Freud Anniversary lecture, "Freud and the Crisis in Our Culture," which one might have supposed would produce the most stubborn resistance, was written in less than three weeks. Toward the end of his life, his writing became alarmingly obstructed. He spent torturing years

224

writing the little critical pieces which preface the selections in his anthology *The Experience of Literature;* I had finally to give him more help with them than with anything he had written since his *Arnold.* Day after day, week after miserable week, he labored at this one assignment: often the most he could accomplish in a day was to change a colon to a semicolon or a "but" to a "however." In the last years of preparing these prefaces, he tried to deceive himself, and me, about the number of them which still remained to be written. "Just three or four more," he would tell me but he refused to count them. He returned to analysis late in life; it was to little avail. What was remarkable in Lionel's sustained admiration for Freud was its contradiction of his own analytical experience. It was not because of any success in his own therapy that he continued to hold Freud in such high esteem, but despite its lack of success. Yet if this represents, as it surely does, a triumph of disinterestedness, it also suggests the extent to which Lionel's approach to analysis was intellectual and even literary rather than clinical: it would have been better for him if he had railed against the failure of his therapy instead of blanketing it as he did in his admiration of Freud. The truth is that instead of approaching Freud as the physician who had created a method for treating the painful actualities of emotional illness, Lionel regarded him as a giant figure in intellectual history, the author of an original and powerful set of ideas. This was the opposite of my own approach to psychoanalysis. I was of course also in analysis, or what I thought was analysis, for a long time, not longer but more consistently than Lionel. For me, Freud was first and foremost a doctor, someone who undertook to heal. For all my appreciation of what Freud taught us about the way in which we become the people we are, I judged and, in the end, continue to judge psychoanalysis not by its contribution to thought but by its ability to cure. It was a constant frustration to me that in moments of emotional confusion or distress I was unable to call on Lionel, with his sharp intelligence and supposed knowledge of analytical method, to help me track down what was troubling me. He had little concern with psychological detection of this clinical kind. In a moment of swagger as a young man, he had written: "I like people's outsides, not their insides," and this remained his natural preference. He was absorbed with the literature of human motivation and much gifted in its comprehension, but in the living of his life he was not drawn to the probing of motive. The disinclination probably carried over into his treatment and hindered its progress.

Neither of us knew anything about Freud in 1929, when we married. While we were living on Bank Street, I had a visit from my Radcliffe friend Theresa Goell; in 1929 she had not yet found her vocation of archaeologist. Theresa was the first person I knew to be analyzed. She spoke of it to me but I had little curiosity about the process; I more or less put it in the same category with my mother's adventure in Christian Science. A couple of years later Lionel and I became Marxists and this put us at an even greater remove from analysis. The two determinisms were felt to be mutually exclusive. For the Marxist, psychoanalysis was a bourgeois indulgence; it represented an excessive individualism and was thus plainly reactionary in intent. For the Freudian, the Marxist dialectic was an evasion of our human dilemma; it was felt to be a means of blinding ourselves to the conditions which shape our personal and social destinies. To the extent that the opposition was a persuasive one, Lionel's and my willingness to involve ourselves with analysis as early as we did, when we were not yet wholly free of Communist influence, can, I suppose, be recognized as yet another indication of our unreliability as revolutionaries. I entered what I thought was analysis with no knowledge of Freud or the method of treatment which he had devised. Neither Lionel nor I yet knew that there were schools of analytic thought which were dissident from Freud—we had not yet heard of Adler or Jung. We assumed, as most people still do when they go into treatment, that all talking therapies were the same and that they had all been inspired by the Viennese master and directly subscribed to his teachings. But we were only ignorant; we had no resistance to psychoanalysis. Certainly we had no innate aversion to it such as then prevailed in the universities. Until well into the forties, Lionel's senior colleagues at Columbia refused to address any form of emotional or mental illness other than of such extreme sort as demands hospitalization and even physical restraint. To admit at this time at Columbia (and, I daresay, at most universities) to a psychological problem was to challenge the authority of mind and it put one at considerable professional risk. Long after Lionel's younger colleagues had come to accept the validity of Freudian thought and even begun to turn to analysis for help with their own emotional difficulties, Lionel would caution them against letting it be known at school that they were in treatment, and he never mentioned his own analysis even to his intimate friends. Unquestionably this was prudent on his part when he was a young teacher and first in analysis. But eventually it went beyond sensible caution. The fact that he preserved this silence when it was no longer necessary points, I think, to a more than ordinary reluctance to acknowledge his emotional vulnerability. Whatever his conscious understanding of the psychological pressures and conflicts to which we are all of us susceptible, on some deeper level of feeling he regarded his own recourse to analysis as a sign of weakness. My susceptibility was less significant: even at the University it was hardly a secret that I was in treatment. But I was a woman and mine were of course cruder symptoms than Lionel's, more difficult to conceal.

I have heard Freudian analysts say that patients get the analysis they deserve. What they really mean by this hard statement is that if you do not choose a therapist from the Freudian establishment, it is because you do not actually wish to be well; you are looking for a crutch or palliative, not for genuine insight into your problems. There is great smugness as well as delusion in this declaration; it fails to recognize that the untutored layman and even the general medical practitioner has no way of knowing who is or is not a qualified analyst and it bypasses the fact that the Freudian establishment, by having held itself so proudly aloof from the task of instructing the public in the difference among various methods of treatment, is itself the major offender in perpetuating the public's ignorance. The Psychoanalytic Society is the professional organization of the Freudians. It is one of the most excluding and enclosed of institutions, cut off not only from the general medical profession but also from all other psychiatric and psychoanalytic organizations—the old division between the Communist Party and the dissident revolutionary groups has a parallel in the separation of the Freudians from the non-Freudians or the less-than-entire Freudians. Yet even where one may be enough knowledgeable to consult the Psychoanalytic Society for guidance in choosing an analyst, one may be at the mercy of error and personal vagary, perhaps even personal malice. One of New York's most respected Freudian analysts, a former president of the New York Psychoanalytic Society, knowingly referred me to an analyst who was morphine-addicted.

If only theoretically, I was an excellent subject for analysis. I was not depressed, obsessive, or compulsive—I am told that compulsive neuroses are hard to treat—and neither my relationship to other people nor my sense of reality was impaired. I was intelligent and verbal and I longed to be rid of my fears. In other words, I was in the condition for which analysis was originally created; it was only much later in its history that the analytical therapy came to be applied in a wider sphere of personality disorders. In my search for cure, I nevertheless went from doctor to doctor over the years, seven in all, and today, at the end of this long road, I still feel that I was never properly analyzed. Three of my doctors died while I was in treatment with them; obviously the profession is not to be blamed for this special fillip to my analytical career. All my therapists were graduates of medical school and seriously engaged in the practice of medicine but none practiced the craft of psychoanalysis as I think it should be practiced. All but two were orthodox Freudians yet in actual fact none fully adhered to orthodox

Freudian procedure—nor of course did Freud himself. In retrospect, I am particularly struck by the inability of all of them to reason about my pathology from their experience of the same symptoms in other patients; I must suppose that they were being overly obedient to the dictate that they not generalize but approach each patient as a unique instance. Psychoanalysis is a language therapy; it depends upon words. None of my doctors was enough alert either to the image-making capacities of the mind or, as a next step, to the ability of the body to reproduce the image-making capacities of language. I, like many other people, frequently express a state of mind in physical symptoms; the condition of my body becomes a metaphor for what I feel. But if, say, I had reported in an analytical session that I was experiencing a strange pressure in my chest, around my heart, while one or another of my therapists might have related the phenomenon to my psychological state, none would have thought simply to inquire why I was feeling heavyhearted. Or were I to have said that I was suddenly burdened by back pain, none would have thought to ask who or what it was that I wanted to get off my back. Yet I once on the telephone rid an acquaintance of an acute spell of dizziness by suggesting that it might be a figure of speech: she had recently had an unusual social success and in consequence was in a whirl. Obviously this dealt not at all with the matter of why she needed to punish herself for her good fortune. But surely it was useful to be freed of her symptom, even if this still left her prone to the need for self-punishment.

On my second visit to Dr. Wechsler he proposed that I undergo hypnosis. He was himself a neurologist, not an analyst or even a psychiatrist, but he professed acquaintance with the new analytical therapy. Even minimally trained in analysis, he should have been able to diagnose my disorder—my panics and early signs of phobia—as a classical anxiety neurosis for which hypnosis was not indicated. The doctor to whom he sent me was youthful, agreeable, and attractive. He wanted to make me well. But he knew little about the dark art in which Dr. Wechsler supposed him to be expert and even less about the talking treatment to which we switched after his first few abortive attempts to hypnotize me. For the better part of a year we met several times a week; I sat across from him at his desk and we talked about my life. It should, I suppose, have been apparent to me—but it was not—that our exchange had no structure and that I was talking to no therapeutic purpose. But I did soon realize that a hint of the illicit was entering our relationship. This frightened and excited me. One late spring afternoon we had the date which for months had been hovering on the horizon. It was still Prohibition and we met in a speakeasy, much as Lionel and I had first met. The date was a disaster. If I did not run home from this danger, it was only because, after one or, at most, two drinks, I was too drunk to run. My doctor sent me home in a taxi.

To be fair, my failed hypnotist never presented himself as an analyst, only as a psychiatrist, whatever that meant in the early years of this century. Still, he assumed and let me assume that in talking about myself I was being psychoanalyzed. My next physician did present himself as a psychoanalyst. He was a classmate of Lionel's at Columbia and was recommended to me by another of Lionel's Columbia contemporaries, who, with his doctor wife, was unparalleled for earnestness and sobriety. They spoke of him not only as an analyst but as a Freudian, and indeed I was now for the first time enrolled for five sessions a week and lay on a couch, trying to obey the instruction to associate freely and say whatever came into my mind. The only caution I was to exercise was not to repress anything. A few years later this doctor would realize that he had not been properly trained in analysis and courageously terminate his analytical practice in order to be professionally retooled. But this lay in the future and in the meanwhile I was surely the worst-served of his patients because I was most the object of his kindness. My fears were entrenching themselves and I was in a panic if Lionel left me alone for even a few minutes while he went to the corner for a pack of cigarettes. My doctor had his office in a Greenwich Village brownstone which was also his home; he occupied it with his wife and infant daughter. He suggested that for part of each day, while Lionel was at school, I come and stay with his family. In any analytic situation, whatever the character of the household, an association with one's analyst's family has an undesirable effect on the transference, that mysteriously generated and charged connection between analyst and patient, but to be introduced into this particular household and to become acquainted not only with this particular wife but also with my doctor's child and his sister and his ill-trained cats and dog was a cruel experience. The household could not have been more disordered. At all hours of the day, remnants of half-eaten meals were strewn about on tables and chairs, on floors and carpets. The household pets relieved themselves as the need seized them and the doctor's infant daughter was let crawl in their mess. Slovenly and willful, the doctor's wife reigned over this chaos, supreme in her domestic power and impervious to the most elementary demands of social propriety. She was overweight and layers of soft white fat rolled out of her clothes. To her husband, she apparently represented—if only at this stage of their marriage—the sweet triumph of biology, but in fact she was already edging toward the severe pathology of her later life. For the several years in which I remained in treatment with this doctor, much of the energy which I should have employed in trying to reach the source of my emotional problems I diverted to concealing my revulsion from his family and the way he lived. Session after session, I lay on the analytic couch battling the urge to tell him what I thought of his wife or, more pressingly, what I thought of him for marrying her. Was it not a rule of this game—*the* rule—that I was to speak freely, repress nothing? I never spoke a word of what I felt. How could I say aloud these awful things I thought? The therapeutic relationship was further deformed by our political differences. It had quickly become clear to me that my doctor was a Communist fellow traveler. His Stalinist friends, at least one of whom, the actor Lionel Stander, would lose his Hollywood position in the McCarthy period, frequently dropped by to visit with his wife or to cadge a meal. My doctor's wife and her visitors talked easily of their politics in my hearing. I was newly an anti-Stalinist and I found it difficult to conspire in their assumption that I agreed with them, but I was dependent on my hostess and stayed silent. And soon the situation became even worse. A year or two after I began my treatment, Lionel became a patient of the same doctor. As if our relationship were not already enough complicated, what with the unwifely demands I put upon him, Lionel and I were now sibling rivals, vying for the attention of the same parental figure. Our analyst had a house in Massachusetts where he spent his summer holidays. He invited Lionel and me to accompany him to the country; we could put up, he said, with a local family and continue our analytical sessions. To my familiarity with my doctor's ménage in New York there now was added an intimate acquaintance with his rural household, including the condition of its outhouse. Today I ask myself whether it was possible that Lionel and I were ever so ignorant of the analytical conventions and of the delicate relation between patient and therapist that we cooperated in such destructive arrangements. The answer is that we were precisely this ignorant, and so was everyone we knew. Our stay in the country that month had at least the virtue of providing Lionel with the model for Laskell's boardinghouse in *The Middle of the Journey*. Laskell's first encounter with his country landlord, when he hears the landlord's strange conversation with his dogs, reproduces Lionel's first encounter with the owner of the house in which we boarded that summer.

When our doctor halted his analytical practice in order to be retrained, he handed me on to Dr. Paul Schilder. I do not recall what happened to Lionel at this stage of his analytical history but I think that he was temporarily out of treatment. I had not previously heard of Dr. Schilder but it was explained to me that he was an outstanding therapist, a leader in the profession, who had recently written a highly celebrated analytical study of *Alice in Wonderland*. With no basis for assessing the value of this recommendation, I went into treatment with him. It was only when he died in a car accident five years later that I learned that Dr. Schilder had himself never been analyzed or undergone the Analytical Institute's rigorous training. The period in which I was in his care was an unceasing test of my strength of will. On the surface his method might seem orthodox enough. I had five sessions a week and again lay on a couch talking about myself. But his treatment was designed not to ferret out the emotional conflicts which generated my symptoms but to prove to me that with determination I could master them. Dr. Schilder was an artist of the counterphobic. Was I afraid to travel around the city alone? Then alone I must travel around the city. Was I afraid of heights? Then I must visit in a penthouse. His role was to assure me that no harm would befall me if I did these things which I feared. My old high-school friend Polly Fadiman once told me that she wished she had my phobias so that she could show the world how quickly they could be overcome. If, like me, she were afraid to travel, she would take the next boat to Europe! She might have been Dr. Schilder's creature. I was myself not far from being the perfect patient. The directions he gave me had the force for me of military commands. I was an enlisted soldier in a volunteer army and I went through battle after battle in which I was myself the enemy to be conquered; and conquer I did, to emerge unscathed, or so I believed. I sometimes asked Dr. Schilder why my treatment was called psychoanalysis since it seemed to involve no analysis but to rely only upon willpower. A psychotherapist is not required to reply to a patient's questions. It is one of the prerogatives of his office that he can avoid an awkward question by calling it yet another manifestation of the patient's illness, an expression of hostility to the analyst himself or of resistance to cure. Dr. Schilder had no need of this protection. He met my question with a question of his own: Was I not now doing the very things which I had previously been afraid to do? What did this mean other than that I was being cured?

I was in treatment with Dr. Schilder in the second half of the thirties. Throughout the decade, Freudian thought was rapidly penetrating the intellectual culture of the country but one accepted or rejected psychoanalysis as a matter of personal choice rather than as a reasoned assessment of its validity; no one of our acquaintance put himself to the serious study of Freud in the way that intellectuals put themselves to the study of Marx. But whatever their ignorance of Freudian thought, the intellectuals we knew felt licensed to have an opinion of the legitimacy of psychoanalysis as both psychological theory and a branch of medical practice. It was as if a body of doctrine which dealt this directly with the personal life demanded only a personal reaction, an assent or dissent. I think it was in 1934 that Lionel began analysis, or what he thought was analysis, but I know of only a single reference to psychoanalysis or to Freud in his work of the thirties. He mentions Freud in his *Matthew Arnold,* published in 1939: the reference is thin and unreverberant. It was not until the spring of 1940 that he published his essay "Freud and Literature" and for some years to come he was virtually alone in the literary community in addressing Freud as a major intelligence and a commanding influence on the culture of the century. Freudian thought excited strong emotions among intellectuals but not much intellection. Intellectuals tended, indeed, to voice their opinion of analysis in the language of religion: one "believed" or did not "believe" in it. I recall once questioning Sidney Hook on his opinion of Freud in just such language: Did he or did he not believe in psychoanalysis? He hedged and I laughingly cut in: "Of course you believe in it, Sidney. But only for women, not for men." Yet the fact is that within the New York literary-intellectual community of the time it seemed to be the men rather than the women who first sought analytic help—with the draft, many of them were exempt from military service because their analysts attested to their emotional instability. On the other hand, the academic response to analysis was, as I have said, conspicuously slow. Long after Freudian thought had deeply penetrated the culture and begun to be incorporated into our intellectual heritage, psychoanalysis remained a target of suspicion and hostility in the universities.

A disquieting subtext of my experience of analysis was my failure to trust my own judgment of these people into whose hands I put myself. Even while I obediently followed the orders of Dr. Schilder, I was never fully confident about his method of treatment. In fact, I never had entire confidence in any of the therapeutic situations in which I found myself. Yet I never left any of them of my own accord. Instead of looking upon my doctors as technicians whom I hired to perform a necessary service and whom I should dismiss if the service was not satisfactory, I behaved with each one of them as if he or she were indispensable to my well-being. Much as a helpless child is tied to the persons who shelter and feed him, I was tied to these people whom I paid to help me. This ultimate dependency of mine on my doctors was a symptom I carried with me into and out of all my analyses. It took jaw-locking effort to control my fears and do the things which Dr. Schilder made me do, and it often occurred to me that without his guarantees I would be unable to function this bravely. But I rationalized my misgivings and persuaded myself that while his method might not be orthodox, it was working—I was doing things I had been afraid to do; I was being cured. In the course of my treatment with Dr. Schilder my previous doctor, who had sent me to him, apparently learned that this had been a mistake; he was now being retrained at the Psychoanalytic Institute and there he must have discovered that Dr. Schilder had never submitted to this rigorous discipline. There is no unhurtful way to separate a patient from an analyst. He made a point of trying discreetly to probe the situation with Lionel. Lionel assured him that I was making excellent progress, and he carried the matter no further. In the early summer of 1938 Dr. Schilder made a trip across Canada with his wife and infant son and invited Lionel and me to join them. Once again I vacationed with my analyst and his family but this time I could not have been in more decorous company. This analyst's wife, herself a psychiatrist, was a model of cautious behavior: if we passed each other in the dining car or on a station platform as we strolled and rested from the confinement of our long train journey, she greeted me pleasantly. Other than for these formal courtesies, she took no notice of me; even when Lionel and I were acciden-tally put at the same dining-car table with her and Dr. Schilder, she kept her quiet distance. I tried to tell myself that she was sim-ply being discreet, that she wanted not to intrude into my profes-sional relation with her husband, yet I worried that she perhaps disliked me and would turn Dr. Schilder against me. There is no way to be in the company of one's analyst's family without its in-terfering in the analytical relationship. The trip was nevertheless a delight. Released from my fear of travel by having my analyst at my side, I drank in the pleasures of being away from my usual surroundings and of exploring a new country. We traveled by the Canadian Pacific Railway to Vancouver. As our train slowly wound through the forests and plains of Canada, I read and slept and happily watched the country unroll beneath our window—what more of a home could one ask for than the compartment of a train? Our porter would tell us if a particularly splendid view was about to open up on the opposite side of the train. If the train took on fresh mountain trout, he saw to it that we had it for our lunch. No one can be prepared for the Canadian Rockies; they rose so precipitously from the plains that at first I mistook the foothills for a building, perhaps a mosque, on the horizon. When we crossed Canada there were as yet no glassed-in observation cars; we went through the Rockies in an open tram, like the summer trolleys of my childhood—one could reach out and dabble one's hands in the snow. The month was June, foaling season in British Columbia: everywhere in the green valleys one saw newborn horses struggling to stand on their uncertain legs. Fragile and awkward, they fell back against the steamy bellies of their mothers. Between Dr. Schilder's family and the family of my previous doctor there was no resemblance. I was nevertheless once more in a situation in which my doctor had lost his therapeutic anonymity. It would have been useful had we analyzed what this meant to me. A year or two later, Dr. Schilder was run over on a New York street and killed. He was on his way to visit his wife in the hospital where she had just given birth to their second child. Putting her affairs in order, Mrs. Schilder wrote me a note demanding that I please pay my bill. The note was unfortunate in tone and should not have been sent—my bill had long since been paid. I wrote back politely but the pain of her implied rebuke was slow to heal. She had of course been given an unwarranted symbolic place in my life. The death of an analyst, whatever the nature of his practice, is traumatic. Dr. Schilder was the first of the three analysts who died while I was in their care.

By the time of Dr. Schilder's death I was dimly aware of the existence of the Psychoanalytic Institute and its exacting standards of training and membership; I even had a vague notion that there was a difference between the orthodox and unorthodox practice of analysis. A close friend was in treatment with Dr. Bertram Lewin, who had recently been president of the Psychoanalytic Society. He was one of its most highly regarded members. Much shaken by Dr. Schilder's death, I turned to Dr. Lewin for advice on how to proceed. We had spoken for only a few minutes when he told me that I was as innocent of analysis as the day I was born—these were the flat words he used to me. To be told that, after ten years of what had been offered to me as psychoanalysis, I was analyzed not at all was cruel news and the fact that I absorbed it with relative ease suggests that I could not have been entirely surprised by it. What I chiefly retain from my interview with Dr. Lewin is the impression that he enjoyed making this communication to me. My friend in treatment with him must often have spoken of me and she could hardly have failed to speak of my treatment with Dr.

Schilder and the strange efforts I made to overcome my fears. Could the good Freudian have been experiencing a moment of professional triumph: See what happens to people who choose their analysts from outside the Freudian establishment! I have, really, no way to explain either Dr. Lewin's harshness of tone or the fact that he included a woman whom he knew to be a drug addict in the list of doctors he now recommended to me, all of them Freudians, colleagues in the Psychoanalytic Society. Scanning the names, I observed that one was the name of a woman and I murmured: "No, I'd rather not go to a woman." He picked me up sharply: "Is it so much worse to be seduced by a woman than by a man?" Talk of this kind becomes familiar and unfrightening in Freudian analysis but it was a thoroughly improper remark to make to someone as innocent of analysis as the day she was born. It confused and angered me and made me defensive. "Very well, then," I announced. "I'll go to a woman." With this careless response I condemned myself to five years of extreme emotional pain. Dr. Lewin knew that Ruth Brunswick was morphine-addicted. The whole Psychoanalytic Society knew it. Yet an organization unmatched for the diligence with which it guarded against any deviation from Freudian principle or practice not only allowed a morphine addict to be one of its members but referred patients to her. Dr. Brunswick was even permitted to be a training analyst; she supervised the early practice of my earlier doctor after he was retrained. The tolerance of the Psychoanalytic Society in her instance has to be accounted for, and the reason I have arrived at is that in her years in Vienna Dr. Brunswick had worked intimately with Freud and he thought well of her. If the Society outlawed her, it could be construed as a criticism of Freud. In addition, Freud had himself been addicted to cocaine and not for just a few weeks or months, as until recently we have been led to believe, but for the better part of a decade. To put Dr. Brunswick's reliability to question because of her drug habit would be tantamount to questioning Freud's reliability during his long period of dependence upon cocaine. Yet finally even this does not constitute an adequate explanation of Dr. Lewin's recommendation of her to someone like myself who, through no fault of my own, had already lost ten years to bad therapy and was desperate for help.

No one spoke to me of Dr. Brunswick's use of drugs while I was in treatment with her. I learned about it only after her death five years later. While I was in her care, I had eye problems. My ophthalmologist was Dr. LeGrand Hardy, who was married to a Freudian analyst, a member of the Psychoanalytic Society, and who was a longtime friend of Dr. Brunswick. I would later learn that at one point he had hospitalized her in an attempt to cure her addiction. My well-being was of no importance compared to what he took to be his professional obligation not to challenge the standing of a fellow physician: Dr. Hardy gave me no indication that I might be with the wrong analyst. I do not attribute Dr. Brunswick's aberrant conduct wholly to her use of drugs; I think that the morphine merely aggravated her native instability. I was still in treatment with her when she died; she was not yet fifty. I counted up the number of sessions I had had with her in the five years in which I was supposed to be seeing her five times a week. It was the equivalent of two and a half years of treatment. She broke as many appointments as she kept, often at the last moment, when I was about to leave the house. At times I would be told that she was too ill to see her patients; at other times no excuse was offered for the cancellation. When we did meet on schedule, she could squander my whole hour in silly chatter or in doing her shopping on the telephone. "No, of course my slacks don't have to have a fly front! Why does a woman need a fly front?" she burbled on the phone to a salesgirl at Saks Fifth Avenue while I waited on the couch for her return to business. When I protested her misuse of my time, she would answer with her too-bright laugh that she never made telephone calls during her other patients' sessions. She had to violate the conventional techniques of analysis in order to break through my incarcerated emotions; by his recourse to willpower

Dr. Schilder had fortified the compulsive elements in my nature and made me rigid. I did not feel rigid or emotionally incarcerated but who was I to say what imprisoned me and made me unable to function as I would have wished to? Often there were sessions in which she would interrupt my flow of associations to lecture me on analytic theory. These didactic excursions she justified by saying that she wanted me to bring to bear upon my treatment all the resources which I could muster, including intellect. It turned out that she was at least correct on this score: as a result of one such theoretical instruction I was able to figure out for myself the cause of my seemingly unmotivated panics. They ended as of that day. This did not lead me to believe in self-analysis, only to question why it was left to me to apply the knowledge she gave me. A half century has passed since my treatment with Dr. Brunswick and panics are no longer fashionable. Hysteria is out of style in this century. But hysterical manifestations still do appear even if they seldom take complete possession of a person as they once did. All neurotic symptoms, Dr. Brunswick told me, represent both a gratification and a punishment. I had no difficulty in figuring out what the punishment was in this most dramatic of my symptoms. But it took much effort on my part, a concentrated effort of the imagination, to figure out what was the gratification. When I had the answer, the panics disappeared. Dr. Brunswick gave me the theory but neither she nor any of my analysts thought to apply it. It was I who thought to apply it this directly and usefully.

The five years in which I was in treatment with Dr. Brunswick were the hardest of my life. Not only when I was at her office but through long sleepless nights I tried to make sense of her bewildering behavior. I felt that there was something gravely wrong with my treatment and with Dr. Brunswick herself, yet I was unable to trust my judgment. I had no previous experience of orthodox analysis by which to measure my treatment and, after all, I had been sent to Dr. Brunswick by a spokesman for psychoanalysis at its most responsible: a president of the Psychoanalytic Society. If his authority was not to be relied upon, whose was? For a long time I had been deceived that I was being analyzed when in fact I had not been analyzed at all. Now that I was in the hands of a certified practitioner, could it be anything but part of my illness to be as critical as I was of the procedure? It was I, not Dr. Brunswick, who was in treatment. I was the one who had the problems: How dependable could be my judgment of my therapy? Back and forth, weary and despairing, I argued with myself. I tried to persuade myself that my treatment was proceeding as it had to. One day during an analytical session, I protested rather more vehemently than usual Dr. Brunswick's interruption of my hours with her telephone calls and personal business. She responded tartly: "You know that if you don't like it here, Mrs. Trilling, you are free to go elsewhere." Is a child free to walk away from a parent? No, but the parent is free to abandon the child. I shook with fear at her implied threat. Even in those terrible years, in a worldly sense I was a competent person, perhaps uncommonly so. I ran our home, I cooked, I cleaned, I took charge of our finances. Even before I began work of my own I helped Lionel in his work. I assumed a considerable responsibility for Lionel's family. Yet in that part of my being where neurosis is born and thrives I had not reached adulthood. In analysis I was always and only a child. Once, in the middle of an analytical hour with Dr. Brunswick, the room was suddenly unnaturally still. I could hear the stillness like the loud ticking of a clock. I jumped up from the couch to look in back of me: there in her analyst's chair Dr. Brunswick must have died. She had not died; she had fallen asleep. She was "on the nod." Opening her eyes, she smiled at me wanly and explained that she had been wide awake and attentive; she had merely closed her eyes to rest them. She soon did die and I learned something of her history. Back in Vienna, an intimate of the Freud household, she had become convinced that she was being slowly poisoned by a house servant. Whether this had a basis in reality or was entirely delusional, I have no way of knowing, nor do I know how Freud came to feel about his gifted student and whether the connection continued or was broken off in response to a change in her behavior. She had not yet returned to America when the Nazis took over in Austria, but she left soon after. At the time that Dollfuss fired on the workers' houses in Vienna, she was analyzing Muriel Gardiner, the heiress to an American meat-packing fortune and a future analyst in this country whose experience in the anti-Nazi underground Lillian Hellman presented as her own in *Julia*. Dr. Gardiner writes admiringly of Dr. Brunswick in her autobiography, *Code Name "Mary,"* which was published shortly before her death. Though she makes it plain in her book that Hellman was never a member of the Austrian underground, her partisanship to Hellman's politics would seem to have restrained her from making a full public accusation against Hellman for appropriating her life. Hellman knew Dr. Gardiner's story from a mutual friend, Wolf Schwabacher, a New York lawyer. He was a law partner of our close friend Jim Grossman.

The years which I spent with Dr. Brunswick are not to be written off as entirely, or even predominantly, a therapeutic waste. Paradoxically it was from this most capricious of practitioners that I had my first glimpse of what is meant by a Freudian analysis. It was agonizing to be in such vagrant care; it should never have been allowed to happen. But deficient and defective as my treatment with Dr. Brunswick obviously was, after my years with her I was not again able to give credence to any therapeutic method other than orthodox Freudianism. She did not cure me of my symptoms but she pointed me in the direction of cure and if, strange to say, what was perhaps most useful to me in my treatment with her were the disquisitions on method with which she interlarded my hours, I remain deeply grateful for these digressions. They instructed me in an analytical technique which neither she nor her successors employed as they should have but which I have used to considerable advantage in thinking about my problems. Most important, it was while I was her patient that I became a writer. In some way which I do not fully comprehend, she helped make it possible for me to have a professional career. I was thirty-six years old when I first wrote for publication. Before that I had been sunk in nonachievement. Something in the analytical situation, it may even have been something in Dr. Brunswick's example, helped me to reverse my course. My literary career started with the contribution of unsigned book notes to the *Nation*. A condition of my employment was that if any book came to me which turned out to be worthy of more than brief mention, I was to write a full-length signed review. This was intended to rescue me from the anonymity of a note writer but the idea of putting my name to a review and being identified as its author overwhelmed me with anxiety. I remember feeling as if I were confronting a world-shaking calamity rather than a career opportunity. It was not the writing but the fact that I would be known as the writer which worried me. Dr. Brunswick's prompt and precise analytical interpretation of what alarmed me brought me through that most significant crisis. She was able to show me that behind my fear of signing a review lay the old parental injunction against exposure and that I very much desired the display which had been denied me in my upbringing. "You can't wait to see your name all over the magazine," she chortled. She was right. The extreme pain of a psychological symptom which we suffer in our mature lives is out of all proportion to its originating cause. In a single dramatic session with the analyst who followed Dr. Brunswick I would discover another of the apparently endlessly ramified consequences of my father's concern that I not exhibit myself: it was the source not merely of my fear of professional notice but, even more tormentingly, it lay at the root of my agoraphobia. How trace the circuitous route of a neurotic symptom from its birth to its full flowering in our adult lives? Surely there was no reasonable relation between the cataclysmic terror with which I contemplated having to sign a review, or the misery which I could sometimes experience merely in walking on an open street, and the forbidden desires of a five-year-old in Westchester.

The years in which I was in treatment with Dr. Brunswick were the years of America's engagement in the Second World War: I grew accustomed to having my sessions begin with her excited pronouncements on the virtues of Lend-Lease or the need for a second front. My next doctor after the death of Dr. Brunswick was Dr. William Dunn. It was now 1945 and Dr. Dunn had just returned from service in the Pacific. I was referred to him by the analyst wife of my eye doctor, Dr. Hardy; she had taken on the duty of placing Dr. Brunswick's patients with other physicians. Dr. Dunn was a psychiatrist at New York's Payne Whitney Clinic as well as an analyst; he sometimes spoke as if he were especially pleased with this double life. He also spoke good-naturedly of his second-class citizenship as a Gentile in so largely Jewish a profession. I should suppose that he was the only psychoanalyst in New York who had the *Social Register* in his office. Dr. Dunn was not a conspicuously astute physician. He frequently reminded me that it was not necessary for an analyst to be as quick-witted as his patient. But he was gentle and kind and conscientious and, in wonderful contrast to his predecessor, he was unfailing in attendance—until he suddenly died of a heart attack. I loved Dr. Dunn's lean New England good looks and his wry humor and I brought into my treatment with him all the pent-up unexplored passion of my infant love for my father. It may be that the fact that he was not Jewish put him at a comfortable remove from my real-life father and permitted me a freer play of phantasy than would have been allowed me were the identification more direct. All of which is to say that within my relation with Dr. Dunn there was contained all the prescribed substance of the positive analytic transference—on the analytic couch, if I had spoken in the first vocabulary of eroticism, I should also have been speaking in the language of our richest sexual development. But in all the years in which I was

Dr. Dunn's patient, I breathed no word of this love, other than once or twice to mutter sullenly something about his being undoubtedly accustomed to sitting in his analyst's chair and listening all day long to his women patients telling him how much they adored him. Sometimes I brought him presents of flowers, yet even my gift-giving never led us to seize this treasure of reanimated childhood emotion and utilize it in my treatment. He had been analyzed by Dr. Karen Horney. Dr. Horney diverged from Freud in attributing to society much of the role in the formation of character which Freud assigned to parental influence. But I have never been certain that it was Dr. Dunn's training with Dr. Horney, or even his own excessive modesty, which made him evade the analysis of my early feeling for my father as it was now reflected in the transference. After all, this oversight was not limited to Dr. Dunn among my analysts. In my childhood I had a recurring nightmare in which I was chased by a golden dwarf intent upon kissing me; if he kissed me, I would die. I spoke of this nightmare with each of my doctors. I had spoken of my father giving me money to quiet me when I was frightened by Bobolinka's death, and I must also have mentioned that my father was shorter than my mother. My nightmare was let vanish into the uninhabited air. None of my analysts, orthodox or unorthodox, analyzed my buried passion for my father, that most crucial emotion of my early life, the source of my capacity for love but undoubtedly the source, as well, of my lasting fear of rejected love.

Lionel and I were growing older. We were forty in 1945 when I began treatment with Dr. Dunn. Lionel's academic career and his literary reputation were both established and I was launched in my career; I remember Dr. Dunn telling me that he tipped the doormen of his building heavily in the hope that they would not reveal to curious journalists the names of patients like myself. Psychoanalysis had made its sober way in the world. Its standing as a serious medical tool was indeed at its peak. But it still had a lurid interest for the gossip columnists. In 1948, while I was in treatment with Dr. Dunn, Lionel and I had our first and only child, a son. Because the problems which still lingered with me tended not to have the palpability of the fears which had troubled me when I was in the care of my earlier physicians, they no longer so readily presented themselves in clinical symptoms of the sort which demand immediate attention; they were coming to seem more and more natural to my personality and to the way I function in the world. To his credit, Dr. Dunn was not satisfied to have me compromise my capacity for a freer life. When I still clung to some of my early symptoms, he worried that he might have overlooked a significant element in my treatment and he suggested that I consult with Dr. Marianne Kris about the problems which remained with me. I no longer recollect what transpired in this consultation but when Dr. Dunn died, Dr. Kris was the obvious person for me to turn to. She would be the last of my doctors and we never pretended that I was actually being analyzed by her. My treatment with Dr. Kris is probably best described as analytically based psychotherapy. The hours were irregular; sometimes I went without seeing her for months or even years. I never lay on a couch; we talked facing each other, our facial expressions part of our understanding of what was going on. She was a most remarkable woman, warmhearted, large-minded, sensitive, sensible, imaginative, a great unraveler of emotional knots. She looked wise and she was wise. Her very calm was therapeutic: it was easy to understand why Marilyn Monroe, whom she also occasionally saw, admired her as she did and bequeathed the bulk of her estate to her for analytical research. She was the wife of Ernst Kris, an art historian and an eminent member of the Psychoanalytic Society—for a long time he was its only member who was not a graduate of medical school. Although a refugee from Austria, she employed her new language with exactness and elasticity. One of her notable gifts, especially helpful to me when we talked about the rearing of my small child, was her ability to supply not only the words but even the tone of voice in which to make an indicated parental communication.

246

Everything which Dr. Kris said was a lesson in the indivisibility of style and content. But to me what was most impressive about her was her professional courage. Hers was the most hierarchical of professions but no analytical colleague was too highly placed to be exempt from her criticism if she thought he was mishandling a patient—Dr. Rudolph Loewenstein, with whom Lionel was in treatment during some of the same period in which I was seeing Dr. Kris, was an intimate associate of Ernst Kris in formulating the post-Freudian ego psychology, but she had no hesitation in stating her belief that he was the wrong doctor for Lionel. She offered no defense of the Psychoanalytic Society against my criticism of it for permitting a morphine-addicted doctor to be one of its members. Analysis, she said, owed the Trillings restitution and for several years, until she began to feel that it perhaps interfered with my treatment, she refused to take money from me.

When I began seeing Dr. Kris, I had been in one or another kind of therapy for more than twenty years. What area of my emotional experience could I have failed to investigate? It developed that there was still much territory to explore. None of my doctors had ventured on the dynamism of my relation with my brother and sister and of the part they had had in shaping my life, even my professional life. My brother was three years my senior, my sister five years my senior. It had of course never been openly stated by my parents that I was not to surpass them, but long before memory it had been silently impressed upon me that I was not to outdistance either of my siblings, my brother because he was a boy, my sister because she was handicapped. Until Dr. Kris brought it to my consciousness, I was never aware of this brake which had been put on my energies. It had continued to function long after there was any possibility of competition among the three of us, and it continues to function, stubborn and compelling, though they are dead: I still hold to my third and minor place in the family procession. I continue to people the world with brothers and sisters whom I must not excel. I apologize to my friends, or at least

247

to those of them who in whatever way reproduce my relation with members of my family, for any good fortune which comes to me; it should, I feel, have come to them and I guiltily try to propitiate them. This corner of my emotional history was opened to me too late for me to do more than chisel away at the loose fragments of so solid an obstacle to my free course in life. Dr. Kris also conjectured that my mother had suffered a nervous breakdown at my birth and that for some of my early life I had not had her presence and care. My mother, who frequently alluded to a nervous breakdown in her past, never said when it occurred, nor did I think to question her on its details. Because of Dr. Kris's hypothesis, I did—as I have said—question my sister about a photograph of me at the age of ten or eleven months, a studio picture in which I am accompanied by an unidentified young woman, not my mother. My sister angrily thrust the picture away from her. She insisted that I never again question her about our childhood.

Since I often asked Dr. Kris for advice and usually took it, it smacks of dishonesty and ingratitude for me to say now that she was too ready with advice. Yet when I look back on our relationship, I see it as one of its serious flaws that she intervened in my life as she did even where, as in literary matters, I had not sought her help. She was neither magical nor magisterial in voicing her opinions, yet inevitably she spoke with the authority of our professional relationship and this is at its source a parental authority and uniquely compelling. There were times when, anything but wise, she expressed views which reflected prejudices bred either in her own Viennese background or in her analytical training. On one visit, for example, I spoke of Lionel's repeated failure to remember to put out the garbage. Putting out the garbage, Dr. Kris interposed firmly, was the work of the woman of the house, not of the man. I was fifty years old when she said this to me and I am not usually accused of intellectual timidity, yet instead of contesting her statement I gave it, at least for the moment, the force of a feasible pronouncement on the domestic relation of the sexes. More than once, Dr. Kris said of my literary criticism that I must "neutralize" it, by which she meant that in my writing as in my life I must be more accepting, less given to the making of judgments; as a critic, I was to be less critical. It was a time when Freudian doctrine identified female normality with "passivity," a counter to the "activity" of the male; I doubt that so invidious an assumption still prevails among Freudian analysts. But in commenting on my work in these terms, Dr. Kris was not just expressing a biased sexual view; she was moving into an area in which she had little competence—psychoanalytical training is not a preparation for literary judgment. Analysis has of course considerably altered since I was a patient of Dr. Kris. Even the Freudians have had to yield to changes in culture as they used not to. On one of my last visits with Dr. Kris—it was at the beginning of the eighties—she indeed spoke of having had to revise her perception of adolescent sexuality. Although at an earlier date she had thought it abnormal for a girl to be sexually active at seventeen or eighteen, now she had come to regard it as abnormal if a girl of that age was sexually inactive. I doubt that the profession would respond today as my analyst friends did in 1962 when I published an essay on Norman Mailer. At that time, to write of Mailer other than as the victim of his pathology was to put oneself, at least so far as the Freudian establishment was concerned, outside the bounds of respectability. Yet even today the crucial distinction between a psychoanalytic interpretation and an analyst's personal opinion is sometimes difficult for a patient to grasp. In a situation in which the analyst is the object of the infant emotions once engendered by one's parents, it is not easy for the patient to keep it in mind that this person who is speaking to him is only another faulty human being like himself, a similarly sad and sorry bundle of conflicting doubts and desires, of tangled principles and prejudices.

By the time I began to see Dr. Kris in the fifties, although psychological therapies were not as institutionalized in the universities as they are today, they no longer belonged in the realm of the scandalous unknown. Lionel nevertheless still made a point of not mentioning his own analysis at college or anywhere. By now he had another reason for this caution: he had a public image to protect, perhaps especially at Columbia. At all stages of education there are teachers who become symbolical figures for their students—they have it in common with analysts that certain of their students vest their phantasies in them. While Lionel himself never proposed that literary criticism was an instrument of power and prestige, his work implicitly suggested a significant public role for the teacher-critic. Mark Van Doren had represented for Lionel's undergraduate generation the happy possibility of being both a teacher and a writer. Lionel represented for his gifted students a literary academic whose thought ranged well beyond the academy, linking literature to the wider political and moral life of the nation. The social relevance and moral intensity which in our American mid-century gave criticism its newly important role in society made Lionel himself into a kind of moral exemplar for his students, someone whose life and character might set the pattern for their own public and private choices. Lionel did not create or encourage this image. Consciously he scorned it. Yet unconsciously he conspired in it. In hidden ways he had been prepared for it by his family. He had had little youthful freedom before his family's financial collapse had thrust the responsibilities of adulthood upon him. Dependent though I was upon him for emotional support, Lionel was never a father to me; for both better and worse, this was not the nature of our relationship. But he was a father to his parents and soon he was a father to his students. Like a father who instinctively conceals his shortcomings from his offspring lest their respect for him be diminished, he was at pains not to reveal the human fallibilities which had sent him into analysis. I very much disliked the image of Lionel as someone immune to profanation. I felt that it lessened and falsified him. I preferred him in all his vulnerable humanity. My annoyance at his willingness to be idealized overflowed one day after a visit we had from a former student of his who was now a colleague. It was late in my pregnancy and the young man's wife, too, was pregnant. He had come to talk with Lionel about the wonders and terrors of approaching fatherhood: Was Lionel as frightened as he was? Did Lionel feel equal to the situation which awaited him? Lionel smiled away his visitor's anxious questions and the young man remarked wistfully that of course there was no parallel in their circumstances: Lionel was a whole person, with no reason for the qualms with which he was himself burdened—he, our young visitor, was only a bundle of bits and pieces. When the young man left, I turned on Lionel in a fury. Who was he to allow such a distinction between himself and the rest of the world? Was he so little fragmented that he belonged to another breed from his young colleague? In a sense I knew that I was being unfair: Lionel never thought himself better than other people. On the contrary. But perhaps somewhere in his being he was still the little boy who had fended off attack by pretending that he was Balder, favorite of the gods. Since his death, I often wonder how, if Lionel had lived to write his memoir, he would have written about this image which his students had of him. It was not an aspect of his life which could properly be avoided. What, in fact, if he had written his autobiography, would he have done about his analysis? In any autobiographical work he would have had to speak of my phobias, which for so long infringed upon his freedom. Could he have written about my analysis without writing about his own? And, forced to speak of his own, what weight would he have given it? I remember that in a session with Dr. Brunswick I happened to repeat Lionel's reference to my analysis as an "emergency." She interrupted sharply. "Why is your analysis any more of an emergency than his?" she demanded. The answer to her question was simple enough: In the practical living of our lives my disabilities were far more disabling than his. They were also more visible. But her question nevertheless underscored the difference between his approach to analysis and mine. Mine was a serious personal problem. His was—what? An intellectual problem?

Obviously I cannot write about Lionel's analytical history with the direct knowledge which I bring to my own. It is my recollection that he stayed with the doctor whom we shared at the start of our analytical experience until that doctor stopped his analytical practice in order to be retrained and that then he resumed treatment with him and remained with him throughout the war. Shortly after the war, while I was with Dr. Dunn, Lionel switched to Dr. Rudolph Loewenstein. With Ernst Kris and Heinz Hartmann, Loewenstein was one of the authors of the ego psychology which became an important extension or augmentation of orthodox Freudian theory. He was an eminent member of the New York Psychoanalytic Society; there was no reason for Lionel to suppose that in being in Dr. Loewenstein's care he was not in the best possible analytic treatment. He stayed with Dr. Loewenstein for some years; then he again changed doctors and went to a woman analyst, Dr. Grace Abbate, with whom he was sporadically in treatment until his death. The move to Dr. Abbate was suggested by Dr. Kris. Frequently in my visits with Dr. Kris I spoke of my lack of confidence in Dr. Loewenstein's treatment of Lionel as it filtered through to me. For a long time Dr. Kris listened to me in silence. Then one day she asked me if Lionel would be willing to consult with her. The consultation resulted in his leaving Dr. Loewenstein for Dr. Abbate. This intervention by Dr. Kris was an extraordinary act of courage and integrity.

I disliked Dr. Loewenstein very much and I am unable to speak well of him. I believe that he did harm to Lionel and, so far as he could, to our marriage by colluding in Lionel's ambivalence toward me. There is nothing unusual in the fact that Lionel's relation to me was colored by his relation with his mother: this is to be expected. But there was a more than expectable element of hostility in Lionel's feeling toward his mother. Fannie Trilling was not beyond criticism. She was strikingly selfish and self-concerned in her rearing of her son, cruelly insensitive to his young pride. In her financial dependence upon us, she was more than selfish, greedy. She made great difficulty for us in the early crucial years of our marriage. But there was much to love and respect in her, and Lionel's attitude toward her was not a fitting response to her maternal behavior taken as a whole. Although with the passage of time he became more relaxed in her company and even managed to acknowledge that she played an important part in encouraging him as a writer, there remained a hard primitive core of hostility in his relation to her—it perhaps represented love turned bitter. It flared into antagonism on very little provocation. For instance, on the day that his novel was published, Lionel took his mother to lunch to present her with a copy. It was a pleasant thing to do and he left the house in good humor. He returned angry: his mother had not taken the book from his hand as eagerly as he wished her to and from her hesitation he had concluded that she never really wanted him to be a novelist. The conclusion was extreme and unwarranted. He was now forty-two years old, too old and presumably too experienced in analysis to allow himself such an indulgence. There was no evidence that Dr. Loewenstein undertook to analyze the origins of Lionel's distrust of his mother or its connection to his unprovoked rages at me. For whatever unexplored reasons of his own, Dr. Loewenstein would seem to have imputed to Lionel an entire objectivity in the judgment he passed on me. This became his own judgment of me as well. All properly trained analysts avoid acquaintance with their patients' families but accidental meetings do take place. I had several such unwanted encounters with Dr. Loewenstein. In each of them he turned away from the introduction with such manifest distaste that I was reminded of my introduction to Lionel's uncles and aunts at his mother's Seder. Dr. Kris's confidence that I was accurate in my report of Dr. Loewenstein's conduct was a great gift to me. In my home I had not been believed; my brother was allowed to establish his own

253

version of my truth. If I have an unusual experience, I still preface any account I may give of it with the warning: "You will not believe this but . . ." It meant more to me than any compliment I have ever had that Dr. Kris assured me that she had never had a patient whose report of reality was more to be relied upon. Lionel's irrational outbursts at me were likely to occur either as a component of one of his bouts of depression or its climax. Even before our marriage, his mother had cautioned me that there was a side of his character against which I must be on guard; if he lost his temper at me, she said, I was to reach for the nearest bottle and hit him on the head with it. I could not imagine what this adoring mother was trying to say to me about her son and I decided that she must be mad. Just so would our close friends have thought me mad had I told them that Lionel, this most peaceable of men and most devoted of husbands, indulged in annihilating verbal assaults on me. The attacks were not frequent, perhaps at most five or six a year, and they always had the same substance: he accused me of being the worst person he had ever met and of having ruined his life. I would come to feel of these scenes that they represented an encapsulated lunacy which from time to time took possession of an otherwise superlatively sane individual. But it took me a long while to assess them this sensibly. It was a heavy charge that he turned upon me and I had a great store of guilt which it detonated. In my devastation, I would usually break into frantic weeping—it was the outcome for which Lionel waited. This consummation attained to, the attack could cease; suddenly his anger disappeared and he put his arms around me and forgave me the injury I had done him. I had indeed done Lionel injury. In the early years of our marriage I needed and took from him far more help than is normally asked of a husband. But if I can be accused of having, by my phobias and the many worrisome illnesses of my young womanhood, robbed him of the carefreeness of youth, this cannot be made to account for either his depression or his rage. Not only his mother's warning to me but also the story which he wrote on our honeymoon testify to the fact that his anger had come into being long before we knew each other; the conditions of our marriage merely provided him with a convenient vessel into which to pour whatever was his old grievance. Lionel's snake story was a story of morbid sexual jealousy expressing itself in morbid bitterness. Although consciously I had not understood its implications for our life together, even at my young age I was strangely troubled by the extremity of its feeling. Nor did his anger disappear with the disappearance of my fears, and the cure of my anxieties did not rid him of his depression. He lived with the burden of a hostility which had long since forgotten its source and I lived with it, too, as he had lived with my neurosis and as how many other people live with similar encumbrances upon their happiness. I know of but one novel, *The Prodigal Women* by Nancy Hale— it was published in the forties—that describes a psychological problem such as afflicted Lionel. I was in middle age before I learned to defuse Lionel's attacks on me by leaving the room when they began: without a visible target, without my pain culminating in tears, they seemed no longer to give him the gratification which they previously offered. Dr. Loewenstein not only failed to treat Lionel's anger at me; he apparently allied himself with Lionel to validate it. This was the perception which led Dr. Kris to urge Lionel to break off his treatment with Dr. Loewenstein and enter treatment with a woman analyst, Dr. Abbate. Through various stretches of time in the late years of his life, Lionel took the subway to Brooklyn for his early-morning sessions with her, but by now he had understandably lost heart for analysis. So had I. As he made his daily journey, in chorus with the sound of the subway wheels the title of Freud's famous essay "Psychoanalysis Terminable and Interminable" must have rung in his ears. In the fall of 1975 Dr. Abbate heard that Lionel was dying and came to visit him. It had been established that he had a fatal pancreatic cancer and I had brought him home from the hospital. They saw each other in private, but when she was ready to leave I took her to the

255

door. I had never before met Dr. Abbate, but at the door she leaned over and kissed me. She said that she wanted me to know how much Lionel had always loved me. It was not something which she had to say, nor was it much to say, but it was enough. Not long afterward, Dr. Abbate herself died.

Until the end of his life, Lionel never yielded in his admiration for Freud. But it was Freud the man of idea, Freud the witness to the tragedy of civilization, whom he esteemed. He was not primarily concerned, as I was and continue to be, with psychoanalysis as a medical practice.

Chapter
TEN

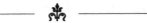

Between 1932 when Lionel was made an instructor at Columbia and 1936 when he came perilously close to losing his Columbia appointment, although he was presumably putting his best energies to his dissertation, he published a substantial number of reviews and even one or two literary essays. He wrote to make money: even the $15 or $20 he was paid for a review were useful additions to our small income. But he also wrote to get away from his dissertation, which was going badly. The books he reviewed were for the most part critical or biographical studies; they dealt, usually briefly, with such figures as Chatterton, Keats, Sainte-Beuve, Charlotte Brontë, Ruskin, Coleridge, Dickens, and his own Matthew Arnold. But he also wrote about subjects which were not immediately related to his academic specialization: in this same period he reviewed a study of the Jews of Germany, a volume about forced labor in the United States, and a group of German novels. This last included novels by Feuchtwanger and Zweig; the review was bravely captioned "A Clue to Hitlerism." Although almost fifteen years would elapse before he followed his snake story with a next story, "Of This Time, Of That Place," he seems to have been increasingly drawn at this time to writing about fiction if not to writing fiction of his own. In 1935, of five reviews which he published, three were reviews of current novels: Silone's *Fontamara,* James Farrell's *Guillotine Party,* and John O'Hara's *Butterfield 8.* In 1936 he reviewed only a single volume of nonfiction, Van Wyck Brooks's *The Flowering of New England.* His reviews chiefly appeared in the *Nation* and the *New Republic;* to appear in these periodicals was a recognized road to literary reputation. But at this point in his career Lionel's work, even the pieces he wrote for the monthlies and quarterlies, received little notice. The *American Mercury,* which had been famous in the twenties under the editorship of Mencken and Nathan, was now briefly revived by Charles Angoff, and Lionel contributed to it as he also contributed to V. F. Calverton's *Modern Monthly.* He excited no attention in either place. In 1936 he published his first full-length essay since the days of the *Menorah Journal:* a study of Eugene O'Neill commissioned for the *New Republic* by its literary editor, Malcolm Cowley. Although Cowley thought well enough of the piece to include it in a collection, *After the Genteel Tradition,* published in 1937, Lionel would later in life refuse permission for it to be again reprinted. He commented simply: "I find I don't like it."

In the spring of 1933, a few months after my father's death, we moved to a graystone on East 77th Street. It was a garden apartment and our new rent was $70, $20 more than we had at the end been paying on upper Claremont Avenue. We thought we could afford the increase because we now had the income from my father's trust fund. But we still had Lionel's family to support and Lionel's financial future was far from secure. Completion of his dissertation was nowhere in sight and without his Ph.D., or even with it, his teaching career was anything but certain. My health also gave us reason for concern. I was substantially recovered from my thyroid operations but I was increasingly the prey of emotional problems. My fear of being alone was entrenching itself and I suffered from frequent panics; at night I was afraid to close my eyes lest my mind become a kaleidoscope of formless images swirling about like Heraclitan atoms in search of their cosmic destiny. No longer involved in the Communist movement, I had nothing to fill my days and, like an unhappy adolescent, I stayed in bed half the morning. Lionel's sister, Harriet, often came to visit us during this period and she would usually arrive to find me still in bed. She compounded my sense of not managing my life or, rather, of not having a life to manage by bringing me breakfast in bed. Lionel, too, brought me breakfast in bed: I would wake at nine or ten to see him standing at my bedside with a tray in his hand. I tried to be grateful for his kindness but in my heart I accused him, as I accused Harriet, of invaliding me. Sometimes I wrote stories to occupy my time but they never satisfied me and I seldom finished them. I wanted them to come to life on the page, with the author's observing intelligence out of view, but I seemed never able to de-intellectualize them and rid them of my intrusive supervision. I suppose that I was already indicating a native inclination to criticism. But the hours which dragged for me were too few for Lionel. From early morning he labored at his desk in what, in our garden apartment, passed for his study, a tiny white-tiled cell beyond the kitchen, no larger than a closet; it had probably been a cold pantry when the house was a private residence. Cool in summer, in winter it had only the nearby kitchen to warm it; dampness rose from its floor and lingered on the tiled walls. This was the worst of Lionel's workrooms, but even as an established writer he never had a proper study. Sometimes he fretted about his desk chair because of his back problems but he never seriously complained about his lack of adequate space to work in, though I suspect that he shared my wistfulness when we visited the Kronenbergers in their house on East 95th Street and contemplated Louis Kronenberger's spacious study—it had originally been the second-floor drawing room of their brownstone. As summer approached I tried to plant a garden in our backyard. The soil was polluted and nothing flowered; sterile dahlias grew to the height of young trees. We replaced some of the concrete in the yard with turf and bought a birdbath; the dusty city sparrows came to bathe and drink. I lay in a deck chair watching them. Nearby, Lionel worked in his cubicle. To complete the emptiness of my life, I did not have even the care of the house to occupy me; we had a housekeeper who came each afternoon to clean and cook dinner. This was the maid whom Whittaker Chambers heard and ordered us to send home when he made his unexplained visit on 77th Street. Herbert Solow had perhaps suggested that he come to see us. Solow was himself a frequent uninvited guest. Like so many of the people we knew, he suffered from extended bouts of depression and during these spells he moved from one friend's house to another, leaving his gift of gloom, like a cat depositing a half-eaten bird at the feet of his master. During one particularly troubling interval, he lay on our living-room couch for the better part of four days, never asleep yet too steeped in misery to talk, coming to life only to eat. It was on the last day of this wintry visit that I made the mistake of offering him a sardine sandwich for his lunch. He sprang from the couch in raging anger. "That's the trouble with you Jewish girls," he stormed at me. "All you can feed a man is sardines!" His Gentile friend Adelaide Walker, he went on to inform me, knew how to feed a man: when Herbert was at her house for a meal, she gave him clam chowder. Expressed anger and depression do not comfortably coexist; for Herbert to open the door to one of them was, at least for the moment, to be rid of the other. He was not happy about being a Jew. He commonly took out his self-hatred on the Jewish women of his acquaintance. Other Jewish writers whom we knew took out their self-hatred as Jews on Lionel: they resented his good looks and manners, his purity of speech, even the fact that he had not had to change his name as they had changed theirs.

With his appointment as an instructor at Columbia, Lionel picked up his old college acquaintance with Jacques Barzun. Barzun was now teaching in the History Department. They had known each other as undergraduates but only casually; now the friendship developed and became deeply important to both of them. In 1934 they began to teach the Colloquium together; it was the honors course which Lionel had taken as an undergraduate when it was first offered in the twenties. On one evening a week a small group of upperclassmen met for two hours to discuss a major work of Western literature or history or philosophy. They were among the best students in the College and these sessions were a significant part of their Columbia experience. Because the Colloquium met on Wednesdays, Wednesday was unlike any other day of the week for Lionel, a day of last-minute hard work and anxiety but also a day of anticipation. No matter how often he taught a book, Lionel reread it in preparation for teaching it; there was considerable challenge in entering into discussion of these important works with Jacques and their gifted students. The two men were markedly dissimilar in background and temperament: Jacques the French-born rationalist, cool, precise, carefully insulated from the movements of contemporary political culture; Lionel the New York Jewish intellectual who, when he first taught with Jacques, had only recently returned from his brief excursion into Communism. The friendly difference between the teachers was helpful to their students, encouraging them to formulate their own ideas. In the fall of 1934 we moved back to the neighborhood of the University, to an apartment on West 114th Street between Amsterdam Avenue and Morningside Drive; the nurses' residence of St. Luke's Hospital has since been built on the site. Jacques, between marriages, moved into the same building with us. In what might seem to be a contradiction of his formality of appearance and manner, he enjoyed intimacy and would gladly have set up his typewriter in the same room with Lionel. It was Lionel who had the greater need of privacy. Jacques has told me that it was a time in our culture when a preference for the modern in art and literature dominated the universities. Neither of the two men recognized any great gulf between the traditional and the contemporary in art. Even before Lionel had entered college he had got from his uncle Hymie an at least superficial knowledge of the new literary and artistic movements in America and Europe, and as a boy in France Jacques had been acquainted with many of the European modernists of the early years of this century—they were familiars of his childhood home. For both Lionel and Jacques the modern lacked the mystery and allure which it had for many of their University colleagues. Certainly it failed to destroy or override their shared pleasure in the Romantics. Because of their interest in the nineteenth-century Romantic poets—Wordsworth, Coleridge, Byron, Keats—Jacques and Lionel came to be known at Columbia as "the Romantic boys," and indeed it was in their work on the Romantic poets that each of them went on to do some of his best writing. Jacques's piece on Byron in his volume *The Energies of Art* remains, I think, one of the best of his critical essays, and Lionel's essays on Keats and Wordsworth are generally given an important place in his work.

Virtually everyone we knew in the thirties and forties was witty. Wit was a guarantee of intelligence; the most serious conversation bounced along on waves of laughter. This was not without paradox. In the living of their lives, the people with whom we associated, most of them professional intellectuals, were far from fun-loving. Yet it was not unexpectable that the New York intellectuals should be witty. Their wit was another natural expression of their love of language and of their speed and dexterity of mind. It was not an overflow of good humor; ours was, in fact, a cruelly judgmental society, often malicious and riddled with envy. I never knew either Jacques or Lionel to be malicious or witty at another person's expense. Their innocent specialty was puns; many years have passed since they taught the Colloquium, but their old-time students still recall some of their more flamboyant classroom improvisations, the evening, for instance, when the name of Malthus triggered a particularly ingenious exchange. "Honi soit qui mal y pense," one of them had declared carelessly. It drew the swift rejoinder: "Honi soit qui Malthus pense," to which the first speaker shot back: "Honi soit qui mal thus puns." At home among intimates, Lionel's humor could be zany. He made up toneless ditties in which he sang of the woes of invented characters: Abie, the fish-peddler, or a baby pig appealing to its mother for deliverance from its porcine fate:

> I don't wanna be a pig, Momma.
> Momma, I don't wanna be a pig.
> I am what I am but I won't be a ham.
> Momma, I'm achin'
> To be somethin' else but bacon.
> Momma, I don't wanna be a pig.

Yet while there was probably more of such nonsensical playfulness in Lionel than in Jacques, of the two Lionel's was the darker nature. Lionel was more anguished by life than Jacques, less content to accept or ignore its promises. His address to ideas was more stringent and challenging. Occasionally Jacques wrote for the intellectual journals which we associate with our more severe life of mind in this century, but in general he was more at home in the pages of the *Atlantic Monthly* or *Harper's*. In his precision of speech and the formality of his personal bearing Jacques appeared to be the more distant of the pair, even the more forbidding; in actual fact, however, he was the more tolerant—what appeared to their students to be Lionel's greater approachability was misleading. He often spoke to me about this difference between Jacques and himself. Each academic year would begin, he told me, with their students intimidated by Jacques and supposing that Lionel was the more sympathetic of their teachers. Then, as the year progressed, the students gradually came to realize that in truth it was Jacques who was the more accessible of the two men and the more comforting, and this development would be paralleled, Lionel said, by the steady growth of Jacques's affection for his pupils, especially those who had turned out to be as bright as they were scruffy. When our son was born, Lionel and I would discover another aspect of Jacques of which we had previously been unaware. He cured Jim's colic: already the father of three, he took us gently in hand and explained what the pediatrician failed to grasp, that the baby's formula was too thin and that his digestive distress was due to being at the same time overcrowded and hungry. Eventually Lionel and Jacques stopped teaching together. After they left the Colloquium they jointly taught a graduate seminar, and it was here or, at any rate, at this juncture that the difference in their response to the contemporary world, especially where there was an unavoidable meeting of culture and politics, began to interfere in their teaching relationship. In 1967 Lionel passingly comments on this in his journal. Speaking of his "need to break new ground or at least to receive fresh news of the intellectual life," he remarks that for his old teaching partner "there really *is* nothing new: the prevalence of intellectual aberration intervenes—the available possibilities of centrality or normality are all in the past." To function as he wished, whether as teacher or writer, Lionel felt that he had to refuse all critical refuge, including the refuge of history.

From the start, one of the things which had cemented Lionel's intimacy with Jacques was the need which both of them had to augment their University salaries. In addition to writing reviews, Lionel did many things to earn money. While we lived on 114th Street he tutored a wealthy young man who was trying to write a novel. He also taught a writing class at the Junior League—this experience inspired a story he wrote many years later, "The Lesson and the Secret." The foremost moneymaking venture of the year was the compilation of a library of excerpts from literary classics to be given away by the *New York Evening Post*. As he left the house to go to the newspaper office to discuss the terms of this assignment, Lionel was still pondering the fee he should ask—he decided to ask for $200. Between the house and the subway, the figure increased to $500 and in the course of the ride downtown it grew yet again, to $750. Then, as he entered the office, all caution fled: he asked $1,000. His price was so readily met that he quickly tacked on another $200 for an assistant. The assistant was of course Jacques. In the next days, armed with scissors and razors, the two men maniacally slashed their way through our bookshelves, here cutting out two pages of Spinoza, there three of Carlyle, here two of Chekhov, there three of Montaigne. Lionel's library would always have a hazardous life. On a quiet evening some years later, in another apartment, I would be sitting alone, reading in the living room, when I heard a strange sound in the bookshelves behind me. The sound was unfamiliar, delicate but persistent. I became convinced that something was eating our books. My childhood fear of not being believed was now dramatically revived. Until Lionel discovered that the cloth covers on many of his books had bare, colorless spots, he refused to take my word that an invasive creature was having its evening meal in his library. Poor Lionel, it could not have been easy to be married to me. The scientific resources of the Museum of Natural History had to be mobilized to determine that our books were providing the nourishment for a giant South American cockroach which had been sneakily nesting in some wet plaster left by the plumber in a bathroom wall adjacent to the bookshelves. Sufficiently desperate for food, the South American cockroach survives on the glue in cloth bookbindings.

The necessity of making extra money never ended for either Lionel or Jacques. The most ambitious and disappointing of their joint enterprises was their successive association in the fifties with two book clubs, the Readers' Subscription and the Mid-Century, both modeled on the Book-of-the-Month Club but geared to a more discriminating public. The idea of a book club for serious readers originated with a former student of Lionel's and Jacques's and the management of the clubs was also in the hands of a former student. There was a third editor besides Lionel and Jacques, W. H. Auden. The editors made no financial investment in these ventures, and their salaries were small, but they hoped to be rewarded when the clubs were successful. This never happened; both projects failed. The most that Lionel ever earned as a book-club editor was $500 a month and for this pay he had not only to read a great many books in order to choose the clubs' monthly selections but also to contribute a critical piece each month to the periodicals which the clubs regularly sent out to their subscribers: the *Griffin,* the magazine of the Readers' Subscription, and the *Mid-Century,* the publication of the Mid-Century Book Club. Although Lionel never felt that the pieces he contributed to these periodicals were of enough weight to include in a major volume of his collected essays, he used several of them in his less austere collection, *A Gathering of Fugitives.* They reveal enough care and thought to raise the question whether at this stage of his career he should have been expending his energies this prodigally. None of the editors knew enough about business to handle the problems which soon arose in the running of the clubs. Only Auden, that most practical-minded of poets, was capable of making an objective assessment of the clubs' management. Because the men who had the business end of the clubs in their charge had once been their students, Lionel and Jacques would not question either their loyalty or their competence, and so great was the admiration for Lionel and Jacques of the supposedly tough-minded lawyer whom they had engaged to guard their interests that he never questioned their judgment. There came a point at which Lionel asked my brother to look into the finances of the Mid-Century to decide whether the club was still viable. My brother, too, let himself be persuaded that the company was sound. Not long afterward, the club folded. What is amusing in the situation is that all three wives— Jacques's, the lawyer's, and I—had no doubt but that the clubs were being mismanaged.

Until 1936 by far the most significant event in Lionel's professional life had been his appointment as an instructor at Columbia. In 1936 he was told that "as a Jew, a Marxist, and a Freudian" he was not happy in his Columbia job and that his appointment would not be renewed. What followed on this devastating news was in itself remarkable and it had an extraordinary effect on Lionel's personality and career. He had not anticipated dismissal and the blow was a heavy one. The fact that in the next weeks he was able to reverse the decision of his department and be reinstated profoundly altered his sense of himself. From this time forward he spoke and wrote differently, bore himself differently, and truly became a different man. He produced a different impression on others. The career by which we now know him dates from the moment in which he refused to be dismissed from Columbia and was able to persuade his senior colleagues to value him as he wished to be valued. I never knew, nor did he, what accounted for the sudden access of self-esteem which made it possible for him to handle his dismissal as he did, but it resulted not only in his reinstatement but also in his taking new command of his life. The success of his confrontation with his department was not a cure for all the ills of his mind and soul. It did not rid him of his sporadic difficulty in writing, nor of his depressions, but he was never again lacking in an authority appropriate to his capacities. In an entry in his notebooks dated June 1936 he wrote:

> Going through change of life and acquiring a new dimension. . . . No longer measure all things by linear Marxian yardstick. But this is symbolic. A new emotional response to all things. New response to people, a new tolerance, a new interest. A sense of invulnerability. The result of my successful explosion at Columbia? The feeling that I can now write with a new illumination, getting rid of that rigid linear method that has irritated me in my reviewing for so long. . . .

"The result of my successful explosion at Columbia?" he asks himself. Decidedly this was the emotional sequence. One wonders how he could even ask the question.

It has been generally assumed by people interested in Lionel's

Columbia career that he was threatened with the loss of his job because he was a Jew and the University did not want Jews as teachers, especially as teachers of English. I tried to make clear in my brief memoir, "Lionel Trilling: A Jew at Columbia," which I published in *Commentary* a few years after Lionel's death, that this is too simplistic an explanation of what happened. It is true that in the thirties Columbia, like the other private universities of the country, operated on a quota system; it took only a small number of Jewish students and had few Jews as teachers. The English Department was especially protected against "outsiders"; it was felt that the Anglo-Saxon tradition could not be entrusted to Jewish instructors. But although the fact that Lionel was a Jew was included in the various statements which bear on why he was not to be reappointed and must therefore be supposed to have been germane to his dismissal, it was not the whole or even the major reason for his being let go. Indeed, his religion probably had as little weight with his department as the other charges which accompanied it, that he was a Marxist and a Freudian. In 1932 when Lionel had been made an instructor, he had been a Communist sympathizer. But this would seem to have worried my father more than it worried the University. If in 1936 he could still say of himself, as he did, that he had been continuing to measure all things by the Marxian yardstick, he says this as a complaint and chiefly he relates it to a rigidity or "linear quality" in his critical manner. For three of the last four years he had been an avowed anti-Communist, or at least an avowed anti-Stalinist, and he is glad to be shed of the detritus of this indoctrination. Even as late as 1939 there were vestiges in Lionel's work of his previous Marxism; the publication for which he then wrote most comfortably was *Partisan Review,* which had been launched as a journal of Marxist opinion—traces of the Marxist habit of thought which still lingered in his work perhaps reflected his association with that magazine. This in no way disturbed his relation to the University. As to the charge that he was a Freudian, this would seem to have been based largely on rumor or speculation. While it is likely that without mentioning his own analysis Lionel spoke of his confidence in psychoanalysis with his younger colleagues or even with his older students, he had not yet written about Freud nor was he teaching Freud's work. All these charges leveled against him by his department were merely the means by which it explained a decision which it would itself have had difficulty in accounting for more accurately. When a senior member of the department said that as a Jew, a Marxist, and a Freudian, Lionel was not happy at Columbia, what he was of course saying was that he was himself not happy with Jews and Marxists and Freudians, but this does not actually tell us why he and his colleagues were so unhappy with Lionel that they did not want to renew his appointment. The fact is that he made them uncomfortable for reasons which they would not have been able to name. They did not know where he was going with his dissertation, nor were they sure that his was the kind of teaching they wanted from their instructors. They did not know the direction which his life was taking. Most important, they felt that he was lacking in force. He did not command their respect. There were other external factors which bolstered their decision to drop him. His presence in the department had been compromised from the first by the way in which his appointment had been made: Professor Ashley Thorndike, then the departmental chairman, had engaged Lionel without consulting his senior colleagues. Why Thorndike had reached out to him in this way, Lionel would never learn. Perhaps he recognized Lionel's potentialities before they were visible to the other members of the department, or it is even possible that he was using Lionel to test the waters to see if a Jew could swim in them. Whatever, his unilateral decision had annoyed the other professors, and their annoyance carried over to Lionel. The department was also aware of Raymond Weaver's entrenched hostility to Lionel. Professor Weaver was famous as the "discoverer" of Herman Melville and he had been one of Lionel's undergraduate teachers. It was while Lionel was still an undergraduate that he had run afoul of him. All but the gaiters, Weaver looked like a bishop and he spoke like a bishop. Lionel had no gift for mimicry but one day he had undertaken to do an imitation of Weaver for his classmates; unseen, Weaver had come into the room and witnessed the performance. Many years later Lionel would contribute a fond recollection of Weaver to a volume of Columbia reminiscences, *University on the Heights,* in which he recalled the days when Weaver was his enemy. "The word has an archaic ring which makes it seem absurd," Lionel wrote, "but Weaver's system of feeling *was* archaic, by choice, and as he made a cult of friendship, so he made a cult of enmity, both very Renaissance in their intensity." And finally there was Lionel's dissertation director, Emery Neff, who perhaps most conspicuously had Lionel's academic future in his keeping. Teachers gain distinction from the distinction of their students. In 1936 Lionel had been working on his dissertation for five years with virtually nothing to show for it. This could not have been pleasing to Emery Neff. The concatenation of circumstances which led to Lionel's being dropped was surely not favorable. Nevertheless, what finally lay behind his dismissal was none of these external factors but something in Lionel's own conduct and bearing. The decision to drop him was altered the moment he altered his behavior. There was one unequivocal truth in the department's explanation of why Lionel was being let go: he was indeed unhappy. But he was not unhappy because he was at Columbia. He was unhappy because his life was unsatisfactory to him. His wife—I—had come through a dangerous illness but had been left with psychological symptoms which signally interfered with his freedom of movement. His family, unable to take care of itself, had thrown all its financial and emotional burdens upon him. More and more he felt of himself that he was being professionally outdistanced by everyone of his generation. He began to believe that he would never realize his ambitions, and he lost pride. His manner, his manner of being, invited denigration. The image he presented to the world was one of powerlessness. For him to change this and impose upon his department an image of determination and deep inner strength was an extraordinary feat of self-renovation. There is evidence in Lionel's notebooks that anger was one of the roads by which his new set of mind was achieved. When I published "Lionel Trilling: A Jew at Columbia," I was not yet aware that Lionel had left his own detailed hour-by-hour memorandum of his dismissal and reinstatement: whom he saw, what was said to him, and what he replied. I had gathered together his untidy journals soon after his death but without reading them; Lionel had never shared these notebooks with me and I was reluctant to invade his privacy. Then in 1984 *Partisan Review* asked me whether there was something of his to include in its fiftieth anniversary issue. I thought it appropriate that he appear there. I had already published his early unpublished essay "The Changing Myth of the Jew," as well as the essay "Why We Read Jane Austen," which was near completion when Lionel died. He had left no other unpublished work and it occurred to me that the journals might yield some publishable material. Christopher Zinn, a graduate student at New York University, went through the notebooks for me and found Lionel's account of his Columbia confrontation.

My 1979 essay "Lionel Trilling: A Jew at Columbia" was in fact written to correct a series of mistaken statements by Sidney Hook in early chapters of his autobiography which had appeared in advance of the book's publication. In one of these excerpts Hook had reported that he first met Whittaker Chambers through Lionel; the meeting, he said, had taken place at a lunch which Lionel had set up to enable Hook to tell Chambers his criticism of the theory of social fascism. While I cannot speak of the matter with certainty, I think it highly improbable that this meeting took place. Lionel was never much interested in the debate of Communist theory and his connection with Chambers was not of a sort to have suggested this kind of social arrangement. Too, Lionel would not have been likely to choose a vegetarian restaurant or any restaurant in the neighborhood specified by Hook as the location of this lunch;

Lionel had no taste for vegetarianism and he was seldom in the East 20's or 30's. My guess is that after so many years, Hook was perhaps confusing Lionel with Meyer Schapiro: Schapiro was not only friendly with Chambers but was much drawn to the discussion of radical theory. He also frequently worked at the Morgan Library, which is in the neighborhood where Hook locates this meeting. But Hook's report of such a lunch is of less interest, and surely less worth disputing, than his strange assertion that when Lionel was threatened with the loss of his job at Columbia, it was he, Hook, who devised the strategy which reversed the decision. In Hook's view Lionel was being dropped because he was a Jew. According to his story he advised Lionel to warn the English Department that Columbia's reputation as a liberal institution would be forever tarnished were Lionel to be dismissed because of his religion. Presumably Lionel took his advice and miraculously this resulted in his reinstatement. But there was yet more. Hook would have us believe that he was not only responsible for Lionel's having retained his instructorship but that several years later, when Lionel had completed his dissertation, he contrived for Lionel's promotion by instructing him to send a copy of his *Arnold* to Columbia's President Butler. The move had eventuated in Lionel's being advanced to tenure. The truth of the matter is that Hook made neither this nor any other intervention on Lionel's behalf at Columbia. Although Lionel had great regard for Hook's intellectual powers, at no time did Hook have anything to do with Lionel's teaching career. Lionel talked freely among our friends about his threatened dismissal and it is not inconceivable that he asked Hook's advice about how to respond to it. But if Hook actually gave him the advice which he outlines in his autobiography, Lionel never followed it. Nor was it Hook who suggested that Lionel send his dissertation to President Butler. This crucial suggestion came from Irwin Edman, who had been one of Lionel's teachers and was now a friend. Edman was thoroughly experienced in the ways of Columbia (which Hook of course was not), yet even so, Lionel resisted the idea of bringing himself to Butler's attention in this way. He would not have considered it if the proposal had come from anyone less versed in Columbia protocol. I clearly recall that Lionel even inquired of Edman how he was supposed to inscribe the book and how he should address Butler in his accompanying letter. These were all matters of which Hook would of course have known nothing. He had no experience of Columbia.

Apparently even the discovery of Lionel's own memorandum of his dismissal failed to convince Hook that it was not he to whom Lionel owed his continuing Columbia career. He never conceded his mistake. Lionel's record of his confrontation with his department was obviously made in haste. The entries in his notebook are written as economically as possible; all the names are abbreviated. Jacques B., or JB, is of course Barzun. Steeves is Harrison Ross Steeves, the new chairman of the College English Department. Mark is Mark Van Doren. Everett is the Bentham scholar, Charles Everett. Weaver is Raymond Weaver. Dick is Harry K. Dick, a senior professor in the department. E.E.N. is Emery Neff. Irwin is Irwin Edman. 65-6 refers to English 65-6, a course in the history of English literature. Colloq. is the Colloquium. The books referred to in the entry of 6 May are *Sons and Lovers* by D. H. Lawrence, *Intermezzo* by Arthur Schnitzler, and *Point Counter Point* by Aldous Huxley. The following is Lionel's memorandum in full. To read it in its entirety is to see that although the fact that Lionel was a Jew undoubtedly contributed to his department's—or, at any rate, Emery Neff's—lack of ease with him at this early stage of his teaching career, it was but one small element in the kind of confused and complex judgment which so often determines a person's advancement or rejection in his place of employment.

Tues April 20 (1936)

Jacques B called to report content of his dinner with Steeves as follows. That I am considered the most brilliant of the younger instructors, that I am most devoted to teaching of all of them & most conscientious. That I have done brilliantly in the colloquium & am irreplace-able in that course: that my two yrs of work in the 19th century were splendid. With freshmen I am not so utterly successful: a little too much for them (not true, I think). The reason for dismissal is that as a Jew, a Marxist, a Freudian I am uneasy. This hampers my work and makes me unhappy. E. E. Neff (a Columbia professor!) concurs in this opinion! (And Mark?)

Tues May 5 (1936)
Interview with Steeves. 1½ hours. Me cool and positive. Him friendly and "realistic."

Explains it as decision of college profs. (i.e. Neff, Weaver, Van D., Everett, Dick). Two reasons adduced: 1. That it is better for me to get out, I being superior to all the other men in the Dept who because of their inferi-ority or mediocrity . . . will easily get jobs at any time. Believe me unhappy here. Act motivated by concern for my welfare. I replied that if this is so I might well have been consulted, that I agreed that it might be well for me to move on, that, however, I had plans which involved a few more years of teaching at C in order to get started on my work of writing. (2) That I had been failing as a teacher. That I irritated many freshman students by talk-ing about literature as sociology and psychology. I asked how his run of the mill teachers taught Babbitt and Point Counterpoint [sic] as anything else. Said that E.E.N. con-sidered that my 1st year of work in 65-6 was excellent but felt I had fallen off in 2nd year. Replied that this con-stituted disingenuousness on N.'s part, for he had assured me that my work had been good, that my removal had been for administrative reasons, that he was trying to get the course for me again. Said at a later time N. dissatisfied with my grad. work. Replied that I considered this equally disingenuous in view of his praise. Said Neff was an excellent friend. Replied Neff knew less about me than almost anyone.

I said that nothing could convince me that I was not a good teacher, & that 90% of my students thought me so. I said I could say this because I had not the slightest intention of trying to convince *him*. Said I thought I was particularly adapted to Columbia as I thought he wanted it to be. He said that he was sure that I was a very good teacher as teaching should be done but that they needed routine men, that the whole dept was to be cleaned out, the most routine men (Eng A & C) to be kept the longest. — Said that my work in Colloq. could not be done better. I said that I was not unhappy at Colum though I might be unhappy, & that my emotions had nothing to do with my teaching. I said he was making an awful indictment of his department if what he said was true. He inclined to agree and include the whole college system.— I asked him how he knew of my condition & its effects on my work. Said it was generally felt. I forced him to say it was a mere intuition. At the end he said would I want to stay another year if the other men agreed. I said I was not asking for it, nor had I the slightest thought of doing so but that I had no desire to be quixotic and that a year would be useful. He said he would see how things *went* (meaning my teaching) and he would delay positive action. I said since I felt that his altruistic motive had to be rejected, and since I preferred to consider that I was being dropped because I was a bad (or too good) teacher, I felt that I could not accept this implication that I was rebuked and would try to improve. He said I was not being rebuked and he would talk to the other men. I said only if he understood and would make clear that I had not asked for an extension of time. He said he understood this.

Tues May 5 (1936) Interview with Mark 5:30–6:15 P.M.
Told him account of interview with Steeves. Listened and approved. Started to say he had no part in the meeting. I warned him that Steeves had said he had concurred. He said that when the attack on me had taken place he had not said anything. Why? Doesn't know. Could only say he admired me, that I was a nice fellow; weight of numbers was against him; had no evidence such as teaching a course with me. Did I not understand that? Might I not act in the same way? Yes I might but I should not feel very proud of it. He felt ashamed, said he.

Weaver had of course spoken against me but W. is usually discounted. Dick had been silent. Everett had said that he had certain reports from students: didn't set much store by them. Steeves rather silent.

(Says Weaver dislikes me because thinks I like to be stepped on too much: too meek. Said W. will be impressed by my standing up to Steeves!) . . .

Telephone conversation with Irwin May 5 (1936) 8:P.M.
Told him of interviews. . . . He told me of having lunch with Edgar Johnson. Neff sits down. Conversation turns to Schappes at C.C.N.Y. Edgar asks what doing about tenure at Columbia? Neff begins to make speech. Some people being fired for incompetence, some for their own good, some because they didn't fit. Irwin asked what about L.T., into what category does he fit? He is not . . . nor . . .—E.E.N. says that is very complicated. "I have followed L's career for a long time with the greatest interest. But . . . His great gift is his literary sense.["] Irwin: Seems good thing in a teacher of literature. E.E.N. But he

has involved himself with Ideas. . . . He is too sensitive . . . Doesn't fit because he is a Jew. At any rate,
he was appointed against the will of the dept!!

Called E.E.N. and made date to annihilate him on
Thursday.

6 May (1936) Interview with H.K. Dick 20 minutes
Stated case as put by Steeves. He replied that he
knew nothing of my teaching, saw no way he could know.
Knew nothing of effect of "happiness" on my teaching:
Said that he had heard some complaints about my emphasis on "Sociology." Said he did not teach "Lovers"
"Intermezzo" or "PCP" any more partly because of
feeling that it might shock boys & that they did not
understand the matters in works [sic]; also there was
consideration of parents' raised eyebrows. Said that the
cause of the movement to drop me was the general policy
of the department to "rotate." Insisted he knew nothing
of my teaching.

May 6 (1936)
J.B. reminds me of E. Neff's old sociological complex. In Eng 5M-6 he could think of nothing in a poem
save what it reflected—democracy, the factory system,
religious conflict etc. Caring nothing for the music or
mood. Of course he used to preach sociology and econ.
in literature to all of us. But my last conversation with
him about poetry brought out the opinion that ideas do
not matter in poetry—the music was everything. Interpretation obvious: in 1924 it was OK to write about Carlyle Mill & the factory conditions. But now it is getting
near and real and he is running for cover into "music."

May 7 (1936) Interview with Everett 11–11:15

Said I wanted to ask him about what he testified in the meeting. He said I must be sure that I do not believe there was unfriendliness to me at the meeting. I said cooly I was neither doubtful nor interested in the matter of friendship. He told me his part: it was as Mark had described it. I told him so. He said he could not do otherwise by his conscience than to tell the truth. I said of course but I said that I could do no otherwise by my pedagogical conscience than to raise hell to say that the way I taught was the right way. I asked him how he taught the books we used. He said he had great difficulty teaching PCP. He said I should not lose my head; that he had been fired once and that the situation had suddenly broken. I said I wasn't much interested.

Interview with Neff May 7 (1936) 12:15–1:30

He very friendly, I cold but amicable. Found it impossible to be furious with him personally but was inflexible in my positions. I gave a very clear and well-put summary of my interviews with Steeves & Van Doren. Told him what I had been told of his declaration about my 1) 65 work & 2) about my thesis.

He said about 1) that Steeves must be mistaken in the attribution. Had only the highest admiration of my work there as he had said to me. Told him to tell this to Steeves, said he wld. About 2) he said he had not wanted to tell me about his reservations about my thesis, because it was still inchoate (when else? I asked) & that he had mentioned them because he felt that my sociological tendencies had hidden my literary gifts in the thesis as in the classroom. But that his reservations were not fundamental.

He said that he did not want me to stay because my

position was bad and likely to get worse. In what way bad? He explained my question about my Jewish-sensitivity: had not meant that: had meant that I was too sensitive to Weaver's "brutality." I said I ignored it. He admitted that there was no fault to find with my teaching that could not be corrected by a word of suggestion to me. What it really got down to was that Weaver pressed hard & my contemporaries had disliked my teaching (and me presumably) & that this had counted. I blew up & asked him if he really meant to say that this minority, part of it unrepresented, had swung a majority. He said things always happened so. I used no uncertain terms.

He told me that the trouble had started with my appointment. Said it had been forced by Thorndike & put through without the democratic consent of the dept. Said he understood I had told Thorndike I was in trouble at Hunter, would get no job & was in desperate financial straits. I denied that I had ever spoken to Thorndike in this way. (Henry Ladd perhaps did.) (This accounts for Weaver's feeling I like to be stepped on?)

Finally I asked him if I might tell Steeves that in his (Neff's) opinion my dismissal had nothing to do with my teaching at all but only with the dislike of Weaver and a few of my contemporaries. He said, heartily, that I might quote him so and even gave me a formulation of that opinion to use.

I said that apparently I was being fired for all the qualities I admired in myself & that I considered the whole matter a triumph for me. He said (defending his success) that it was not a triumph but luck. —I did not admit at any point the decency of his getting me fired for my own good, though his absurd mind is sincere about it, I believe. He said the whole matter was not to have been as peremptory as it was with a short time set and hinted vaguely that it might be adjusted as to time. The whole business he had thought would be a warning not a dismissal: nonsense.

There remains to see Steeves and tell him what I now know and to insult Weaver, publicly if possible.

Note that Mark concurs with Steeves about Emery's position and intention!

Not everything which Lionel reported to me at the time as having transpired in these interviews is recorded in his journal. He told me, for instance, that in the middle of his interview with Emery Neff, Neff jumped up to shut the transom: Lionel was talking loudly and had called someone, either Weaver or Neff himself, a bastard, and Neff was afraid that passersby would hear him. He also omits from these notes what to me was the most extraordinary statement he made to his senior colleagues: his declaration that the English Department had never had, and never would have, anyone as good as he was. It was a monumental, indeed almost alarming, assertion for him to make in 1936 when we consider how little he had in actual accomplishment or reputation to support it. But his department had not been alarmed. It would seem to have been captivated by this change in deportment in someone of whom Weaver had said that he liked to be stepped on. Like most people, Lionel's senior colleagues preferred the company of the strong. Weaver was of course the member of the department to whom Lionel's transformation spoke most compellingly. In his description of Weaver many years later, Lionel would write: "He set great store by anger, which seemed to him a means of self-definition, an active as against a passive state." After Lionel's angry challenge of the department, Weaver made no further move for Lionel's dismissal. Soon his old hostility turned into warm friendship—if because of his homosexuality any tension remained in his attitude toward his former student, the weight of his feeling was now on the side of championship. Difficult as it may have been to be a Jew at Columbia in those distant days, it was a great deal more difficult to be a homosexual. Weaver was anguished by his sexual deviance but handled it with courage and manliness.

Lionel's journal has but one more reference to his threatened dismissal. A month after the last of his interviews with his department, when he now knows that he is not going to be let go, he writes of himself that he is "going through change of life and acquiring a new dimension." He conjectures that perhaps this is a result of his "successful explosion" at the University.

Even before his high drama at Columbia and his assurance that his job would continue, at least for a while, Lionel and I had begun to allow ourselves a bit more ease in our lives. In 1935 we rented a house in Babylon, Long Island, for the month of August and the following summer we spent several months in the neighboring town of Amityville. It would be several decades before we traveled in Europe; in the intervening years, our summer vacations largely consisted of going to Riverside Park in the early evenings and sitting on the grass watching the lights come on across the river. Other than when we were abroad, I never knew Lionel to take a vacation from work. A summer holiday, whether on Long Island or, after Jim was born, in Westport, Connecticut, merely meant a change of desk, and when I began to write, this became the pattern of my life as well; I still work every day on what I call my holidays. In both Babylon and Amityville we were without a car: we traveled to Long Island by railway, and to get about we walked or took a taxi. It was not then unusual to rely upon public transportation: few people we knew in the mid-thirties had cars. The Fadimans were summering in a house across the road from us in Babylon and had no car; neither did their visitors Sam and Bella Spewack, though the Spewacks were highly successful journalists and Broadway playwrights. My parents had had a car as far back as the First World War; I remember giving lifts to anyone in uniform and, most excitingly, I recall the night of the Armistice, when our brave little Chandler joined a flotilla of cars which inched its way down Ocean Parkway to Coney Island. The cars were tied together by the paper streamers which suddenly appeared from nowhere, and everyone was laughing and singing, boisterously happy. Neither of my parents learned to drive; in common with most of their Flatbush neighbors, they employed a chauffeur. At the age of fourteen or fifteen I had what purported to be a driving lesson from our young chauffeur, but I was in love with him and to demonstrate my helpless femininity I squealed with feigned terror and took my hands off the wheel as we approached a busy crossroads. He reported this to my mother and I was forbidden ever again to drive. Lionel's family had never owned a car; Lionel bought his first car and learned to drive when he was fifty-four. He liked to boast that he had taught himself to play tennis from a book, but he received professional driving instruction and passed his test on his first try. Once he was licensed, however, it was as if he were possessed by the devil of lawlessness. He not only drove too fast; he also flaunted his lack of regard both for rules and for common sense. On highways he ignored the demarcation of lanes and gave no notice of his intention to switch from one side of the road to another. The drivers whose lives he was putting at risk would shout at him, "What the hell do you think you're doing?" and Lionel would look at me in perplexity and ask why people were getting so excited. When he did stay in lane, he drove so close to the outer edge of the road that his tires grazed the curb; the car might at any moment be thrown into a spin. Even as a pedestrian, Lionel had a deficient sense of direction. I never knew him actually to get lost between Claremont Avenue and his Columbia office, but anyone whom he undertook to help negotiate these few blocks may to this day be wandering the city. When, as was often the case, he was a marshal at Commencement, there was the strong possibility that he would guide his distinguished guest to Broadway and the West End Café instead of to the platform. On highways he regularly overrode his exits and in the city he just as regularly missed his turns; he had a developed instinct for driving the wrong way on one-way streets. Witnessing his tortuous efforts to back into a parking space, I reminded myself that steering—steering anything: a horse, a bicycle, even a pair of roller skates—was a mystery into which he had never been inducted. After a few years he gave up driving and sold the car. I cheerfully accepted his accusation that I had undermined his confidence.

There was no doubt a connection between Lionel as driver and Lionel as swimmer, though swimming was an activity of which he had considerable experience. He swam very well but without any consciousness that cautions were sometimes demanded of swimmers. In Amityville we swam from a small strip of sand near where we lived. It was not a public beach and there were no lifeguards. Lionel worked at his desk in the mornings and early afternoons; in midafternoon we played tennis and swam. Elliot and Sylvia Cohen had taken the house next to ours, and David and Bettina Sinclair were living around the corner. Usually it was late afternoon by the time we got to the Sound; the pleasure boats were returning to their moorings. Swimming powerfully, never lifting his face from the water, Lionel swam directly into their path. The Cohens and Sinclairs were as frightened as I: we all of us would stand at the edge of the water screaming at him. But Lionel never heard us and when we spoke with him later we were unable to persuade him that he must occasionally lift his face from the water and see what he was heading into. He was also a maddening tennis player, who put himself to the game with life-endangering determination. Virtually everyone who now appears on a tennis court has a better command of the game than any one of us had when we were young. There has been a generational improvement in the way that tennis is played. Lionel was not a good tennis player even for his time, but he was also not the worst. His problem, a serious one, was his overzealousness: compensating in energy for what he lacked in skill, he raced furiously around the court, never where he should properly have been, yet never refusing a ball. After he had played a few games, his face would be purple and his lips black; his eyes had all but disappeared into their dark caverns. Wherever we played, whether in the country or in the city, the people with whom we played tennis seem not to have been well-chosen. Like croquet, tennis seemed to bring out the worst in our friends: it encouraged Bettina's bright-eyed Radcliffe competitiveness and it made an anti-Semite of David Sinclair—he was not an intellectual, and tennis became the arena in which he demonstrated his contempt for the inferior physical prowess of his brainy Jewish opponents. Most often our New York tennis partners were Elsa and Jim Grossman. However disturbing his performance, Lionel at least knew what a tennis stroke was supposed to look like. For Jim Grossman, form was folly. He came to the tennis court as to a court of law, to win. Gripping his racquet in mid-handle, he darted about the court like an exploding firecracker. He never drove or lobbed; he popped. Unfailingly he got under every ball and returned it: pop, pop, pop, it went over the net. He was not playing tennis; he complacently acknowledged that he was playing hit-the-ball. Dedicated though they were to a higher ideal than this, Lionel's exertions were a menace to his health—or so I rationalized my secret desire that he give up the game. I was especially embarrassed by his inability to keep score. During the war we often spent our spring and summer weekends at Lost Lake, near Brewster, where Bettina had a house with her second husband. The absorbing occupation of the Lost Lake community was tennis. It was a profanation of their game to have to play with Lionel, but it was an even greater tax on their tolerance when they had to suffer his confusions as a referee in their tournaments. He regularly volunteered for this position.

If it was Lionel's bad fortune to have me so close a witness of his down-spiraling career in tennis, it was his good fortune that I was excluded, even as a spectator, from the sport to which he in later life transferred his enthusiasm, trout fishing. His former student Quentin Anderson, who had become a friend and Columbia colleague, introduced Lionel to trout fishing. They usually fished on Long Island and were joined by Jack Thompson, who taught at Stony Brook; sometimes as well by Charles Everett of the Columbia English Department. I think that as much as Lionel enjoyed working a stream, he delighted in the paraphernalia of trout fishing, the clothes one wore, the elaborate gear he prepared for fishing trips, and the rituals which soon grew up around them: there was an Italian roadhouse at which the fishing party had to stop for beer and sausage on its way to the stream and again on its trip home. Lionel might not be much given to mythologizing himself or his life; he left this to other people. But he mythologized fishing and gave it a unique place among his activities. He was awed to learn that a Canadian friend, the psychoanalyst Bruce Ruddick, knew Roderick Haig-Brown, the famous Canadian authority on fly fishing. Ruddick arranged for them to meet but the occasion was not a success; Lionel was too impressed with Haig-Brown's expertness as a fisherman to dare talk about fishing and Haig-Brown was apparently too impressed with Lionel as a literary critic to dare talk about writing. I had a catastrophic social evening of my own connected with Lionel's trout fishing. Once, when he and Quentin Anderson and Jack Thompson and Charles Everett went off to fish together, I invited their wives to dinner. These were lively and gifted women but the venture was disastrous. Perhaps it was premature: this was before women's liberation and women had not yet imagined the possibility of a social engagement without men. We were not four women enjoying each other's company but four fishing widows putting ourselves in readiness for the funeral pyre.

Lionel's Columbia job was restored to him but he did not know for how long. In 1936–37 the future was still as uncertain for him as it had always been; before it could take shape, there was a dissertation to write. But it was different to be working on his dissertation now. It was still a chore but it was no longer a doom. Shortly after Lionel's confrontation with his department, we moved from

114th Street to 620 West 116th Street, near Riverside Drive. In our seven years of marriage, it was our sixth move and turned out to be of extended duration. We stayed in these four rooms for nineteen years, seven of them after Jim was born, though Jim's arrival forced Lionel to give up his study and rent a workroom elsewhere. In the early fifties, while we were still on 116th Street, Quentin Anderson one day remarked to Lionel that we ought to move; the way he put it was that a man in Lionel's position owed it to himself to live in a better apartment than ours. Both Lionel and I found this a startling statement. It had not previously occurred to either of us that there was anything wrong with the way we lived or that Lionel had a position to maintain. I often think of this when I read references to what was supposed to have been our privileged life.

ELEVEN

In 1937 William Phillips and Philip Rahv, fresh from their break with the Communists, took over the previously Communist-controlled *Partisan Review* and launched it as a Marxist but anti-Stalinist journal. Lionel appeared in its first issue and for more than two decades he was one of its regular contributors. It is the *locus classicus* of the work of his middle years. Six of the sixteen essays in *The Liberal Imagination,* which was published in 1950, and three of the nine essays in his 1955 collection, *The Opposing Self,* first appeared there. Lionel was thirty-two years old in 1937 and he had published extensively in the best literary magazines of the period; his work was acceptable to the most exacting editors. But it was seldom solicited and it was little responded to. He came into public view only with the publication of his *Matthew Arnold* in 1939. One wonders, then, why he was invited to contribute to the first issue of the new journal, and the obvious explanation is that the editors were not yet in a position to venture far afield for their writers. Among the other contributors to the first number of the magazine were Delmore Schwartz, Lionel Abel, William Troy, Arthur Mizener, and James Agee; none of them had yet established his reputation. It was through his work in *Partisan Review* that Delmore Schwartz would become known in the literary community; Mizener's well-received biography of F. Scott Fitzgerald, *The Far Side of Paradise,* did not appear until 1951; and it was not until after the publication of *Let Us Now Praise Famous Men,* his book with Walker Evans, that Agee came to public notice. In the contributors' box of the first issue of *Partisan Review,* Lionel is identified only as a teacher at Columbia and a contributor to Malcolm Cowley's *After the Genteel Tradition.*

In addition to Phillips and Rahv, the names of F. W. Dupee, Dwight Macdonald, Mary McCarthy, and George L. K. Morris appeared on the masthead of the new magazine. Talk had it that Morris, a member of a distinguished and wealthy New York family, supplied the magazine with much of its early funding. No doubt all of the editors participated in the formulation of policy. But in the first years of its life, Macdonald was perhaps the most visible of them in the pages of *Partisan Review:* it was his initials which were likely to be attached to the most thundering of its editorials, in particular those in opposition to impending war in Europe. Launched though *Partisan Review* was with a brave declaration of independence, the heavy shadow of the Communist Party hung over its boast of freedom. "*Partisan Review* is aware of its responsibility to the revolutionary movement in general," the magazine announces on its first appearance, "but we disclaim obligation to any of its organized political expressions. Indeed we think that the cause of revolutionary literature is best served by a policy of no commitments to any political party." What the new magazine means by "revolutionary literature" we are not told in this first editorial statement, nor will this ever be defined except negatively, by what the magazine refuses to include in its pages. Still addressing—and challenging—the Communist Party's domination of the country's intellectual culture, the new periodical continues its statement of purpose: "Marxism in culture, we think, is first of all an instrument of analysis and evaluation; and if, in the last instance, it prevails over other disciplines it does so through the medium of democratic controversy." In its first year, the subtitle of the new journal is "A Literary Monthly." The next year, shifting to quarterly publication, it describes itself as "A Quarterly of Literature and Marxism." This accurately defines its intention: until America enters the Second World War, the chief emphasis of the magazine, certainly in matters of politics, is Marxist. Yet for all its revolutionary fervor, it is for its insight into the hidden communications of literature that *Partisan Review* is from its start most valuable. The ways in which politics and culture bear upon each other are many and subtle and, from its inception, the first occupation of the new journal is to explore the connection between the two, especially in the writing of those who knowingly or unknowingly submit themselves to the influence of Stalinism. Throughout its life, even when *Partisan Review* will no longer be Marxist, its high literary dedication and its concern with the politics of culture will be what give it its distinctive character.

Partisan Review's statement of purpose is at once enough limiting and broad to accommodate anyone of left-wing persuasion who is not locked into the sterile orthodoxies of Stalinism, and it produces a lively first issue. Edmund Wilson traces the parallel between Flaubert's socialism in *The Sentimental Education* and Marx's treatment of the revolution of '48 in *The Eighteenth Brumaire*. Dwight Macdonald examines the way in which the *New Yorker* deals with class in America: the piece so much impresses that magazine that it gives him a lifelong place on its staff. Delmore Schwartz publishes a story, "In Dreams Begin Responsibilities," which catapults him into early fame. James T. Farrell presents a chapter from a "novel in progress." Lionel's contribution is a review of Robert Briffault's *Europa in Limbo;* the novel is clearly third-rate but in the pious political atmosphere of the time it has been praised for its portrayal of the decadence of capitalist Europe during the First World War. The review is not impressive; Lionel's dismissal of Briffault's mindless reading of history is chiefly interesting for its ritualistic deference to Marx. Of the author of this "license-and-rape" theory of social upheaval Lionel writes: "Mr. Briffault, I take it, is supposed to be a Marxist and this makes the vulgarity doubly culpable. If there is one thing the dialectic of history teaches it is an attitude on cultural matters the very opposite of [his] splenetic one. But that attitude is difficult and complex." With his first piece for the new magazine, Lionel is recording his taste for difficulty and complexity, a preference which will be emblematic of his work throughout his career. Happily, his tone of disdain will soon disappear.

The new *Partisan Review* arrived in a world which had considerably altered since 1933 when we had left the National Committee for the Defense of Political Prisoners. The country was no longer in political and economic crisis; under Roosevelt's resourceful leadership, the worst of the Depression was behind us. Four years earlier, Nazism had been only a menacing possibility in Germany; now it was in full vicious command. Over the decade Stalin had consolidated his despotic rule of the Soviet Union; now he fortified his dictatorship with his infamous Moscow trials, the most recent and dramatic of them the trial of the old Bolsheviks Zinoviev and Kamenev, whom he accused of conspiring with Trotsky and the German Gestapo to topple the Soviet regime. Spain was divided in an anguishing civil war. Although England and America refused to intervene on behalf of the Spanish Loyalists, there was no lack of sympathy for them in either country; in America an army of volunteers, the Lincoln Brigade, was organized to go to their aid, and along with this military battalion went an army of American and English writers and journalists intent on publicizing the heroic struggle. In retrospect, surely the most arresting feature of the period was the absence in the democracies of any liberal protest against Nazism comparable to the liberal opposition to Franco's fascism in Spain. In 1937 we were not entirely ignorant of the situation in Germany. Hitler's "final solution" had not yet been embarked upon—this would have to wait another five years, until 1942—but the Nuremberg laws had been enacted in 1935 and the effective elimination of Jews from German life was already well in train. Although the Nazi concentration camps were still only labor camps, not extermination camps, like Auschwitz or Buchenwald, their grim character was no secret from the rest of the world. The plight of the Jews of Germany had even entered its fiction. Feuchtwanger's novel *The Oppermanns,* a thinly disguised account of the fate of his family under the Nazis, had appeared in this country as far back as 1934. Lionel had reviewed it in August of that year. But even though we knew what was happening in Germany, we failed to *feel* what we knew. It had an only minor place in our moral-political consciousness. If one could afford it, one perhaps supplied the affidavits which were required for the entrance of German refugees into the United States, but this was an act of personal philanthropy much more than it was an expression of public outrage. With clenched fists and upraised arms, we and our fellow-traveling friends had pledged ourselves to the defeat of the capitalist oppressors. There were no arms being raised nor fists being clenched, none that I saw, in defiance of the Nazi dictator. The liberals of this country failed even to raise their voices in protest of Roosevelt's restriction on the admission of German refugees to the United States. Einstein came to America in 1935 and was followed a few years later by Thomas Mann. They were received as honored guests, not as victims; in the glare of their celebrity we lost sight of the tyrant from whom they fled. The little that Lionel and I knew of the actuality of Nazism—and I have no reason to suppose that we were untypical—was what we could adduce from the weary but uncomplaining middle-aged men who peddled domestic supplies, dish mops and towels, soaps, sardines, a wonderful raspberry syrup called *himbeersaft,* from apartment to apartment in New York. These were the lucky Jews of Germany: they had lost their land and language and their means of livelihood but they had managed to get out of their country early; they were still alive. None of them spoke of what they had suffered in Germany or of what they had escaped. It was as if they had been instructed not to inflict their sorrows on the country which had given them refuge. Perhaps they had read a piece by Clare Boothe Luce in *Life,* mocking German refugees for talking their "bird talk" in our streets. The American press in the early and mid-thirties dealt with Hitler as it dealt with Stalin: it told us little of Stalin's murderous regime and it told us little of Hitler's virulent anti-Semitism. This would come back to me during the war in the Persian Gulf when the press, representing itself as our only source of reliable information, was in such full cry against the government because it had curtailed the military access of the newspeople; I asked myself what justification the press had had in the history of our century for now thinking of itself as the sole guardian and purveyor of truth. Almost alone in the profession, Dorothy Thompson broke the silence which surrounded the whole subject of Nazism. Repeatedly she went on the air to warn this country of Hitler's malignity and growing strength. The American public was not pleased with her news: a popular joke of the period was that she was having her menopause on the radio. Even many years later, at Dorothy Thompson's death, a veiled note of disapproval would creep into the obituaries of this premature and too-urgent anti-Nazi—the *New York Times* could find no space for a letter I wrote in commemoration of her foresight and courage. Yet even while we were this heedless of Hitler's atrocities, the stationery of the League Against War and Fascism, that most prominent and successful of Communist-front operations, spilled over with the names of the writers and artists and entertainers who supported it. With Russia not yet prepared for war, Stalin would have us believe that any war, even war against fascism, or perhaps particularly war against fascism, was as abhorrent as fascism itself. In fact, the two were inexorably linked. Stalin's secret protection of Hitler, which had begun in the first years of the decade with his refusal to allow the German Communist Party to make a united front with the German Social Democrats to halt the Nazis, continued through the signing of the Soviet-Nazi pact in August 1939, right up to Hitler's invasion of Poland.

Between the founding of *Partisan Review* in 1937 and its issue of Summer 1939, on the eve of the outbreak of war in Europe, Nazism is not mentioned in the magazine. Hitler's name does not appear in its pages. The word "fascism" appears frequently but as an abstraction—the magazine would seem to have been unable to take German fascism out of the realm of political theory and concretize it in the reality of Hitlerism. It had no difficulty of this kind in dealing with the Communism of Stalin. To this it brought a firsthand experience of the Communist-controlled radical movement of our own country: the editors had been burnt in that fire. For the magazine itself and those of us who were in its orbit, anti-Stalinism had become our expertise and our moral mission. We understood the character of life in Stalin's Russia and the influence of Stalinism in the culture of the democracies as few intellectuals understood it then or since. Among liberals, the anti-Communist position has regularly and prejudicially been associated with political reaction. Undoubtedly even in the thirties some of the opposition to Communism was generated on the right, but *Partisan Review* was far from being on the right. It was launched as a left-wing journal, a journal of revolution, and it remained a revolutionary journal until America was at war. At no time did it have an organizational alliance with any party of the left. It veered, however, toward Trotskyism. Among dissident revolutionary movements this was the faction of choice. Only with America's entry into the war would *Partisan Review* alter its political course and cease to be a journal of Marxism. From this point forward, it would permanently divorce itself from revolution while locating itself unspecifiedly left of center. There was never a time, not in the thirties or forties or ever, that its anti-Communism—or Lionel's or mine—had its source in the fear of a Communist revolution in our own country. Once the wishful dreams of the thirties were dispelled, no one of normal intelligence could suppose that a workers' revolution was going to take place in the United States. A Communist revolution in our own country had indeed never been a Communist goal. Even in the sixties, when the slogan "Better Red than Dead" would be popular among American left-wing intellectuals, although in a debate sponsored by *Commentary* this position could be literally and rousingly defended by Stuart Hughes and C. P. Snow, it was usually addressed not so much to the actual threat of a Communist takeover in America as to a defense of the Communist enterprise in general. The threat we and our friends feared as anti-Communists was not imaginary. We feared Stalin's influence upon American liberal thought. Nazism never had an intellectual constituency in the democracies, not even at the height of Hitler's power. Hitler's only following in the United States was a lunatic fringe of German-American Bundists. But the support which the Soviet Union had in the West was formidable. Its propaganda network penetrated deep into our society; its purpose was to undermine our democratic resolve vis-à-vis the Soviet Union. *Partisan Review* was not unique among American periodicals in its opposition to Stalin's Communism but it was unique in its perception of the part which Stalinism played in our culture and in its understanding of the uses of culture in Soviet politics and foreign policy.

Lionel's personal revolution, the "change of life" in the wake of his Columbia confrontation on which he reports in his notebooks, was at first more apparent in his correspondence than in his published writing, even his writing for the new magazine. At Columbia he had a new office mate and friend, Alan Brown. Alan was a Harvard graduate five years Lionel's junior. This new young instructor had considerably more sophistication in the area of cultural politics—the sphere in which issues of culture connect with matters of public policy—than most of the people in the Columbia English Department. He not only shared Lionel's anti-Stalinism but, yet more reassuring, the two could talk about politics without falling into the theoretical hagglings which provided so much diversion for Lionel's friends downtown. In addition, he was someone who could appreciate the play of personalities in Lionel's dealings with their senior colleagues. In the year which was so crucial for Lionel at Columbia, Alan contracted tuberculosis; he spent the academic year 1936–37 curing at Saranac Lake in the Adirondacks. Departing for Saranac with his wife and infant daughter, Alan took with him the comforting knowledge that his job at the University was being held for him and that he would be paid during his absence; Professor Ernest Hunter Wright, head of the University English Department, had written him: "Professor Steeves [head of the College department] and I have arranged with Dean Hawkes and Mr. Fackenthal [Provost of the University] to grant you a year's leave of absence with pay. The other members of the College staff are very kindly arranging to take care of your work during the interval." The formulation is disingenuous. It is made to appear that the University is continuing Alan's salary and that his courses are being distributed among other members of the department, presumably for extra pay. What actually happened was that four members of the junior staff, Lionel among them, took over Alan's classes without pay so that his salary would not be cut off. Each added, that is, a fifth course to the four he already taught. Alan knew nothing about this until many years later. Lionel wrote regularly to Alan during his absence, reporting the news of the University and commenting on political developments in the world. While letter writing was not Lionel's best means of communication, his letters to Alan at Saranac tend to be more relaxed and discursive than is usual in his correspondence, and they more accurately catch the rhythms of his speech. They also—sometimes at the risk of sounding like reasoned briefs for an argument—tell us a good deal of how Lionel was thinking about current affairs at this stage of his life. But there is humorous relief as well. Like Lionel, Alan was working on his Ph.D. The two bored candidates exchanged comic verses on their shared ordeal of producing

dissertations. The title of Lionel's poem is "The Scholar's Tale."
In a donnish conceit, he describes it as "a newly discovered frag-
ment of L. Trilling" and a "reprint from PMLA":

> One spends long years in the nice warm bog
> Of the quiet life of the pedagogue,
> Grinning at life and life's sad perversity
> From behind the walls of a liberal university.
> One grins and one sits and one notes on cards
> Significant facts about minor bards
> Who lived and sang to provide the data
> For the theses that advertise Alma Mater.
> One sits and one notes for no larger fee
> Than the bliss of becoming a Ph.D.

And the poem concludes:

> The thesis is done! The cocoon yields a scholar!
> It's a nice clean trade. (How filthy the dollar!)
> And for years of sitting behold the reward:
> One's thesis thin and one's arsis broad!

In August 1936 we vacationed in Amityville on Long Island. From
Amityville Lionel wrote to Alan:

> . . . Your letter made me quite nostalgic: I spent so
> many summers at Saranac, camping on the lake—Eagle
> Island, you can see it from the head of the lake—and I
> know how exciting the air and the country are this time
> of the year. We have our first touch of fall today so yours
> must have come some time ago.
> A letter isn't any place to talk about the Russian bus-
> iness [the latest Moscow trials]; it needs a novel or an
> autobiography. Everybody I know is very confused and

dejected; I know that, though for long my feelings about Russia have been mixed enough to make me try to be philosophical, I feel now that I must completely overhaul all my ideas and my whole character. But there are a few objective things that one can say.

First—there is the political significance of the event. You will remember that at the Kiroff trial some of these fellows admitted to a "moral" or "logical" guilt of Kiroff's death. General feeling is that they were coerced to this. Now why the sudden revival of the whole business with the attack on Stalin Almighty included? We must remember that the Trotskyist party in Spain is very powerful and its influence very wide. According to some, it is the spearhead of the radical forces. In France the Trotskyists, though numerically small, are rather influential. At any rate, they are the militant group of the proletariat and they feel that the Popular Front is going to end up as a betrayal of the working class. Their agitation has been met by police suppression by the Blum government— at the instigation of the Stalinists. In short, Russia fears Trotskyist revolution; it fears revolution in any form, of course, but especially the Trotskyist power that may emerge. The Russian trials are an attempt to discredit Trotskyism. In effect, it is a sabotage of the revolutionary movement. There is also the possibility, claimed by some, that the Trotskyist—or some dissident—movement is strong in Russia itself.

Second: Most of the people involved in the trial have either repudiated Trotsky or have been repudiated by him. I myself do not believe in Trotsky's complicity. I am not entirely sure how far the mutual repudiation went, however, for I get this at second hand.

So much for objective fact or what may be fact. We may then imagine coercion at work to produce the kind of hideous spectacle [of] the trial. As you say, it is inconceivable that these old Bolsheviks should not thunder out their political reasons when they had the opportunity. But would the opportunity have been given to them if the officials were not sure that there would be no thunder? We can imagine threats of reprisal to families unless this particular show were gone through, implicating Trotsky and blessing Stalin; even with death a certainty, these men would knuckle under to protect wives and children.

On the other hand, there is, as you say, religious hysteria. When it becomes not only a crime but a sin to be in opposition—I mean not counter-revolution but just political opposition, say, about the *rate* of collectivization—then I suppose men may possibly get the horrible emotions of the defendants forced on them.

Well, but all this settles nothing for me: except to convince me that I must always have a reservation of faith in anything. The revolutionary heroes—and they certainly were that—were disgusting. Russia was disgusting. Perhaps every revolution must betray itself. Perhaps every good thing and every good man has the seeds of degeneration in it or him. And life—he said, with that self-deprecating air of badinage with which he delivered always his finest bits of wisdom—is a perpetual struggle. Never a being, always a becoming.

Which leads me to report that the book now moves along and I hope before school opens to have a major portion in the hands of a publisher. I should like to have it accepted for publication before I submit it to the university committee.

Jacques Barzun has gotten himself married.

I dipped into the Huxley book [probably *Eyeless in Gaza*] and, like you, fell and had to finish before I could work. Beatrice [Beatrice Brown, Alan's wife] is right: it isn't as good as PCP *[Point Counter Point]* but only in a literary sense does it fail. I found it an extremely moving and respectable failure. Is there any other man who writes for grownup people? He doesn't solve his problem and he even doesn't pose it too well. But there the problem is, the problem of human virtue. And I find it funny how distressed people are by the book, how they only want to talk about its literary weakness and dismiss the problem with a flip word, embarrassed. I have an essay I want to do on liberal and radical faith: it will use Ibsen as a spring board.

We are getting tired of this place and will probably abandon it after Labor Day. We are going to live in the same apartment, proud because we are the only tenants in the house whose rent hasn't been raised, on the ground that we were such desirable tenants! It makes us feel like two fat and middleaged people in a story by de Maupassant.

I haven't read Gone with the Wind and damned if I will lose any more time on novels.

I hear from Ez [Ez Lecky, who had also been a young instructor in the department] who seems enjoying himself but there still are no prospects.

Are you allowed movies? We Went to College might have been a swell comedy but it fizzled. Hugh Herbert delivering a lecture on Adam Smith opens the picture and that's grand and then he plays the cello in a concert at a faculty tea and that's fine but thereafter it falls away. However, Una Merkle gives an excellent performance as a faculty wife which pleased Diana very much and we both said Beatrice would like it.

Keep on getting well even more rapidly; Diana joins

me in this exhortation and we both send our best greet-
ings to Beatrice.

In its pleasant movement from politics to books to movies, this
letter to Alan is on the whole anything but "dejected." Its ease is
typical of Lionel's discourse with his friends. But the politics with
which it deals, specifically the trial of the old Bolsheviks, weighs
heavily on him. As a document in Lionel's political development,
the letter is puzzling. Why as late as 1936 should the trial in Moscow require Lionel to overhaul his ideas and character? Why at
this moment of his life does he counsel himself to have a "reservation of faith" in his response to all things? Presumably he had
had a major reservation of faith in Soviet Communism for the last
three years. At this date his reflection that "perhaps every revolution must betray itself" sounds not only tardy but unctuous. Zinoviev and Kamenev have confessed to political actions which are
manifestly at odds with everything in their lives as seasoned revolutionaries and this raises the question of their motive and/or their
moral probity. But by now Lionel must surely be aware that it is
not in the ranks of revolution that one looks for moral probity, not
as he would define it. The trial of the old Bolsheviks took Lionel
by surprise; it took everyone by surprise. But surprise or even dis-
gust does not propose the need for self-revision. And as to the
terms in which he speaks here of Trotskyism, they seem to go
beyond thinking of this opposition to Stalin as only a stick with
which to beat the party now entrenched in the Soviet Union. All
of us who had had an experience of Stalinism in practice knew
from the earliest days of the Spanish Civil War that Stalin's people
were bent on destroying their opponents among the Spanish Loyalists. We knew that Stalin was determined to keep the struggle
against Franco under his own command. But in this letter Lionel
sounds as if he were doing more than simply recognizing that the
Trotskyists were a prime target of official Communism. His tone
suggests assent in Trotsky's political position. He did indeed prefer

Trotskyism to Stalinism but he was not a Trotskyist. He was not this much of a revolutionary.

A few months later Lionel reports to Alan on the progress of his *Matthew Arnold*. Overoptimistic, he says that he expects "to get the bulk of it to the publisher's in a couple of weeks . . . I find," he says, "I have to get myself into a very special world in order to work on the thing. However, I am much encouraged by its quality and its quantity—though emery neff [sic] is I think a little cool about its slow progress, though also, I think, at my continuance next year." But he soon swings again from shop talk to politics:

> On politics I can give you little clarification unless you
> are so very confused that you force me to look & feel
> clear by contrast and by closeness to some of the facts.
> My difficulties, however, are philosophic & long-range. I
> see the greatest obfuscation going on under a cloud of
> seemingly "realistic" idealism. The Spanish business,
> underneath, is most depressing for those who, like me,
> know something of the situation but I live surrounded by
> the clouds of complex & subtle misrepresentations of the
> Nation, the New Republic, Malraux and Louis Fischer.
> But one has only to open one's mouth to have all the lib-
> erals, good, nice people, feel that one is a new kind of
> reactionary. . . . I remain willfully on the outskirts of
> things because I want now to keep my time & vacuum
> free for the book.

The temptation to get involved in the political activities of the moment, whether downtown or on the University campus, is of course considerable. But such activities eat up one's days and one's mind and Lionel avoids them. It is not, however, solely on behalf of his dissertation that he withdraws from political involvement. His private occupations would always have priority for him over the seductions of political camaraderie. Even before being engaged on his dissertation, he protected his "vacuum." My phobias were an unhappy help in this regard; it was not by choice alone that Lionel was home at his desk so much of the time. The need to stay with me abetted his wish to stay clear of the group activity which was so signal a part of the time-squandering appeal which radicalism had for the intellectuals of our generation. Yet physically removed as he was from this radical busywork, he was never out of touch with the current movement of ideas and he responded to it with the full force of his moral and intellectual energy.

In the heated atmosphere of the thirties, the launching of *Partisan Review* as so boldly anti-Stalinist a journal brought strange criticism from strange quarters. Even *Poetry* magazine—that inflammatory periodical!—made itself heard from Chicago, questioning whether the new journal was *really* revolutionary. The revolutionary barricades had become everybody's jungle gym. With Jovian certainty, *Partisan Review* replied to its critics:

> Our program is the program of Marxism, which in general terms means being for the revolutionary overthrow of capitalistic society, for a workers' government, and for international socialism. In contemporary terms it implies the struggle against capitalism in all its modern guises and disguises, including bourgeois democracy, fascism, and reformism (social democracy, Stalinism).

Between bourgeois democracy and fascism, the magazine admits no useful distinction; capitalist America is no less an enemy of the working class than Nazi Germany. For the next two years, until war actually breaks out in Europe, *Partisan Review* will with increasing stridency call upon its readers to refuse the impending European conflict as no more than a struggle between rival imperialisms. Capitalist war must be turned into class war.

Expectably enough, Dwight Macdonald, the most fiery of the

editors of *Partisan Review* in the early days of the magazine, was the author of its most rousing editorials. Although Lionel and I knew Macdonald for many years, we never advanced in intimacy with him. For that matter, we were intimate with none of the early editors of the magazine except Rahv and Phillips; we came to know Fred Dupee over time, especially after his marriage, but at first we knew him only from *Partisan Review* parties. George Morris was seldom present on these occasions; his life lay elsewhere. He was married to Susy Frelinghuysen, a blond Jeritza-like creature who eventually became known as a painter but who, in the early days of *Partisan Review,* planned a career in opera; I heard her do a more than creditable Tosca. Uncommonly skilled as a journalist, Macdonald occupied a central place in the New York intellectual world in the middle years of this century but he had little part in Lionel's and my life; so far as I recollect, we visited him and his wife, Nancy, only once. It was when they gave a New Year's Eve party; typically, Dwight charged the guests an admission fee of fifty cents. The New Year's Eve party must have taken place after Trotsky's assassination: on the wall of the living room hung a large picture of Trotsky with an ax through his skull. Nothing was easier than to be angry at Macdonald, whether in or out of print, but it was difficult to stay angry with him; he was too childlike, too seemingly innocent. Certainly he was innocent of the consequences of his ideas. It says as much of the intellectual culture of his time as it does of him that he was never either then or later called to account for the positions he advocated in his wonderfully clear brisk prose. This "child" invited us to the grimmest of destinies, now class war, now anarchy. After the start of the European war he disagreed with Phillips and Rahv about America's participation in the war and broke with *Partisan Review* to found, with Nancy, his own magazine, *Politics.* Dwight's irresponsible passion for politics, however, outlasted even this periodical. In 1968, with the outbreak of the campus disturbances at Columbia, he was at once on the scene, loaded for bear. He had no connection with

Columbia; to him it mattered not at all if the institution lived or died—he had found himself a revolution. Report had it that he was hauled up in a basket to a window in the barricaded Mathematics building. He and I quarreled during this period: he had sent me an appeal for funds for the SDS, Students for a Democratic Society, the student organization which masterminded the uprising, and he found my indignant refusal to help the SDS "hilarious"—what more laughable than to want a university to endure? I doubt that Lionel and Dwight ever exchanged a serious word or attempted to. I once heard Lionel at a pre-Christmas party at the Rahvs' jokingly try to persuade Dwight to buy Nancy a Christmas present. "A Christmas present?" Dwight emitted one of his whoops of laughter. "What kind of a Christmas present?" Lionel suggested a black silk nightgown—black underwear was a first knowledge of sin for our generation. Briefly a look of perplexity flashed across Dwight's face; then he again gave one of his infectious guffaws. Macdonald was far more trustworthy as a critic of literature than as a writer on politics. His literary taste was free of whatever was the reckless impulse behind his political ardor. He was the editor of *Partisan Review* who persuaded the magazine to accept Lionel's story "Of This Time, Of That Place."

Mary McCarthy was not an editor of *Partisan Review* for long; she left its editorial board in the spring of 1938, only a few months after the magazine was launched, but she continued to be one of its most valued contributors. I very much envied Mary as a writer. There was a shine on everything she wrote, and whatever she wrote was always a statement of her sense of her own power. Yet I felt of her criticism that it was insufficiently based in reality and, of her novels and stories, that she was a writer of fiction more by disciplined intention than by grace. Even the book of hers which I most liked, *Memories of a Catholic Girlhood,* seemed to me to be more contrived, even fictionalized, than a re-creation of lived experience. Although when she and Bowden Broadwater, with whom she was living at the time, invited Lionel and me to dinner she was rude to me, it was not with the purposeful rudeness of her good friend Hannah Arendt. Year after year Hannah made believe that I did not exist even when we were a few feet apart, staring into each other's faces—but Hannah was attracted to Lionel, as Mary did not seem to be, and was therefore more resentful of me. Yet on one of the few occasions when I undertook to talk seriously to Mary, she was thoroughly disagreeable. My essay "The Other Night at Columbia," which was an account of a poetry reading by Allen Ginsberg, had recently appeared in *Partisan Review* and was being met with considerable hostility; finding myself next to her at a party, I asked Mary what she had thought of the piece. Her reply, senseless except as an insult, was that no one knew from whose point of view the piece was written and that I should have started it by identifying myself as the wife of Lionel Trilling. In 1968 the two of us debated the "solution" to America's involvement in Vietnam in the *New York Review of Books*. While we agreed that America had no choice but to pull out of Vietnam, we were profoundly at odds about the consequences of an American withdrawal. The Vietnamese "boat people" did not yet exist but I foresaw just such a tragic fate for any South Vietnamese who would resist a Communist takeover. For Mary, the domination of South Vietnam by North Vietnam was the cheeriest of prospects. A Communist dictatorship held no terror for her; in her view the only people who would suffer at the hands of Hanoi would be people who had collaborated with America and these apparently deserved whatever happened to them. I had virtually no support for my position in our exchange; the readers of the *New York Review of Books* seemed wholly to side with Mary. I was nevertheless unhappily certain that time would prove me correct. Mary never understood why, when her Vietnam articles were to appear in book form and I was asked for permission for my part of our exchange to be printed in the volume, I consented as readily as I did, only specifying that my part in the debate be printed in its entirety. I knew that I would be vindicated by history.

One never recovered from one's surprise that Fred Dupee had not only been a member of the Communist Party but, even more startling, an organizer on the New York docks. The son of a Middle Western banker, his appearance and personality were ineradicably stamped with his too-tender upbringing. But his soft looks and manner masked a considerable tough-mindedness. He was not given to the Talmudic hasslings of Rahv and his political cronies but he held his own better than most in our rough corner of the intellectual world—no one in the New York intellectual community and certainly no one in the Columbia English Department could have managed Allen Ginsberg's poetry reading at Columbia as Dupee did, bridging with such quiet authority what might otherwise have been a dangerous division between tradition and subversion in Ginsberg's audience. Early in our acquaintance, before I had become a writer, I thought Fred was condescending to me when he drew me aside at a small literary gathering to talk with me about the fabrics I had chosen for our living-room chairs; but actually he loved houses and everything involved in their decoration. When he left *Partisan Review,* Dupee became a valued member of the Columbia faculty. All the *Partisan Review* editors eventually became college professors; their literary distinction was readily rewarded with academic posts. With his young wife, Andy, and his two small children, he lived in the Columbia-owned apartment on Claremont Avenue to which Lionel and I would move in 1955 and in which I still live. In the room which became Lionel's study, he coached me for my first public talk in 1951, telling me how I was to stand and how I was to hold my hands—I was to speak from the same platform with Arthur Koestler and Arthur Schlesinger at Freedom House. I have never known any other intellectual, male or female, not the most generous of them, who would have taken that kind of trouble for a friend. It is not the way intellectuals live their lives.

A great deal has been written about that oddly matched but so well-joined pair, the founding editors of *Partisan Review,* William Phillips and Philip Rahv, each in his own way so gifted and yet blocked in the final fulfillment of his possibilities, each so independent of mind but so easily influenced by the tendencies and preferences of the cultural moment, each so deeply immersed in politics and yet so remote from the practicalities of government. The swarthy, blunt-featured Rahv had grown up in Russia; I think he then briefly moved to Palestine. He was not fat but he was big and with his wide face and broad shoulders he gave the impression of bulk. Notwithstanding his expensive clothes, there was something primitive, even animal-like in his appearance—my mother would have called him a mujik, by which she would have meant that he had the stolidity and guile of a Russian peasant; one saw the craftiness in his smile. Rahv had a tropism to money not of his own earning; he went through several wives, most of them wealthy; the one we knew best was Nathalie Swan, an architect. After he and Nathalie were divorced, he married a descendant of John Jay Chapman and with her moved to Boston, where he consorted with those of its first families who appreciated his powers of mind as he appreciated their social elevation. With Nathalie to help him with the more onerous chores of preparing a meal, Philip loved to cook: for a time he and I carried on a modest cooking competition. This clever man was also a small-minded man, envious and malicious. It took longer than I suppose it should have for Lionel and me to discover his untrustworthiness. Everyone around *Partisan Review* had his licensed malice and made jokes at the expense of his friends—puncturing yet another reputation, Rahv would laugh from the deepest recesses of his belly. The time came, however, when malice became the ascendant element in his character; the new magazine he launched in Boston, *Modern Occasions,* became for its short life the vehicle of his personal hatreds. Featured in its first issue was an extended attack upon Lionel by a then-unknown teacher of English, Mark Krupnick. Like "The Duchess' Red Shoes," Delmore Schwartz's attack on Lionel in *Partisan Review,* Krupnick's piece was of course solicited and predesigned.

One would not have taken Rahv for an intellectual except perhaps—were he less well-dressed—in a novel by Dostoevsky. William Phillips, on the other hand, looked every inch the modern literary man; he was lean, handsome, appealingly ascetic. Poor, from an unhappy home, he remembered his childhood with bitterness. As an undergraduate he had attended City College; he did his graduate work at New York University. Phillips was wittier than Rahv, more cautious in his dealings with people. He was excessively hypochondriacal: he had been a college athlete, a member of his varsity swimming team, but even when we first knew him as a young man he worried inordinately about his health, especially about what he ate; in restaurants he was certain that the kitchen was going to introduce some diabolical ingredient into the plain food he had ordered. At the same time that he thought the medical profession manifestly unreliable, his deference to any doctor he saw or to any medical instruction he had been given was total; he reminded me of Lionel's mother who, having been assured after a gallbladder operation that she could safely eat cottage cheese for her lunch, never again ate anything else for her midday meal. As an editor, he seemed always to be similarly looking for the literary authority who would assure the health of his magazine. All periodicals live by their ability to respond to the taste of their readers; a successful editor is nothing if not a pulse-taker. Phillips could spot a shift in the intellectual culture before it took shape. While Rahv might flout the best interests of the magazine in order to gratify some devious private purpose, William's devotion to *Partisan Review* was absolute. If the magazine got much of its bite and its tone of exhilarating controversy from Rahv, it was no doubt Phillips who saved it from the unpleasantness which poisoned Rahv's journal. Certainly it was Phillips who, with his wife Edna, a high-school teacher and school administrator, kept the writers for *Partisan Review* within a recognizably domesticated universe. One could talk with William and Edna about an illness, a family crisis, a social dilemma and they knew what one was talking about. Rahv was not this well connected to the familiar world. During my pregnancy I started to tell him and Nathalie of an amusing incident which had taken place at my obstetrician's office. Rahv interrupted me to ask me what an obstetrician was. "You mean you go to a *stranger* to have a baby?" he demanded incredulously. The Rahvs took their illnesses to the neighborhood druggist.

Until America was actually engaged in the conflict in Europe, *Partisan Review* was fiercely opposed to the war. It was not alone in taking this stand. It was a Marxist journal and culturally anything but isolationist, yet in its opposition to America's involvement in the war it joined a strange chorus. Isolationist sentiment took a variety of forms in this country, encompassing views as divergent as that of Charles Lindbergh and his wife, Anne Morrow, who accepted Nazism as the wave of the future, and that of the Socialist leader, Norman Thomas. Virtually up to the moment that America was brought into the war, popular sentiment against the war was so strong that in the 1940 presidential campaign, although France had already fallen, Roosevelt could not safely go beyond the "short of war" policy which he had proposed in the early spring: had he expressed the wish to intervene on behalf of the British, it would have severely jeopardized his chance of winning the election. *Partisan Review*'s position had nothing in common with the isolationism of the Lindberghs, but neither did the magazine share Roosevelt's sympathy with the anti-fascist allies. It was intransigently revolutionary. In its view the war against Hitler was no different than the war of 1914; it was a war between rival imperialisms. All war which was not class war was imperialist war. One of the most vehement of the editorials which appeared in *Partisan Review* in this period was its denunciation of the English intellectuals who condemned Chamberlain for his appeasement of Hitler at Munich:

> The liberal and radical intellectuals have thrived for two
> decades on exposing the meaning and instruction of the
> last Great War. Yet today they are urging upon us the

very same social-patriotic policies, the identical supra-class illusions which they claim the catastrophe of 1914 had taught them to renounce forever. . . . It would almost seem that the peculiar function of the intellectuals is to idealize imperialist wars when they come and to debunk them after they are over.

Lionel and I did not at all believe that war against Hitler was war between rival imperialisms. We were deeply partisan with the Allies and dismayed by Chamberlain's action at Munich. The day that France fell, I remember feeling that the world had come to an end. Yet though we saw Rahv and Phillips frequently, I have no recollection of our quarreling with them about their opposition to the war. Was it they or we, I now wonder, who were able to concede on so vital an issue.

On the eve of the outbreak of war in Europe *Partisan Review* published a symposium, "The Situation in American Writing." Today it makes startling reading. There were many respondents and the answers had to be published in two sections. The first installment appeared in the issue of Summer 1939; the contributors were John Dos Passos, Allen Tate, James Farrell, Kenneth Fearing, Katherine Anne Porter, Wallace Stevens, Gertrude Stein, William Carlos Williams, John Peale Bishop, Harold Rosenberg, and Henry Miller—the magazine had by now its pick of writers. Lionel made his contribution to the second installment, which appeared in the issue of Fall 1939. The other respondents in this second group were Sherwood Anderson, Louise Bogan, R. P. Blackmur, Horace Gregory, Robert Fitzgerald, and Robert Penn Warren. Of the replies to the seven questions asked by the editors, those in response to the last of them are of most historical interest: "Have you considered the question of your attitude towards the possible entry of the United States into the next World War? What do you think the responsibilities of writers in general are when and if war comes?" The answers divide between a strangely self-referring and even querulous pacifism and agreement with *Partisan Review*'s already well-advertised antiwar position. Henry Miller sees "no problem confronting the world which might not be solved peaceably." (How the "problem" of Hitler is to be solved peaceably he does not tell us.) Sherwood Anderson submits that, as a literary man, he does not believe in any war: "In a time of war any man working in the arts is sunk. His lamps are out." Louise Bogan writes: "In the event of another war, I plan to oppose it with every means in my power." James Farrell cheerily cites the Albanian who during the last war was asked how he felt about it and replied: " 'What? Two dogs are fighting for a bone, and you ask the bone how it feels?' " As late as the summer of 1939 Gertrude Stein assures us that "most probably there will not be another general European war." The response of Robert Penn Warren is the most economical and graphic: "I think that if we get into the next war we are suckers." To the shallow assertiveness of most of the replies, Wallace Stevens brings at least some measure of political realism, bred no doubt in his familiar life of commerce: "I don't think that the United States should enter into the next World War if there is to be another, unless it does so with the idea of dominating the world that comes out of it, or unless it is required to enter it in self-defense."

Lionel answers the last of the seven questions first. "I find," he writes, "that it is the only one that I 'face.' The possibility of war is the great objective and subjective fact which confronts every writer." War spells for him the halt and perhaps the extinction of writing: ". . . for the war-period at the very least, there will be a cessation of literary activity in any true sense. . . . [In the postwar period] there is every likelihood that the writer will either be silenced or enslaved." He avoids any out-and-out statement against an impending war in Europe and, like all the contributors, he fails to mention Hitler—nowhere in the symposium is there a hint of recognition of the true character of Nazism. The enemy in this conflict into which we must not allow our country to be dragged is faceless and unnamed. In fact, he is nonexistent; there is no enemy other than ourselves. In step with the other contributors, Lionel appraises the war only from the point of view of its effect—its dire effect—on writing: the writer, he says, will be enslaved. It turned out of course that our worried writers were mistaken in predicting that the war would put an end, even a temporary end, to literature. The literary production of this country during the war was, if anything, more copious than in time of peace and it had a larger and more eager audience. *Partisan Review* flourished during the war to which it was so much opposed. The current of left-wing thought apparently swept Lionel off his accustomed course: important as literature had always been for him, it was not his habit to give it this pre-eminence among the concerns of mankind. Democracies do not silence or enslave their writers, only dictatorships silence or enslave, and his apocalyptic warning that, as a result of war, writers would be silenced or enslaved echoes the fashionable left-wing belief that war inevitably ensues in fascism. The idea that fascism is the consequence of war, even a war *against* fascism, lasted long and traveled far among the intellectuals of Lionel's and my generation. It was with morbid fascination that, once America was in the war, we and our friends contemplated what the future had in store for our young airmen when they would no longer have their giant bombers to command and had to resume their old civilian lives. How could one expect them to return to their factories and gas stations?

Partisan Review had it both ways. On the one hand, it argued that there was no difference between democratic capitalism and fascism and, on the other hand, it assured us that if the capitalist democracies went to war, fascism would be the outcome. "War is the Issue!" the magazine headlined a letter to its readers soliciting their support for a newly formed organization, the League for Cultural Freedom and Socialism. The call appeared in the same issue with the second installment of the symposium on American writing and was signed not only by the editors of the magazine but also by an impressive list of intellectuals and public figures, among them John Dewey, Suzanne La Follette, Meyer Schapiro, James Burnham, William Carlos Williams, Clement Greenberg. "So far as it lies in the power of the New Deal, American blood and treasure will be lavishly expended to help France and England crush once more their ancient imperialist rival," the letter proclaims. It continues:

> We loathe and abominate fascism as the chief enemy of all culture, all real democracy, all social progress. But the last war showed only too clearly that we can have no faith in imperialist crusades to bring freedom to any people. Our entry into the war, under the slogan of "Stop Hitler!" would actually result in the immediate introduction of totalitarianism over here. Only the German people can free themselves of the fascist yoke. The American masses can best help them by fighting *at home* to keep their own liberties.

At least the existence of Hitler is finally recognized. If only by implication, we are at last permitted a distinction between Hitler's fascism and "real democracy." But the appeal is still couched in the familiar language of Communist incitement and in thrall to Communist doctrine. The liberties which are being threatened "at home" are not specified, nor are we told how the German people are to be freed, if not by military intervention. Indeed, even after the fall of France the magazine's vocabulary of exhortation remains unchanged. Between the issues of Summer 1939 and Fall 1939 the magazine drops its designation as a Marxist journal, but it is not yet weaned from Marxist doctrine and the Communist idiom. It still consigns democratic capitalism to the dustbin of history. Capitalist tyranny and imperialist expansionism are still the sole enemy.

[Our choice] is not between victory under Willkie-Roosevelt or defeat by Hitler, but rather between defeat under Willkie-Roosevelt or victory under a native fascist regime (perhaps led by one of those individuals). The lesson of France seems clear: democratic capitalism is historically obsolete, and in a struggle with fascism it must either be defeated . . . or else it must itself go fascist as the price of victory.

The Communist argument for the substitution of class war for a war among nations is made in a rhetoric which not only bridges any difference between presidential candidates with a hyphen but labels both of them as potential fascists.

Lionel is not among the signatories of this letter. It may be that he was not invited: his radical credentials were perhaps not improved by his reply to one of the earlier questions in the symposium. A first question put to the contributors was: Had their work had its source in an allegiance to any group or class or system of thought? Lionel replied:

My own literary interest—and I suppose that in a writer this is an allegiance—is in the tradition of humanistic thought and in the intellectual middle class which believes that it continues this tradition. Nowadays this is perhaps not properly pious; but however much I may acknowledge the historical role of the working class and the validity of Marxism, it would be *only* piety for me to say that my chief literary interest lay in this class and this tradition.

Six years have elapsed since Lionel was briefly a Communist, three years since his Columbia department charged him with being a Marxist. Through most of this time he has been engaged on his *Matthew Arnold*. The *Arnold* has now been published. If it is informed by Marxism, the influence is surely a subtle one: it perhaps helped him to understand the importance of economic power in the functioning of society. But this shadowy Marx is not the Marx of class war, nor the Marx with whom a writer for *Partisan Review* had to touch base as a member of the intellectual left. Contributing to *Partisan Review* in 1939, it took some independence of mind to locate oneself in the "intellectual middle class" though that class be defined not as a bulwark of capitalism but as the guardian of "the tradition of humanistic thought." The magazine practiced the humanistic tradition more than it preached it, but Lionel was running counter to at least its expressed principle. Yet even as he renounced the ruling faith of *Partisan Review,* he made a last obeisance to it. He saluted "the historical role of the working class and the validity of Marxism."

Macdonald was the author of many of the editorials in *Partisan Review* during these years leading up to the Second World War but even those which he wrote had of course to be acceptable to the other editors. Today they make strange reading in a magazine which has come to be regarded as the best intellectual journal of the American mid-twentieth century. But the important point about *Partisan Review* even as far back as the prewar years is the fact that it combined its questionable judgment in matters of politics with a rigorous intelligence in matters of culture. It was its nonpolitical content which would have allowed those who did not share its editorial opinions to forgive its political irresponsibility. We keep it in mind that despite his political preferences, so diametrically opposed to those of *Partisan Review,* T. S. Eliot chose this magazine for the first publication of his "East Coker." It appeared in the issue of May–June 1940.

In July 1937 Lionel wrote to Alan Brown on the progress of his dissertation: "But the work goes well, no periods of sterility and a kind of pertinacity to get what I want (or nearly) that pleases me. The book, I think, is good. . . . I dream of suddenly coming to a place and realizing it's finished." He did at last reach that place; the arrival was not without drama. The dissertation was submitted, defended, and found acceptable. Lionel's doctoral committee gave no indication that the work in any way exceeded its expectations; praise had to await the book's public reception. The job done, Lionel collapsed. The manuscript was to have been handed in at the University on Monday morning. Sunday was to be devoted to incorporating the many small suggestions which had been noted in its margins by its departmental readers. At seven on Sunday morning, then again at eight, and once more at nine, I woke Lionel; that is, I endeavored to wake him. It was not possible. He was breathing normally and it was obvious that he was alive, but he responded not at all to my urging that he wake. His eyes remained closed; he was unmoving. I put warm washcloths to his face, without effect; when I switched to cold, he still failed to open his eyes. I brought a cup of tea to the bed and tried spooning it into his mouth. His eyes still shut, he let the tea dribble down his chin. Frightened, I called the doctor and while I waited for his arrival I phoned our friends the Grossmans to ask them to come and help me with Lionel's manuscript. After examining Lionel closely, the doctor assured me that he was not ill, just profoundly exhausted. For the present he must be allowed to rest, but if he was not awake by five that afternoon, I must force him from bed. For the rest of the day, while Elsa and Jim and I worked on Lionel's manuscript, preparing it for delivery, Lionel slept. He had taken a leave from life. In the late afternoon we coaxed him from bed. For an hour he sat in the living room, bemused, watching us at our labors. Not then or ever did he acknowledge that there was anything unusual in his behavior or that he had a reason for gratitude to the Grossmans or me. The next morning he wakened fresh as a baby. Ten years later, on completing his novel, he would repeat this performance, but at least this time there were no last-minute revisions to be taken care of. He had the right to collapse in fatigue when he handed in his dissertation. Between the spring of 1936, when he had been threatened with the loss of his job, and the completion of his *Arnold* in 1938, in addition to his teaching and his work on his dissertation, he had done a substantial amount of other writing, reviews not only for *Partisan Review* but also for the *Nation* and the *New Republic* and for a publication called the *New York Teacher,* and a second essay, this one on Willa Cather, for the series commissioned for the *New Republic* by Malcolm Cowley. He also wrote an introduction to the Modern Library edition of three plays of Eugene O'Neill, "Anna Christie," "Emperor Jones," and "The Hairy Ape." He was due a day of rest.

At the time that Lionel took his Ph.D., a candidate for a doctorate at Columbia had to publish his dissertation in order to receive his degree. The requirement could make for hardship and expense; achievement was not always rewarded with publication and candidates were often forced into what is known as vanity publishing. I have an only spotty memory of Lionel's efforts to publish his *Arnold.* I seem to recall that he offered it first to the Atlantic Monthly Press, which rejected it. His next submission, to W. W. Norton, was more fortunate. The reader at Norton was Eleanor Clark, who had recently graduated from Vassar; she recommended that the book be accepted. Mr. Norton agreed, however, only on condition that Lionel contribute $250 to the cost of publication. It was a great deal of money for us to provide, almost ten percent of Lionel's Columbia salary, and it was also an extravagant demand on Norton's part, considering that the publisher would break even if the book sold eight hundred copies. But Lionel had no choice. We borrowed the money and in early 1939 his *Matthew Arnold* was published both here and in England. In the more than half century since this original appearance it has never been out of print. The critical reception was almost universally favorable; it is not granted many doctoral dissertations to be reviewed this widely and prominently. One should perhaps have been able to foresee that the English response would be even more enthusiastic than the American. The *Times Literary Supplement* gave it its lead review with the bold caption "A Word to the Anglo-Saxon Democracies." The *New York Times Book Review* commended it but it had reservations to voice. The reviewer was H. F. Lowry: together with Arnold Whitridge, a grandson of Matthew Arnold and a member of the Yale English Department, Lowry controlled the Arnold papers in this country. Whitridge and Lowry had refused Lionel access to these unpublished documents, but Lowry now held Lionel accountable for the gap in his scholarship. The response in America which gave Lionel most pleasure was Edmund Wilson's review in the *New Republic*. Remembering that it was Wilson who had given him his first encouragement to write a book about Arnold, Lionel was pleased that Wilson approved the finished product; he agreed with Wilson that he should perhaps have paid more attention to Arnold as a poet. In *Partisan Review* the book was warmly praised by William Phillips.

It was pivotal in Lionel's career as a teacher that, resistant though he was to Irwin Edman's suggestion that he send a copy of his dissertation to President Butler, he followed the advice. Butler was a formidable and imperious figure; the present-day academic world would not accommodate him. Like Eisenhower after him, he aspired to the presidency of the United States, but unlike Eisenhower, who became President of Columbia merely as a stepping stone to the higher office, Butler built the University from which he hoped to launch his political career. Much of Columbia's distinction as a private university is owed to him, particularly the creation of its graduate schools. But the radical thirties were not a congenial time for Butler. Communism dominated the campus and even outside the University he came to be seen as more a figure of reaction than of progress. The night that Lionel sent his book to President Butler, I had a waking dream in which Butler, having read it, rushed to the office of his provost, Frank Fackenthal, with the exclamation: "You mean that we have an instructor in this University who can write a book like this? He must be promoted immediately!" Later, I learned that my phantasy had been almost literally enacted. The President had his strategies for making his wishes known in the University. He invited Lionel, a lowly instructor, to dinner at his home with the Dean of the College and with Professor Wright, who was head of the University English Department. The message was clear. I described the evening in "Lionel Trilling: A Jew at Columbia":

Every spring the Association for University Teas gave a reception at the Faculty Club for the President and his wife. Several weeks before the event this spring an engraved invitation arrived at our house: Lionel and I were asked to dinner at the President's the evening of the reception. No one we knew had ever been at the Butlers' for dinner, perhaps not even Irwin Edman—I remember I had to go afield for advice about dress, but that could have been because Irwin had no wife I could consult. I felt I was taking my life in my hands in even calling the Secretary of the University, a white-haired gentleman who suggested a plumper, smoother Cordell Hull, to inquire whether it was white or black tie that was indicated for our occasion. "White tie, I should think," said Mr. Hayden in a voice that froze the heart. It was decided: Lionel would hire tails and I would buy a ballgown. A terrible thought came to me: need I wear long white gloves? I called the fashion department of *Vogue* which assured me that there was no occasion or place that any longer required long white gloves unless it was the Court of St. James's. This convinced me: long white gloves would be worn at President Butler's. I called the fashion advisor at Bonwit Teller and got the same reply but this time I was more specific: "What about dinner at the home of President Butler of Columbia University?" "Well, yes," came the reply. "That might be a good idea."

Public figures and University people were obviously

319

not to be mixed; on the evening of our dinner the guests were entirely from the faculty, I think there were twenty people present. For dinner at eight, Lionel and I carefully arrived at 8:02. We were the last to arrive and were rather urgently propelled toward the closed drawingroom doors by a footman. The doors were flung open, we were announced by a butler. The receiving line consisted of the President and his wife. "Let me congratulate you, sir, on your splendid English reviews," was the President's greeting to Lionel. "There's only been one," said Lionel. "There have been two, sir," the President corrected him. In the meantime I was being welcomed, if that's the word, by his wife. "Do you know everyone here, my dear?" I made a lightning survey of the room. "I am afraid I don't know anyone." "That, my dear, is because you never come to any of the teas or receptions." In the dining room it was possible to study the company. All the women but one wore long white kid gloves, the hands now rolled back. Lionel was the obvious purpose of the evening. . . .

Through dinner the President ate nothing; he drank a great deal of Scotch. The food was delicious: his wife was a Frenchwoman of mature years built with the kind of one-piece sloping bosom that made a properly solid armature for a lavender cut-velvet Worth gown, very expensive, elegant, and unbeautiful, that was then in favor among higher-echelon ladies of two continents, and I knew about her table from the grocer we shared. One day when I had been offered a bargain in loose carrots from a corner basket and I had rejected them as "horse carrots," he had confided to me that these were the ones Mrs. Butler bought for the servants' kitchen; nothing was too good for her own table. There were several footmen to serve so that the meal went swiftly. At its end the women repaired to Mrs. Butler's sitting room upstairs while the men had cigars and brandy in the President's library. The President sat on a bench with his back to the fireplace, Lionel told me, and did all the talking. He was growing old; under any circumstances it would have been easier to talk than listen. In a circle in front of him the men attended what he had to say.

What the prefatory monologue consisted in was of no import, it was where it inescapably led that mattered: Butler recounted the correspondence he had had with the Chancellor of the University of Berlin when the two universities, Berlin and Columbia, had decided on an exchange of philosophy professors. Columbia proposed to send Felix Adler and the Chancellor had written to protest a Jewish visitor. Lionel recreated the scene. Having got this far in his narrative, Butler had put down his brandy glass and firmly planted his hands on his knees, fixing his eyes on Professor Wright as he boomed: "And I, gentlemen, I wrote back: 'At Columbia, sir, we recognize merit, not race.' " Silence. The party rose to join the ladies and move on to the Faculty Club reception. In the summer, "under his summer powers," President Butler appointed Lionel an Assistant Professor of English, the first Jew in that department to become a member of the faculty.

Soon after his promotion, Lionel had word from his old teacher and dissertation director, Emery Neff, that Neff wanted to speak with him: Could they meet at our apartment and would I, too, be present? He at once explained the reason for his visit without apology or embellishment; he wanted the two of us to understand that it was his hope that Lionel's appointment would not be used to open the department to other Jews. He could not have been more straightforward. Did it take courage, I wonder, for this odd little man, for whom there had always seemed to be a wide and fearsome sea between his own Midwestern farming background and the Columbia metropolis, to make this statement, or did it merely reflect his own inviolate sense of racial superiority? He made it plain that he spoke only for himself; he had not been sent by his colleagues. Lionel and I said nothing. We sat and stared. He soon left. Emery Neff's visit took place in the early autumn of 1939, soon after the outbreak of war. In the decade which followed the war, the situation of Jews in American universities altered profoundly in response to our new consciousness of the hidden dangers in even the most perfunctory social or professional racial discrimination. Soon after the war Lionel could grinningly tell me that the English Department had just hired an instructor named Hyman Kleinman. We thought of Neff. Lionel was lucky in his name as in his good looks. Thorndike might not have made his appointment if Lionel had been more distinctively Jewish in appearance. But it was not because of his name or good looks that Lionel retained his place at Columbia and won the time to reveal his abilities, and it is not because he was an "acceptable" Jew that Butler had him promoted.

In 1940 there was instituted the first peacetime draft in America's history. Lionel was thirty-five and beyond the age for registration. But the next year the draft was extended to include men of thirty-six. Lionel was classified 1-A but not called up; his board took the word of my doctor that my health was too precarious to allow him to be drafted. Although Lionel never referred to it, I doubt that he forgave me for exempting him from military service. His parents had denied him a full experience of boyhood and I denied him the full experience of his adult generation. What the army would have done with him had he been called up, it is not difficult to guess: it would probably have assigned him to desk work or teaching. There is little likelihood that he would have seen active duty. But he would have been in uniform and living in barracks with the other men, sharing their discomforts and obeying his superiors as they obeyed theirs. Neither Lionel's students nor the younger writers around *Partisan Review* were this eager to be called up. Few of the younger intellectuals we knew felt that it was their war. Once America was at war, *Partisan Review* conceded to the general sentiment of the country. So far as I know, none of the people who in 1939 wrote so earnestly against the war continued to oppose it. But by one means or another most of the intellectuals of our acquaintance evaded the draft, usually by pleading emotional instability; we knew only one person, Jim Grossman, who volunteered for military service, and his action was felt to be eccentric. Lionel became an air-raid warden but it was an unsatisfactory substitute for the army. Sometimes students or other young people came to ask his advice on what should be their attitude about being drafted. He told them that in his belief it was a just war and one in which they should be willing to be engaged. Among those who sought Lionel's opinion and cheerfully took his advice was Melvin Lasky, who later became the editor of *Encounter* in England. It confirmed what Lasky already felt but hesitated to trust because it ran counter to general intellectual opinion. In the army Lasky quickly qualified for officers' training. He came to see us soon after he was commissioned, very proud of his military issue. He had been a poor boy and he winningly explained to us that he had never before had such good leather shoes and gloves.

Chapter
TWELVE

I became a writer by accident early in 1941 as the result of a telephone call to Lionel from Margaret Marshall, the literary editor of the *Nation;* she was calling to inquire whether he knew someone who could write the brief unsigned fiction notes for her magazine. I overheard Lionel's end of the conversation: he told her that he would look around for a possible candidate. When he hung up I offered myself for the job. I have no idea of why I was moved to make such a suggestion. It had never until that moment occurred to me to be a professional writer, least of all a critic. It was not that the putting of words to paper was an entirely foreign occupation to me. I had always been at ease with words and in one form or another I suppose that I had always been writing. At camp I wrote skits and lyrics for our camp songs and I edited our magazine, and in high school I sometimes wrote poetry—it was not of high quality. I was campus reporter for the *Boston Herald* as a freshman at Radcliffe, but I had no desire to continue with writing for a newspaper after that single year. The plays and stories I wrote early in my marriage were written only to fill time; I never intended them to lead to a literary career. I identified criticism with the life into which I had been catapulted by my marriage. Lionel and his literary friends had all of them had a very different training from mine; until I entered their world, I had not even heard of many of the books on which they had cut their critical teeth. Yet curiously enough, while I ceded the professional field to them, I never doubted my own competence to judge their work. I had no hesitation in reshaping Lionel's prose; in draft after draft of his *Matthew Arnold,* I removed, added to, or otherwise altered what he had written. What I was trying to bring to his writing was a greater directness and a greater fluidity. I wanted it to have at once more spine and more grace. I was not undertaking to shape his ideas other than as style is inevitably an extension of thought. Lionel never resisted this intervention. Indeed, until he no longer required it, he welcomed it, counted upon it. This was generosity as well as good sense on his part: over the years, when I have tried to provide similar editorial help to various of our men friends, they have taken it as an assault on their masculinity. The practice of literary criticism, however, asks for more than editorial skill. Behind my confidence that I knew good writing when I saw it lay a considerable if unexplained faith in my ability to judge the whole of a literary performance. This was now much bolstered by Lionel's willingness to recommend me for the *Nation* position; if he had indicated any doubt of my ability to do the work, I would have at once withdrawn my candidacy, and I would not today be the person I am. Even with Lionel at my side, it was my writing which gave the middle years of my life much of their focus and meaning and since his death it is my work which has sustained me at an age when lack of purpose is the death of the living. Difficult as it is to support old age with pride even when one has a loved companion, for a woman alone it is a fierce test of courage: only the luckiest of us have work with which to meet it. In work, especially work at which one has some measure of success, a woman can at least pretend to find a substitute for the sexual power which she must lose with the years.

I was worried that Margaret Marshall had engaged me without proof of my competence, out of regard for Lionel, and I exacted a promise through Lionel that she would not keep me on because of him. But this was only my first brief concern. When it was explained to me that if, in the course of my reading, I came across a book which deserved more attention than just a brief note, I was to review it at full length in a signed review, I was thrown into a panic. Fortunately I was in analysis. Had I not had this means of coping with my extreme of fear, my career would surely have ended before it had begun. I was not afraid of writing a full-length review; I was afraid of signing it. The thought that my name would be in print revived in me, in all its infant force, my father's prohibition against self-display. Through the years it had taken up its residence in the dark recesses of my mind, emerging as required to proclaim its inviolability: had it not disclosed itself a decade earlier with the illness which lodged in my throat and kept me from being a singer? The degree of my panic stimulated my analysis and I quickly discovered the source of my terror. Simultaneously and even more important, I learned that my fear of public display was a screen for my desire for public attention. "What you really want," my analyst said, laughing, "is to see your name all over the magazine." It was true: in less than a year I asked for and was given my own column. But although I was able this quickly to shed the anonymity in which I might otherwise have taken permanent refuge, my cure was never wholly complete. In some measure I must still associate public performance with the forbidden intimacies of the body; I have not moved my writing career forward as I might have. Lionel was aware that I worked under an unspecified restraint upon ambition. Had he known how to help me surmount the limits which had been put upon me and which I now put upon myself, he would cheerfully have given me this assistance. His encouragement could not overcome my upbringing. I am still unable to attend a concert or lecture or any public performance without at some moment having my throat tighten with the temptation to scream and thus divert, in a most unpleasant way, the attention of the audience from the onstage display to my own imprisoned self.

I preferred writing my reviews to reading the books which came to me. The first novel I wrote about at full length was a late book of H. G. Wells: I was in such a hurry to get started on the writing that I rushed to the typewriter when I was only halfway through the book and had to do my review again from the beginning. Now that I was to sign what I wrote, the question arose of what name I should use, my maiden name or my name as Lionel's wife. Socially I was always known by my married name. We consulted our friends at *Partisan Review*. They were united in the advice that I write under my maiden name; they feared that I was going to be an embarrassment to Lionel. But Lionel was adamant that I write as his wife. From the day I first appeared in print, there was never a moment when his confidence in me wavered, and if one is moved to interpret this as evidence of his own professional security, it should be kept in mind that in 1941, when I began at the *Nation,* he had made only a first step to public recognition; he had only just published his *Matthew Arnold.* His essays of the forties, which would make up *The Liberal Imagination,* had not yet been written.

It would be pleasant if I could say that Margaret Marshall gave me my column because she admired my work. Actually the situation was not so simple: she needed to be relieved of some of her editorial responsibility and my request gave her the means of doing this. Forty or fifty novels came to the *Nation* each month; she had to inspect all of them and to decide which were to be reviewed and by whom. In addition, she had to make the same assessment of an even larger number of nonfiction books. While I would not have been given the space and prominence if she thought that my work did not warrant it, she was not rewarding me. She was allowing me to help her. Peggy was a wonderful person to work for. She never pressed her critical opinions upon the people who wrote for her; she never altered my copy by so much as a comma without my consent. In her years as literary editor of the *Nation,* she made its "Books and the Arts" section—the back of the book, as it was always referred to—into a remarkable feature of the magazine, gathering around her an extraordinary group of columnists: B. H. Haggin as the music critic, Clement Greenberg as her art critic, James Agee her film critic. Fred Dupee and Randall Jarrell alternated as reviewers of poetry, and Mary McCarthy and Peggy herself wrote about the theater. Yet she made no literary reputation for herself and left no personal mark on the cultural history of the time. When she left the *Nation* in the fifties, she became an inconspicuous editor at the publishing house of Harcourt Brace & World. The wonder is, I suppose, that she did as well with her life as she did, considering the extreme depression under which she functioned. Clinically it was of a quite different sort from the depression which Lionel had to combat. Peggy's was implacable; it invaded the whole of her personality, virtually annihilating it. There were times when her spirits were so borne down that she was unable to speak: she once spent an entire evening at our house without uttering a word. Other times she was incongruously lively, even coquettish. She had been raised a Mormon and she was usually modest in her bearing, but she was ambitious, perhaps excessively so relative to her capacities—this may have contributed to her emotional immobilization. Her envy of women who were manifestly successful was not always hidden. She was bitter, for example, that more credit was given to Mary McCarthy than to her for a series of articles on the contemporary critics which the two of them worked on together for the *Nation.* Throughout the years in which I knew her, she was working, or trying to work, on a book about Constance Rourke, the author of *American Humor* and an early feminist with whom she strongly identified. The work was never carried very far; there was nothing publishable at her death. Sometimes she wrote a political piece for the magazine. I thought that she wrote better about politics than about literature or the theater. While I had my column, if a novel came to me by a well-known writer, I would always offer it to Peggy to write about herself or to assign to another reviewer if she wished to. She never took advantage of this for herself and rarely for anyone else. I was the beneficiary of her impairment.

I was never in the *Nation* office; the books were sent to me at home, four, six, eight at a time. I watched them pile up on the living-room table—I had no workroom of my own. I never discarded a book without reading at least a few pages. At the start I was a slow reader; in a few months I tripled my speed. Presumably a process of selection had already taken place before the books were sent out for review and only those with a claim, or pretension, to seriousness were sent to us. Few, however, rated serious attention. In all the years that I was connected with the *Nation*— and I was there for close to a decade—I was never free of the worry that I might overlook a good book by an unknown author. Would I have recognized, say, a John O'Hara or even an F. Scott Fitzgerald before they had made their reputations? I doubt that I missed a new talent, but I probably overpraised writers of only minimal gift. But in the writing world I was viewed as a harsh critic. A Viennese novelist, a refugee from Nazi Austria, was said to have remarked that he had lost his country, his home, his language, but that he had had at least one good fortune: he had not been reviewed by me.

Among Lionel's literary friends one scarcely rose to the level of appearance (to borrow James's happy phrase) unless one's name was in print. I quickly became a member of this exclusive club: if Fred Dupee had now taken me aside to talk about the new coverings of my living-room chairs, I would not have supposed, as I once had, that he was patronizing me. The editors of *Partisan Review* frequently gave parties. They were torturing affairs for any woman who attended them as a marital appendage rather than in her own literary right; both Edna Phillips and Nathalie Rahv, who had to act as hostesses for their editor husbands, would one day confess to me that in order to get through these evenings they had to fortify themselves with several stiff drinks. Now at *Partisan Review* parties it was as if I had all at once acquired new powers of mind or a new endowment of personal charm; the other writers could talk to me without the fear that they were squandering time which might be used more gainfully. It may be that the circulation of the *Nation* or of the *New Republic* is greater today than it was in the forties, but in the forties these magazines had a place which they have now lost to television and to magazines which can promise their contributors more celebrity. I knew no one in the forties who did not consistently read one or both of them. There was no writer of our acquaintance who was not glad to write for these weekly periodicals: Edmund Wilson established his critical reputation with his literary essays in the *New Republic,* which were later collected in *Axel's Castle.* The *Atlantic Monthly* and *Harper's* were also intended for conscientious readers and they similarly avoided the twin pitfalls of cultural conformity and professional specialization, but they had none of the immediate influence of the two weeklies. It was the *Nation* and the *New Republic* which kept one current with political developments both here and abroad and which confirmed and sharpened one's judgment on books and the arts. In particular, it was their political authority which was held in high regard: it traveled as far as Washington. It was said of the *Nation* during the Roosevelt years that what appeared in its pages today was government policy tomorrow. There was nothing light-mindedly fashionable about reading the *Nation.* It was an obligation of intelligence.

The *Nation* not only described itself as a liberal periodical but this was how it was everywhere described. Yet in fact, during the years in which I wrote for it, politically speaking it was two magazines in one, both of them liberal but with a different understanding of what this meant. The front of the book, its editorial section, was deeply colored by its Communist bias. The back of the book, its literary section, was anti-Communist. These were not stated programs but they were clearly apparent; everyone who read the magazine was likely to be aware of the division. It inspired Elliot Cohen's famous witticism: "How can the *Nation* long endure, half Slav and half free?" Readers of the magazine would readily announce to which section it was that they gave their loyalty. The publisher of the *Nation* was Freda Kirchwey. Although she was nominally my boss, I met her only once, by accident, at a public gathering. Kirchwey was much under the influence of her lover, Julio del Vayo, a Spanish exile and a passionate advocate of the Soviet Union. Even when del Vayo had held office in Negrin's Communist-controlled government in Spain, he had never called himself anything but a Socialist. It is possible that he was a Soviet agent. Yet extreme as was his influence upon Kirchwey, at least throughout the forties she held fast to her principles of free speech. The literary section of the magazine was the domain of Margaret Marshall, and Kirchwey would not interfere in how it was run. Often the division between the front and the back of the book produced an amusing contrast. There was a week in 1943, for instance, in which the *Nation*'s editorial page called for a cessation of criticism of our brave Communist ally but I began my column: "Except for members of the Communist Party, or a few sentimentalists who think that the fine victories of the Russian Army justify the sins of Stalinism, and of course Martin Dies, it is hard to know who can take seriously Ruth McKenney's long and serious new novel, *Jake Home*." My divergence from the magazine's editorial line drew no rebuke from Freda Kirchwey or even, so far as I know, a comment. Indeed, when Margaret was planning a sabbatical, Kirchwey suggested that I take over the literary section of the magazine in her absence; it was Margaret who vetoed the proposal. Eventually the situation changed: Kirchwey began to impose her views on the back of the book and Peggy found it impossible to stay in the job. But this was in the fifties, after I had left. The back of the book, as I knew it, did not represent any organized political position. We were not a political faction but a group of individuals; apart from our loyalty to Peggy, we were united only by our shared rejection of cant, especially the cant of Communist fellow traveling.

Among Peggy's columnists, the one with whom I was best acquainted was her music critic, Bernard Haggin; Lionel and I had met him at Yaddo. Haggin was an angry man; it took considerable patience to be friends with him. Tall, square-shouldered, square-headed, with wiry black hair which fitted close to his skull like a cap, he had the features and bearing of an Egyptian prince. But he was never in regal repose. He took authority from Shaw for his reiterated opinion that the critic was every man's enemy, his hand turned against everyone's. "Tell him to take his finger out of my eye!" was his strange way of indicating a difference of opinion with a musical or literary colleague. His priorities in the living of his life were as strangely his own as his language of invective: one summer on Long Island, when we had arranged that he come out on Friday evening to spend the weekend with us, he wired us on Friday afternoon to say that it was not possible for him to arrive until Saturday morning because he had just learned that his mother was making his favorite vegetable soup for Friday-night dinner. When he was not in a rage, he could be charming and even entertaining. He had a gift for satiric anecdote and a most infectious way of enjoying his own stories. In his bare, spotlessly clean apartment in upper Manhattan near Fort Tryon Park, he repaid the hospitality of his friends with evenings of recorded music. He selected the programs for these home concerts with the greatest care and, sitting over his fine record player, he was as gravely concentrated as the captain of an ocean liner on the bridge of his ship. Our long friendship suffered a premonitory threat when I published a piece in the *Nation* about Caruso—I was apparently permitted to talk about music but not to write about it. Our son's birth was what finally terminated the relationship: Haggin was not prepared to accept the competition for our attention. He signaled the final break by denouncing me roundly for providing liquor for our guests who drank but never having chocolates for him.

Neither Lionel nor I was close to the *Nation*'s film critic, Jim Agee, although we sometimes spent an evening with him; we learned that it was dangerous to invite Agee to our apartment for a visit because he never went home. Rangy and loose-limbed, in appearance he was a younger, handsomer Abe Lincoln, but in reality he was a premature child of the sixties; despite the fact that in addition to writing for the *Nation* he worked for Henry Luce at *Time*, he remained an untarnished figure of rebelliousness. He was a prodigious drinker, but it was not with drink or drugs, it was with language that he undertook to extend the boundaries of consciousness. He seduced language, he made love to language and showered it with gifts, often unwisely. Drink never impeded his talk; liquor was its ally. When he stood up after a long evening of drinking, he would sway gently, like a strong young tree. We had first become aware of Agee on the publication of his book about sharecroppers in the Depression, with its stark and stunning photographs by his close friend Walker Evans. Lionel warmly reviewed *Let Us Now Praise Famous Men* but his appreciation of it was at first not widely shared; on its original appearance in 1941 the book sold six hundred copies. Both Lionel and I liked Evans more than we did Agee. Evans sometimes wrote for *Fortune* as well as photographing for it. He had a harder intelligence than Agee; for example, when both of them reviewed *Mission to Moscow,* a famous politically charged film based upon a book about the Soviet Union by our former ambassador to that country, Joseph Davies, it was Evans who recognized its bias. Agee took refuge in his accustomed pure-mindedness from having to deal with the political message of the film. Beyond his other virtues, Evans was also the best dancer in the intellectual community. The story is told of Agee that after urging Evans to share his, Agee's, wife, Agee sat by weeping as he watched the two of them make love. This is perhaps apocryphal but it captures something which always troubled me in Agee, some element of false or contrived innocence.

Could it have been the evening of my first meeting with the

Nation's art critic, Clement Greenberg, that he and Lionel nearly came to blows? We recently encountered each other after a lapse of many years and I asked Greenberg to refresh my memory of what had precipitated his old quarrel with Lionel. Still righteous, he told me that he had attacked Lionel for having neglected to call Henry Adams to account for his anti-Semitism—this puts him at the head of the list of people who over the years took it upon themselves to tell Lionel how one properly acts as a Jew. Lionel was a peaceable man but he was several times drawn into near-physical clashes with acquaintances of ours. Once, at a *Partisan Review* party, I came up behind him just in time to hear Alfred Kazin demand: "When are you going to dissociate yourself from that wife of yours?" He meant, of course, that Lionel was to dissociate himself from my politics. Perhaps mistakenly, I restrained Lionel's uplifted arm. Another time, it was his tennis racquet which he raised in anger, at Dwight Miner, a colleague in the History Department at Columbia; Miner had refused to relinquish the court which was long past due to us. The strain with Greenberg lasted for most of the decade but the two were at last reconciled, if only symbolically, in unforeseen consequence of a practical joke played upon them. We were wakened one night by a telephone call which purported to come from Delmore Schwartz: he was in difficulty and asked Lionel to come downtown to help him. Lionel and Delmore were only marginally friendly. It was unlikely that he would appeal to Lionel for help, and before rushing into the night Lionel took the precaution of checking at Delmore's apartment. The call was indeed a hoax: Delmore was safely asleep in his bed. By now we were fully awake and we went into the living room to smoke and talk. It was close to five in the morning when suddenly the doorbell rang and there stood Clement Greenberg. He, too, had received a call. His purported to come from Lionel, asking his assistance with Delmore, who was said to be at our house in a state of extreme agitation. With Greenberg's arrival the *ronde* ended but Lionel never forgot Clem's readiness to come all the way from the Village in the middle of the night to help him. Though we never could establish who perpetrated this elaborate ruse, Lionel and I were certain that it was the novelist who, alone among the writers around *Partisan Review,* was aware not only of Lionel's uneasy relationship with both Schwartz and Greenberg but also much talented in mimicry and given to practical jokes.

In the forties celebrity was not the much sought-for peak of the literary life which it is today, not among serious writers. This is not to say that writers were then less interested in success than they are now, but only that serious writers were distinguished from the general class of writers in wanting, not celebrity, but fame. Fame was enduring recognition and even the promise of immortality; celebrity was of the moment and could vanish as fast as it came. In more immediate terms the serious writer measured success by how he was judged by his peers: behind his typewriter stood a formidable tribunal of critics who were also likely to be his close friends and associates. In the literary and intellectual life as I knew it, far from its adding to one's reputation to be widely read and talked about, it put one under suspicion of having compromised one's standards. The risk was particularly great if one made money. It was not the desire for celebrity, it was the desire for fame which Lionel was writing about in his journal. I did not become famous as the fiction critic of the *Nation,* but I had a surprising degree of success in quarters where it most mattered to me. Emily Dickinson was denying the legitimate wish for public acknowledgment when she wrote: "How dreary to be somebody / How public like a frog." I became "somebody" and the condition was not "dreary." It was exceedingly pleasant. Looking back today over my *Nation* reviews, what first strikes me about them is how outspoken they were in their statement of my own tastes and judgments. Reviews this self-referent could not have been written except in a featured column and in the first person, but it astonishes me that with so little ground for authority I claimed so much right to be heard. Apparently, whatever my private timidities, my public voice was firm and courageous. From the start, without instruction, I knew better than to burden my readers with detailed synopses of the books I was reviewing and I never castigated the characters in a novel for being unsuitable as moral companions. Lionel was rebuked at Columbia for his sociological approach to the novel. I was fortunate to be outside the academy: I was even more liable to this accusation, but no one brought it. It is hard for me to recapture the early heady experience of becoming a public person, someone whose name was recognized on introduction, at least among literary people. Publishers took me to lunch to ask me to write books for them. I was interviewed and photographed by the fashion magazines. Leo Lerman came to interview me for *Vogue* and stayed to become a lifelong friend. The *Nation*'s promotion department singled me out from among its regular writers to advertise the magazine. It gave me a large party for which, although she did not herself attend, Freda Kirchwey contributed her handsome apartment on Washington Square. I was several times invited to be a judge in literary competitions. The most bizarre of these invitations came from Metro-Goldwyn-Mayer, which was holding a contest for a new novel to be made into a film. The first prize was $250,000, a sum of then-unheard-of magnificence. The woman who phoned me with the invitation to be a judge in this M-G-M contest explained that I would have to read no more than seven or eight final manuscripts and that I would be paid seven fifty a book. I repeated the amount carefully: "You mean seven hundred and fifty dollars a book?" Oh no, she hurried to correct me: seven dollars and fifty cents. When I refused the paltry fee, she inquired icily: "Why, how much do they pay you at the *Nation?*" My pay at the *Nation* was two cents a word, and I could also sell my review copies. There were weeks in which I made as much as $35.

The index of my 1978 volume, *Reviewing the Forties,* for which I made a selection of my *Nation* pieces, reveals an imposing array of writers whom I reviewed: Jean-Paul Sartre, Arthur Koestler, James T. Farrell, James Gould Cozzens, Saul Bellow, Eudora Welty,

Sylvia Townsend Warner, Katherine Anne Porter, John Marquand, Sinclair Lewis, Truman Capote, Edmund Wilson, Alan Paton, Angela Thirkell, Ayn Rand, Elizabeth Hardwick, Helen Howe, J. B. Priestley, Eleanor Clark, Christina Stead, Robert Graves, Robert Penn Warren, John Hersey, Elizabeth Bowen, Somerset Maugham, Carl Sandburg, William Maxwell, Jean Stafford, Vladimir Nabokov, William Saroyan, Herman Wouk, Joyce Cary, Anaïs Nin, Dawn Powell, Evelyn Waugh, Carson McCullers, George Orwell. All of these had novels published in the forties and I wrote about them. How then did it happen that I left the magazine, as I did in 1949, not because I was tired of writing reviews, but because I was tired of reading the books which came to me for review? The answer lies, I suppose, in the disproportion between the known and unknown authors I had to deal with. For every book by a writer of established reputation, I had to go through a hundred by people of less or no interest and even with known writers I was not always in agreement with the established judgment. The novels I could read with pleasure or even with curiosity were, I am afraid, few in number; I came to feel that the greater the literary pretension, the soggier the performance. In 1939 the talented popular author Grace Zaring Stone took the pseudonym Ethel Vance to write an anti-Nazi thriller, *Escape,* which launched a new category of fictional entertainment. While *Escape* was no doubt ahead of its time in its recognition of the Nazi menace, to read it today is to be reminded of how little we knew or could imagine about Hitler even on the eve of the Second World War. Commonplace though they might be in their execution, political thrillers provided me with welcome relief from the run of current fiction. Sometimes I had to write about books by friends; I always found this troublesome. But to fail to write about the book of a friend could make for even worse problems. I remember a week in which I did a roundup of ten inconsequential novels in order to give a six-line mention to a book by a friend. Edmund Wilson was never more than an acquaintance, but having to review his *Memoirs of Hecate County* gave me, I recall, great difficulty because of his stature as a critic and because he had gone out of his way to be kind to me early in my career. A year or so after I began at the *Nation* I published my first literary essay. It was about Alice James, the then little-known younger sister of William and Henry. Wilson waited for me at a party to tell me that he had enjoyed the essay and to urge me to concentrate on more-extended critical writing rather than on reviews. On its appearance *Memoirs of Hecate County* was charged with obscenity, and Lionel was one of the people who testified at its trial. He told me about the plight of the judge, who was impaired in his hearing, so that the obscenities being put into evidence by the prosecuting attorney had to be shouted at him. But it was one thing to oppose literary censorship and another to deal with Wilson's novel on its merits, especially since my dislike of *Hecate County* considerably derived from my sense of the unpleasant emotions which had animated its author. My review became a major exercise in circumlocution. I suppose that all regular reviewers long for a "discovery." I was not alone in discovering the talent of Isabel Bolton; Wilson was at that period the book critic of the *New Yorker* and he, too, wrote in praise of her novel *Do I Wake or Sleep.* Isabel Bolton's remarkable little book was surely the best novel by a new writer to come to me in my career as a reviewer. The author was past sixty when it was published. The novel is about the confrontation between American innocence and European experience, a Jamesian theme, but Miss Bolton's thoroughly intelligent and beautifully crafted book went well beyond being a Jamesian school piece. Yet despite Wilson's appreciation of it and mine, *Do I Wake or Sleep* quickly sank from sight; its publishers lacked our faith in it. Her excellent next novel, *The Christmas Tree,* a penetrating study of the possible psychological origins of homosexuality, was also permitted to disappear. Christopher Isherwood was the runner-up to Isabel Bolton as the happiest of my new encounters. He was younger than Miss Bolton and fared better in his career: his *Prater Violet,* which I reviewed in 1945, is still in print and his subsequent work is of course widely known.

It was not possible to write about the novels of the forties and avoid the politics of the left, whether trumpeted or cloaked. The attitude toward politics of writers and intellectuals had importantly changed since the early days of the Depression. With the creation of the Popular Front in 1935, Communism was no longer aimed at the overthrow of capitalism. It no longer had revolution as its goal. The united front, which Stalin had so disastrously refused in Germany when Nazism first emerged in that country, was now more than encouraged, demanded. The order from Moscow was that Communist parties in the West cooperate with all people of good will, whatever their party connection. The American Communist Party obediently surrendered its political militancy and its cultural militancy as well: where it had earlier called for a literature which would celebrate and support the working class, it now sought a more common denominator and found it in the figure of the "little man," a virtually classless representative of the democratic hope but also of the failed promises of capitalism. The so-called proletarian novel had never flourished in American soil; the American writer would seem to have been unable successfully to imagine a proletarian hero. He was even less successful with the little man as hero: it apparently takes more than a virtuous victim to bear the weight of a significant work of fiction. To tell the little man's story there even came into being what I called a little-man prose, a soft, lilting language of self-effacing decency. Itself disarmed, it was presumed to be disarming.

> A star fell and hit me . . . I had figured it all out suddenly. Logic—schoolroom logic. What was lacking in the world was faith. A faith like old-time religion. A faith honest, earnest, and true to all these things handed down from a mountain in Sinai . . . a return to a faith of the

little people, a love of mankind, an understanding, a tolerance of the rights of people. Of the rights of lovers and
children and fields . . .

The passage is taken from a peculiarly ill-conditioned example of
the little-man genre, *The Land I Live* by Stephen Longstreet, but
it is not untypical. Released by the Popular Front from the duty to
write about the proletariat, a class foreign to his experience, the
middle-class novelist was also free now to write about himself. The
forties saw a spate of but thinly disguised autobiographical fiction,
all of it with its base in the radical commitment, most of it confessional and even self-condemnatory. One of the chief targets in the
hearings of the House Un-American Activities Committee at the
end of the decade would be the playwright Michael Blankfort. His
novel *A Time to Live,* which I reviewed on its appearance in 1943,
was almost comic in the range and passion of its self-indictment:
his protagonist had fiddled away his time at playwriting when he
should have devoted himself to revolution and he had remained a
doubting fellow traveler when he should have joined the Communist Party. In a tasteless play of fancy, Mr. Blankfort even has the
wife of his spokesperson die of leukemia, a disease in which the
white blood corpuscles destroy the red. Hiram Haydn, who would
later in the forties become editor of the *American Scholar,* the journal of the Phi Beta Kappa Society, was another conspicuous contributor to this literature of repentance. Of Mr. Haydn's novel *By
Nature Free,* I wrote:

Persuade a writer that anything in the world—politics,
sociology, economics, religion—is expected of him
except literature and you can hardly expect him to practice literature without guilt. While in the Twenties and
even in the early Thirties it was the whole point of
the biographical novel that society was responsible for
the unhappy condition of the author-hero, ten years

of "social conscience" topped off by a new world
war have reversed the situation: now it is the author-
hero who is responsible for the unhappy condition of
society.

Throughout my stay at the *Nation* my anti-Communism was seldom far from the surface of my reviews. It seemed, however, not to interfere with the reception of my column as it would to-day though today the Soviet Union no longer exists and the anti-Communist position has only a historical significance. I explain the difference by the fact that in the forties we were still in the pre-McCarthy era. Though anti-Communism was certainly not a fashionable position among intellectuals, it was not yet thought to be discreditable. McCarthy took anti-Communism out of the realm of debate and, by his example, created for liberals an automatic association between anti-Communism and reaction. Before McCarthy, although anti-Communism was not a prevailing sentiment among our best-educated classes, it was still a viable political position; it was never assumed of it that it necessarily went hand in hand with political conservatism. All declared Socialists were anti-Communists, and with a few exceptions our anti-Communist friends were declared liberals. Lionel and I never regarded ourselves as anything but liberals, and it was how we would have been generally described, as liberal anti-Communists. The phrase was a comfortable one; it had in it no hint of paradox. Lionel was not being disingenuous or self-ironizing in calling his 1950 volume of essays *The Liberal Imagination* and no one of any political sophistication questioned his dual use of the word "liberal" in that book, now to define his own political point of view, now to refer to the Communist-inspired liberalism which he was putting under critical inspection. Throughout the forties it was widely recognized among intellectuals that there were two kinds of liberals: anti-Communist liberals and fellow-traveling liberals. The back of the *Nation* was known to be anti-Communist but it was never accused of speaking for the right. Insofar as the regular contributors to the back of the magazine were conscious of being in disagreement with its editorial policy, we felt that we represented a liberal dissent from the mindless Communist-controlled liberalism of the front of the book. Compared to fellow-traveling liberals, anti-Communist liberals were few in number and had far less power in the culture. Then as still, we were also disbelieved. In 1947 there came to me for review the first volume, *The Age of Reason,* in a projected fictional trilogy by Jean-Paul Sartre. Comparing Sartre's search for an authority with which to replace the sexually tainted parental authority with Aldous Huxley's similar need to escape the heavy burden of our sexuality, I wrote of Sartre: "While one hesitates to conjecture that the very fierceness of the Existentialist protest against authority may disguise a longing for it, we recall that Heidegger, the German Existentialist, became a Nazi. And we take note of the fact that the Communist Brunet in *The Age of Reason* is given, almost all unconsciously, a very different moral quality from the other characters. Huxley chose God; might not the Existentialist choose the State—the proletarian dictatorship, say, though not the fascist dictatorship? Might not the final act of freedom be the free choice to give up all purely personal freedom?" The prediction, so soon to be confirmed, outraged Sartre's publishers and no doubt many of the *Nation*'s readers as well. But whatever the distaste or disbelief with which anti-Communist opinion was received in the general liberal community, anti-Communists were not excluded, nor did we exclude ourselves, from the intellectual mainstream of the country. McCarthy substantially changed all this. He was a great gift to the Soviet Union; in cultural terms the greatest gift our country could have made to Communism. He robbed anti-Communism of its base in liberalism and brought to it the opprobrium which attached to his own mode of operation. In the wake of McCarthy, all anti-Communism, liberal no less than illiberal, became vulnerable to the demeaning charge of McCarthyism. I recall the surprise with which I heard a friend of ours, a person of moderate liberal opinion, speak of John L. Lewis, head of the AFL – CIO, as a "Neanderthal man" because of his intransigent opposition to Communism: it was the fifties and McCarthy had thus polluted our political rhetoric. McCarthyism had a lasting effect in polarizing the intellectual community and in entrenching anti-anti-Communism as the position of choice among liberals. As recently as 1990 one of our popular novelists, a moving figure in the writers' organization, PEN, could declare that anti-Communism was the worst evil of our century. It is highly improbable that he intended this as a statement in favor of Communism. I take him to have been saying that it was anti-Communism which had drawn us into the war in Vietnam and that it was as a consequence of Communism and the Cold War that America had spent on armaments the money which it might better have spent on necessary social programs. The charge cannot be lightly dismissed, but it fails to address the large question of what would have happened to our country and to this writer and his family, among other lovers of democracy, had the Soviet Union been permitted to triumph in the West. There is a curious abstractness in the liberal condemnation of anti-Communism, which has become increasingly marked since the collapse of the Soviet Union. It is as if there were no connection between the reality of Soviet Communism, in particular Stalin's Communism, and the opposition it engendered among some few intellectuals in the democracies. While on the one hand liberalism acknowledges and deplores the evil of the Communist dictatorship, on the other hand it treats anti-Communism as an object of its scorn. The illogic of this attitude was plainly underscored in the celebration of Vaclav Havel, the president of the new free Czechoslovakia, on his visit to America. In greeting Havel as a representative of the new and better dispensation in Middle Europe, the anti-anti-Communists were apparently able to ignore the fact that Havel had spent long years in jail because of his "evil" occupation as an anti-Communist. Political logic, however, has seldom been the ready resource of writers and intellectuals. There comes to mind a symposium which was held by *Commentary* in the early sixties on the topic "Better Red Than Dead." This was when Norman Podhoretz, then newly the editor of *Commentary,* was still a partisan of the New Left and devoted to rescuing the magazine from the anti-Communism of its founding editor, Elliot Cohen. Together with the British author C. P. Snow, Stuart Hughes argued the affirmative in that debate. He was prepared to surrender the United States to Soviet Russia rather than die battling Communism. Yet he was not prepared to leave the matter there. He foresaw a heroic role for people like himself in an underground opposition to the ruling regime; the memorable moment of the evening was his reply to the question: What would happen to people like him under a Communist dictatorship in America? With schoolboy ardor, Hughes responded that he and his friends would take to the hills with their rifles. It would appear that he invited the Soviet Union into America so that he could be in opposition to it.

One of the periodicals for which I wrote with some frequency during the McCarthy era was the liberal anti-Communist weekly the *New Leader,* edited by Sol Levitas. In the pages of the *New Leader* I described my dual position: I was against both Communism and McCarthyism. They were enemies of each other, but I was the enemy of both. Double positions of this kind are not popular; it appears to be too much to ask of us that we hold two opposing ideas in our minds at the same time. I also briefly described my position on McCarthy in an issue of *Partisan Review.* It brought a surprising letter from Philip Graham, the husband of Katherine Graham—it was he who was then the publisher of the *Washington Post.* At a Washington dinner party he had been lamenting the support which McCarthy was presumed to have gained among the New York intellectuals, and he had named me as one of McCarthy's adherents, but when he came home from the party he happened on my piece in *Partisan Review* and he wrote now to apologize for his misstatement and to assure me that he would call the other people at the dinner party to retract his unfounded accusation. Reviewing my collection *Claremont Essays* when it was published in England in 1965, the English critic Christopher Ricks also undertook to set straight my political record. He wrote that, having been told in America that I was a right-winger, he had gone through all my published work to find evidence for the charge. He had found none. Far from supporting McCarthy, I thought that his procedures and those of the House Un-American Activities Committee were a serious threat to freedom and an offense against the democratic process. But they were not a witch hunt, as they are so often said to have been. Witches do not exist. Communists and Communist fellow travelers did exist, the latter in abundance.

It was generous advice which Wilson gave me when I published my first literary essay, that I now turn to more extended critical writing instead of concentrating on book reviews, but I was not enough sure of myself as a writer to take his advice until several years later. Like most serious intellectuals, Wilson was an intellectual snob, what would now be pejoratively referred to as an elitist. He wanted me to write for the discriminating monthlies and quarterlies, but I began to contribute to the women's magazines and the large-circulation periodicals: *Vogue, Harper's Bazaar, McCall's, Mademoiselle.* In the early fifties the editor of one of the popular women's magazines would tell me that there had been a recent moment in which the editors of all the large-circulation journals in this country had had to decide whether to seek a more general public or, as she put it, "raid *Partisan Review.*" The magazines which chose the latter course increased their readership; those which strove to become more popular lost circulation. What she was describing was the moment in the cultural life of this country in which what had previously been a virtually unnavigable distance between the world of high seriousness and our more popular culture began suddenly to narrow. The literary magazines had up to this time held the superior ground. They now lost much of their dominance: the next decades saw them steadily relinquish their power to periodicals designed to reach a wider, less demanding audience. Today the authority and influence, which were once the property of magazines with a circulation of four or five thousand, are enjoyed by popular journals such as the *New Yorker* or *Vanity Fair*. It was not until the late forties that I began to write for *Partisan Review:* I suspect that I was their first contributor who had also appeared in *Glamour*. Although I liked to boast that wherever I wrote, my work was the same, I think I was deceiving myself. Where one cannot assume that one is writing for people with the same education as oneself and the same intellectual concerns, one is bound to limit one's range of reference and to relax the tension in one's prose. I have only once published the same piece in both a popular journal and a literary magazine: a piece I wrote on the death of Marilyn Monroe appeared simultaneously in *Redbook* in America and in the distinguished Anglo-American journal *Encounter* in England. It was Marilyn Monroe, not I, who bridged the gap between the two periodicals.

There were times when it was possible to read hostility into Margaret Marshall's long periods of depressed silence. There was only one occasion, however, when any bad feeling toward me rose to the surface. Discussing Margaret's projected sabbatical, Freda Kirchwey had suggested that I replace Margaret during her absence. "She suggested *you*," Margaret reported the conversation incredulously. In her view the proposal was so patently absurd that I was bound to share her entertainment, and to my shame I did in fact laugh, or at least smile, along with her. Perhaps I invited treatment of this sort. I was similarly mocked and drawn into self-mockery when Ursula Niebuhr, the English-born wife of the renowned theologian Reinhold Niebuhr, reported a compliment which had been paid me by T. S. Eliot. The Niebuhrs were friends and neighbors of ours on Claremont Avenue. They frequently entertained visitors from England and during a visit from Eliot, Lionel's name had apparently come up in the conversation. Eliot remarked that he was unfamiliar with Lionel's work but that he was an admirer of mine. Repeating so bizarre a statement, Ursula was unable to contain her amusement. Like the kinsman of Major Molyneux in Hawthorne's story of that name, I joined in her denigration of me. For her replacement at the *Nation* while she was on leave, Margaret chose the poet Randall Jarrell. He was an acute critic of poetry; she could reasonably expect that he would bring distinction to the post. The magazine did not suffer from the appointment, but he disliked my work and I, too, soon took a sabbatical. On the arrival of the Jarrells in New York, we had invited them to dinner. I traveled across town to Madison Avenue to procure a special dessert, a coconut cream pie. As I brought the pie to the table, Jarrell inquired brightly: "What's that? Pus?" Lionel and I were also invited to a small welcoming party given for the Jarrells by the Rahvs. I had a new pocket watch which Lionel had given me as a present; it wound by being opened and shut, and I passed it around the little circle in which we were sitting because Rahv was curious to see how it worked. Afterward Lionel told me that he had known that when the watch reached Jarrell, Jarrell would drop it on the floor. British intellectuals are more accomplished than Americans at being rude. An early English visitor in New York after the war was Cyril Connolly, the gifted author of *Enemies of Promise* and editor of the short-lived British literary magazine *Horizon*. We had Connolly to lunch with the Barzuns. Marianna Barzun, who adhered to outmoded laws of etiquette, wore her hat at table, which may have stimulated Connolly's wish to outrage the company. With the food shortages in England in mind, I had prepared a rich chocolate cream for dessert. Connolly never tasted it. He elaborately indicated that he had no intention of tasting it, by lighting a cigar and flicking his ashes into it.

Although it was the forties and the women's movement had not yet begun, all the publishers who took me to lunch in the hope of signing me up for a book wanted me to write about women. They were not specific about the content or direction of such a book but they appeared to sense the existence of a large market for a book on the subject. I never wrote a book about women until, many years later, I wrote a book about *a* woman, Jean Harris. I never wrote a book of any kind until I wrote *Mrs. Harris: The Death of the Scarsdale Diet Doctor* after Lionel's death. From time to time the idea for a book would occur to me. There was a period in which I contemplated a book about Jane Welsh Carlyle, wife of Thomas Carlyle; she was a strangely modern instance of old-fashioned frustrated female talent. For a time I also toyed with the possibility of writing about Freud's friend and pupil Lou Andreas-Salomé. I wrote reviews and critical essays and I wrote articles of various length and depth. In the sixties I collected what I thought to be the best of my essays in a volume, *Claremont Essays*. While I was still working for the *Nation* I edited the volume on D. H. Lawrence for the Viking Portable Library; I also published a selection of Lawrence's letters. In 1950 I was awarded a Guggenheim Fellowship for a book in which I proposed to study the interplay between my family culture and the general culture of the time in which I grew up. The book was never written except as there may now be a reminiscence of it in this volume. I contributed to other people's books; I did not write a book of my own. There are several possible explanations for my failure to engage in a larger enterprise than reviews and articles. The most ready to hand is obviously Lionel's looming presence in my life. But if it was Lionel who inhibited me, the responsibility lies with me, not with him. He placed no barriers in my literary path. Far from putting any restraints upon me, Lionel constantly encouraged my career and delighted in its every advance. He was much quicker to my literary defense than to his own, and he countenanced no suggestion that he impose his authority on me: when a well-known London psychoanalyst once wrote to demand that he put a stop to my criticism of psychoanalysis, he greeted this request with amused contempt. The question most often asked of me by interviewers is: How did it feel to be Lionel's wife? How, they mean, did it feel to be a critic in my own right but married to a better and more famous critic than I? My honest if unfashionable answer is that it felt fine. We were never in competition as writers. We were never in competition of any sort. It sometimes happened that I would be downgraded or overlooked in his favor but this was anything but his doing. The English biographer of E. M. Forster, P. N. Furbank, wrote and thanked Lionel for help which in fact I had given him. On their superficial meetings, Lionel had been scarcely aware of him and he was enough annoyed by Furbank's misdirected gratitude to write back in reprimand. We once both contributed to a symposium in a semipopular magazine for which Lionel was paid a fee twice the size of mine. I protested my payment but this was not because I thought that I should receive the same pay as his but because I independently wanted more money than I was being given. If there was a single rivalry between us it was one of which I never spoke to him and which I mention here only with some wryness: the men I knew seemed always to be more taken with Lionel than with me. I never had any doubt in my mind but that, of the two of us, he was the more important writer. He had more to say than I and a great deal more resonated from what he wrote. Having been better educated than I, he moved through the centuries and through the intellectual disciplines as I could not. Lionel felt of my work that it was not enough appreciated and that this was chiefly due to his presence in my life. But he did not mean this in the sense in which it would be generally understood. He did not mean that I was overshadowed by his reputation. He was talking about the nature of our marriage, the fact that I not only wrote under my married name but always appeared in public as his wife, never as someone with her own literary identity. He would point out to me—but he never talked about it with anyone else—that there was no other woman writer in our circle who was so unremittingly coupled with a man as I. Myself, I had and have a simpler explanation of why my marriage may have detracted from my literary recognition. People will celebrate one member of a household but not two. To celebrate two members of a single household doubles the strain on generosity. Women, in particular, were likely to feel that I had enough good fortune in being married to someone as attractive and agreeable and distinguished as Lionel without, in addition, having distinction of my own. It has indeed been my impression that more envy has been directed to me than to any woman writer of our acquaintance, Hannah Arendt, Lillian Hellman, Mary McCarthy, all of them infinitely more successful than I, and that Lionel was the cause. The situation was most crudely revealed in the letter I received from Hannah More Everett, the wife of Charles Everett. Everett was for a time head of the Columbia English Department; he was also an occasional fishing companion of Lionel's. Hannah More was a markedly fastidious woman of unanticipated wit. She was said to be an accomplished pianist though no one heard her play; she would not have called this much attention to herself. She piqued my curiosity; I thought of her as someone of much spirit, much repressed. A few years before her death, Hannah More wrote a brief memoir. She made no attempt to publish it; she said that she had written it just for her nieces. But she gave it to Lionel to read with the understanding that it was not to be shared with me. To me, she wrote a letter which it is still painful for me to recollect. With an impertinence which much contradicted her usual refinement, she wrote to remind me that a woman's first duty was to her husband; I must forget about my own writing and devote myself undividedly to Lionel. Another such intervention, this time by Lionel's publishers, the Viking Press, was even more surprising though less encompassing in its purpose than Hannah More's letter. In the late fifties I published an article, "The Case for the American Woman," in *Look,* a highly popular magazine of the period. It was a solicited piece, a reply to a series of articles which had been running in the magazine; the articles charged American women with pushing their husbands to extremes of exhaustion, often fatal, in order to satisfy their lust for money. We were ourselves always short of money. Every few months I drew up a list of our debts, which Lionel and I contemplated with despair. Almost always, miraculously, something would turn up to rescue us at the brink of disaster. *Look* offered me $9,000 for three articles in defense of women. I agreed to do one for $3,000. It was more money than either Lionel or I had ever been paid for anything and we were ecstatic, Lionel even more so than I. In my piece I declared that American homes were mental hospitals; the women were the nurses, their husbands the patients. The statement drew a storm of protest. Viking was not directly in touch with me. It protested to Lionel that I was damaging his reputation and must not be allowed to continue.

Actually, with my upbringing I had to be married to a man who was more successful than I. I should not have known how to manage if the scales had been tipped differently. The limits which I would put on my career were similarly determined in my upbringing; my literary life was just one more territory through which I dragged the heavy anchor of my childhood instruction. I did not have to be married to someone who was as good a critic as Lionel to put a brake on my ambitions. Whether in deference to my sister's disabilities or my brother's masculinity or merely in obedience to the family Puritanism, which decreed that less was better, I was reared to curb my energies. If we can say that I was born with ten units of personal power, I never used more than five. What would have happened to my marriage if I had used all ten, I obviously cannot know. But I surmise that the marriage would not have endured as it did. Lionel's and my life together was precisely tuned to the needs of each of us. It met the requirements of our weaknesses no less than of our strengths. This is the magic of all marriages which survive, that they answer the demands prepared for them many years earlier, well before the partners have any acquaintance with each other. I did eventually write a book of my own, *Mrs. Harris*. It made few, if any, generalizations about my sex. I have never supposed that I have any special wisdom to impart on the subject of women. I separate from the feminists of our present day in thinking of men, not as the opponents of women, but as their companions in the same hard business of being human. If, as is surely the case, they have had advantages in this difficult enterprise which have been denied to women, it has not made them any happier. I am not convinced that it is harder to be a woman than it is to be a man. I have also had far too many pleasures and privileges in being a woman to think of myself as a victim in the way in which feminist doctrine now seems to dictate. By and large, I have been much more troubled by the petty superiorities which men assert over women than by the grand social injustices: the fact, say, that quick as I am in calculation, I have to stand by while a confounded man fumbles for our taxi fare or, with my reliable sense of direction, I have to yield to a male navigator determined to drive us a hundred miles out of our way. In the spring of 1971 I took part in a meeting at New York's Town Hall in which Norman Mailer defended his book *The Prisoner of Sex* against a panel of women. To most women in the women's movement Mailer was the enemy; several women who were invited to speak that evening refused to share a platform with him. Norman and I had met many years earlier at a party at Lillian Hellman's where he had turned to me at the dinner table with the opening remark, "And how about you, smart cunt?" I am usually addressed with appalling respect: he got my attention. We became good friends and at the time of the Town Hall meeting we were still friends; he had not yet capitulated, as he did a few years later, to Hellman's requirement that no friend of hers be a friend of mine. The star of our evening at Town Hall was Germaine Greer, the highly popular author of a volume of feminist polemic, *The Female Eunuch*. Greer had, in my view, complicated her position on the condition of women by making it widely known on the eve of her encounter with Mailer that she wanted to go to bed with him. The Green Room of Town Hall, in which Mailer and the panelists gathered, was suffused with sexual intimation. Ever gallant, Mailer was holding up Greer's book for the cameras instead of his own. Not all feminists make reliable "sisters": throughout the delivery of my talk—so my friends in the audience would later tell me—Greer upstaged me by passing notes to Mailer; he never heard my speech and had to ask me the next day if he could read it. The Town Hall meeting was more a "happening" than an occasion for sensible discussion. The Hall was crowded and the audience rowdy and obscene, in the fashion of the late sixties. I reprinted my talk and described the encounter in my 1977 volume, *We Must March My Darlings.* The evening was also recorded in a film, "Town Bloody Hall," which was many times shown at the Whitney Museum in New York. The occasion marked, I think, the end of an earlier decade. It had not been my decade: I was a sightseer at the sixties. My own long-ago generation was that which followed the triumph of woman suffrage after the First World War. Women had won the vote and they had won many new social and personal freedoms, and for the most part we were content. With disbelief I recall that as a college sophomore I and my Radcliffe contemporaries were lectured to by our dean, Mrs. George Pierce Baker, wife of the famous Harvard professor of drama, who, speaking to us of the importance to women of a college degree, promised us that our college educations would not only help us to be more efficient housekeepers but also provide us with something to occupy our minds as we went about our domestic chores: washing our dishes, we would cleverly stack them on the drainboard to be rinsed with but a single kettle of boiling water; drying our dishes, we could recite to ourselves our favorite poems of Shelley or Keats. Although in the next years women of my age and education were urged not to allow themselves to disappear into domesticity, our success as women was still measured by our success as wives. Today, after a century of revolutions, of which the most successful has been the sexual revolution, I wonder how much this judgment has really changed. Superficially, much has really changed: in the public sphere women edge into new positions of power, and in the domestic sphere the demand grows for men to share in the rearing of their children and in the running of their homes. Certainly life has been made more tolerable for women who do not marry. Yet if we are to trust the cultural signs, the evidence, for instance, of television and the movies, whatever a woman's accomplishment outside the home, it is still by her success with men and, specifically, her success as a wife and mother that she is finally judged.

Viking's Pat Covici was the most amiable of the publishers I came to know while I was writing for the *Nation* and the most persistent in urging me to write a book for him. It was easier for Pat to lie than to tell the truth but this was part of his charm for Lionel and me. We often went to his house for dinner. Sweating profusely, he would produce his unspellable Hungarian noodle dish, or was it Romanian, like Pat himself? Other than to contribute my Lawrence volume to the Viking Portable Library, I never became a Viking author, but with the publication of his novel, *The Middle of the Journey,* Lionel began a long association with the firm. Lionel, too, contributed to the Portable Library; he did their volume on Matthew Arnold. We were both of us paid the standard fee for a Portable, $1,000. No royalty was specified in the contract, and the fact that Lawrence was one of the more prolific of modern writers and that it took me more than six months to read through his forty-five volumes of long and short fiction, critical essays, travel writing, and poetry did not bear on the financial arrangement. After Covici's death in 1964, such trifling business as I had with Viking was taken over by Marshall Best. In 1970, twenty-three years after the publication of my Lawrence Portable, Best wrote to tell me that inasmuch as the sales had now exceeded a hundred thousand, the firm was granting me a small royalty; I would be receiving an advance of $250 against future earnings. I had been content with my original agreement but, as I now wrote to Best, an advance of $250 on a book which had sold over a hundred thousand copies was an insult. Best was not the cuddly bear that Covici had been. There even came the moment when young Tom Guinzburg, who had become head of the firm on the death of his father, Harold, had to save me from Best's plan to take the Portable Lawrence away from me and have a new volume edited to meet the requests of professors of English throughout the country.

In 1950, no longer at the *Nation,* I had done my first important essay-review for *Partisan Review.* It was called "Men, Women and Sex" and was a review of Margaret Mead's *Male and Female.* Mead's book was poorly written and not easy to deal with; I had to read it twice to be sure that I understood its argument. I met Margaret Mead only once, at the home of Eliseo Vivas, Lionel's old Wisconsin acquaintance. Much of the evening was given to a discussion of religion. While Mead was not herself religious, she told us that she sent her daughter to church so that she would not be deprived of an experience which appeared to have been necessary to all people at all times in history. Lionel and I felt that if she herself was not a believer, sending her child to church was only a contrivance; it altered and even invalidated its significance as a religious act. The argument lasted most of the evening and carried us a considerable distance beyond its starting point; before we had done, both sides had modified their views. Margaret Mead looked tough and had, of course, a formidable reputation, but what I chiefly recall of the evening was her apparent vulnerability: at one stage of the discussion she wrongly supposed that we were attacking her, and her lips began to tremble as if she were about to cry. After the appearance of my Mead essay, I wrote with increasing frequency for the literary journals. The transition demanded no major self-renovation; by now I, too, regarded myself as an intellectual. But I have never brought to the designation the unqualified pride with which Mary McCarthy invests it in the memoir on which she was working at her death. Today, when the intellectual world as I knew it in the middle decades of the century no longer exists, I deeply mourn its loss. I loved intellectual talk: the easy discursiveness, the free range of reference, the refusal of received ideas, the always-ready wit. I cherished the exigency of the intellectual life as it used to be lived and I ask myself now: What is this poor thing called mind? My attitude toward intellectuals themselves, however, has always been ambivalent. I always supposed that an intellectual met Diderot's definition of a philosopher, that he was a man of reason; that is, someone who not only reasoned well but lived a reasonable life. I expected intelligence to be matched by honorableness and I continue to regard any failure of integrity on the part of an intellectual with the kind of dismay with which religious people regard human folly in a man of the cloth. It never ceases to surprise me how little able intellectuals are to apply their gifts of mind to life's actualities or, even more important, how little their strength of mind is matched by grace and generosity of spirit. Writing about the relation between art and neurosis, Lionel pointed out that artists are surely no more subject to psychological disorder than scientists; the difference is that artists leave a record of their disturbance as scientists do not. This perhaps also applies to intellectuals: it may be that intellectuals are no more malicious or self-absorbed or self-seeking than other people, but their actions are more public. It troubles me that intellectuals seem to experience the ordinary human emotions through reading rather than through living. They go to books for the knowledge of their human kind and remain in ignorance of what is going on around them. Philip Rahv, who had to be told what an obstetrician did for a living, was only an egregious instance of such blindness to social fact. It has not been reassuring to be a longtime witness to the political histories of some of the best-known figures in our intellectual community, their weavings and waverings, their movement from one extreme of the political spectrum to another: anti-Communist liberals suddenly giving their support to Hanoi, hard-line Socialists joining the Children's Crusade of Gene McCarthy, onetime Trotskyists becoming the staunchest of right-wing Republicans. As a young man, Lionel met an old Russian anarchist who warned him that the only thing that intellectuals really cared about was power. I am not certain that this is true, but perhaps it is. I am more impelled to believe that the intellectual, like everyone else, is animated by the wish to be in accord with those around him who, in his view, best represent the requirements put upon him in his childhood. Identification with the parent of one's own sex, unconscious though it may be, provides us with the strongest motive for our behavior. That mildest of creatures George Novack, who became a lifelong Trotskyist, was the son of a failed gangster. I read in his emotional history a text which is applicable to us all.

The great terminating event of the forties for the New York intellectuals was the Hiss case. Whittaker Chambers, a contemporary of Lionel's at Columbia, most recently an editor at *Time,* confessed to having spied for the Soviet Union and accused Alger Hiss of having similarly engaged in Soviet espionage. Hiss was one of the architects of the United Nations and a former official in our State Department. For the people around *Partisan Review* the Hiss case was located in familiar territory; most of us had for some brief time been Communist fellow travelers or sympathizers. We knew that the Soviet Union counted upon the unlawful help of its well-placed supporters in the democracies and we were even acquainted with the vocabulary of espionage, bandying such words as "drop," "control," "microfilm." Far from its being difficult for us to credit Chambers's accusation of Hiss, his charge, like the parallel charge which would eventually be confessed to by Sir Anthony Blunt, the keeper of the Queen's Art Collection in England, brought to us a shock of recognition: there but for the grace of God went any one of us. William Phillips took me to an expensive lunch to ask me to write their Hiss piece for *Partisan Review.* I was flattered but badly frightened. I nevertheless accepted the assignment and I wrote the piece without difficulty. For years the Hiss case represented for America, if only in small, what the Dreyfus case had represented for France. While it could not be said to have divided this country as the Dreyfus case divided France, nor of course to have produced a Proust to record its effect on the society, it dramatically divided our best-educated and politically conscious population. My piece in *Partisan Review* was not an analysis of testimony, such as I would try to supply a few years later in writing about the Oppenheimer hearings before the Atomic Energy Commission. It was a political memorandum and chiefly dealt with the relation of liberal idealism to the reality of Soviet totalitarianism. In dividing on the guilt or innocence of Hiss, American liberal opinion ignored the evidence on which he was convicted of perjury. The division was an ideological, almost automatic, separation between those who measured their political enlightenment by their tolerance of the Soviet Union and those who had old acquaintance with Stalin's objectives and methods.

Throughout its early and best decades, *Partisan Review* spoke of itself as anti-Stalinist in its politics but radical in its culture. I am afraid that I have little taste for what one usually means by the radical in culture, yet looking back over all my work I realize that although the individuals and events about which I wrote were perhaps not always wholly adversary to the established culture, they were to a significant extent subversive of it or in conflict with it. Whittaker Chambers was a self-confessed spy. Robert Oppenheimer, while himself not guilty of treason, moved by political preference among treasonable people. Profumo and his well-placed friends in England represented scandal in high places. Norman Mailer was the self-advertised spokesman for hipsterism. Allen Ginsberg and the "beats" described themselves as druggies and crazies. Timothy Leary, once a member of the Harvard faculty, had made his more recent career promoting LSD. Jean Harris was a convicted murderer. The campus uprisings at Columbia were defended on the ground that they were a "shove to establishment." Such were the people and subjects of which I chose to write, and if this manifest appeal of the illegal or illicit does not put me in the company of Rebecca West, whom I so much admire and who wrote so brilliantly about people who had rejected the established values of their society, it at least points to the darker interests I shared with her. I met Rebecca West's son, Anthony, before I met Rebecca West herself, at a party at Leo Lerman's. It was shortly after the Second World War and Anthony, her son by H. G. Wells, had just arrived in America. He seemed to know no one at the party and I went over to talk to this young visitor standing alone before the fireplace. Our casual exchange was broken in on by Pearl Kazin: she was working at *Harper's Bazaar* and she interrupted us to ask my companion if he had any recent information about his mother for the contributors' box of her magazine. This was how I learned his identity. Looking down at her from his great height, Anthony replied a bit heavily: "I know nothing about my mother." He added: "She doesn't speak to me." "Oh dear," said Pearl in distress and made as if to withdraw. But he continued: "She doesn't approve of my having come to America." Referring, I suppose, to his illegitimacy, he said: "My mother is afraid that it will hurt her reputation if Americans are reminded of me. She wrote Harold Ross at the *New Yorker* warning him against me." By now Pearl had fled, leaving the field to me. I remonstrated with Anthony: "We think very highly of your mother over here; I'm sure she knows that. It's hard for me to believe what you're saying." But he was not to be dissuaded. "My mother acts as if I shouldn't exist," he assured me. "I was arrested in Cornwall during the war and accused of being a fascist because I had Oswald Mosley's phone number in my address book. I phoned my mother and told her I was being held as a spy and she laughed and said: 'Well, are you?' " I wanted to laugh as well, but it was plain that Anthony did not share my appreciation of his mother's humor. "Look!" I at last insisted. "You really shouldn't go around talking this way about your mother to people you don't even know. It's not good for her and it certainly isn't good for you." My appeal was of course not heeded; he would continue to make a career of attacking his mother. So far as I could make out, neither Harold Ross nor anyone else had ever tried to keep Rebecca West's son out of public view; he was given every encouragement to make a literary career. Several years later I met Rebecca West when she came to America to lecture at Columbia. She had cabled to invite me to lunch, and after that we saw each other whenever she was in this country or I was in England. Between visits we corresponded. We spent many sad hours talking about Anthony's need to put this wall of resentment between himself and her. His infant love for his mother had taken a bad turn: in its frightening power it had transformed itself into hatred.

No doubt there are quarters in which my reputation has not yet recovered from my report for *Partisan Review* in 1959 of Allen Ginsberg's poetry reading, "The Other Night at Columbia." I had heard about the stage antics of Ginsberg and his "beat" friends at previous public performances, and well before his return to his old college I knew a great deal about him from his having been a student of Lionel's in the forties. He had occupied Lionel outside the classroom rather more than was usual in Lionel's relation with his students. While an undergraduate, he had been suspended for a year for various improprieties and infringements of college discipline. These had included his having written "Fuck the Jews" on a dusty window in one of the University buildings, an act of irreverence which no longer reads well in our present climate of opinion and which is therefore suppressed by his biographers. Even after college he had continued to involve his old school and teachers in his misbehavior. Eventually he was arrested for robbery, or perhaps it was for receiving stolen goods, and not only Lionel but Jacques Barzun and Harry Carmn, then dean of the College, went to considerable lengths to keep him out of jail: instead of being sent to prison he was given a free year of treatment at Columbia's psychiatric hospital. He was not grateful for this reprieve. I wrote of Ginsberg's subsequent relation with Lionel:

> Two motives, it would seem to me, impelled him: the wish to shock the teacher, and the wish to meet the teacher on equal ground. To talk with one's English professor who was also a writer, a critic, and one who made no bones about his solid connection with literary

tradition, about one's descent from Rimbaud, Baudelaire or Dostoevsky was clearly to demonstrate a good-sized rationality and order in what was apparently an otherwise undisciplined life. Even more, or so I fancied, it was to propose an alliance between the views of the academic and the poet-rebel, the unity of a deep discriminating commitment to literature which must certainly one day wipe out the fortuitous distance between boy and man, pupil and teacher.

At the time of the reading, Ginsberg was already widely known but he had not yet graduated to his present-day three-piece suits. He and his stage companions, Peter Orlovsky and Gregory Corso, were still in jeans. Academic certification still lay in the future. The evening ended with Ginsberg reading a love poem to Lionel. Lionel was not in the audience; he was kept at home by a meeting of the staff of his book club. It was in the ironic contrast between the stage capers of Ginsberg and his friends and the conformable scene to which I returned when I came home that I found much of the meaning which the evening had for me. For me, perhaps no less than for Ginsberg, it had been an evening of ambiguities. As I weighed the choice between rebelliousness and acceptance, the beats held their own on many scores. The respectable presence at our apartment of W. H. Auden, one of the editors of the book club which was meeting there, had special ironic force, reminding me as it did that the making of poetry is not a comradeship but a highly individual assertion. No doubt unkindly, I wanted Auden to know that I had been moved by Ginsberg, but the established poet wanted none of this. "Really, Diana!" he rebuffed me. In the first days after the publication of my piece, word reached me that Ginsberg very much liked it. To my amusement he had found it "motherly." But he was soon persuaded that he had been condescended to, even insulted. The movement of opposition to my essay began with a letter to *Partisan Review* from Josephine Herbst, a minor novelist of the period, who has recently been given posthumous stature by an accomplished biographer. "The real subject [of the piece]," wrote Herbst with but a poor hold on syntax, "was not about the Beatniks at Columbia but about something far more insidious; the limitation and lack of imaginative comprehension embedded in the academic powerhouse mind. I have seldom read anything," she wrote, "that drips so conspicuously with unctous [sic] self-approval." The disapprobation with which my piece was met around *Partisan Review,* not only by Herbst but by that magazine's reviewer of my volume *Claremont Essays,* the collection in which I reprinted "The Other Night at Columbia," was not, as Herbst would have it, a response to an "academic powerhouse mind" or to my supposed "self-approval." It was occasioned, I think, by my refusal to grant Ginsberg and his friends any special privilege because they were poets. I treated them, not as abstractions, but as persons who were as fully responsible as myself for the choices they made in life. This robbed them of their role as victims and it robbed readers like Herbst of their virtuous role as defenders of the victimized. Reviewing *Claremont Essays* in *Partisan Review,* a British critic, G. S. Fraser, singled out this essay for critical disapproval but added: "If the essay had been a short story, I would have hailed it as one of the great contemporary American short stories." I take him to be saying that it is only in fiction that people are to be thus burdened with their humanity. A few years earlier, in early 1953, I had published, also in *Partisan Review,* a piece called "An Autumn Journal." It consisted of reflections and comments on a variety of topics which had happened to capture my attention. It, too, dealt with people, even those with whom we have our daily casual encounters, as if they were fully human and responsible and it, too, had been met with embarrassed mirth by friends of the magazine. William Phillips perhaps clarified at least one principle at work in discriminating between what did and what did not qualify for inclusion in *Partisan Review*. We were talking about a war movie I had just seen in which the hero had foiled all attempts of the enemy to steal our war secrets. The film had ended with a burst of patriotic music and an American flag flying in the breeze. "It's the kind of movie which you know is meretricious but nevertheless gives you goose pimples," I said to William, and I went on to ask: "Why do we not write about this kind of emotion in our serious film criticism? We all of us experience it." William replied: "That's the kind of thing you talk about with your mother. You don't write about it for *Partisan Review*." Lionel liked "The Other Night at Columbia" best of anything I wrote. He frequently reread it. If only temporarily, Ginsberg seemed to forgive me for the attack which I was thought to have made on him. When I attended a psychedelic celebration by Timothy Leary, the apostle of LSD, Ginsberg came to my side to help me understand what was going on and he was always friendly when, if he happened to be in the Columbia neighborhood, he dropped by to see Lionel. On one such visit, he brought with him an accordionlike instrument to which he sang so dolefully and unceasingly that I was in acute discomfort. I finally diverted him by proposing that we move to the kitchen and eat some cold fried chicken which I had in the refrigerator. At the kitchen table, breaking into our random talk, he suddenly assured me that he was a good person. "I'm a good person, Diana," he repeated earnestly. I was taken aback but I replied in all sincerity that I knew he was a good person, other than for the fact that he proselytized for drugs. I stated my belief that while it might be all right for people like him or Aldous Huxley to experiment with addictive drugs, it was another matter to urge them on people who might not be able to handle them. As if he had foreseen this turn in our conversation, Ginsberg went to the living room and retrieved a mesh carrying bag which he had had with him on arrival. It contained government pamphlets on the dangers of alcohol, and he proceeded to cite their statistics in proof of the destructive power of drink: it was the use of alcohol, not the use of drugs, which must concern us. I saw Ginsberg briefly after Lionel's death but I did not see him again at any length until a year or two later, when we were invited to dinner together by Anne Hollander. Orlovsky was again with him and Allen was again carrying the mesh bag which he had been carrying on his visit to our apartment. This time the bag contained underground publications of his work and the work of his friends: at the end of the evening, he insisted on inscribing each of the little books to me. But they were not inscribed with affection. He was angry at me, bewilderingly so. Just as abruptly as he had broken in on our conversation in the kitchen to assure me that he was a good person, he had burst in on our quiet dinner with a furious political tirade: it was I and my anti-Communist friends, he said, who, in taking over the docks of Marseilles and replacing the Communist dockworkers with gangsters and drug dealers, had flooded the streets of New York with their deadly merchandise. It was because of people like me that the number of junkies in New York had now so dramatically increased. I tried to reply to him in a reasonable fashion: I had not taken over the docks of Marseilles. I was not responsible for the junkies on the streets of New York. But how does one reasonably answer so mad a harangue? At home that night I lay awake pondering the meaning of his outburst. Suddenly the image of his mesh bag sprang to my mind and I remembered the earlier occasion when he had gone to fetch it in response to my statement that while he could perhaps manage drugs, there were other people who could not. I had not mentioned Gregory Corso on that visit, nor even thought of him, but I now recalled that I already knew that Corso had become heroin-addicted. His life was in ruins. Small wonder that Ginsberg was angry at me: I had triggered in him what must have been an overwhelming guilt. It was as if I had charged him with Corso's addiction and he tried to rid himself of his guilt by transferring it to me: it was anti-Communists like me who made a junkie of Corso. I have not again seen Allen since that unhappy encounter, but he did once write to me; he sent me a friendly postcard. He may not have been aware of it, but it had been written on Yom Kippur, the Jewish Day of Atonement.

Chapter

THIRTEEN

In 1971 Purdue University held a series of seminars at which practicing critics discussed their life and work. Lionel was invited to give one of the sessions; he did not prepare a formal lecture but wrote out the first pages of his talk and some notes for what would follow. I have reprinted these notes as an Appendix to the posthumous volume, *The Last Decade,* in the Uniform Edition of his work. His remarks at the start of his talk were to be understood, he said, in the very simplest and most literal sense: "I am always surprised when I hear myself referred to as a critic. After some thirty years of having been called by that name, the role and the function it designates seem odd to me. I do not say alien, I only say odd. With the passing years I have learned to accept the name . . . and even to be gratified by it. But it always startles me, takes me a little aback . . . If I ask myself why this is so, the answer would seem to be that in some sense I did not ever undertake to be a critic—being a critic was not, in Wordsworth's phrase, part of the plan that pleased my boyish thought, or my adolescent thought, or even my thought as a young man. The plan that did please my thought was certainly literary, but what it envisaged was the career of a novelist. To this intention, criticism, when eventually I began to practice it, was always secondary, an afterthought: in short, not a vocation but an avocation." He goes on to say that this is probably not the occasion to try to explain why he did not pursue the career of a writer of fiction and indeed that such an occasion may not ever present itself. He feels that he must nevertheless speak of the matter here because it is definitive of the nature of his work in criticism: "My conception of what is interesting and problematical in life, of what reality consists in and what makes for illusion, of what must be held to and what let go, was derived primarily from novelists and not from antecedent critics or from such philosophers as speculate systematically about the nature and function of literature." Whether the autobiographical memoir which Lionel had been about to start would have provided him with the occasion to attempt an explanation of why his literary career took the direction which it did, in contradiction of his earlier desire, we of course have no way of knowing.

Engaged as they are by Lionel's polemic or, better, carried forward as they are by the impetus which it gives to their own polemical energies, most of the critics who have written about his work dwell—as I have already noted—on *The Liberal Imagination,* to the neglect of his later work, the more purely literary essays. They also tend to overlook his fiction, the stories he wrote at various stages of his career and his novel, *The Middle of the Journey,* or certainly to subordinate his fiction to his criticism. *The Middle of the Journey* is primarily regarded as a tributary to the general stream of his critical writing and even the best known of his stories, "Of This Time, Of That Place," is chiefly comprehended as a test of the political correctness of his attitude toward madness. Neither in dealing with his fiction nor in dealing with his late literary essays have the people who have written about his work been properly aware, it seems to me, of the extent to which Lionel's idea of what is "interesting and problematical in life" derived from his reading of the great novelists of the past and, to my knowledge, only one has usefully addressed himself to Lionel's ambitions as a writer of fiction. This exception is Lewis P. Simpson, an editor of the *Southern Review,* whose essay, "Lionel Trilling and the Agency of Terror," appeared in the Winter 1987 issue of *Partisan Review.* Despite its fashionable title, Simpson's essay is direct and plainspoken. An excerpt from Lionel's notebooks had been published in the anniversary issue of *Partisan Review* in 1985 and a second excerpt appeared in the same issue with Simpson's piece—the first section alone had been available to him. Simpson was not personally acquainted with Lionel. The editor of a literary journal which exists at a considerable remove from the intellectual life of New York, he was dependent upon published sources for his understanding of the social and cultural context of Lionel's work, and this no doubt accounts for such errors in his piece as his identification of Lionel's experience as a Jew with that of other Jewish writers of his time whose background and religious upbringing had been very different from his. When Simpson quotes Lionel's remark in one of his notebooks that "being a Jew is like walking in the wind or swimming: you are touched at all points and conscious everywhere," he fails to realize that the entry was made when Lionel was a very young man writing for the *Menorah Journal* and much under the influence of Elliot Cohen, and that with the passage of time his consciousness of himself as a Jew returned to its earlier character. But what distinguishes Simpson's essay is its recognition of the gulf which existed for Lionel between creative and critical writing—in an earlier century it might have been referred to as the conflict between imagination and reason— and the unhappiness he suffered because he had not made his career as a novelist. In a 1933 entry in his journal Lionel describes a letter he has seen from Ernest Hemingway to Clifton Fadiman: "A crazy letter, written when he was drunk—self-revealing, arrogant, scared, trivial, absurd: yet felt from reading it how right such a man is compared to the 'good minds' of my university life—how he will produce and mean something to the world . . . how his life which he could expose without dignity and which is anarchic and 'childish' is a better life than anyone I know could live, and right for his job. And how far-far-far I am going from being a writer—and how less and less I have the material and the mind and the will. A few—very few—more years and the chance will be gone." When he made this entry, Lionel was twenty-eight years old but Simpson correctly speaks of its tone of "despairing prophecy." Though he will go on to find the lost novelist, or at least something of the novelist's imaginative capacity, in Lionel as a critic, before doing this Simpson analyzes what it may have been in Lionel's personal disposition which frustrated his hope of being a writer of fiction. "Even though he was still in his twenties," Simpson writes, "Trilling did not have, and had never had, the Bohemian option of 'exposing' his life 'without dignity'—of writing a letter when he was drunk or even of getting drunk." The observation is not correct in literal detail: Simpson was not privy to Lionel's private life and was not aware of the problem about drinking which beset Lionel in his middle years, his inability to give up alcohol though he had to recognize that even in smallest quantity it badly altered his behavior. But the soundness of Simpson's essential point remains: Lionel had not had the Bohemian option—if that is what one wants to call it—of exposing his life without dignity. As a young man, he frequently got drunk but, as far as I can say, he never wrote a letter in this condition, certainly not to a stranger, as Fadiman was a stranger to Hemingway. Writing of Hemingway's letter to Fadiman, Lionel uses the word "writer" as if it were synonymous with "novelist." Is it his belief, then, that only the novelist is a writer? Is the critic not a writer? The literary vocation, he assures us, has been his since boyhood; but what he means by the literary vocation is the vocation of the novelist and he has not fulfilled it. By the time Lionel spoke at Purdue, forty years had gone by since he had made this entry in his journal but his view of his career is unchanged. While he does not specifically say of himself that he is a critic and thus not a writer, the judgment is implicit in the veiled pathos of his statement.

The failure to make his career as a novelist may not have wholly accounted for the feeling of failure which shadowed Lionel's life even at its most successful. Yet surely it was his sense of having been denied the inner freedom which he supposes might have allowed him to be a novelist which constituted his persisting emotion of deprivation and made him find in Hemingway's the "better life than anyone I know could live." In the second excerpt from the notebooks, the selection which appeared in the same issue with Simpson, there is a further reference to Hemingway, similarly significant for the light it sheds on Lionel's sense of failure as a writer. On 3 July 1961 he records: "Death of Ernest Hemingway. Except Lawrence's 32 years ago, no writer's death has moved me as much— who would suppose how much he haunted me? How much he existed in my mind—as a reproach? He was the only writer of our time I envied. I respected him in his most foolish postures and in his worst work (except *The Old Man and the Sea*)." That the literary career of D. H. Lawrence might represent for Lionel the career which he had himself failed to achieve is not hard for us to understand; the author of *Sons and Lovers* and *Women in Love* is one of the undisputed masters of twentieth-century fiction. But Lionel's high regard for Hemingway is more than a surprise, a shock—who indeed would suppose it? It was not, however, the judgment of the critic which Lionel was directing to Hemingway; it was the admiration and envy of someone who felt that Hemingway pre-eminently stood for what he had himself sacrificed in his life and work. In Freudian terms, Hemingway represented the triumph of id over superego, with the resultant release of his creative powers. By id Freud meant that side of our nature which is devoted to the uninhibited gratification of instinct. Its monarch is Eros. By superego he meant conscience, the internalization of parental and social law and of the values which are dedicated to the control of the imperious demands of impulse. No contest in his own life or in the life of man was more actual for Lionel than the struggle between the need to live life under the rule of internalized law and the wish to live life in the service of instinctual gratification. With the first of these opposing modes of being, he identified criticism. With the second, he identified the writing of fiction— fiction was freedom from the stifling restraints of conscience. Intellectually Lionel of course knew that a life of impulse is its own form of tyranny and that the freedom he envied in Hemingway was, in Lawrence's phrase, just "another rattling of chains." But he dismissed intellect as his guide; in choosing his path as a writer, intellect had led him where he did not wish to go. In 1950 the *New Yorker* published a profile of Hemingway by Lillian Ross. It was heartlessly brilliant, like the record of a too-candid camera. It included a description of a tour of the Metropolitan Museum which the reporter had made in the company of the famous author: Hemingway punctuated the excursion with boisterous swigs of whiskey. Lionel all but flung the magazine at me. His voice was tense and bitter: "And you expect *me* to be a novelist!" In the dark recesses of his heart where unhappiness was so often his companion, he was contemptuous of everything in his life which was dedicated to seriousness and responsibility. In 1949 or thereabout he made note in his journal of a conversation he had had with Allen Ginsberg about a forthcoming book by Ginsberg's friend Jack Kerouac: "I predicted that it would not be good & insisted. But later I saw with what bitterness I had made the prediction— not wanting K's book to be good because if the book of an accessory to a murder is good, how can one of mine be?—The continuing sense that wickedness—or is it my notion of courage—is essential for creation." It was to decency that Lionel felt that he had sacrificed his hope of being a writer of fiction—conscience had not made a coward of him, it had made him a critic. Was I the only person in the world who knew this about Lionel? Did his friends and colleagues have no hint of how deeply he scorned the very qualities of character—his quiet, his moderation, his gentle reasonableness—for which he was most admired in his lifetime and which have been most celebrated since his death? Discussing Lionel as a writer of fiction in his study *Double Agent: The Critic and Society,* Morris Dickstein writes: "Trilling's constitutional ambivalence is related to his ordeal of being a Jew in a gentile world, teaching English literature in a gentile university. This problem of identity was a theme in Trilling's early stories, but he turned away from it in his mature fiction, with fateful results." Dickstein's fashionable statement tells us nothing about Lionel. There was much "ordeal" in Lionel's life but nothing was less an ordeal to him than being a Jew, whether within or outside the University. Lionel's internal conflicts were not of this variety. Simpson would appear to be alone among critics in recognizing what was truly a struggle in Lionel's life and in perceiving the strangely simplistic disjunction which Lionel made between the circumspect life of criticism and the life of unhampered instinct, of drunkenness, irresponsibility, unimpeded sexual freedom, from which flowed (as Lionel would have it) the capacity to be a novelist. I could not have wished Lionel to be a drunkard in order to be a novelist. The power to write fiction does not lie in the bottle. But I could have wished him to have a thousand mistresses were this to have released him from the constraints upon him as a writer of fiction. I would willingly have been his female Leporello and sung his conquests.

I did not share Lionel's improbable admiration for Hemingway—not that he was much a subject of conversation between us—but I remember that sometime in the fifties I had the idea of writing a piece about him from the point of view of a woman. This was many years before women's liberation and, so far as I know, no woman had put Hemingway's work under this kind of examination. I was not wildly committed to the project but I thought it would be interesting, as a woman, to write about an author who was conspicuous among the male writers of our time for his boast of masculinity. Lionel vetoed the proposal. "They'll slaughter you," he predicted. "They" were the editors and male readers of *Partisan Review,* the periodical for which I would have intended the piece. I accepted Lionel's judgment that the idea was not one which I should pursue.

I was surely not the right wife for someone with Lionel's conscience, or perhaps I mean his stern self-prohibitions. I was myself too much burdened by superego and by the need to keep a firm rein on instinct. "A housekeeping goddess of reason," Robert Lowell would call me in replying to my lengthy report of the 1968 uprisings at Columbia, "On the Steps of Low Library." It was his ultimate courtly insult. Eliot Fremont-Smith must also have been groping for some such clue to what bothered him in my work when he reviewed my volume *We Must March My Darlings* for the *New York Times* and said of me that I was the kind of person who would probably never steal a Star Wars bookbag—he was writing from San Francisco, where he was attending a book fair at which these bags were apparently being sold. Obviously what both men were responding to in my work was its implicit if not expressed moral judgment. Though I have difficulty in remembering jokes, there is a story which has remained with me since the thirties of a man who is handing out leaflets on a street in Nazi Germany. A passerby takes the flyer from him, examines it, and protests that there is nothing written on it. "That's all right," the man who gave him the blank paper replies. "They know what I mean." There is good reason for me to remember this story; it is the story of my life: I need say no word for people to know that I am passing judgment on them in whatever area of their unease. The judgment is assumed to be severe, adverse. Both in his writing and his teaching, Lionel, too, was supposed to be speaking in the voice of moral authority. People of small imagination interpreted his reasonableness and the value he placed upon orderliness as a deference to propriety and convention. Those of more generous spirit recognized it as a necessary affirmation of law. I have heard gifted students of his say that Lionel taught them renunciation: I take this to mean that as person and as writer he represented for them the rule of conscience over license, especially over libidinous license. Certainly he made no effort to rescue id from the harsh authority of superego. He understood the bargain which Freud had made on behalf of civilization. On Freud's death, W. H. Auden wrote a moving tribute to the father of psychoanalysis. He concluded his memorial poem:

> One rational voice is dumb: over a grave
> The household of impulse mourns one dearly loved.
>> Sad is Eros, builder of cities;
>> And weeping anarchic Aphrodite.

The lovely lines rest upon a fundamental misreading of what Freud actually believed and said. Lionel's clever students knew better. They understood that impulse would not have mourned over Freud's grave, nor Eros been sad. The bargain which Freud made was a tragic one, as he himself knew; it required that Eros stay at its useful work but that anarchic Aphrodite be beaten into an at least relative submission. Just so, the "reality" which is invoked, either explicitly or implicitly, everywhere in Lionel's writing is not a playground for instinct. "Reality imposes on human beings the necessity of renunciation of pleasure," wrote Norman O. Brown in *Life Against Death*. His book, published in 1959 and now little remembered, was a central document of the unruly sixties, the decade from which orthodox Freudianism has not recovered and will probably never recover. Despite Lionel's secret regard for Hemingway, he could not subscribe to the de-civilizing principle of *Life Against Death*. He was not prepared to cede our traditional notions of order and responsibility or to return with Norman O. Brown to the Eden of polymorphous perverse infancy. He was nevertheless far from ready to associate himself with our psychoanalyst friends, all of them orthodox Freudians, who felt no need to take note of Brown's attack upon the usually unexamined premises of civilization. In charge at this time of Phi Beta Kappa ceremonies at Columbia, Lionel invited Brown to be the Orator at the spring induction of new members. The occasion also demanded a ceremonial Poet and for this office Lionel selected Robert Lowell. Lowell was first to perform and read his newly completed poem, "For the Union Dead." He read it, in fact, twice, so that the audience might better understand it. When it was Brown's turn to speak, he made a rousing appeal for mankind to free itself of the encumbrances of reason and join the blessed band of the mad. His talk was a revivalist's call to the celebration of the pagan mysteries and not the least extraordinary of its features was the fact that it was being delivered from the platform which Brown shared with Lowell, whose life was a constant anguished struggle to retain his sanity. A few days later, I was seated next to Brown at a luncheon given for him at Barnard. I mentioned this anomaly. Brown was dismayed. He pushed back his chair and all but leapt to his feet. He knew nothing of Lowell's illness, he assured me; had he been aware of it, he would not have spoken as he had. For the author of *Life Against Death* there was apparently nothing wrong in urging madness upon the world. What was unfitting was to apostrophize it before one of its sufferers.

It is not necessary to accept the whole of Lionel's case against the destructive powers of conscience in the development of his writing career to recognize that, excessive though he may have been in choosing Hemingway as his guide to a life of freedom, he was not fanciful in feeling that the controlling influence of intellect had more than its fair share in contriving his literary destiny. Even in his first stories for the *Menorah Journal,* which appeared between 1925 and 1929, it is clear that mind—conscious intellect—is triumphant over the fictional imagination. His earliest story, "Impediments," gifted as it is, is as much an argument as a work of fiction. It is Lionel's argument with himself as a Jew, an argument precipitated by his new connection with Elliot Cohen's magazine, this so-important association for a very young man who hoped to be a writer. "Impediments" was written while Lionel was still in college and is about two college students, close friends, who are fiercely at odds about their commitment to their religion. For one, the fact that he is a Jew is the determining force in his consciousness, the prism through which he sees all of life. For the other, the author's obvious spokesman, his religion is little more than an accident of birth; even as he accepts it, he hedges it around with skepticism and question. The story was based on Lionel's relation with his college friend Henry Rosenthal. Henry had been brought up in strictest orthodoxy and still clung to this rearing; he had not yet gone through the dismal ritual of eating his first ham sandwich and vomiting—this must wait for some years, until his break with his family tradition. As the two students jockey for ascendancy in their debate, Lionel steadily yields to his antagonist. There is built into their moral contest the added advantage which his opponent can claim as the less socially privileged of the two of them: Lionel's Henry-figure was brought up in poverty. It soon becomes plain in the story that the secular vision, with its reservations and ambiguities, is but a poor match for the monolithic power of unquestioned and unquestioning faith. As Lionel's literary career develops, his preference for complexity, difficulty, and modulation becomes its virtual hallmark. But even in his first story we encounter the contradictory attraction which unambiguous passion would always have for him. In "Impediments" the attraction is not expressly stated; it is disclosed in the defeat of the author's protagonist. But later in his career, most notably in his celebration of Isaac Babel, the Odessa Jew "with spectacles on his nose and autumn in his heart" for whom acts of violence are made luminous by their directness of feeling, Lionel has no such hesitation in revealing the appeal which unmediated emotion has for him. His admiration of Lord Nelson no doubt had the same source: he spoke of wanting to write a piece about Nelson and in Paris bought a medal of the Admiral which he kept on a bookshelf in his workroom. "Impediments" is a story of much talent. The economy of means by which the reader learns about the different backgrounds of the two students and about the bitter bond of affection which underlies their conflict is a youthful indication of the technical skill which, from the start, he could bring to the writing of fiction. Nonetheless, the story is propelled not by the drama of character in conflict but by the drama of conflicting idea. Lionel was nineteen or, if we are to trust the date of a letter he wrote to Elliot Cohen in which he refers to the story, even younger than this when he wrote "Impediments." It was a crucial moment for him: he was on the threshold of his literary life. It was great good luck to have a magazine which wanted his work but it was also unfortunate to have Elliot Cohen's encouragement in the use of fiction as a means of arguing issues which might more appropriately be left to the frankly didactic medium of criticism.

On superficial inspection, or perhaps only because of its title, Lionel's next story for the *Menorah Journal,* "Chapter for a Fashionable Jewish Novel," may appear to be a more traditional fictional effort. Its characters are presented to us in social action rather than in debate. It is also possible to read the story, though not with much satisfaction, as an exercise in the "Proustianism" which Jim Grossman associates with Lionel as an undergraduate. At DeWitt Clinton High School, Lionel had come to know several German-Jewish boys who were the sons of well-established professional men. Their families had been in this country for several generations. These were the classmates with whom Lionel had hoped to go to Yale; through them he was introduced to the kind of Jewish society which in those years must surely have been his mother's ideal of the world she wanted for her son. This was Jewish life as it was lived in well-kept brownstones on tree-shaded streets rather than at the dreary northern extreme of Central Park West. Here were fathers who were not borne down by the financial burdens which pressed so heavily upon the manufacturer of fur-lined coats and here were mothers who stayed perpetually young and who flirted, not without serious intent, with the friends of their high-school-aged sons—except, of course, that of this Lionel's mother would have known nothing. Unlike Proust and his Guermantes, Lionel was not seduced by this German-Jewish society but, if only briefly, he was charmed by its iconography. The story is almost embarrassingly attentive to class. In fact, the distinguishing features of class play something of the same role in "Chapter for a Fashionable Jewish Novel" that religious argument plays in "Impediments": its attention to class gives the story its density of thought. Young as he was, Lionel was himself aware of this teacherly similarity between the two stories and critical of the flatness of the second story. On October 23, 1924, he wrote to Elliot Cohen (still "Mr. Cohen" to the young author): "This is the story of which I told you; it is, as I also told you, not very good. Essentially, it deals with the same matter as *Impediments* but it does so indirectly, ramblingly and without much intensity or passion; it lacks all the compact 'lyric' qualities that a short story should have. The people in it are very obvious and simple and not very clever. I would not so malign your alma mater [Elliot Cohen was a Yale graduate] as to suggest that these people are as they are merely because they are in and about Yale, nor so exalt my own as to imply that the Impediments people are interesting only because they went to Columbia. Quite honestly, now that the thing is written and finished I do not consider the bare situation around which it is built to be good material for a story. As a pig's ear it does well enough, but as a silk purse it is not too admirable. However, I am not sending it to you as a story but as a Human Document or as a tract. In that character perhaps you can find some use for it. If the title is the only thing that annoys you, you will find me entirely agreeable to any change you may suggest." The October 1924 date on the letter is confusing. "Impediments" was published in the *Menorah Journal* in June 1925. "Chapter for a Fashionable Jewish Novel" followed a year later, in the issue of June–July 1926. If Lionel did not make a mistake in the date of his letter, it would mean that both stories had probably been written before he reached his nineteenth birthday and that they were held for a considerable time before publication. Even at this tender age, Lionel perceives that behind its thick curtain of social observation, "Chapter for a Fashionable Jewish Novel" is a "tract." It lacks the intensity of "Impediments." To me, the boldness of Lionel's address to his editor and the letter's air of self-possession are even more arresting than its critical astuteness; there is in it something of the same tone which Lionel will use when, about to be dropped as a Columbia instructor, he will win over his department to his own sense of his capacities. With or without its outcome in the compact lyricism which Lionel thinks necessary to a short story, conscious intellect continues to dominate his fiction. His succeeding two stories for Elliot Cohen, "Funeral at the Club, with Lunch" and "Notes on a Departure," both of them written in his graduate year at Wisconsin, are stories of Jewish isolation and alienation. I find them false to Lionel's experience as a Jew. To be sure, he was not by birth a member of the ruling culture of Madison, Wisconsin. In addition to being Jewish, he was Eastern, urban, and of the striving manufacturing class, which probably had but poor representation in that community. But native to the place or no, he had a fine year in Wisconsin. Everyone has moments of isolation, insiders no less than outsiders. There is nothing unique to Jews in the sense of foreignness which Lionel attributes to his spokesperson in these stories, nor was Lionel likely to have experienced such moments of loneliness or nonparticipation because he was of a different religious background from most of the people around him. I felt, and still feel, that his Wisconsin stories were contrived to meet the specifications of a Jewish magazine.

On one of our first dates I asked Lionel why he was taking a Ph.D. if he planned to be a novelist. In 1928 this was how he still projected his future. Lionel's reply was that the novel had changed in our century and that the novelist had now to be an educated man; even the poet must be instructed in history and philosophy and anthropology. He had no doubt been reading Huxley, Wyndham Lewis, Joyce, T. S. Eliot—he read Eliot's "The Waste Land" aloud to me on one of our early dates. Lionel read poetry beautifully, as well as, or perhaps even better than, the poets themselves. Almost as if he foresaw that my vision would become impaired and that I would be dependent in these last years of my life on recorded books, he very much wanted to read for the Library for the Blind of the Library of Congress and wrote offering himself. The letter was never replied to and he made no further effort. I understood nothing of Eliot's use of symbol and myth in his poem but the poem made me cry. It was not the poet's daunting intellect which reached me; I cried because of the music of his poem. I wanted Lionel to set up his fictional workshop in the spacious world of the great social novelists of the nineteenth century where mind did its work in secret, selecting, ordering, perhaps commenting, but always subordinating itself to the lived life on the page. It now sometimes painfully occurs to me that my frequently stated taste in the novel may have had a share in deterring Lionel as a fiction writer. Between his graduate year in Wisconsin and 1942, he wrote no fiction whatsoever. He spent the decade of the thirties writing his *Matthew Arnold* and shaping his critical style. Then, secure at the University, he once more turned to fiction: he wrote the story "Of This Time, Of That Place." Together with his volume *The Liberal Imagination,* it is probably his best-known work: it has been much anthologized and it is taught in college English courses. "Of This Time, Of That Place" was published in the same year, 1943, as Lionel's study of E. M. Forster but I am uncertain which of them was written first. Certainly the story was produced readily enough; whatever he wrote in the forties, he wrote easily. But the publishing history of "Of This Time, Of That Place" had to have troubled someone who had not written fiction for fifteen years. He first sent the story to the *New Yorker,* where it was rejected. Only after it was successfully published elsewhere did the *New Yorker* indicate an interest in Lionel as a writer of fiction and even then the interest was not productive. I also seem to recall that "Of This Time, Of That Place" was turned down by one or two other magazines before Lionel submitted it to *Partisan Review*—he had hoped for a new and larger audience. Although he was now very much at home at *Partisan Review,* the magazine apparently preferred his criticism to his fiction: its two chief editors, William Phillips and Philip Rahv, hesitated over "Of This Time, Of That Place." It was Dwight Macdonald who finally persuaded them to take it. Many decades later Macdonald still spoke of it to me as a "masterpiece." Lionel was paid $25 for it.

Late in life Lionel would publish a literary anthology, *The Experience of Literature,* in which he reprinted "Of This Time, Of That Place" with a prefatory comment. The story is about madness and Lionel tells us in this preface that it had its origin in encounters he had had early in his teaching career with two students much like his characters, Tertan and Blackburn, the former irretrievably deranged and the latter so grotesquely conformable that it is hard to say whether he is in possession of some unique genius of social accommodation or whether he, too, is insane. The voice of the author is that of Joseph Howe, a young poet and an instructor in the Midwestern university which is the scene of the story. Both students are in one of Howe's classes. As the story opens, Howe has just come under attack for his divergence from prevailing poetic practice. The criticism being directed to him threatens his standing at the university. From his own knowledge of how it feels to be the object of unfriendly judgment, the troubled Tertan extravagantly identifies with Howe. His "understanding" is an embarrassment to his teacher; it adds to the uncertainty of Howe's position. The superb Blackburn, on the other hand, tries to use Howe's diminished reputation as a means of blackmailing him into raising his grade; his elaborate attempt to manipulate Howe is no less lunatic than Tertan's voluble affection. Torn by pity for Tertan yet aware that the boy is inevitably moving beyond the reach of reason, Howe finally reports his condition to the college authorities. There can be no outcome for Tertan except confinement to a mental hospital. Full of contempt as he is for Blackburn, Howe must watch him go on to a successful graduation. From its first publication, "Of This Time, Of That Place" was misread and interpreted out of recognition. In response to its initial appearance, Lionel received many strange telephone calls, often in the middle of the night. Who in the story, his callers demanded, was really mad? Surely it was not the brilliant, lovable Tertan. Tertan could not be insane; he was too gifted, too poor and pure, too clearly a social victim. Obviously what Lionel had to be saying in the story was that it was Howe who was mad, for why else would Tertan's teacher have colluded with the college authorities to consign Tertan to a mental institution? No one suggested the possibility that there were two mad persons in the story: Tertan was mad but also Blackburn was mad. The difference was that Blackburn's aberrancy promoted his professional fortunes and was therefore not easily recognized as lunacy. This many years later, even in the face of Lionel's own exposition of his story, the need persists for reassurance that Tertan was not insane but only a helpless casualty of the cruel social process. We apparently still concur in Norman Mailer's statement of the sixties that in a sick society it is the sick who are well, not only metaphorically, like Blackburn, but actually. A few weeks after Lionel's death the Modern Language Association devoted a session of its annual meeting to "Of This Time, Of That Place." Robert Boyers, editor of the literary journal *Salmagundi,* presented a paper which argued not only that Tertan was wholly sane but that Lionel, in having Howe join the college in sending Tertan to a mental hospital, was the culpable agent of a brutal social force. This was to ignore Lionel's own commonsensical pronouncement in *The Experience of Literature* that "an awareness of the relation between an actual person and a created character can have no part in our assessment of a work of fiction." To Boyers, Trilling *was* Howe. In his strangely personal championship of Tertan and in his attack upon Lionel for mistreating Tertan, Boyers placed himself firmly in the company of those who suffer, as Lionel put it, "our modern anxiety at confronting a painful fate which cannot be accounted for in moral terms and which cannot be said to result from some fault of society." Lionel was the author of the story. It was he who had made it up, and in *The Experience of Literature* he states unequivocally: "Nothing, I fear, can reverse the diagnosis of Tertan's illness." In the downward spiral of the boy's life, as his author conceived it, there could be no alternative to permanent hospitalization. It has sometimes been suggested that the character of Tertan was drawn from Allen Ginsberg. There is no basis for this opinion; Lionel had not yet met Ginsberg when he wrote the story. While Lionel was still alive, "Of This Time, Of That Place" was bought for television. It was to be the pilot of a television series about campus life in a Midwestern college. The film was made and shown but it had none of the quality of Lionel's story and nothing came of the projected series.

If the *New Yorker* had reacted more favorably to "Of This Time, Of That Place" or if *Partisan Review* had been more enthusiastic about it than it was, would Lionel's career have taken a more definitive turn toward the writing of short stories? Negative responses have a disproportionate weight for most of us. Lionel did, however, go on to write two more stories after Tertan's story, "The Other Margaret" and a story called "The Lesson and the Secret." The second of these was not of great consequence. It was inspired by a writing course which Lionel taught at the Junior League in New York—it was one of his less likely attempts at earning extra money. I think it was intended to be part of a novel. There were two novels, as I recall, which Lionel began at this period, or perhaps a bit later. In one of them the central character was a grand old man of letters or art; the other was set in an ancient civilization, perhaps that of Greece. Neither had a promising start and Lionel soon discarded them. "The Other Margaret" is, in a sense, a return to fiction as a form of argument or pedagogy. It addresses an enduring moral-social problem, the relation between one's social location and one's moral accountability. There are two Margarets in the story: one is a well-loved daughter of the middle class, Margaret Elwyn; the other is the Elwyns' maid. In her progressive schooling Margaret Elwyn has been taught that because the other Margaret is black and poor and trails a history of racial oppression, she is not responsible, as someone of different social origin would be, for her manifest acts of hostility toward her comfortable white employers. Upon Elwyn, the child's father, falls the delicate task of correcting so faulty an assumption and of instructing his daughter in the complex truth of moral responsibility, a truth which transcends even the looming truth of class. To the simple dictate of liberalism, Lionel opposes the demand that we deal with the disadvantaged as persons like ourselves—similarly available to moral choice and similarly liable to moral judgment—and not as objects of our pious sympathy. "The Other Margaret" is less a "felt" story than "Of This Time, Of That Place" and it failed to achieve the popularity of its predecessor. Its publishing history was no less discouraging. Following the appearance of "Of This Time, Of That Place," the New Yorker had asked to see any fiction which Lionel produced, and Lionel sent "The Other Margaret" to them. The New Yorker was unhappy with the story as it stood. It wanted the climactic scene between Elwyn and his daughter to be reached more quickly, and it proposed that Lionel eliminate both the opening episode at the picture framer's and Elwyn's bus ride home. Lionel refused to make these changes; the New Yorker's taste for focusing its stories on a single episode or a single moment of emotional revelation had, he felt, always limited the range of its fiction. Discouraged, he passed "The Other Margaret" on to Partisan Review, where it was joylessly accepted. It was at this point in his life, I believe, that Lionel made one of his several attempts over the years to engage a literary agent, but without success. He had already published his Matthew Arnold and was writing with some consistency for the literary journals, but there was no interest in his work on the part of the agents whom he consulted.

The Middle of the Journey sprang full-grown from Lionel's brow, like Minerva from the brow of Zeus—or so I think of it. Lionel had made abortive starts on two novels and I remember that he several times spoke of wanting to write a novel, or perhaps it was a play, about the assassination of Trotsky, but I have no recollection that he had ever spoken to me of the novel he did actually write or of his even telling me that this was the work on which he planned to spend his upcoming sabbatical. Not only was *The Middle of the Journey* written without my having any knowledge of its inception; it was virtually completed before I knew what it was about. Of its composition I have but one memory, a strenuous memory: my intervention in its final pages where Lionel describes the impending return to New York of Laskell, the protagonist of the story, and Laskell's farewell meeting with Emily Caldwell, the woman to whom he had made love at the river. For reasons which I presume were hidden even from himself, Lionel was unable to inject any note of tenderness into this farewell encounter. Through rewriting after rewriting, Laskell was inexplicably angry at Emily. Together with her shiftless husband, Duck, and their young daughter, Susan, Emily Caldwell is among the local people whose lives become entangled with those of a group of left-wing New York intellectuals summering among them in Connecticut. The most articulate of the city people, dismayingly so, is Gifford Maxim. Maxim has been known to the others as a passionate Communist sympathizer. In fact, he was a Soviet spy. At the start of the story he has lost his Communist faith and is in flight from the agents of the Soviet underground. To Arthur and Nancy Croom, the friends with whom Laskell is visiting while he recuperates in Connecticut from a severe illness, Maxim's defection, when they become aware of it, puts him beyond the reach of their imaginations. The moral lives of the Crooms are defined by their Communist dedication.

While Emily Caldwell, with her silly social and cultural pretensions, has no claim to their tolerance, they invest her worthless husband, Duck, with all the virtues of character which they consider native to a class less advantaged than their own. Laskell is Lionel's voice in the novel: his political moderation and the quiet humanity which he counters to the fiery emotions of a Gifford Maxim or a Nancy Croom closely approximate Lionel's own temperament and approach to politics. As the summer wears on, the novel picks up much drama and even melodrama; as in the novels of E. M. Forster, there is even sudden death. By the end of the book, Duck has been exposed in all his baseness, and Gifford Maxim in all his dangerous ideological bombast.

With one or two notable exceptions, *The Middle of the Journey* was favorably received by the critics in this country. On its publication in England it was perhaps even more favorably written about. But not even in England was it foreseen that it would still be in print more than half a century later. Its most hostile American review appeared, curiously enough, in Lionel's friend Elliot Cohen's *Commentary;* the reviewer was Robert Warshow, an assistant editor of that magazine and its gifted film critic. The substance of Warshow's attack was that Lionel had wrongly made the characters in his novel Gentiles instead of Jews. Everyone knew that most Communists were Jews: Why had Lionel peopled his story with non-Jews? The Hiss case, with its full complement of non-Jewish Communists, was still in the future. *The Middle of the Journey* was published by Viking; it had little support from its publisher. Indeed, even taking into full account the subjective factors which may have been at work in frustrating Lionel's wish to be a novelist, one has to recognize that the negative response to his novel by the people at Viking was bound to have played a decisive part in his never again writing any fiction. No relationship in the working life of a writer is more important than his relation to his publisher: the subject has not been sufficiently remarked upon. While ultimately a writer must of course provide his own incentive, his publisher has a primary role in fortifying or thwarting his hopes. It is the publisher who rescues the writer's work from the obscurity of the creative process and gives it its public existence. He is the first and perhaps loudest voice of public opinion. No energy which an author musters on his own behalf can equal the assurance given him by an enthusiastic publisher, someone who values his work enough to put his money on it. If the message of the publisher is negative or even only halfhearted, the author cannot but be impeded in will. Pat Covici, Lionel's immediate editor at Viking, was always friendly to Lionel. But Covici was not a person with whose literary judgment one was prepared to rest; he was not held in that high regard even at his own firm. I am uncertain of the hierarchical arrangements at Viking when Lionel was their author, but it is my impression that even in the forties Marshall Best outranked Covici and that with the passage of time Best became even more powerful. But above Marshall Best in the organizational pyramid was Harold Guinzburg and perhaps even above him was Ben Huebsch with whom Lionel had only a distant and formal acquaintance. Lionel was fond of Covici; he introduced Saul Bellow to him and Bellow stayed with Viking until after Covici died. John Steinbeck seems to have been similarly loyal to Covici. But no good will on Covici's side could hide the fact that Viking took little pleasure in publishing *The Middle of the Journey*. Lionel did not deceive himself that there was much money to be made from his novel, but by 1947 he had enough literary reputation to expect that he would be published with a bit of pride. No pride was visible at Viking nor, when the Hiss case broke a few years later, did the firm seem to recognize that there was a connection between Lionel's novel and that dramatic event. Anyone who had known Chambers had of course recognized him in Lionel's character Gifford Maxim. With the Hiss case, readers jumped to the mistaken conclusion that the characters of Arthur and Nancy Croom in Lionel's book were drawn from Alger Hiss and his wife, Priscilla. In 1975, shortly before Lionel's death, *The*

Middle of the Journey was reissued by Secker & Warburg in London and a year later this new edition was brought out in America by Scribner's. In a new introduction which Lionel supplied for this new edition, although he confirmed the fact that his Gifford Maxim was based upon Chambers, he plainly stated that when he had written his novel he had not even heard of Hiss. Nancy and Arthur Croom, those extraordinary previsions of Priscilla and Alger Hiss, were entirely fictional creations. In this introduction he spoke of Chambers as a "man of honor." It was a careless phrase and was subsequently used to discredit the politics of Lionel's book. Obviously no spy can be called a man of honor, whatever the high ground on which he betrays his country. I take Lionel to have been saying that in his opinion Chambers was too honorable to make a false accusation against Hiss.

Day after day in 1949, as the Hiss—Chambers case continued to dominate the front pages of the newspapers, Lionel waited for his publisher to revive interest in *The Middle of the Journey*. This never happened and Lionel began to wonder whether it was just another instance of a publishing house dragging its feet or whether it reflected a political bias: Was the firm perhaps reluctant to bring the book to further public attention? It took fifteen years for his political suspicion to be substantiated. In 1964 Lionel became the Eastman Professor at Oxford and, living in England, we got to be friends with Fredric Warburg of Secker & Warburg. Warburg told us the disturbing circumstances which had surrounded his purchase of *The Middle of the Journey* from the Viking Press; the story he told us is repeated in somewhat briefer form in his autobiography, *A Gentleman's Profession*. On a purchasing trip to New York, Warburg had followed his custom of calling upon Ben Huebsch to see whether Viking had any books on its forthcoming list which he might want to buy for England. Huebsch listed the books he was about to publish, but without mentioning *The Middle of the Journey*. Warburg, however, had heard that the firm was bringing out a novel by Lionel and inquired about it. "Oh, you wouldn't be interested in it," Huebsch shrugged off the question. Warburg had nevertheless insisted that he wanted to read Lionel's book and had come in the next morning to say he wanted to buy it. At this, Huebsch had laughingly asked: "What do you want of me in return?" The story was not a happy one, and it had a coda. In the seventies I received a grant to conduct a series of interviews on the advanced literary-intellectual culture of New York in the mid-twentieth century. One of my most fruitful interviews was with a New York bookseller, Walter Goldwater. Goldwater had been a convert to Communism in the early thirties and had spent a disillusioning year or more in Russia. In Moscow he had become friends with my friends Bettina and David Sinclair. Speaking on tape, Goldwater referred to the International Publishers in New York, a well-known arm of the Comintern, the international organization of the Communist Party. He mentioned some of the prominent people who had supported this agency of the Soviet Union. Among them was Ben Huebsch. I interrupted: "Do you mean Ben Huebsch of the Viking Press?" Yes, this was the Ben Huebsch of whom he spoke. It surprised him that I was surprised and that I had not known that Huebsch was an ardent longtime Communist.

Was Marshall Best also a Communist sympathizer? I have no idea. Pat Covici died while we were in Oxford; even before Pat's death, Lionel had most of his business dealings with Best. The documents of these dealings even as late as the sixties, when Lionel's critical reputation was well established, make painful reading. Before we left for Oxford in 1964, Lionel asked Viking for an advance. Behind Best's demeaning response to this request there may have lain an old political difference but his insulting tone could also have been dictated by mean-spiritedness. Lionel replied at some length in a letter dated March 23, 1964:

> I find I must deal with certain impediments to the kind
> of relationship that I know you and I both believe should
> properly exist between an author and a publisher. The

first of these obstacles is, I think, best summed up in your remarks to me when you evaluated my present behavior in terms of the investment Viking had long made in me and all that the firm had done to "build me up." It is my opinion that, as between us, these cannot be weighty considerations except as they offend my sense of justice. For you will recall that I came to you after the publication of my first two books, the *Matthew Arnold* and the *E. M. Forster,* by which I had already laid the foundation of my reputation. Authors, I know, are not notable for modesty: I must nevertheless ask you whether you yourself or any fair-minded onlooker could honestly say that it was much of a publishing risk to take on a writer whose earlier publications had won the reception of these two books? I am not aware of any special efforts the firm has made to advance my fortunes as a writer. My sense of the situation is that I have given you three books *[The Middle of the Journey, The Liberal Imagination,* and *The Opposing Self]* and that you brought them out in the proper, decent way that is associated with the respected Viking imprint; but I cannot be aware that anything except the existence of the books themselves has made my reputation. As to considerations of money—which is what I take you to have meant when you spoke of investment—I must be conscious both of the fact that you have responded to my request for certain advances in the past in a very pleasant, easy way and that you have not grown rich through me. But I now owe you, as of your last statement, $1680 in advance of earnings. It is not a sum which suggests to me that the financial risk, as I understand such things, was an extreme one.

He continues by reminding Best that over the years of his connection with Viking the firm has refused four books which he offered it: a new edition of his *Matthew Arnold,* his *Freud and the Crisis of Our Culture, A Gathering of Fugitives,* and the trade edition of *The Experience of Literature.* "In each instance," he points out, "the book was felt to have sufficient worth, literary if not always financial, for another publisher to take it eagerly and without my committing to him any further work of mine." He also reminds Best that although Viking had contracted with him for a Portable Keats, when the firm decided not to include Keats in its Portable Library it had taken it for granted that it could transfer the advance made for that book to his general advance against future work and that Lionel had made no protest of this move. He concludes:

> Yet again, there is—what is very difficult for me to accept—the minatory and truly humiliating tone in which you tell me how much money you will advance me on what terms. You speak of proof of my reliability being needed, and this, I suppose, is meant to refer to my slowness in producing the books you say you are proud to publish. You are right: I do not produce books as fast as either you or I would like. But do I need to explain to you, with your experience of the strange business of authorship, that if there is one attitude on the part of a publisher which is calculated to impede a writer's progress with his work as well as degrade his relationship to his publisher, it is the attitude of reproof which you convey to me, both implicitly and explicitly, in your letter? I will not adduce for you at this point my standing in the literary community as my reason for resentment at being addressed like a delinquent child, ungrateful for the many past favors he has received and not deserving of the continued confidence of his elders. I will only tell you that if, for a good many years now, I have had the sense, which I have tried to put down, that (despite Pat's continuing

friendly interest) there has been on the part of the firm a deficiency of respect for my work and me, the impulse by which I suppressed my actual judgment of the situation has now been made impossible.

Then why, one asks, did Lionel not at this late date, or even at a subsequent date, leave Viking, terminate the relationship? Virtually any publisher in the country would have been glad to have him as an author. Yet Lionel remained with Viking until his death. At his death, I promptly ended the connection. Even in the 1964 letter, laying out his case against the firm, Lionel offers a means by which Best can clear the situation in regard to both "publishing enthusiasm" and money. On the financial side, the sum he at present needs is $5,000, "a sum of which your offer falls short by $1600." At the beginning of 1965, he will need another $2,500, "a sum which you speak of in a very conditional way." Though he refers to his literary reputation, he seems to be insufficiently convinced of his worth to risk terminating the old publishing connection. It is not a good tone which he takes with Best; we are reminded of his deportment at the time that he was being let go at Columbia. There were situations and relationships in which he could not function as a free and mature person. It is possible that he might have altered Best's treatment of him as he altered the opinion of the Columbia English Department. But there was something other than timidity or self-doubt present in Lionel's continuation at Viking: loyalty to his old friend Jim Grossman. Jim was lawyer for the Viking Press. He was the member of his law firm who had close charge of all the legal affairs of the publishing house. Jim was much valued by Viking not only for his legal skills but for his remarkable range of literary and historical knowledge and he in turn vested virtually the whole of his sense of his professional accomplishment in his connection with the Viking Press. It was Lionel's belief that a rupture in his own relation with Viking would be damaging to Grossman. For a long time there was no evidence that this was the case, but it eventually developed that Lionel was correct in this strange surmise. In 1966, long after the Hiss case had disappeared from the news, Viking published a book called *Friendship and Fratricide*. The author was a California psychoanalyst, Dr. Meyer Zeligs; the book was offered as an analytical study of Whittaker Chambers. Zeligs had no acquaintance with Chambers. To analyze him without knowing him violated a fundamental premise of his profession, but on the ground of his presumed analytic insight into character and unconscious motivation, he put together an elaborate defense of Hiss and an extended indictment of Chambers. Lionel and I knew that Zeligs's book was soon to be published and we had some advance notion of its tenor, but we had not yet seen it when Jim Grossman came to us with a message from Viking. The firm had requested him to ask that neither of us review the Zeligs book nor otherwise speak of it publicly. The impropriety of the message was staggering and it was plain that Jim was anything but comfortable in delivering it. Yet deliver it he did and grimly awaited our response. For a moment Lionel and I sat speechless. Then I pulled myself together to reply slowly that in the light of our long friendship we would of course do what he asked of us. We neither of us ever wrote about the Zeligs book. Meyer Schapiro reviewed it for the *New York Review of Books* as it needed to be reviewed.

In the ever-shifting world of literary success, *The Middle of the Journey* achieved its quiet permanence. More than half a century after its publication, it is still remembered as a distinguished work of political fiction. It is chiefly admired, however, for its intellectual-political content rather than for, say, its depiction of the social habits of the little country community in which the story is set or for the charming portrayal of its minor characters: the Folgers with their dogs and their precious Miss Walker, or Mickey, the resolute two-year-old son of the Crooms. These are the passages in the book in which I find the sad unfulfilled promise of Lionel's career as a novelist. The reality to which Lionel made such frequent allusion in his criticism was more than the repository of prohibitions which some of his students took it to be. It was life itself, humanity in all its strained effort to come together for support and warmth. Lionel was still a student when the novel of this kind of reality lost prestige for any writer who proposed to address the modern world. In a literary culture which suggested that in order to be a novelist one had to prepare oneself by the study of philosophy and history and anthropology, there was little place for the Folgers or the brave toddler of *The Middle of the Journey*. Such a culture separated mind from these human objects of its contemplation. Lionel lacked the genius of a Joyce to bring the traditional novel into alignment with the demands of our atomizing and sterilizing century. Lewis Simpson was correct in saying that the powers of social observation and of psychological understanding which Lionel might have employed in the writing of fiction he channeled into criticism.

Chapter

FOURTEEN

*T*he *Liberal Imagination,* which appeared in 1950, takes its title from the introductory chapter of a book about E. M. Forster which Lionel wrote for New Directions in 1943, "Introduction: Forster and the Liberal Imagination." In a recent study of Lionel's work, Forster is said to have been his favorite novelist. This is not accurate. The fact that Lionel wrote a book about Forster does not mean that he held him in this high esteem. Lionel enjoyed Forster's novels, or certainly he enjoyed them as a young man. At the time he wrote his book, Forster was scarcely known beyond a small literary coterie in his native England; Lionel introduced him to a new, wider audience in this country. His close analysis of Forster's novels helped shape his critical approach to literature. But Forster never had the place in Lionel's affections of such novelists as Dickens, Dostoevsky, Tolstoy or Henry James or Jane Austen; at his most appreciative, Lionel did not attribute to him the stature of these earlier writers. When he completed his study he did not return to him as a subject, nor do I recall his rereading him for recreation.

Lionel wrote his *E. M. Forster* with unaccustomed speed; it was finished in six weeks. But it was written in unaccustomed circumstances. My sister had had a cancerous toe amputated and was staying with us until she could care for herself. Lionel gave up his study to her and rented a workroom elsewhere in our building. He stayed there for long hours each day, which was fortunate for him. I tried to work at home in our living room as I always had, but my sister listened from down the hall and if I stopped for even a moment she would call to me in coy admonition: "Diana, I don't hear your typewriter!" At the time that Lionel wrote his book about Forster, the two men had not yet met or even corresponded. After the book's publication they did occasionally exchange letters; I remember that there was discussion about how they were to address each other. But the nearest they came to intimacy was when Lionel once or twice sent Forster a food parcel during the food shortages in England after the war. Philip Rahv is reported to have spread the story that while Lionel was writing about Forster he had no idea that Forster was homosexual and that he learned about it, to his chagrin, only when Forster came to New York and invited him to a gay party. This was a malicious invention. As Lionel explained to Truman Capote on their accidental meeting, he had begun to suspect that Forster might be homosexual while he was writing his book but had not pursued the idea. They met for the first time in the spring of 1949 in our apartment on West 116th Street. Forster had come to New York, and Lionel invited him to dinner; Forster preferred that we not invite other guests. It was a thoroughly relaxed evening. After dinner Forster helped me clear away the dishes and also asked that we wake the baby for him to see. Jim was ten months old and a reluctant sleeper; it was not our habit to wake him once we got him settled for the night. But we felt that we could not refuse Forster's request. The infant cradled in his arms, Forster moved softly around the living room. At one point he leaned the baby's face into a bowl of purple lilacs and Jim became frightened and began to cry: Forster comforted him so tenderly that I wished that I could engage him as the baby's nurse. He commemorated the visit with an inscription to Jim in our copy of the *Collected Tales*. A few years later, in the fifties, Lionel made his first trip abroad and visited Forster at King's College, Cambridge, where Forster had been given rooms and where he would live for the rest of his life. The reunion was not as agreeable as their original meeting had been. On the earlier occasion Forster had seemed pleased that Lionel had "discovered" him for America, but now his reputation had considerably grown and he acted as if Lionel, in writing about him, had used his prestige to elevate himself. As Lionel was leaving King's that day, Forster gave him a present of a book, *My Dog Tulip,* by his friend J. R. Ackerley, the author of the much-admired novel *Hindoo Holiday* and the editor of the BBC magazine, the *Listener*. The book was a perverse little memoir of Ackerley's release from obsessive homosexual cruising by his love for his Alsatian setter. Lionel forgot the book in a taxi. When he reported this to Forster, Forster pounced upon him with the glee of a parlor analyst: How could there not be an obvious meaning in Lionel's wish to forget the Ackerley book? Lionel's last meeting with Forster took place in the spring of 1965, when we were spending the year in Oxford, and all three of us, Lionel and Jim and I, went to tea in his rooms in Cambridge. Jim was now sixteen and in school in London. We supposed that it would give Forster pleasure to see the infant whom he had once carried around in his arms now grown to young manhood. But Forster was old and whatever the emotions aroused in him by Jim's visit, they were not pleasurable. He had a tea cake in a tin box, which he doled out to us in the thinnest possible slices. A perpetually starved adolescent, Jim waited patiently to be offered a second slice. When it was not forthcoming, he asked Forster if he might cut another piece of the cake for himself. Forster replied harshly that he would be the one to do the serving.

The introductory chapter of Lionel's *E. M. Forster* reveals the basic direction of his thought at this time or, at least, one of its strands: his concern for the insufficiencies in the current practice of liberalism. "If liberalism has a single desperate weakness," he writes, "it is an inadequacy of imagination." The theme will be reiterated and adumbrated throughout his essays of the forties. In areas of political and social speculation, where even to raise a question is inevitably to generate further question and where the search for "solutions" invalidates the very purpose of the investigation, it is the folly of contemporary liberalism to suppose that there are ready answers to all the perplexities of the moral life. For Lionel, perhaps the chief virtue of the novels of Forster is their awareness of the complication and even the contradiction in our experience as moral beings. "All novelists deal with morality," Lionel writes in praise of Forster, "but not all novelists, or even all good novelists, are concerned with moral realism, which is not the awareness of morality itself but of the contradictions, paradoxes and dangers of living the moral life." Forster, says Lionel, goes beyond the recognition of good and evil in the moral universe to the awareness of their coexistence. He has the knowledge of good-and-evil, a brave knowledge which we do not often encounter in our progressive culture. For Lionel, Forster's primary accomplishment as a novelist is beguilingly modest, in some sense even negative. It lies in his quiet withdrawal from the fierce struggles of will which rage so relentlessly in our civilization.

For anyone acquainted with Forster's later writing, there is bound to be a considerable irony in Lionel's celebration of Forster's transcendence of the liberal orthodoxies: his later work speaks clearly in the voice of contemporary progressivism. But this is when he is no longer writing fiction. Forster was a relatively young man when he wrote the novels with which Lionel deals in his book and by which we now know him. The last of them, *A Passage to India,* appeared in 1924, when Forster was forty-five. After that he produced only a single other full-length work of fiction, his disappointing homosexual novel, *Maurice,* which he deposited in the British Museum under closure until his death. The nonfiction of his later years was written in a different world than he inhabited as a novelist, one in which the enlightened culture demanded a conformity which had not previously been required of writers. While as a younger man he had been able to bring a valuable complication to the liberal ideal, with the passage of time he had fallen captive to the certitudes of our liberal mid-century. Indeed, in his relations with Forster in the fifties and sixties, Lionel must have come to understand that there was perhaps other reason than only that of professional grudgingness, political difference, to account for the distance which Forster put between them.

I was startled, not long ago, when a young historian who came to talk with me about Lionel's work opened the interview with the confident pronouncement that *The Liberal Imagination* had freed a generation of students from their acquiescence in Communism and helped them find a new political direction. I wondered which students he had in mind. In the course of his long career at Columbia, Lionel taught several generations of undergraduates. During the forties, the period in which he was writing the essays in *The Liberal Imagination,* his gifted students included Fritz Stern, John Hollander, Jason Epstein, Richard Howard, Steven Marcus, Norman Podhoretz, Louis Simpson, Byron Dobell, Robert Gottlieb, Robert Shulman, Joseph Kraft—and this is to name but a few of them. Surely they represented a wide range of political views. Not all of his outstanding undergraduates were students of literature—Fritz Stern was a student of history and Bob Shulman was a student of science—but all of them were sharply alert to what was happening in their contemporary society and well informed on the changing currents of political thought. While Lionel no doubt influenced these burgeoning young intelligences and may in some instances have even altered their political views, it must be remembered that he was also a father figure to many of the young men he taught and that this meant that at some point in their relation to him they were bound to rebel against his authority. But it was the minimalism of my visitor's statement, rather than its facile comprehensiveness, which especially troubled me. Was this how

The Liberal Imagination was now being read, solely as a political argument? Was this how it had been read even in the past? Unquestionably Lionel's 1950 collection was an attack upon Stalinism; later in his life, Lionel himself declared that *The Liberal Imagination* had been written with this political intention. Nevertheless, to read it only as political polemic was, it seemed to me, to ignore the source of its distinction. The book is not a tract or diatribe and to address oneself only to its political content is to miss what connects it with the work of Lionel's later years in which politics play little or no part. Other than in the one essay, "George Orwell and the Politics of Truth," Lionel's dissent from Stalinism figures not at all in *The Opposing Self,* the collection of critical pieces which he published in 1955, and if politics make an appearance in his 1965 collection, *Beyond Culture,* it is wholly by indirection. Yet the later essays are plainly the product of the same critical intelligence and the same sensibility, also the same moral urgency, as inform the first collection. For me, it is Lionel's moral-intellectual purpose, far more than his political purpose, which gives his work its character and its unity. His warning of the limits imposed upon us by the liberal orthodoxies has a wider reference than only that of Stalinism: he attacked Stalinism because at the time he wrote the essays in *The Liberal Imagination* it was in the culture of Stalinism that the hindrances put upon the moral imagination by the dictates of progressive doctrine were most plainly visible. This does not mean that he supposed that a deficiency of moral realism was to be found only on the Stalinist-dominated left. Writing about the characters in Forster's novels, he was not writing about people whose minds had been corrupted by Communism: four of Forster's five novels were written before the Russian revolution and most of the characters in his fiction are not even liberals, as we now understand that designation; they are ordinary decent people who have been emotionally rigidified by the familiar dehumanizing processes of Western society. Forster liked to jog his characters out of the confines of their familiar lives by plunging them, as in the case of *A Room with a View* or *A Passage to India,* into a foreign culture whose roots were more firmly planted in biology than those of their own Anglo-Saxon universe or, as in the case of *Howards End,* by introducing them to a messenger from a less-protected social class. Though in his lecture to the New York Psychoanalytical Society in 1955, "Freud and the Crisis in Our Culture" (later titled "Freud: Within and Beyond Culture"), Lionel will welcome the part played by biology in limiting the powers of culture, he is not deceived even in his earlier work by such myths of salvation as Forster fell back upon to rescue or redeem the people in his fiction. He understands that biology imposes its own absolutism. I have said earlier in this book that I do not join in the general opinion that *The Liberal Imagination* is Lionel's most important work. While the collection is far more than only a prolegomenon to his later essays, I read it as the introduction to a body of critical writing which becomes steadily richer in expression and implication as it moves beyond political-cultural immediacy.

If the explicit communication of *The Liberal Imagination* is its attack upon Stalinism, its implicit and, I think, more significant communication is that of its style. Style, in Arnold's view, is not to be separated from a writer's moral intention. The style of Lionel's essays is intimately connected with their moral purpose. *The Liberal Imagination* gave a new dignity and a new moral dimension to the old Communist/anti-Communist conflict. Its prose invited reflection, and it rejected both political invective and comforting certainty. If it freed his students from the hold which Stalinism might otherwise have had on them, it also urged them to a new understanding of the relation between our political views and the character of our personal being.

From time to time it has been suggested that because of his anti-Communism Lionel was a progenitor of our present-day neoconservative movement. While I, no more than anyone else, am able to say beyond dispute what would have been the direction of

Lionel's politics if he had lived into the decade of the eighties, I am of the firmest belief that he would never have become a neo-conservative and that, indeed, he would have spoken out against this outcome of the anti-Communist position. In the preface to *The Liberal Imagination* he states unequivocally of his essays in the volume that they were written from within the ranks of liberalism. His criticism of liberalism, that is, is criticism from within the family. Nowhere in this volume or in anything which followed *The Liberal Imagination* do we find a deviation from the liberal commitment. In *The Liberal Imagination* Lionel uses the word "liberal" in two opposing meanings: at moments he employs it in its traditional nineteenth-century connotation, while at other times he uses it to describe a politics of the left which has been corrupted by its submission, conscious or unconscious, to Stalinism. His own stand is in the traditional liberalism of the nineteenth century and, complicate the situation though he undoubtedly does, he remains a traditional liberal until his death. Nothing in his thought supports the sectarianism of the neoconservative movement. Everything in his thought opposes its rule by doctrine.

I date the start of the neoconservative movement from the presidential campaign of 1972. In the late summer of that year, as Lionel and I were about to leave for a year in England, we received a telephone call from Gertrude Himmelfarb, the much-respected historian, and wife of Irving Kristol, soliciting our signatures for an advertisement in the *New York Times* in support of Nixon. She wanted us to join other former Democrats who had become disenchanted with the Democratic program and party. Although Lionel and I were uneasy about McGovern, we refused to support Nixon. In fact, in the next year, when Lionel became the first recipient of the Jefferson Award in the Humanities, he sought reassurance that he would not be officially entertained at the Nixon White House. An invitation from Nixon would have presented him with a dilemma: he did not wish to show personal respect to Nixon but he did not wish to be lacking in respect for the presidency. It was my impression that in soliciting our signatures in support of the Republican candidate, Bea Kristol, as she is known to her friends, was markedly uncomfortable. Her voice on the phone was embarrassed, as if she foresaw our refusal and the reason for it. We were close friends with both Bea and Irving for many years, and it is my enduring regret that our political disagreement has all but ended the relationship. I would not have predicted the course of the Kristols' politics: we knew them as thoughtful conservatives, Burkeans, not right-wing Republicans or Republicans of any stripe. To be sure, even as a recently disillusioned Trotskyist, Irving Kristol was strangely cynical. His disenchantment with Communism slowly colored the whole of his view of the world—it was as if he were trying to rid himself of any vestige of his youthful idealism. Yet one would not have supposed that he was headed to his present politics of self-interest. In our knowledge of them, both Irving and Bea were generous-spirited, and neither of them was sectarian-minded. In 1965, in company with Daniel Bell, Irving launched his magazine *The Public Interest;* he asked Lionel and me to act as its joint literary editors. Even then we were reluctant to associate ourselves with his generally conservative stance and we did not accept the offer. Lionel did not live long enough to witness the rise of the neoconservative movement, but I have little question that if he had been alive and working in the eighties, he would have been highly critical of this swing to the right by our old friends. Neoconservatives like to protest that they are not a movement, only a group of individuals who have been brought together by their shared perception of the follies of the left. Back in the thirties and forties, Communist sympathizers and fellow travelers similarly protested that they were not a movement but merely individuals who happened to be in social-political accord.

By 1950, when *The Liberal Imagination* was published, Lionel was a full professor at Columbia: his promotion to an assistant professorship in 1939 with the publication of his *Matthew Arnold* had been followed by promotion to an associate professorship in

1945. He was made a full professor in 1948. Toward the end of his life, he would grow tired of teaching and speak wistfully of an earlier time when his teaching had been so satisfying an occupation. He felt that with the passage of the years he had lost his old personal identity at the University and become a "figure," an institution. His students no longer felt free, as they once had, to exchange ideas with him; his younger colleagues no longer gathered casually in his office to visit with him. His writing rather than his teaching always had priority in his life. He made it a point to teach in the afternoons, reserving his morning hours, when he was freshest, for his own work, as he thought it. He often counseled the young men in his department against allowing the college to swallow up their energies. His teaching was nevertheless far from a routine duty. Although he liked to say that he taught subjects, not students, he was much concerned for the present and future welfare of the people he taught; he spent virtually every Sunday writing letters of recommendation for jobs or fellowships for them. He preferred, however, that his relation to his students be kept to the classroom and not overflow into his life outside the University. Inevitably, as time went on, some of his students became his friends, several were valued colleagues, but so long as he was teaching them, he wanted as far as possible to keep the connection that of teacher and pupil. I recall only one undergraduate who successfully breached the barrier between college and home: Bob Shulman became precociously a friend by offering himself as a tennis partner. Yet despite the separation which Lionel made between his writing and his work at college, his teaching played an important part in the development of his criticism; he was fully conscious of this and would undoubtedly have written about it in his memoir. His teaching not only kept him steadily in contact with the great minds of the past but it had direct bearing on his thought. This is to speak, however, of his undergraduate, not his graduate, teaching. He disliked lecture courses such as were usually required in the graduate school. He went "across the street" to teach only when it was unavoidable. What he liked best was to teach small undergraduate classes or seminars in which he could engage his students in discussion, throw out an idea and have it questioned or perhaps given a new direction. It was in the give-and-take of the college classroom that he worked out many of his critical positions. The Colloquium, which he conducted for so many years with Jacques Barzun, was especially useful as a testing ground for his ideas because of the sharpness of mind not only of his teaching partner but also of their students. The lively interchange to which he was accustomed in his undergraduate teaching at Columbia was not duplicated at Oxford, where one lectured to silently respectful listeners. He was not tempted by the offer of a professorship at Oxford: the Goldsmith's Professorship at New College was being vacated by David Cecil and was accepted, instead, by Richard Ellmann. Author of a biography of Joyce, one of the two or three best biographies produced in this century, Ellmann moved to England and to his new teaching assignment shortly after his wife, Mary, herself a person of some literary promise, was physically incapacitated by illness; in addition to his college responsibilities, he took on all the duties of their household, marketing, seeing to the preparation of meals and, beyond this, making their home a warm center for the entertainment of friends and visitors to Oxford. Outside the home, he carried his crippled wife everywhere with him. In 1972 when Lionel returned to Oxford as a Visiting Fellow at All Souls, I often ran into Ellmann in Oxford's open market, happily shopping for a dinner party—to witness his courage was a privilege of my life. I loved Oxford and would have been glad to have settled there permanently. Lionel also loved Oxford, but he did not wish to teach or to write there. It was important to him to live his working life among people with whom he had a shared past. Although much of his literary heritage had its source in England, he was finally not prepared to move there.

The forties were the decade in which Lionel became fully established at Columbia and the decade in which he did some of his best-known work. In the forties I, too, became a writer. It was the decade of the Second World War; one might suppose that the war would be the background to all our personal experience during this period, the central event to which all other events, public or private, would be subordinated in memory. Even in the midst of the Battle of Britain, life of course went on in London: people worked, shopped, went to the movies or the library, visited the doctor or the dentist. But I doubt that any activity in which they engaged is readily separated in their recollection from the bombings which were its accompaniment. I was a mature woman in the forties, but the war as I knew it returns to me only in the most fragmentary snatches, an embarrassing number of which have to do with food—surely the food shortages were not that significant! The point is that for America the war took place on distant soil. We doused the lights and pulled down the shades in air-raid drills, but no bombs fell on us. For the second, but not the last, time in this century we were at war without having to endure, or even really fear, the destruction of our cities and the devastation of our countryside. American lives were lost in the war, many of them, but chiefly they were lives which had been conscripted for the sacrifice; they were not civilian lives. A fraction of the population put itself at mortal risk for the rest of us. The rest of us slept soundly in our beds. The war behind them, the English avoided any mention of it; on a visit to Holland, Lionel and I found it a relief that at least the Dutch allowed themselves to remember that they had had a Nazi enemy. But mute themselves though they might, even the English could not eradicate the physical residue of war. When we got to London in 1964, almost twenty years after the war, there were still great holes in the street where bombs had fallen. Though flowers might bloom where death had rained down from the sky, the holes remained in evidence of the ordeal which everyone had shared—no exemption for civilians. On our side of the Atlantic, we had no such immediate and general knowledge of war. The distance this creates between us and countries less fortunate than us is wider than any ocean. If I wonder why I feel as if the second war is less vivid for me than the war of my childhood, so much further from me in time, I remind myself that at its start I was in Europe and held bullets in my hand and saw bloodied heads at the windows of the trains in the Berlin train station.

The New York intellectuals can scarcely be said to have been caught up in the war spirit or the war effort. They had much anti-war sentiment to wipe from memory. The way in which Lionel and I learned of the attack on Pearl Harbor can be understood as a metaphor for the relation of the New York intellectuals to the war. On that Sunday afternoon, our music-critic friend, Bernard Haggin, had listened to the Philharmonic broadcast. He had then come to have supper with us. As we saw him to the door at the end of the evening, he casually inquired whether we had had any further news. News of what, we asked, and so it was that we discovered that America was at war. We had been together for several hours but the attack on Pearl Harbor was apparently of insufficient importance for him to mention it. Even among intellectuals Haggin was no doubt uncommonly self-absorbed—when his father died, we learned about it only when he asked us if we knew someone who could use a tuxedo. But to some degree all the advanced intellectuals of our acquaintance—and this includes most of its core figures—shared his assumption that they were of an essentially different order of being from the rest of mankind and thus exempt from the usual concerns of their time and society. To the nineteenth-century artist's scorn of bourgeois values the twentieth-century intellectual added a new contempt for all commonly held attitudes and all established authority. It is perhaps this set of mind which explains the appearance on the cover of the *New York Review of Books,* in the sixties, of directions for making a Molotov cocktail or, say, the uncritical reception of Edmund Wilson's rationalization of his failure to pay his income tax.

Was it our war? This was the charged question so often asked by the intellectuals in Lionel's and my small corner of the universe and echoed, to more immediate purpose, by the younger intellectuals eligible for the draft, in particular the younger readers of *Partisan Review*. Although in 1939, when the war began in Europe, *Partisan Review* was only two years old, it was already a major force in the advanced culture of this country. One did not have to agree with all its editorial opinions to regard it as the base from which one took off on one's own independent intellectual journey. Until the actual outbreak of war in Europe, *PR* had been in vehement opposition to it. The only kind of war a Marxist magazine could sanction was class war; any military action between nations was the war of rival imperialisms. But even the non-Marxists of our intellectual generation had of course long been schooled in the belief that the First World War was fought, not to make the world safe for democracy, but for the profit of the munitions makers. This disenchanting lesson permanently influenced the way in which we viewed our citizenship. Love of country was no longer an appropriate emotion for a serious intellectual. Heroism of any sort, but specifically such as is called for in war, could no longer be an ideal. With the outbreak of war in 1939, a rift developed among the editors of *Partisan Review* on how the magazine should respond to it. Eventually Dwight Macdonald, the most vocal and intransigent of the editors in his opposition to the war, left to found his own periodical, *Politics*. During these early years of *Partisan Review*, Lionel and I had many fundamental disagreements with the positions it took. We had not for a long time been Communists and we had no wish for a workers' revolution, Trotskyist or any other variety. We did not equate Churchill and Roosevelt with Hitler, as *PR* did, and far from supporting Chamberlain's appeasement of Hitler at Munich, we were much opposed to it. The war was not *Partisan Review*'s war until America was well into it. But from the start, Lionel and I believed that it was our war. Little as we knew about the horrors of Nazism relative to what we would all of us learn at the end of the war, we believed that Hitler had to be got rid of and that this could be achieved only by military action. It was nevertheless impossible to be as friendly as we were with Phillips and Rahv and as complicit in the cultural attitudes of the magazine and not be affected by its antiwar sentiment. We were not opposed to the war but we put between it and us the distance which intellectuals are always supposed to keep between themselves and their society. Yes, Lionel assured the young men who asked him if he thought it was our war: it was our war to fight and win. Privately he wished that he could himself be in the army. Still, when our close friend Jim Grossman enlisted, we were confused and embarrassed. Successful lawyers looked for majorities and colonelcies, positions of power; they did not volunteer as privates. We knew no one else who, like Grossman, responded to a call of conscience.

Repeatedly *Partisan Review* had warned its readers that America's participation in the war against Hitler would result in the end of democracy in our own country. The price we would pay for joining the imperialist war against fascism would be to become fascist ourselves. The prediction was unfounded: America did not become fascist in consequence of the war. The pilots and bombardiers who returned from the war were glad to give up their giant instruments of destruction and to re-enter civilian life. Indeed, the young and not-so-young men who came to the universities on the G.I. Bill were strikingly unbellicose, eager to be educated in the professions of peace.

It had never occurred to me that I would not have children and I assume that Lionel similarly took it for granted that we would one day have a family. But I have no recollection of our setting a timetable for this important next step in our lives or of our even discussing it as an eventuality. As a girl, I had counted off the petals of daisies, chanting the familiar "Loves me, loves me not," and, even more eagerly, I crumpled the yellow seeds and tossed them into the air, catching them on the back of my hand; their number

411

foretold how many children I would have. I wanted it to be many. Yet I cannot remember speaking of this desire with Lionel. It was not a deliberate omission or an oversight. It was how life was for us. Our circumstances in the early years of our marriage—first my physical illness, then my emotional problems—made pregnancy unwise or certainly put any decision about having children into the future. We lived the whole of our early lives under the rule of postponement: life was not in the present, it was always ahead of us. Somewhere in the future we would be the people we intended to be. The years were going by, yet the fact that the time for child-bearing might be running out on me never entered my mind. I was never accidentally pregnant. I was all but unique among the women I knew in never having recourse to a back-street abortion. A majority of the writers and intellectuals of our acquaintance, and even a number of Lionel's colleagues at the University, were childless on principle. Their lives had no room for such constraints. Emery Neff, Lionel's dissertation director, cautioned the young members of the English Department against the dangers of intruding parenthood into their academic careers, and when I at last had a child, Charles Everett, also of Lionel's department, turned his eyes away from the infant's carriage lest he have to recognize that biology had been in process.

My forty-second birthday was behind me when I woke one morning with the startling realization that if I ever meant to have a child, it had to be now. The thought had come unbidden; I have no explanation of why I had this sudden access of reason. I at once sought medical confirmation that it was not too late for me to become pregnant and that I was healthy enough for child-bearing. The obstetrician gave me this assurance, but he warned me that after so many years of using contraceptives I might have difficulty in conceiving; his own wife had decided to have another child late in life and it had taken her over a year to become pregnant. I became pregnant that evening. It was mid-November. At the end of December, the obstetrician with good grace conceded that I had bypassed his warning.

The last days of 1947 are memorable in the annals of New York weather: the city was in the grip of an unprecedented ice storm. On New Year's Eve the streets were empty, glassed over; everywhere trees were breaking under their weight of ice. Lionel and I had no plans for the evening. His mother had developed an allergy to something in her apartment and had temporarily taken refuge with us. We were content to remain home with her. I had already told her my exciting news but I had not yet told my sister and brother that I was pregnant. It was my habit to call my sister at midnight on New Year's Eve. That night, after greeting her, I told her that I was going to have a baby. For a moment she said nothing. Then she said: "I've always told you that you're very clever, Diana, but you're not fit to have a child!" Lionel's mother was in bed in Lionel's study and I was using the telephone at her bedside. She reached out to try to stop me as, in a paroxysm of rage, I screamed into the telephone: "You bitch! You bitch!" It was too late to control my anger. I had hemorrhaged. I was standing in a pool of blood.

Were it not for Lionel's mother, I would have lost the baby. Without her support, I should not have been able to resist the obstetrician's conviction that my pregnancy had self-terminated: a poor implant, he said, was a poor implant and had best be got rid of; he would send an ambulance to take me to the hospital for a curettage. On a night such as this, the ambulance drive alone would be enough to end a pregnancy. Lionel's mother gave me the courage to refuse the doctor's order. She insisted that she had known many women who had bled as badly as I and yet held on to their babies. What I must do was go to bed and stay still for the next days; she would take care of me. The doctor warned me that if I did not follow his instructions he could not take responsibility for my life. Very frightened, I replied that I would take responsibility for my own life. I went to bed as Lionel's mother had suggested that I do. But first I called my internist to tell him what was happening. He lived on the other side of the Hudson but immediately set out through the icy night to stay at my side. In the morning the obstetrician arrived unannounced. When he left he was less worried than when he had come. For a week I remained in bed, unmoving, while my mother-in-law cared for me and inspected the blood I lost to be certain that I had not lost the baby—it was not clotted. At the week's end, I was retested: I was still pregnant. From this time forward, my obstetrician could not have been more concerned with my care. During my long week of anxiety, Walter Winchell carried the news of my pregnancy in his gossip column: he had had word of it from a friend of Lionel's sister. It was difficult, at a time of such uncertainty, to take calls of congratulation.

We are today accustomed to women having children, even first children, in their late thirties or even in their forties, after they have launched their careers and settled into the pattern of their married lives. But when I was pregnant, it was virtually unheard of for someone to have a first child at such an advanced age except by unhappy accident. I never felt or looked better than when I was pregnant. I had not a moment of discomfort other than weakness in my legs, yet my condition was generally regarded as precarious, perhaps irresponsible. Lionel and I had no sense of danger. In fact, so far as Lionel was concerned, it might perhaps have been useful if he had been a bit worried—the more I advanced in pregnancy, the more he acted as if nothing special were going on in our life or in my body. Once Jim was born, Lionel was the most devoted of fathers: nothing in his own life took precedence over the needs of his son. But waiting for his child's birth, he wholly removed himself from what was going on. I had to wear a maternity corset in my final months of pregnancy in order to support my back. It was an old-fashioned kind of corset, with laces which tied behind me, impossible for me to manage without assistance. Helping me obviously filled Lionel with distaste. I had to ask a friend who lived a few doors away to stop by each morning to lace me up. When I became heavy and it was awkward for me to rise from a lying-down position, Lionel seemed never to be there to help. He had no desire to listen to his baby inside me; he never felt him kick or move. He had no experience whatsoever of the child's gestation; he began to love it only when it was outside my body. It was no doubt more important that he was the dedicated father he became than that he was so isolated from the process of the baby's birth, but I still feel the deprivation of having had so unshared a pregnancy. Because Lionel could not let it be real for him, he made the experience less real for me. I must suppose that he was trying to conceal from himself the memory of his mother's pregnancy with Harriet: for seven years he had been an only child, alone in his mother's affection. I suspect that he never forgave her or any woman the injury of having been betrayed by his mother's having another child. Throughout his life he was prone to the kind of jealousy which a child feels at the birth of a younger sibling. At the time of Jim's birth, fathers were not expected to participate in the delivery of their children. This was my good luck: I cannot imagine Lionel as a Lamaze partner. Pat Covici charmingly told me that he loved pregnant women because they looked so aristo-cratic. In my lumbering fashion, I did indeed feel aristocratic; I wished that Lionel took more pride in me, or in some manner showed that he was pleased with me for bearing his son. I wanted him with me at the hospital when I first got there, or thought I did; I felt that I was being given most-favored-nation treatment by my obstetrician because he permitted Lionel to sit with me in my hospital room when I first arrived. As soon as my contractions became severe I sent him away; I did not want him to be made uncomfortable by the sight of my pain—in my generation this was how a woman was supposed to feel. The birth itself went well. "What they euphemistically call easy" was how Mia Fritsch, Jim Agee's wife, put it when she called to inquire how things had gone for me. It was perhaps too easy for Lionel's poor mother. The excruciating length of time it had taken her to give birth to Lionel had always been one of her claims to special gratitude on his part and on the part of the world. As for my sister, she apparently wiped out the memory of our awful exchange on New Year's Eve. It was as if it had never been. Lionel undertook to be friendly when he had to be with her, but he never forgave her for almost robbing him of his child. He was unwilling to understand that life had not been generous to her and that it was difficult for her to have a younger sister who was so much more fortunate than she.

Lionel had no theories about men and women sharing the duties of parenthood; he took it for granted, as I did and do, that the care of children chiefly devolves upon their mothers. But there was no aspect of Jim's life with which he was not concerned and no area of his own life which had priority over any claim which Jim made on him—as infant, as toddler, as schoolboy, Jim had his father's attention for the asking. On weekends Lionel was the most visible of the neighborhood fathers at our sandbox on Riverside Drive. It was he who was on call during Jim's long sleepless nights: there were many days when he did his work on no more than three or four hours of sleep. Of these nighttime vigils in which he read quietly at Jim's bedside while Jim lay with eyes wide open, trying with all his little might not to give up the control of his infant universe, Lionel would later say that they were among his pleasantest memories. It had been wonderful to be alone with his son, reading, while the whole world slept.

During pregnancy I had devised a dozen plans for how I would organize my days so that I could efficiently combine writing with motherhood. It took a while, too long, for me to let my life take its natural shape. If they could afford it, middle-class women at that time had nurses to take care of their babies, at least in their first weeks. I discovered that baby nurses were mad, all of them. A few years later, recalling my samples of the species, I began a group profile of our baby nurses for the *New Yorker,* but I could not make the piece amusing. My experience had been too grim. In the hope that a young person might be less tyrannous than the older baby nurses with whom I had tried to deal, I engaged a nineteen-year-old graduate of the training program at the New York Foundling Hospital to help me with Jim. Jane might be pleasanter to live with than her older predecessors but she was no less resolute in her authority and when she left to marry I made no further effort to have anyone to help with Jim's care for more than a few hours of the day. A woman writer is of course better situated than other working mothers for bringing up children. She can be home and keep an eye on things and she has the flexibility to meet emergencies. But by the same token, her working life is exposed to constant interruption. I did more writing in the fifties, while Jim was small, than earlier in the decade, but it took a certain amount of trial and error before I settled into a satisfactory routine. Lionel had never had a proper workroom; he was always crowded. I had no workroom at all until he died and I moved into his study. I worked in the living room in the midst of family traffic. For a short period when Jim was little I felt that I needed more quiet than he permitted me and I rented a room in the apartment adjacent to ours and tried to work there. He was only two, and I supposed that he would not know where I went when I shut the door behind me. But he soon figured out that we were divided only by a wall. He beat a tattoo on the wall until I came home. I gave up the rented room and in one way or another, largely by improving my concentration, I learned to work at my living-room desk, whatever might be going on around me.

Often Lionel and I spoke of how strange it was that none of our friends who had had children had told us of the extraordinary joy of being parents. No one told us of the incomparable beauty of an infant waking in the night, flushed with sleep, or of the wrench of aching love with which one saw one's child reach out his trusting hand for help. No one spoke even of the wonder of a child's growth: the first step, the first word, the first assertion of an independent self, a self on its own in the world. These friends of ours had of course supposed that we would never have children. They were sparing us the knowledge of what we missed.

In 1950, the middle of our century, Lionel was in the middle of the journey of his life, or should have been. He was forty-five and could have been expected to live to ninety, another forty-five years. Instead, he lived only to the age of seventy. He had always been in good health and had had no important illness except the scarlet fever which he had before we married and a serious bout of pneumonia in Oxford, sometimes back pains, sometimes a grippe or flu, just in time to spoil his Christmas holiday. The dark rings under his eyes and the worn look which often troubled people who knew him only passingly were not signs of a worn body; they were signs of a troubled spirit. He was in excellent physical condition until the last months of his life, when he was stricken with the pancreatic cancer from which he died. He died in November 1975. The specter of his death had appeared to me in early summer of that year while we were vacationing in St. Andrews in Canada. The walk from the house we had rented to the village where we shopped was less than a mile. There had to be something wrong for Lionel to take account of this distance as he now did, and to walk more slowly than I. One of the distinctive things about Lionel was the firm speed with which he walked. When he went to the backyard for wood for our fireplace, he brought in a single log. At the end of July I decided to cut short our stay. We returned to New York. Pancreatic cancers do their work quickly. He was in the hospital only a few days; until he died in November, we cared for him at home. It was my intention, when he died, to write an article in protest of the prohibition against giving morphine even to a dying patient lest he become addicted. Here at last I record my indignation at this cruel stupidity. The drugs which were permitted Lionel kept him from sharp physical suffering but they did not release him from consciousness. In human decency, this was what was called for.

There is a sense in which Lionel was lucky to die when he did. He was never made to suffer the humiliations of old age; he died while his life had dignity. He was lacking in the skill to grow old and had never accepted old age as part of life. Even in its premonitory stages he experienced it as a personal affront. On our sixty-fifth birthdays we went together to register for Social Security at our local Social Security office. It was a dismal place and we were in unhappy company. The young woman with whom we dealt looked up sharply from her desk and said: "You two look the way people are supposed to look." Lionel took no comfort from the judgment she had passed. He hated to be numbered among those who no longer mattered. He despised the category of "senior citizen" and refused to take advantage of the reduction in transit fare or theater tickets.

Soon after Lionel died, two of our friends of slightly younger age, one a poet, the other a critic, came to visit me. It was a condolence call: they sorrowed over Lionel's death. But they also mourned the turn which their own lives had recently taken—each had lost his wife to another man. Calling on me, they contemplated the loneliness which they would now be sharing with me. How lacking they were in imagination! Everyone knows that any man who wants a wife can readily have one, younger than himself if that is what he looks for. No man, whatever his age, need be alone. Loneliness is for women, for widows, and only the luckiest of us, a handful, have anything but memory to sustain us through the empty years. To live with Lionel was to have at my side someone with whom I could share every thought, even the most trivial. The miracle of marriage, if it works, is that it makes you the most important person in the world for at least the one other person. Your well-being, your desires and frustrations, your amusements or disappointments matter to your marital partner as they can never matter to anyone else in your grown universe. The miracle of Lionel's and my marriage was that this companionship transcended the frustrations and emotional problems and angers which otherwise might have engulfed it. Seventeen years have now passed since Lionel's death, and hour by hour, minute by minute, I still listen for a clock which no longer ticks. I sometimes think that what I miss most is the companionship of his mind. Lionel was a person of remarkable insight and intellectual range. I have not found a substitute for his unhurried and unostentatious thoughtfulness. He lived in the world of ideas and he constantly brought me its news. He valued his intellectual endowment all too lightly and I am afraid that I also undervalued it. The intellectual culture of this country as Lionel and I knew it in the earlier decades of the century no longer exists. It had begun to disappear even in Lionel's lifetime: it may be that when he complained that the younger men at the University no longer engaged him in easy intellectual exchange, what he was noting was not so much a response to his reputation as a change in the temper of the times. The New York intellectuals had their moment in history and it has passed. Theirs was uniquely the age of criticism. Their criticism went everywhere. They had no gods, no protectorates or sacred constituencies. They were a small, geographically concentrated group, but if they did nothing else, they kept the general culture of the country in balance. It is no longer in balance. No weight is now being put against the popular culture. The gap which once existed between the professional intellectual and the academic narrows. Our best intelligences retreat into the universities and into their special fields of learning. They give up what earlier in this book I called the life of significant contention. Instead, they settle for the life of expertise.

The strange difficult ungenerous unreliable unkind and not always honest people who created the world in which Lionel and I shared, and to which we tried to contribute, are now most of them dead. I inscribe their names here, on this poor monument: Elliot Cohen, Herbert Solow, Henry Rosenthal, Philip Rahv, Dwight Macdonald, Mary McCarthy, Hannah Arendt, Sidney Hook, Edmund Wilson, Malcolm Cowley, Fred Dupee, Margaret Marshall,

Delmore Schwartz, William Barrett, James Agee, Bernard Haggin, Irving Howe. The list is of course much longer. People such as these, minds such as theirs, should be replaced. Our society needs them.

Index

Canada: travels to, 103, 236–37, 418
Capitalism, 340
  blamed for individuals' problems,
    183–84, 341
  Partisan Review's attitude toward war
    and, 309–10, 312–14, 410–11
Capote, Truman, 110, 338, 398
Carlyle, Jane Welsh, 349
Carlyle, Thomas, 81, 349
Carman, Harry, 361
Caruso, Enrico, 35, 108, 333
Cary, Joyce, 338
"Case for the American Woman, The"
  (DT), 351–52
Castle, Irene, 63
Catcher in the Rye, The (Salinger), 82
Cather, Willa, 82, 317
Cecil, David (Lord), 407
Celebrity: vs. fame, 336–37
Chamberlain, Neville, 309–10, 410
Chambers, Whittaker, 216–21, 260,
  271–72, 358–59, 388–89, 394
"Changing Myth of the Jew, The" (LT),
  189, 271
"Chapter for a Fashionable Jewish
  Novel" (LT), 89–90, 378–80
Charterhouse of Parma, The (Stendhal),
  18
Chatterton, Thomas, 257
Chaucer, Geoffrey, 76
Child's Garden of Verses, A (Stevenson),
  39
Childermass, The (Lewis), 143
Christian Science, 49, 226
Christmas Tree, The (Bolton), 339
Churchill, Winston, 410
CIA, 181
City College of New York, 26, 82, 168,
  308
Civilization and Its Discontents (Freud),
  86
Claremont Essays (DT), 73, 346, 349, 363
Clark, Eleanor, 317, 338
Class, 188, 289. *See also* Middle class
  in LT's stories, 90, 379
"Clue to Hitlerism, A" (LT), 257
Code Name "Mary" (Gardiner), 242
Cohen, Blanche (Mrs. Isidor), 131–34

Cohen, Deborah (LT's aunt), 18, 26–27,
  31, 38, 112, 113, 170, 171, 253
Cohen, Della (LT's aunt), 18, 26–27, 31,
  38, 112, 113, 114, 171, 253
Cohen, Elliot, 92, 141–42, 154, 173, 283,
  420
  as *Commentary* editor, 345, 387
  death of, 93
  DT submits story to, 126–27
  and Jewish identity, 117, 144, 194
  LT's friendship with, 145, 149, 167
  and LT's *Menorah Journal* stories,
    88–89, 369, 376, 378, 379–80
  as *Menorah Journal* editor, 88–89, 91,
    92, 117, 137–40, 161, 194
  as model for character in *Unpossessed*,
    137–38
  on *Nation*, 332
  politics of, 91–92, 138, 194–95, 198,
    205, 209–12
Cohen, Fannie. *See* Trilling, Fannie
Cohen, Franny, 123
Cohen, Hyman (LT's "Uncle Hymie"),
  24, 26–28, 31, 37, 121, 170
  art collection of, 26, 27, 114, 261
  and LT and DT's engagement, 112–14,
    253
Cohen, I. Bernard, 26, 123
Cohen, Isidor (LT's uncle), 26, 28, 31,
  114, 131–32, 253
Cohen, Israel (LT's grandfather), 24–25
Cohen, Larry (LT's uncle), 26–27, 28, 31,
  112, 114, 253
Cohen, Lester, 142
Cohen, Louis. *See* Kirkman, Louis
Cohen, Maude (LT's aunt), 18, 26, 112
Cohen, Teddy (LT's uncle), 26
Cold War, 344. *See also* Anti-
  Communism
Coleman, McAlister, 200
Coleridge, Samuel Taylor, 76, 81, 257,
  262
Collected Tales of E. M. Forster, 399
Columbia University. *See also Names of
  professors and administrators at*
  Colloquium at, 85–86, 261–64,
    273–75, 407
  intellectual climate of, 79–82, 407

del Vayo, Julio, 332
Dennis, Nigel, 220
Denver Quarterly (magazine), 35
Derrygally (Boonton, NJ), 184–86, 195
DeSilver, Margaret, 137
Deutsch, Helene, 49
DeVane, William Clyde, 143
Dewey, John, 179, 213, 313
Dick, Harry K., 273, 274, 276, 277–80
Dickens, Charles, 36, 85, 102, 257, 397
Dickinson, Emily, 336
Dickstein, Morris, 373
Diderot, Denis, 357
Do I Wake or Sleep (Bolton), 339
Dobell, Byron, 401
Dr. Transit (Schneider), 214
Dos Passos, John, 82, 198, 310
Dostoevsky, Fyodor, 36, 76, 362, 397
Double Agent (Dickstein), 373
Dreiser, Theodore, 82, 198
Dreyfus case, 358
Drinking, 11–14, 16, 17, 106, 133, 230,
  370
Drugs, 178, 187, 228, 238–44, 251,
  364–65, 418
"Duchess' Red Shoes, The" (Schwartz),
  30, 307
Dunn, William, 244–46, 252
Dupee, F. W., 288, 303, 306, 329, 330,
  420
Durante, Jimmy, 88
Dzerzhinski, Feliks, 205

E. M. Forster (LT), 110, 224, 381, 391,
  397–401. *See also* Forster, E. M.
"East Coker" (Eliot), 315
Edman, Irwin, 114, 272–73, 276–78,
  318, 319
Education of Henry Adams, The (Adams),
  24
Eighteenth Brumaire, The (Marx), 289
Eimi (Cummings), 202
Einstein, Albert, 291
Eisenhower, Dwight, 318
Eliot, George, 36
Eliot, T. S., 76, 82, 85, 315, 347–48,
  381

Ellmann, Richard and Mary, 407
Emerson, Ralph Waldo, 76
Encounter (magazine), 323, 347
Enemies of Promise (Connolly), 348
Energies of Art, The (Barzun), 262
England, 18, 408
  as Cohen family's residence, 9, 24, 28
  DT and LT in, 79, 120, 389–90, 399,
  407
Epstein, Jason, 401
Erskine, John, 85
Escape (Vance), 338
Europa in Limbo (Briffault), 289
Evans, Walker, 38, 288, 334
Everett, Charles, 273, 274, 276, 278, 285,
  351, 412
Everett, Hannah More, 351
Experience of Literature, The (LT), 135,
  225, 382, 383, 384, 392

Fackenthal, Frank, 295, 318
"Facts of Life" (Goodman), 45
Fadiman, Clifton ("Kip"), 83, 152, 161
  desire for position at Columbia by, 85,
  193
  Hemingway's letter to, 369–70
  on marriage, 149, 168
  relations of, with DT and LT, 1, 11, 119,
  122, 184–85, 281
Fadiman, Polly, 1, 11, 119, 122, 184–86,
  233, 281
Fame: vs. celebrity, 336–37
Farber, Dorothy, 74, 75, 109
Farrell, James T., 258, 289, 310–11, 337
Far Rockaway (NY), 37, 39
Far Side of Paradise, The (Mizener), 288
Fascism: and war, 312, 411. *See also*
  Nazism; Spain
Faulkner, William, 82
Fearing, Kenneth, 310
Female Eunuch, The (Greer), 353
Feminism, 21, 352–54. *See also* Woman
  suffrage; Women; Women's movement
Feuchtwanger, Lion, 257, 291
Fields, W. C., 88
Films, 161, 189, 299, 334
Finnegans Wake (Joyce), 147

First World War, 39, 77, 81, 410
  as dividing line between generations,
    16–17, 150
  DT's memories of, 46, 56–57, 281–82,
    409
Fischer, Louis, 301
Fitzgerald, F. Scott, 19, 82, 150, 288
Fitzgerald, Robert, 310
Flaubert, Gustave, 76, 289
Flowering of New England, The
  (Brooks), 258
Fogg Museum (Harvard University), 76,
  77, 79, 80
Fontamara (Silone), 258
Forbert, Charlie (DT's uncle), 47, 53
Forbert, Sadie Helene (DT's mother's
  maiden name), 52
Ford, James W., 200
Ford Foundation, 132
Forster, E. M., 90, 110, 350, 387,
  397–403. *See also E. M. Forster* (LT)
"For the Union Dead" (Lowell), 376
Fortune (magazine), 334
Foster, William Z., 200
Franco, Francisco, 290, 300
Frankel, Charles, 86
Fraser, G. S., 363
Freeborn, Mr. and Mrs., 120, 122, 123,
  126, 159
Freeman, Joseph, 216
Frelinghuysen, Susy, 303
Fremont-Smith, Eliot, 374
Freud, Sigmund, 25, 49, 100, 245,
  371–72, 375. *See also* Psychoanalysis
  Brunswick's relationship with,
    238–39, 241–42
  DT's approach to, 225, 256
  lack of study about, by DT and LT's
    friends, 234
  LT's regard for, 86, 223, 225, 226,
    234–35, 255, 256, 266, 268–69
  practice of psychoanalysis by, 228
"Freud and Literature" (LT), 234
"Freud and the Crisis in Our Culture"
  (LT's lecture), 224, 403
Freud and the Crisis of Our Culture (LT),
  391–92
Frick Art Reference Library, 98

Friendship and Fratricide (Zeligs), 394
Friends of Mr. Sweeney (Davis), 12
Friends of the Soviet Union, 196
Fritsch, Mia, 415
"Funeral at the Club, with Lunch" (LT),
  143, 380
Furbank, P. N., 350

Gardiner, Muriel, 242
Gathering of Fugitives, A (LT), 135, 266,
  392
Gender differences
  in DT and LT's generation, 107–8, 134,
    149, 150, 155–56, 175–76, 209, 248,
    326, 349–56, 415, 416
  Freudian views of, 248–49
  in old age, 419
  in those seeking psychoanalysis,
    234–35
Gentleman's Profession, A (Warburg), 389
"George Orwell and the Politics of
  Truth" (LT), 402
Germany. *See also* Nazism
  American restrictions on Jewish
    refugees from, 291–92
  DT's childhood travels to, 56, 104
  Ford Foundation trip to, 132
  and Nazism, 207–8, 211, 290–93
  Social Democratic Party in, 207, 211,
    292
Ginsberg, Allen, 205, 305, 306, 359,
  361–66, 372, 384
Glusker, David, 219
Gobineau, Joseph-Arthur de, 143
Goell, Theresa, 105, 226
Gold, Mike, 124
"Gold Spot Pals" (radio show), 106
Goldwater, Walter, 390
Goodman, Paul, 45
Gottlieb, Robert, 401
GPU, 219
Grace (Comrade), 199, 207, 213
Graham, Philip and Katherine, 345–46
Graves, Robert, 338
Great Depression, 290. *See also*
  Communism
  effect of, on DT's father, 2, 64–65, 135,
    165–66, 168, 169, 188

Meredith, William, 109
Merkle, Una, 299
Metro-Goldwyn-Mayer, 337
Metropolitan Museum, 98
Metropolitan Opera, 109
Micheles, Vera. *See* Dean, Vera Micheles
Mid-Century (magazine), 266
Mid-Century Book Club, 265–66
Middle class, 77, 416–17. *See also* Class
   attacks on, 35
   LT and DT as members of, 47, 139–40,
     168–72, 199
   LT's relation to, as a writer, 314–15
Middle of the Journey, The (LT)
   autobiographical elements in, 16
   LT's collapse after completion of, 316
   models for characters in, 159, 218, 232,
     387
   as political novel, 30, 90, 181, 386–89
   reception of, 368, 387–88
   and Viking Press, 355–56, 387–94
   writing of, 386–87
Mikol, Bettina, 48, 66, 74, 109. *See also*
   Sinclair, Bettina
Millay, Edna St. Vincent, 150
Miller, Henry, 310–11
Miner, Dwight, 335
Misérables, Les (Hugo), 48, 101
Mission to Moscow (film), 334
Mrs. Harris (DT), 349, 352, 359
Mizener, Arthur, 287, 288
Modern Language Association, 383
Modern Library, 317
Modern Monthly (magazine), 258
Modern Occasions (magazine), 307
Modernism, 84–85, 261–62
Monogamy, 149–51. *See also* Adultery
Monroe, Marilyn, 246, 347
Montaigne, Michel de, 76
Morality, 29–31, 171–72, 374–75,
     399–403. *See also* Conscience;
     Honesty; Manners
Morningside (magazine), 83
Morris, George L. K., 288, 303
Morrow, Felix and Ann, 185–87, 205
Moscow Trials, 213, 290, 296–98, 300
Mount Holyoke, 76, 80
Moynihan, Daniel Patrick, 132

Mozart, Wolfgang Amadeus, 109
Mumford, Lewis, 183, 214
My Dog Tulip (Ackerley), 399

Nabokov, Vladimir, 90, 338
Names, 2–3, 8–11, 96–97, 185, 328, 350
Nathan, George Jean, 139, 258
Nation (magazine), 86, 161, 179, 301
   DT's writings for, 108, 181, 184, 243,
     325–43, 348, 349, 355, 356
   LT's writings for, 189, 258, 317
   Marshall's sabbatical from, 347–48
   politics of, 331–32, 341–42
National Broadcasting Company, 106,
     107, 110
National Committee for the Defense of
     Political Prisoners. *See* NCDPP
National Student League, 196
Nazism, 207–8. *See also* Hitler, Adolf
   and Heidegger, 343
   Hellman's claims about her role
     against, 242
   liberals' lack of concern about,
     290–94, 302, 309–14, 410–11
   Lindberghs' views on, 309
Nazi-Soviet Pact, 207, 293
NCDPP (National Committee for the
     Defense of Political Prisoners)
   DT and LT's break with, 208, 212–14,
     216–21, 290
   DT and LT's involvement with, 181,
     194–96, 198–99, 205, 207–12
   members of, 91
Neff, Emery, 412
   anti-Semitism of, 321–22
   as LT's dissertation director, 193, 270,
     301
   and LT's fight to remain at Columbia,
     273, 274, 276–77, 278
Nelson, Lord, 377
Neoconservatism, 92, 182, 403–5
New Directions (publishers), 397
New Freeman (magazine), 189
New Leader (magazine), 345
New Masses (magazine), 215
New Republic (magazine), 131, 189, 258,
     301, 317, 318, 331
New Rochelle (NY), 4, 45, 56

Saroyan, William, 338
Sartre, Jean-Paul, 90, 337, 343
Scarlet Sister Mary (Peterkin), 142–43
Schapiro, Meyer, 83, 85, 272, 313, 394
Schilder, Mrs. Paul, 236–37
Schilder, Paul, 232–38, 240
Schlesinger, Arthur, Jr., 206, 306
Schneider, Isidor and Helen, 214–16
Schnitzler, Arthur, 273
"Scholar's Tale, The" (LT), 296
Schwabacher, Wolf, 242
Schwartz, Delmore, 30, 287–89, 307, 335–36, 421
Scott, Evelyn, 178–79
Scottsboro case, 208–11, 213
Scoundrel Time (Hellman), 199, 220
Scribner's (publishers), 389
SDS (Students for a Democratic Society), 304
Secker & Warburg (publishers), 389
Second World War, 244, 322–23, 408–11
    Partisan Review's politics in, 293, 303, 309–13
Seder. *See* Passover
Sentimental Education, A (Flaubert), 289
Sex. *See also* Homosexuality
    attitudes toward premarital, 14–16, 150–51
    DT and, 15, 65–67, 104–5, 150–51
    DT's father's views of, 14, 15, 51, 104–5, 115–16, 143–55
    innocence of, at Radcliffe, 65–67
    as topic of discussion for intellectuals, 149–51, 184, 214
Shakespeare, William, 76
Shaw, George Bernard, 82, 333
Shelley, Percy Bysshe, 102
Shulman, Robert, 401, 406
Silone, Ignazio, 258
Simon & Schuster (publishers), 1
Simpson, Lewis P., 369–71, 373, 395
Simpson, Louis, 86, 401
Sinclair, Bettina, 119, 148, 202, 151, 283–84, 390. *See also* Mikol, Bettina
Sinclair, David, 48, 119, 202, 283–84, 390
Sinclair, Upton, 48, 202

Singing, 101–2, 106–9
"Situation in American Writing, The" (*Partisan Review*), 310–11
Six Who Pass While the Lentils Boil (Kreymborg), 151
Slesinger, Tess, 126–27, 137–38, 151
Snow, C. P., 294, 345
Socialist Party, 180, 200, 202, 207–8, 342
Social Security, 419
Society, 72–73, 90–91. *See also* Conscience; Culture; Manners; Morality
Society for the Prevention of Cruelty to Animals, 59
Solow, Herbert, 83, 141, 151, 420
    and the *Menorah Journal*, 137–38, 161, 194
    as model for character in *Unpossessed*, 137–38
    personality of, 117, 145, 167, 260
    politics of, 138, 140, 194, 205, 212
    and Whittaker Chambers, 219–21
Sons and Lovers (Lawrence), 273, 277, 371
Southern Review (magazine), 369
Sovern, Michael, 86
Soviet Union. *See also* Chambers, Whittaker; Comintern; Popular Front; Russian revolution; Stalin, Joseph; Trotsky, Leon
    and American Communists, 180–81
    Communist oppression in, 182, 202
    Joseph McCarthy a gift to, 343–44
    Nazi pact with, 207, 293
    support for, in the West, 294, 358–59
Spain, 290, 300, 301, 332
Speakeasies, 11–12, 13, 16, 133, 230
Speaking of Literature and Society (LT), 189
Spectator (magazine), 83
Spewack, Sam and Bella, 281
Spinoza, Baruch, 147
Stafford, Jean, 338
Stalin, Joseph, 179, 202. *See also* GPU; Moscow Trials; Soviet Union; Stalinism
    dictatorship of, 182, 195, 197, 220, 290, 359
    and Hitler, 207–8, 211, 292–93, 340

437